A NEW ERA FOR MENTAL HEALTH LAW AND POLICY

The Convention on the Rights of Persons with Disabilities (CRPD) has generated new ideas and standards in healthcare and disability law and policy. In the mental health context, the CRPD directs governments to ensure people with mental impairments are treated equally before the law, including ensuring people have access to the resources necessary to enjoy their rights. But what this means in practice remains unclear. In addition, current domestic laws that authorise involuntary psychiatric interventions stand at cross-purposes with the CRPD, which requires respect for the 'will, preference and rights' of persons with disabilities 'on an equal basis with others'. This book explores the implications of the CRPD for law, policy and practice that responds to the complex issues raised by mental health impairment and disability. It argues that the support framework of the CRPD holds potential to address persistent shortcomings in mental health law and policy.

Piers Gooding was educated at the University of Melbourne, Monash University and King's College London. He has held a number of teaching and research appointments, including at the Melbourne Social Equity Institute and Melbourne Law School, University of Melbourne, the Centre for Disability Law and Policy, National University of Ireland, Galway, and the Faculty of Law, Monash University. His research focuses on disability law and policy, with a special focus on the UN Convention on the Rights of Persons with Disabilities.

CAMBRIDGE DISABILITY LAW AND POLICY SERIES

Edited by Peter Blanck and Robin Paul Malloy

The Disability Law and Policy Series examines these topics in interdisciplinary and comparative terms. The books in the series reflect the diversity of definitions, causes, and consequences of discrimination against persons with disabilities while illuminating fundamental themes that unite countries in their pursuit of human rights laws and policies to improve the social and economic status of persons with disabilities. The series contains historical, contemporary, and comparative scholarship crucial to identifying individual, organizational, cultural, attitudinal, and legal themes necessary for the advancement of disability law and policy.

The book topics covered in the series also are reflective of the new moral and political commitment by countries throughout the world toward equal opportunity for persons with disabilities in such areas as employment, housing, transportation, rehabilitation, and individual human rights. The series will thus play a significant role in informing policy makers, researchers, and citizens of issues central to disability rights and disability antidiscrimination policies. The series grounds the future of disability law and policy as a vehicle for ensuring that those living with disabilities participate as equal citizens of the world.

Books in the series

Ruth Colker, *When Is Separate Unequal? A Disability Perspective*, 2009

Larry M. Logue and Peter Blanck, *Race, Ethnicity, and Disability: Veterans and Benefits in Post–Civil War America*, 2010

Lisa Vanhala, *Making Rights a Reality? Disability Rights Activists and Legal Mobilization*, 2011

Alicia Ouellette, *Bioethics and Disability: Toward a Disability-Conscious Bioethics*, 2011

Eilionoir Flynn, *From Rhetoric to Action: Implementing the UN Convention on the Rights of Persons with Disabilities*, 2011

Isabel Karpin and Kristin Savell, *Perfecting Pregnancy: Law, Disability, and the Future of Reproduction*, 2012

Arie Rimmerman, *Social Inclusion of People with Disabilities: National and International Perspectives*, 2012

Andrew Power, Janet E. Lord, and Allison S. deFranco, *Active Citizenship & Disability: Implementing the Personalisation of Support*, 2013

Eliza Varney, *Disability and Information Technology: A Comparative Study in Media Regulation*, 2013

Lisa Schur, Douglas Kruse, and Peter Blanck, *People with Disabilities: Sidelined or Mainstreamed?*, 2013

Jerome E. Bickenbach, Franziska Felder, and Barbara Schmitz, *Disability and the Good Human Life*, 2014

Peter Blanck, *eQuality: The Struggle for Web Accessibility by Persons with Cognitive Disabilities*, 2014

Robin Paul Malloy, *Land Use Law and Disability: Planning and Zoning for Accessible Communities*, 2014

Arie Rimmerman, *Family Policy and Disability*, 2015

Paul Harpur, *Discrimination, Copyright and Equality: Opening the E-Book for the Print-Disabled*, 2017

Arie Rimmerman, *Disability and Community Living Policies*, 2017

Anna Arstein-Kerslake, *Restoring Voice to People with Cognitive Disabilities: Realizing the Right to Equal Recognition Before the Law*, 2017

Aisling de Paor, *Genetics, Disability and the Law: Towards an EU Legal Framework*, 2017

Piers Gooding, *A New Era for Mental Health Law and Policy: Supported Decision-Making and the UN Convention on the Rights of Persons with Disabilities*, 2017

A New Era for Mental Health Law and Policy

Supported Decision-Making and the UN Convention on the Rights of Persons with Disabilities

PIERS GOODING
The University of Melbourne

CAMBRIDGE
UNIVERSITY PRESS

CAMBRIDGE
UNIVERSITY PRESS

University Printing House, Cambridge CB2 8BS, United Kingdom

One Liberty Plaza, 20th Floor, New York, NY 10006, USA

477 Williamstown Road, Port Melbourne, VIC 3207, Australia

4843/24, 2nd Floor, Ansari Road, Daryaganj, Delhi – 110002, India

79 Anson Road, #06-04/06, Singapore 079906

Cambridge University Press is part of the University of Cambridge.

It furthers the University's mission by disseminating knowledge in the pursuit of education, learning, and research at the highest international levels of excellence.

www.cambridge.org
Information on this title: www.cambridge.org/9781107140745
DOI: 10.1017/9781316493106

First published 2017

Printed in the United Kingdom by Clays, St Ives plc.

A catalogue record for this publication is available from the British Library.

ISBN 978-1-107-14074-5 Hardback

Contents

Acknowledgements

I would like to thank a number of colleagues in particular, namely Professor Bernadette McSherry, Professor Gerard Quinn and Dr Penelope Weller. Their generosity, both personal and professional, was a constant source of encouragement for my work.

I also owe thanks to a number of people with whom conversations and collaboration informed this book (though I take full responsibility for any flaws in my arguments and interpretations). I am grateful to Dr Eilionóir Flynn, Dr Annegret Kämpf, Dr Ronli Sifris, Dr David Webb, Dr Anna Arstein-Kerslake, Professor Ron McCallum, Professor Michael Perlin, Catalina Devandas-Aguilar, Alberto Vasquez, Professor Peter Blanck, Professor Amita Dhanda, Dr Lucy Series, Dr John Chesterman, Dr Liz Broznan, Dr Gunvant Patel, Dr Michelle Browning, Dr Eoin Daly, Dr Oliver Lewis, Tina Minkowitz Esq, John Watkins, Professor Peter Bartlett, Dr Gavin Davidson, Professor Jill Stavert, Dr Lisa Brophy, Rosemary Kayess, Professor Genevra Richardson, Dr Linda Steele, Dr Fleur Beaupert, Professor George Szmukler, Dr Sascha Callaghan, Dr Christopher Ryan, Kay Wilson, Gábor Gombos, Professor Jerome Bickenbach, Dr Éva Szeli, Kristijan Grdan, Professor Theresia Degener, Lei Ning, Dr Jo Watson, Cath Roper, David Oaks, Wayne Weavell, Flick Grey, Merinda Epstein, Leah Harris, Daniel Mackler, Dr Rosemary Callander, Cher Nicholson, Dr John Brayley, Dianne Chartres, Dr Lucy Knox, and Deb Rouget.

Some of the work was undertaken during a period as a visiting research fellow at the Dickson Poon School of Law, King's College London, in 2012. I am grateful to the Menzies Centre for Australian Studies for this opportunity.

Additional proofing support was generously provided by Cate Read and the Melbourne Law School Research Service, for which I am grateful.

For personal support over the period of writing this book, I am grateful to my family, Heather Shand, Chris and Darcy Gooding, and to Rosemary Crowhurst. This book is dedicated to the memory of Graeme Hugh Gooding.

Related Publications

This book incorporates material that the author published in the following journal articles:

G Davidson, L Brophy, J Campbell, S Farrell, P Gooding and AM O'Brien, 'An International Comparison of Legal Frameworks for Supported and Substitute Decision-Making in Mental Health Services' (2016) 44 *International Journal of Law and Psychiatry* 30

P Gooding, 'Change and Continuity in Mental Health Law: the Long Road to the United Nations Convention on the Rights of Persons with Disabilities' (2014) *Web Journal of Current Legal Issues* 20

P Gooding, 'Navigating the "Flashing Amber Lights" of the Right to Legal Capacity in the *United Nations Convention on the Rights of Persons with Disabilities*: Responding to Major Concerns' (2015) 15(1) *Human Rights Law Review* 45

P Gooding, 'Supported Decision-Making: A Rights-Based Disability Concept and Its Implications for Mental Health Law' (2013) 20(3) *Psychiatry, Psychology and Law* 43

P Gooding and T Bennett, 'The Abolition of the Insanity Defense in Sweden and the United Nations Convention on the Rights of Persons with Disabilities: Human Rights Brinksmanship or Evidence It Does Not Work?' (2017) *New Criminal Law Review* (forthcoming)

P Gooding and E Flynn, 'Querying the Call to Introduce Mental Capacity Testing to Mental Health Law: Does the Doctrine of Necessity Provide an Alternative?' (2015) 4(2) *Laws* 245

B McSherry and P Gooding, 'Torture and Ill-Treatment In Health Care Settings: Lessons from the United Nations' (2013) 20 *Journal of Law and Medicine* 712

Abbreviations

ALRC	Australian Law Reform Commission
AOT	Assisted Outpatient Treatment
DCP	Division of Clinical Psychology, British Psychological Society
CACL	Canadian Association of Community Living
CRPD	Convention on the Rights of Persons with Disabilities
CRPD Committee	Committee on the Rights of Persons with Disabilities
CTO	Community Treatment Order
ECHR	Convention for the Protection of Human Rights and Fundamental Freedoms
ECT	Electroconvulsive Therapy
HSCC	South Australia Health Services Complaints Commission
MHCT	Mental Health (Care and Treatment) (Scotland) Act 2003
MI Principles	Principles for the Protection of Persons with Mental Illness and for the Improvement of Mental Health Care
NMHL	National Mental Health Law 2010 (Argentina)
OHCHR	UN Office of the High Commissioner for Human Rights
OPA	South Australia Office of the Public Advocate
VLRC	Victorian Law Reform Commission

Foreword

Mental health law has proven to be exceptionally appealing for policymakers. According to the 2014 World Health Atlas, 51% of WHO Member States have a stand-alone mental health law. The European and Western Pacific regions have the highest percentage (more than 70%), while the African and American regions have the lowest (50–55%). Notably, almost half of them were enacted or modified around the year of the adoption of the UN Convention on the Rights of Persons with Disabilities. Indeed, following the WHO Mental Health Action Plan 2013–2020, many States have passed mental health law as a way to 'codify the key principles, values and objectives of policy for mental health' and 'strengthen effective leadership and governance for mental health'.

Nevertheless, as this book puts forward, mental health laws are not in line with human rights. Despite its increasing rights-based rhetoric, mental health legislation legitimizes coercion in health care, conferring clinical authority on mental health professionals to involuntary detain and treat persons with psychosocial disabilities. Moreover, in the last two decades, this coercive power has expanded beyond the psychiatric hospital, and around the world there is a worrisome rise of coercive care in the community through the so-called community treatment orders. As Dr Gooding suggests, mental health laws have become very sophisticated, but their outcome remains the same: persons with psychosocial disabilities – as well as autistic persons, persons with intellectual disabilities and persons with dementia – are still disproportionately exposed to human rights violations in the context of mental health services. The limited focus of 'rights-based legalism' – mostly concerned with safeguarding compulsory medical treatment – have not changed power imbalances in mental health care.

The UN Convention on the Rights of Persons with Disabilities ('CRPD'), adopted in 2006, challenges coercion in psychiatry, raising the need to rethink the existence of mental health laws. The CRPD moves away from medical and paternalistic approaches in relation to the rights of persons with disabilities towards a human rights perspective. Instead of questioning the existence of an intellectual or mental impairment, which is part of human diversity, the CRPD questions the existence of structures and practices that are contrary to the full enjoyment of the rights of persons with any of those conditions. The focus is no longer on what rights an individual with a disability has, or what rights can be limited, but rather on how to ensure that all persons with disabilities enjoy all their human rights on equal basis with others.

Furthermore, the CRPD has upheld a universalist perspective of the right to liberty and security of person that supersedes previous 'soft law' standards such as the Principles for the Protection of Persons with Mental Illness and the Improvement of Mental Health Care (MI Principles). The CRPD recognizes that all persons with disabilities, including those with intellectual and psychosocial disabilities, enjoy all human rights and fundamental freedoms on equal basis with others, such as equal recognition before the law, personal liberty and security, integrity and free and informed consent. The CRPD further prohibits unlawful or arbitrary deprivation of liberty of persons with disabilities and states that the existence of a disability cannot justify a deprivation of liberty.

In this vein, States should not limit any longer the political and social responses necessary for the inclusion of persons with disabilities in the provision of mental health services. On the contrary, a holistic assessment of the social barriers and challenges is needed. At the same time, responses from mental health services need to change to ensure the full respect and protection of the human rights of persons with disabilities. Coercion, in particular, needs to be acknowledged as a failure of the system to provide adequate support. States need to put their efforts toward eliminating coercion in the mental health care, repealing legislation authorizing forced commitment and treatment and ensuring access to support for all persons with disabilities.

The CRPD has already impacted the work of the United Nations on this matter. Different treaty bodies, special procedures and agencies are having their standards progressively adapted in line with the CRPD.[1] The World Health Organization (WHO), for example, has recently withdrawn from its webpage the 'Resource Book on Mental Health, Human Rights and Legislation', which

[1] *See* A/HRC/34/32; A/63/175; A/HRC/30/37, paras. 38–41; CRPD/C/GC/1, paras. 40–41; CEDAW/C/IND/CO/4–5, para. 37, CCPR/C/GC/35, para. 19; CAT/C/CAN/CO/6, para. 19.

has been very influential in drafting mental health laws worldwide, 'because it was drafted prior to the coming into force of the UN Convention on the Rights of Persons with Disabilities and is therefore not compliant with the latest human rights norms and standards'.[2] Whereas many Sates with strong tradition of psychiatric coercion might find those standards challenging and will require more time to fully implement them, there is a growing number of countries formulating new legislation and policies based on those standards. Costa Rica, for example, has recently abolished all forms of substituted decision-making and expressly forbidden all forms of involuntary treatment for persons with disabilities.

In addition, as this book exemplifies, there are many good practices that also demonstrate that a paradigm shift is possible. Service models such as Open Dialogue have created significant evidence on the benefits of a non-coercive community approach. The Swedish personal ombudsman system ('PO Skåne') have also developed expertise in supporting people with psychosocial disabilities during states of extreme emotional distress, without coercion. Different forms of peer support have also proven to be successful in supporting individuals with psychosocial disabilities to exercise their rights in the context of mental health services.

It is important to stress that the 'absolute ban' on involuntary psychiatric practices does not mean that general administrative, civil and criminal legislation do not apply to persons with disabilities. For example, if an individual with a psychosocial disability inflicts tangible harm on others, the general administrative, criminal or civil rule should be applied in those cases as long as these interventions are applied on equal basis with others, do not constitute direct or indirect discrimination against persons with disabilities, and reasonable and procedural accommodations are provided if needed. However, the notion of 'potential dangerousness' should not be applied at any case as a ground for detention, as it violates the presumption of innocence. In this regard, I recommend exercising caution about creating new 'disability-neutral grounds' for coercion that may open the door to new forms of social control that could be disproportionately applied against persons with disabilities. I see an opportunity to end coercion and implement active, engaging services that could fill the gap in terms of support.

Against this background, this book represents a substantial contribution to the discussions around the fate of mental health law in the CRPD era. The CRPD obliges us to rethink mental health law in order to ensure a legal framework that guarantees the rights and freedoms of persons with disabilities.

2 *See* www.who.int/mental_health/policy/legislation/en/

As they exist today, mental health laws represent a threat to the rights of persons with psychosocial disabilities rather than a protection. There is a need to stop the spread of mental health laws and instead promote the inclusion of mental health in the general health legislation; this must be done under a human rights–based approach. Different aspects covered by mental health legislation, such as promotion and prevention, community-based interventions and budgeting, can be mainstreamed into other pieces of legislation or removed altogether. We do need a moratorium on mental health laws, and to start working on guidelines to ensure the implementation of a human rights approach in all mental health services.

Catalina Devandas-Aguilar
UN Special Rapporteur on the Rights of Persons with Disabilities

Introduction

Since the coming into force of the Convention on the Rights of Persons with Disabilities ('CRPD'),[1] the need to rethink mental health law, policy and practice from a human rights perspective has never been stronger. The CRPD is historic. Not only does it hold the record for the highest number of opening signatures in the shortest space of time, its development was also uniquely participatory. Unlike previous human rights treaties, those whose rights were at stake were closely involved, with disabled people's organisations, in particular, playing a key role in negotiations.[2] The CRPD is also historic for bringing mental health issues more forcefully than ever before into the fold of international human rights law.

This development is timely given the major issues facing mental health 'systems' in the developed West. In England, the Schizophrenia Commission described the acute system as 'broken and demoralised'.[3] In Canada, the Mental Health Commission describe a 'system that is not working well', in which 'the status quo is not an option'.[4] In Australia, the National Mental Health Commission described the 'fundamental structural shortcomings' of the mental health system, a conclusion reportedly 'reached by numerous other independent and governmental reviews'. The commission stated: 'Despite [billions spent] on mental health every year, there are no agreed or

1 Convention on the Rights of Persons with Disabilities, opened for signature 30 March 2007, Doc.A/61/611 (entered into force 3 May 2008).

2 R Kayess and P French, 'Out of Darkness into Light? Introducing the Convention on the Rights of Persons with Disabilities' (2008) 8(1) *Human Rights Law Review* 1.

3 Schizophrenia Commission, 'The Abandoned Illness' (Rethink Mental Illness, 2012) 3 <www.rethink.org>.

4 Mental Health Commission of Canada, Canada, Changing Directions, Changing Lives: The Mental Health Strategy for Canada (2012) 9.

consistent national measures of whether this is leading to effective outcomes or whether people's lives are being improved as a result'.[5]

These evaluations will be familiar to anyone interested in mental health policy worldwide. People who have used mental health services (or found them inaccessible) are likely to be acutely aware of these shortcomings, as are those who have felt violated by involuntary psychiatric interventions.

There are indications of significant and unmet demand for effective support. In England, the Secretary of State for Health reported that the yearly admissions of people with a 'primary and secondary diagnosis of mental health conditions' to emergency departments had increased from 330,000 in 2002 to more than one million from 2014 onward.[6] In Canada, the national Mental Health Commission reported that 'mental illness is a leading cause of disability',[7] while the Australian Bureau of Statistics ranks a 'psychological/psychiatric condition' as the *primary* reason for Australians to receive a disability support pension.[8] At the global level, the World Health Organisation has reported that 'mental and substance use disorders are the leading cause of disability worldwide'.[9]

In one sense, these reports warrant caution. Public attitudes and professional practice towards mental health have changed greatly in recent decades. Year-on-year statistics may reveal an increase in rates of diagnosis and reporting rather than increasing rates of impairment, illness and distress. Concerns have also been raised about the biomedical approach underlying many of these reports, and the potentially *disabling* effects or sectoral interests served by portraying the issues as a public health crisis. Irrespective of these disagreements, it is generally agreed that there is a significant and, in many cases, unmet public demand for mental health support of some kind.

Non-consensual psychiatric intervention is implicated in the shortcomings of mental health policy. Legislative schemes for the compulsory detention

5 National Mental Health Commission (Australia), 'Report of the National Review of Mental Health Programmes and Services: Summary', 30 November 2014, 18 <www.mentalhealthcommission.gov.au>.

6 United Kingdom Parliament, HC Deb, 'Mental Illness: Written Question – 216612', 8 December 2014.

7 Mental Health Commission of Canada, 'Why Investing in Mental Health will Contribute to Canada's Economic Prosperity and to the Sustainability of our Health Care System' (2014).

8 Department of Social Services, 'Characteristics of Disability Support Pension Recipients', Australian Government, June 2013.

9 World Health Organisation, 'Ten Facts on Mental Health' (2014) <www.who.int>.

and psychiatric treatment of people with severe mental health issues in certain circumstances are now commonplace in developed countries.[10] While rates of coercive interventions vary and are difficult to validate,[11] some reliable data exists. In common-law countries, a significant number of mental health–related hospital admissions occur on an involuntary basis. In England, for example, the Care Quality Commission reported that 51 per cent of all mental health inpatients during 2014–15 were subject to the Mental Health Act 1983 (England and Wales).[12] The National Health Service reported 63,622 instances of detention under the act in the year to April 2016.[13] This figure constituted a 47 per cent increase since 2006, the year comparable records began,[14] and the year 2014–15 saw a 10 per cent increase over the previous year and the highest ever year-on-year increase.[15] *Outside* the hospital, in people's homes and residences, reports have also emerged of increased involuntary psychiatric interventions in jurisdictions that use compulsory community treatment.[16]

It is also noteworthy that class, race and gender are implicated in involuntary psychiatric intervention.[17] For example, across Britain as a whole, higher rates of detention were reportedly experienced by women and people from

[10] B McSherry and I Freckelton (eds), *Coercive Care: Rights, Law and Policy* (Routledge, 2014) 3.

[11] For example, the Canadian Institute for Health Information ('CIHI') reports that it 'does not have sufficient data to produce rates for involuntary and voluntary treatment for any province. Although CIHI data sources have some data on this subject, the coverage is partial.' Personal correspondence with Harry Kang, senior analyst, Rehabilitation and Mental Health Methodologies and Specialized Care, Canadian Institute for Health Information, 5 February 2016.

[12] Care Quality Commission, *Monitoring the Mental Health Act in 2014/15* (2015) 6 <www.gov.uk/government/publications>.

[13] Community and Mental Health Team, NHS Digital, Inpatients formally detained in hospitals under the Mental Health Act 1983, and patients subject to supervised community treatment uses of the Mental Health Act: Annual Statistics, 2015/16 (30 November 2016) <www.content.digital.nhs.uk>.

[14] Ibid.

[15] Care Quality Commission, above n 12, 4.

[16] See, P Appelbaum, 'Law and Psychiatry: Twenty-Five Years of Law and Psychiatry' (2006) 57(1) *Psychiatric Services* 18; A Molodynski, J Rugkasa and T Burns, 'Coercion and Compulsion in Community Mental Health Care' (2010) 95 *British Medical Bulletin* 117; S Johnson, 'Can We Reverse the Rising Tide of Compulsory Admissions?' (2013) 381(9878) *The Lancet* 1603.

[17] B Audini and P Lelliott, 'Age, Gender and Ethnicity of Those Detained under Part II of the Mental Health Act 1983' (2002) 180 *British Journal of Psychiatry* 222; L Snowden and F Cheung, 'Use of Inpatient Mental Health Services by Members of Ethnic Minority Groups' (1990) 45(3) *American Psychologist* 347; P Prior, *Gender and Mental Health* (New York University Press, 1999) 155–7; Y Stolk, H Minas and S Klimidis, 'Access to Mental Health Services in Victoria: A Focus on Ethnic Communities', *Victorian Transcultural Psychiatry Unit* (2008) 3.

'the Black or Black British ethnic group' and 'Asian or Asian British'.[18] In New Zealand, according to Melissa McLeod and colleagues, Māori people experience seclusion under mental health law at the highest population-based rate reported internationally.[19]

Some commentators suggest that resource scarcity is a higher-order concern than non-consensual psychiatric intervention. Elyn Saks, who has written about her own personal experience of unwanted forced treatment, has argued that '[t]he central problem facing the mental health system today is not treating unwilling patients but failure to provide treatment to willing patients. There is simply not enough care for those that want it'.[20]

The current vulnerability of local and international economic systems may exacerbate such unmet need. Financial limitations may well represent a barrier to rights-based systems of support, particularly where some evidence suggests a rise in population mental health issues following fiscal austerity.[21] Yet even if resource scarcity is made a first-order concern, coercive interventions continue to shape broader service provision. Saks herself acknowledges that admission policies favour those who meet civil commitment criteria, whereby 'current policy no doubt leads to much shading of the truth among patients and doctors alike: say the magic words, or you won't be admitted'.[22] Others have reported that fear of involuntary commitment or eagerness to be discharged can lead to the concealment of distress or suicidal thoughts, which, perversely, cuts off potential support.[23]

A picture of cyclical disadvantage emerges. Funding gaps for voluntary services increase the likelihood of emergency crises. Emergency crises then 'warrant' coercion under the terms of mental health law, and institutional resources

[18] Health and Social Care Information Centre, Inpatients Formally Detained in Hospitals Under the Mental Health Act 1983 and Patients Subject to Supervised Community Treatment, England – 2014–2015, Annual figures (2015) 16, 17 <www.hscic.gov.uk>.

[19] The Māori are the indigenous people of New Zealand. M McLeod, P King, J Stanley, C Lacey, R Cunningham and S Simmonds, 'The Use of Seclusion for Māori in Adult In-Patient Mental Health Services in New Zealand', The National Centre of Mental Health Research, Information and Workplace Development, Te Pou o te Whakaaro Nui, 2013.

[20] E Saks, *Refusing Care: Forced Treatment and the Rights of the Mentally Ill* (University of Chicago Press, 2002) 72.

[21] B Barr, P Kinderman and M Whitehead, 'Trends in Mental Health Inequalities in England during a Period of Recession, Austerity and Welfare Reform 2004 to 2013' (2015) 147 *Social Science and Medicine (1982)* 324.

[22] Saks, above n 20, 72.

[23] D Webb, *Thinking About Suicide: Contemplating the Urge to Die* (PCCS, 2010) 170; MS Swartz, JW Swanson and MJ Hannon, 'Does Fear of Coercion Keep People Away from Mental Health Treatment? Evidence from a Survey of Persons with Schizophrenia and Mental Health Professionals' (2003) 21(4) *Behavioural Science Law* 459.

are diverted to compulsory treatment. Restrictions are imposed on an already marginalised population who must forfeit their right to refuse extreme measures that they do not want: unwanted medication with very serious risks and side effects, electroconvulsive therapy and psychosurgery. Susan Stefan, who interviewed and surveyed 244 suicide attempt survivors, argues that

> our policies and practices regarding suicide create an irrational incentive structure where people understand that they have to attempt suicide to get help, help which is of questionable utility, while community-based approaches that are less expensive and work are underfunded. We have a system that doesn't work for anyone – neither the people who are supposed to be providing help, nor the people who are supposed to be receiving it.[24]

These observations highlight how laws – in this case, the apparent suicide-prevention mechanism of mental health law – can authoritatively create the power structures, institutions and incentives for mental health services.[25]

As such, tremendous strategies are required to align law, policy and practice in the mental health context with human rights aspirations for the twenty-first century. This book asks what the CRPD can contribute to this aim. It asks whether the broad support framework of the CRPD, and its articulation of equality, autonomy, human dignity and solidarity, provides a conceptual and practical alternative to existing legal configurations that emphasise 'substituted decision-making'. 'Substituted decision-making' roughly refers to paternalistic, 'best interests' formulations for responding to mental distress, disorder and disablement. As well as examining the practical and conceptual implications of such a shift, this book identifies what forms human rights-based support might take, or may currently exist, in law, policy and practice.

A THE CRPD AND MENTAL HEALTH

The subject of human rights has expanded greatly since the Second World War and is now a fundamental part of our legal, political and moral landscape. The CRPD was the first international human rights treaty of the twenty-first century and adds to a suite of international human rights instruments. These instruments have the potential to influence not only state laws and practices but also the work of a diverse range of government and non-government institutions, including influencing decisions about research, reporting,

[24] S Stefan, *Rational Suicide, Irrational Laws: Examining Current Approaches to Suicide in Policy and Law* (Oxford University Press, 2016) xxi.

[25] C Unsworth, *The Politics of Mental Health Legislation* (Oxford University Press, 1987).

action, recommendations and arbitration. Philip Alston and Ryan Goodman have described the 'youth' of the human rights regime in general,[26] which would place the CRPD in its infancy. Yet CRPD negotiators benefitted from the accumulated knowledge surrounding all human rights treaties of the twentieth century (including prominent critiques of human rights).[27] Further, negotiators were able to draw on the consolidated input of people with disabilities and their representative organisations. More than one hundred disabled people's organisations were accredited to take part in the final stages of negotiations.[28] This lent to the process the collective insights of a long-standing global social movement and the political buy-in of its regional, national and local networks.[29] These foundations – and the unprecedented scale of endorsement by countries around the world – offer a strong basis to move from the majestic generalities of human rights law towards the hard work of implementation at the national and local level.

The CRPD does not contain a definition of disability, although it does provide a 'de facto' definition. Article 1 describes mental health-related disability with reference to 'those who have long-term physical, *mental*, intellectual or sensory impairments which in interaction with various barriers may hinder their full and effective participation in society on an equal basis with others'.[30] This definition emphasises the evolving character of human development and sets out a non-exhaustive list of aspects of the human being. The preamble refers to disability as 'an evolving concept … [that] results from the interaction between persons with impairments and attitudinal and environmental barriers that hinders their full and effective participation in society on an equal basis with others'.[31]

These descriptions raise the important point of terminology. Terms such as 'consumer', 'psychiatric survivor' and 'patient' imply different values. Some critical theorists argue that speech can alter normative facts – for example, where derogatory presuppositions and expectations frame conversations.[32] The

26 P Alston and R Goodman, *International Human Rights* (Oxford University Press, 2013).

27 As well as general human rights instruments, the CRPD builds upon previous international texts related to persons with disabilities, including the Standard Rules on the Equalization of Opportunities for Persons with Disabilities – 1994 (not a legally binding treaty) and the World Programme of Action on Disabled Persons – 1982 (not a legally binding treaty).

28 M Sabatello, 'The New Diplomacy' in M Sabatello and M Schulze (eds), *Human Rights and Disability Advocacy* (University of Pennsylvania Press, 2013) 239, 240.

29 Ibid. 239–58. See also Kayess and French, above n 2.

30 CRPD art 1 (emphasis added).

31 Ibid. (e).

32 See, e.g., R Delgado, 'Words That Wound: A Tort Action for Racial Insults, Epithets, and Name Calling' in MJ Matsuda et al. (eds), *Words That Wound: Critical Race Theory, Assaultive Speech, and the First Amendment* (Westview Press, 1993). Mary Kate McGowan has presented

extent to which terms like 'mental illness' and 'psychosocial disability' perpetuate or address disadvantage remains debatable, and will depend greatly on the context in which they are used. Naming a group can demarcate grounds for protection (for example, through anti-discrimination law) or help to garner resources (for example, by directing goods to those in need). Consider the quite extraordinary statement reportedly made by Judy Rapoport, former head of child psychiatry at the US National Institute of Mental Health: 'I am incredibly disciplined in the diagnostic classifications in my research, but in my private practice, I'll call a kid a zebra if it will get him the educational services I think he needs'.[33]

It is also self-evident that ascriptions in the mental health context can harm.[34] Diagnoses can pathologise ways of being or, alongside prejudicial legislation, legitimise grounds for discrimination. (Consider that homosexuality and bisexuality appeared in the Classification of Diseases of the World Health Organisation as late as 1992[35] or that in Britain until 2013, members of Parliament detained on grounds of mental disorder could have been compelled to vacate their seats.)[36] Mental health terminology is likely to remain controversial where people with severe mental health issues continue to be among the most marginalised and excluded in society. Arguably, debates over terminology will dissipate once systems of social organisation that generate disadvantage are addressed.[37]

For the purposes of this book, it seemed more appropriate to draw primarily from terminology advanced in UN jurisprudence, even if it is not commonplace.[38] Since the CRPD came into force, the term 'psychosocial disability' is

an account of the way speech can affect identity-based oppression by altering 'the conversational score' in such a way that it oppresses members of a certain group. MK McGowan, 'Conversational Exercitives and the Force of Pornography' (2003) 31(2) *Philosophy and Public Affairs* 155–89.

33 R Ginker, *Unstrange Minds: Remapping the World of Autism* (Basic Books, 2007) 131.

34 See, e.g., The Lancet Psychiatry, 'Medicalisation and Its Discontents' (2016) 3(7) *The Lancet Psychiatry* 591.

35 Royal College of Psychiatrists, 'Royal College of Psychiatrists' Statement on Sexual Orientation' (Position Statement PS02/2014, April 2014) 2. More recently, the Indonesian Psychiatrists Association has reportedly classified homosexuality, bisexuality and transsexualism as mental disorders, which it says can be cured through proper treatment. L Yosephine, 'Indonesian Psychiatrists Label LGBT as Mental Disorders', *The Jakarta Post*, 24 February 2016.

36 R Kelly and H Armstrong, 'Repeal of Section 141 of the Mental Health Act 1983', House of Commons Library SN/PC/6168, 19 February 2014.

37 G Quinn, 'Reflections on the Value of Intersectionality to the Development of Non-Discrimination Law' (2016) 16 *The Equal Rights Review* 63, 67.

38 Exceptions include terms adopted by authors cited or defined in law, as well as the occasional use of other terms typical to the mental health context, such as 'mental disorder', 'mental health crises' and 'mental health issues'.

increasingly being used, including by the Office of the High Commission for Human Rights, the World Health Organisation, the CRPD Committee, various governments and a range of disabled people's organisations.[39] This term is by no means uncontroversial, nor does it refer to a coherent and easily defined human experience[40] – although neither, I would hasten to add, do long-standing clinical terms such as 'mental disorder'.[41] Many people who have experienced severe mental health issues, even the majority, may not think of their experience in terms of disability. Nor might mental health professionals be inclined to use disability to frame their practice. As the book investigates the overlap and difference between the CRPD and mental health law and policy, and between notions of 'disability' and 'mental illness/disorder', I will explore these tensions and ambiguities in detail. I will also refer to persons with intellectual and cognitive disability, even though such differentiation can be misleading. Again, neat distinctions are rarely possible. Many people with intellectual or cognitive disabilities may also experience psychosocial disability.[42]

Over the past decade, the idea of a broad support framework in line with the CRPD has gained international momentum in academic monographs, journal articles, case law, regional courts and bodies, in the formation of centres and institutes, in the operation of conferences and symposia, and in

39 World Health Organisation, Comprehensive Mental Health Action Plan 2013–2020 (2013) 6; Human Rights Committee, Promotion and Protection of All Human Rights, Civil, Political, Economic, Social and Cultural Rights, including the Right to Development, 32nd sess, UN Doc A/HRC/32/L.26 (adopted 29 June 2016) [2]; Committee on the Rights of Persons with Disabilities, *General Comment No 1: Article 12: Equal Recognition before the Law*, 11th sess, UN Doc CRPD/C/GC/1 (19 May 2014) 11 [9]; UN General Assembly, OHCHR, Tenth session, Agenda item 2, 'Annual Report of the United Nations High Commissioner for Human Rights and Reports of the Office of the High Commissioner and the Secretary-General: Thematic Study by the Office of the United Nations High Commissioner for Human Rights on Enhancing Awareness and Understanding of the Convention on the Rights of Persons with Disabilities', Distr. GENERAL A/HRC/10/48 (26 January 2009) [49]; International Disability Alliance, 'Letter on Functional Capacity to the CRPD Committee', (International Disability Alliance, 2010) <www.internationaldisabilityalliance.org>.

40 See H Spandler, J Anderson and B Sapey (eds), *Madness, Distress and the Politics of Disablement* (Policy Press, 2015).

41 For example, the Diagnostic and Statistical Manual of Mental Disorders, Fourth Edition, Text Revision, states that 'no definition adequately specifies precise boundaries for the concept of "mental disorder" … different situations call for different definitions'. Further, 'there is no assumption that each category of mental disorder is a completely discrete entity with absolute boundaries dividing it from other mental disorders or from no mental disorder'. American Psychiatric Association, *Diagnostic and Statistical Manual of Mental Disorders (Text Revision): DSM-IV-TR* (American Psychiatric Association, 4th ed, 2000) xxx–xxxi.

42 M Bach and L Kerzner, *A New Paradigm for Protecting Autonomy and the Right to Legal Capacity* (Report to the Law Commission of Ontario, 2010) 15 <www.lco-cdo.org>.

UN activity. The Commissioner of Human Rights for the Council of Europe released an issues paper that sought to convey the practical implications of providing CRPD-based support in the mental health context:

> We may already be used to thinking about reasonable accommodation in terms of ramps and work place adjustments, but the concept also applies to the decision-making process where individuals interact with each other ... [P]ersons with intellectual or psychosocial disabilities may not, at the outset, understand the implications of certain transactions and interventions such as taking a loan, terminating an insurance policy or consenting to or refusing a medical operation. In such cases, the bank, insurance company and doctor have an obligation to take positive measures (to the limit of disproportionate or undue burden) to accommodate the individual, to ensure that he/she is put in an equivalent position with others.[43]

The analogy of the 'decision-making ramp' simply captures how the CRPD reframes decision-making and self-determination using principles of equality and non-discrimination, including strong provision for accessibility and 'reasonable accommodation'.[44]

However, decision-making is only *one aspect* of a much broader range of support promoted in the CRPD. Some support may relate to decision-making, some may not. Support might include personal advocacy, peer support services, access to healthcare treatment, housing, statutory representation agreements and, in exceptional circumstances – when it is necessary to make a decision about a person when his or her wishes are unknown or unclear – using the best interpretation of a person's 'rights, will and preference' to guide decisions.[45] Given this broad scope, the framework of support advanced in the CRPD is unsurprisingly contested.

Commentators refer to the CRPD to make radically different claims: from replacing mental health legislation and abolishing forced treatment, to refining the grounds for involuntary intervention and improving procedural safeguards. For example, Tina Minkowitz has argued that non-consensual psychiatric intervention constitutes torture and cruel, inhuman and degrading

43 Council of Europe Commissioner for Human Rights, 'Who Gets to Decide? Right to Legal Capacity for Persons with Intellectual and Psychosocial Disabilities', Comm DH/Issue Paper, Strasbourg, 20 February 2012, 12.

44 Article 2 of the CRPD defines 'reasonable accommodations' as the 'necessary and appropriate modification and adjustments not imposing a disproportionate or undue burden, where needed in a particular case, to ensure to persons with disabilities the enjoyment or exercise on an equal basis with others of all human rights and fundamental freedoms'. CRPD art 2.

45 Ibid., art 12(4). Committee on the Rights of Persons with Disabilities, above n 39, 5 [21].

treatment.[46] She calls for a moratorium on all forced treatment, the delivery of reparations to survivors and the creation of a framework of supported decision-making for all.[47] In contrast, John Dawson has described the prohibition of substituted decision-making and determinations that a person lacks mental capacity as 'unrealistic', and makes the case for a 'more conservative interpretation' of CRPD requirements.[48] Similarly, Adrian Ward has argued that Article 12, which is central to the support framework of the CRPD, was the result of 'inept drafting', leaving those it was meant to protect more vulnerable to abuse than before.[49]

In part, the support framework is contested because some of its core concepts are new and somewhat ambiguous. One such concept, 'supported decision-making', is advanced by UN treaty bodies as the preferred response for persons otherwise subjected to the powers of civil commitment laws.[50] This widely used term does not appear in the CRPD yet has become prominent in major debates about the implications of the CRPD for mental health law, policy and practice. The CRPD Committee refers to a 'supported decision-making regime' as the overarching support framework in law and policy required by the CRPD.[51] Others have used the term 'supported decision-making' to describe practices designed to strengthen the self-determination of persons with disabilities, including systems of mutual aid and peer support developed in parallel to state-based services.[52] Still others have applied the term to professional practices[53] or to statutory arrangements for appointing decision-making

[46] T Minkowitz, 'The United Nations Convention on the Rights of Persons with Disabilities and The Right To Be Free From Non-consensual Psychiatric Interventions' (2007) 34(2) *Syracuse Journal of International Law and Commerce* 405.

[47] Ibid.

[48] J Dawson, 'A Realistic Approach to Assessing Mental Health Laws' Compliance with the UNCRPD' (2015) 40 *International Journal of Law and Psychiatry* 70. See also M Freeman et al., 'Reversing Hard Won Victories in the Name of Human Rights: A Critique of the General Comment on Article 12 of the UN Convention on the Rights of Persons with Disabilities' (2015) 2 *Lancet Psychiatry* 844; J Dute, 'Should Substituted Decision-making be Abolished?' (2015) 22 *European Journal of Health Law* 315.

[49] A Ward, 'Adults with Incapacity: Freedom and Liberty, Rights and Status: Part 1' (2011) 5 *Scots Law Times* 21.

[50] See, e.g., Committee on the Rights of Persons with Disabilities, above n 39, 6 [26]; UN Office of the High Commissioner for Human Rights, 'Chapter Six: From Provisions to Practice: Implementing the Convention, Legal Capacity and Supported Decision-Making', *United Nations Handbook for Parliamentarians on the Convention on the Rights of Persons with Disabilities* (Geneva, 2007) 89 <www.un.org>.

[51] Committee on the Rights of Persons with Disabilities, above n 39, 6–7 [29].

[52] See Center for the Human Rights of Users and Survivors of Psychiatry, 'Good Practices' <www.chrusp.org>.

[53] S Pathare and LS Shields, 'Supported Decision-making for Persons with Mental Illness: A Review' (2012) 34(2) *Public Health Reviews* 1.

assistants.[54] These few examples indicate that 'supported decision-making' does not point to any singular agreed-upon meaning; instead, it refers to a collection of various demands. These demands centre upon boosting the agency of persons with disabilities, offering them resources for making choices among good options about how to live.

The CRPD Committee has directed States Parties to 'take action to develop laws and policies to *replace* regimes of substituted decision-making by supported decision-making',[55] including by abolishing mental health legislation.[56] According to the CRPD Committee:

> Historically, persons with disabilities have been denied their right to legal capacity in many areas in a discriminatory manner under substitute decision-making regimes such as guardianship, conservatorship and mental health laws that permit forced treatment. These practices must be abolished in order to ensure that full legal capacity is restored to persons with disabilities on an equal basis with others.[57]

The CRPD Committee echoes the comments of the UN Office of the High Commissioner for Human Rights and the UN Special Rapporteur on Torture.[58] In 2013, the latter called on all countries to:

> Impose an absolute ban on all forced and non-consensual medical interventions against persons with disabilities, including the non-consensual administration of psychosurgery, electroshock and mind-altering drugs such as neuroleptics, the use of restraint and solitary confinement, for both long- and short-term application.[59]

Similarly, in 2016, the UN Special Rapporteur on the rights of persons with disabilities, Catalina Devandas-Aguilar, and on the right to health, Dainius Pûras, called on states to 'do away with non-consensual psychiatric treatment'.[60] In less conclusive terms, the Human Rights Council,

[54] M Bach and L Kerzner, *A New Paradigm for Protecting Autonomy and the Right to Legal Capacity* (Report to the Law Commission of Ontario, 2010) 84 <www.lco-cdo.org>.

[55] Committee on the Rights of Persons with Disabilities, 'Compliance Review: Tunisia', 5th sess, UN Doc CRPD/C/TUN/CO/1 (adopted 15 April 2011) 4 [23] (emphasis added).

[56] Ibid.

[57] Committee on the Rights of Persons with Disabilities, above n 39, 2 [7].

[58] Ibid. [49].

[59] JE Méndez, Report of the Special Rapporteur on Torture and Other Cruel, Inhuman or Degrading Treatment or Punishment, UN Doc A/HRC/22/53 (1 February 2013) [81].

[60] Office of the High Commissioner for Human Rights, '"Dignity Must Prevail" – An Appeal to Do Away with Non-consensual Psychiatric Treatment World Mental Health Day – Saturday 10 October 2015', Geneva, 8 October 2015.

which adopted a Resolution on Mental Health and Human Rights in 2016, emphasised:

> that persons with mental health conditions or psychosocial disabilities, in particular persons using mental health services, may be subject to, inter alia, widespread discrimination, stigma, prejudice, violence, social exclusion and segregation, unlawful or arbitrary institutionalization, overmedicalization and treatment practices that fail to respect their autonomy, will and preferences.[61]

The Human Rights Council expressed equal concern that 'such practices may constitute or lead to violations and abuses of their human rights and fundamental freedoms, sometimes amounting to torture or other cruel, inhuman, or degrading treatment or punishment, and conscious that greater commitment is needed to address all the remaining challenges in this regard'.[62] The comments of different UN agencies reveal differences in views, particularly regarding a definitive stance on coercive psychiatric intervention (which I will discuss in Chapter 2). However, there is a clear consensus among UN agencies on 'the need for States to take active steps to fully integrate a human rights perspective into mental health and community services'[63] and to 'provide access to support for decisions about psychiatric and other medical treatment'.[64] Despite such directives remaining uncontroversial and widely endorsed, details of the practical implication of such support remain unclear.[65]

Establishing theoretical coherence and normative practices takes time, and key questions about the CRPD and mental health law remain open.[66] For example, under proposals for a 'supported decision-making regime', how should the law work when someone is unaware of the harm of her or his actions? What should happen when a person wishes to jump off a building because she believes doing so will save the world? If an intervenor blocks that person, should he or she be charged with assault or deprivation of liberty? If not, how should the law respond? In the general health setting, what happens when a person with hypothermia in a state of confusion refuses treatment to correct his temperature? Turning to the issue of public safety, it is not hard to

61 Human Rights Committee, above n 39 [2].

62 Ibid.

63 Ibid.

64 Committee on the Rights of Persons with Disabilities, above n 39, 6–7 [29].

65 P Gooding, 'Supported Decision-Making: A Rights-Based Disability Concept and Its Implications for Mental Health Law' (2013) 20(3) *Psychiatry, Psychology and Law* 43.

66 See, e.g., B Kelly, *Dignity, Mental Health and Human Rights: Coercion and the Law* (Ashgate, 2015).

imagine how mental health crises and other extraordinary mental states could lead to violence against others.

These matters tend to give rise to a fundamental question in debates about supported decision-making and the broader support framework of the CRPD; that is, when can coercive responses be justified? There seems to be a broad consensus that at least *some* crises warrant *some* form of coercive intervention. Yet the literature on the CRPD includes little to identify what those crises are, how they might be determined or what CRPD-compliant 'coercion' might look like. In part, this gap has opened up where proponents of universal legal capacity do not wish to 'lock in' exceptions, which historically have placed people with disabilities on a slippery slope towards having their rights denied[67] – but what are the consequences of this avoidance?

Other questions about the model remain. Common concerns include the possible manipulation of decisions by so-called supporters, the need for safeguards to address violence and exploitation perpetrated *against* persons with psychosocial disabilities, and questions as to responsibility when supporters or supported persons make mistakes. What of the very real concerns of families and other informal supporters who will query the push for 'dignity of risk' for individuals, and ask, 'Who will be around to pick up the inevitable pieces, service providers'?[68]

Again, there are few easy answers, and any efforts to provide them will require careful public deliberation, including by government, service users and people with disabilities, families, professionals and others. Academics can assist by clarifying key issues and offering avenues to resolve major dilemmas – an aim to which this book is directed.

B RESEARCH SCOPE AND AIMS

This book is meant as an addition to work already under way that draws together mental health scholarship and practice, international human rights law and disability studies. It takes account of changing trends in law and policy, as well as critical developments in scientific knowledge; in views on disability, health, illness, safety and risk; and in the consolidating input of persons with disabilities and their representative organisations.

Part I of the book will consider the origins, aims and major conceptual and practical issues of mental health law today. Chapter 1 will focus on the

67 G Quinn, 'Personhood and Legal Capacity: Perspectives on the Paradigm Shift of Article 12 CRPD' (Paper, Harvard Law School, 20 February 2010) 21 <www.nuigalway.ie>.

68 Ibid. 5.

purpose and procedure of mental health law, and Chapter 2 will examine the implications of the CRPD not just for civil commitment law, but for broader efforts to secure the rights of persons with disabilities. Chapter 3 will list the major criticisms of mental health law, in order to better identify the issues that the CRPD support framework could remedy. Part II of the book will turn explicitly to the support framework of the CRPD, examining its core concepts (Chapter 4) and the emerging strategies for implementation in mental health policy and beyond (Chapter 5), as well as the extent to which these might address the major dilemmas in mental health law. Conceptual discussion will be balanced with considerations of real-world application: Chapter 6 will list a range of programs, policies and laws that apply different elements of the framework in practice. Chapter 7 will consider key criticisms of the support framework of the CRPD and offer a number of strategies to address these concerns, as well as highlight remaining pitfalls and ambiguities. The final chapter will draw together themes from the previous chapters and present a final set of recommendations to policymakers and others, indicating where law and policy could be better aligned with obligations under international human rights law, and where an organised public might rearrange social responses to distress, disorder and disablement.

The scope will be restricted to common-law jurisdictions in Western, high-income countries, such as the United Kingdom, Canada, Australia, New Zealand and Ireland, all of which are signatories to the CRPD.[69] In common-law systems, the term 'mental health law' can potentially describe a body of laws that extends across criminal law (the insanity defence/fitness to plead), contract law (invalidation due to incapacity), tort law (psychiatric injury) and civil commitment law (involuntary treatment and detention).[70] For the purposes of this book, I use 'mental health law' to refer to civil commitment laws: statutes that legalise the detention and involuntary treatment of people with apparent or diagnosed mental illness in certain circumstances.[71] The broad cross-jurisdictional focus can be justified on two grounds. First, international trends shape mental health laws, even as their powers and duties are set out in national or state legislation.[72] Second, the CRPD raises remarkably

[69] Of these countries, only Ireland has yet to ratify the CRPD (as of June 2016). Where relevant to key themes, I will also refer to the United States, which has not ratified the CRPD.

[70] See, generally, J Stapleton, *Disease and Compensation Debate* (Oxford University Press, 1986).

[71] There are exceptions to this generalisation, where some mental health statutes require a formal diagnosis, whilst others merely require the 'appearance' of mental illness to come into effect.

[72] See L Gostin et al., *Principles of Mental Health Law and Policy* (Oxford University Press, 2010) v; B McSherry (ed), *International Trends in Mental Health Laws* (Federation Press, 2008); see

similar challenges across high-income common-law jurisdictions, particularly the fundamental challenge it poses to domestic mental health law.

Considerations of time and space prevent a broader focus on 'low- and middle-income' countries.[73] Bhargavi Davar has argued that commentators in the Anglosphere often present debates about the CRPD and legal capacity in universal terms.[74] This ignores major social, cultural and political differences that affect what it means to achieve equal recognition before the law.[75] Certainly, the different historical picture of the 'West', which saw a proliferation of mental asylums through modernity, raises different concerns. Non-Western low- and middle-income countries tend to be more concerned with developing inclusive and community-based mental health support than with issues of state sanctioned compulsory treatment and detention.[76] Nevertheless, the investigation in this book will be relevant worldwide, given its interrelated concern with, on the one hand, forced treatment, deprivation of liberty and restriction of legal capacity, and, on the other, inclusive and community-based support services, the right to health and accessibility, and other positive obligations under the CRPD.

Another axis here is mental health and liberalism, including prominent critiques of liberalism. Current legal doctrine embeds a traditional liberal model of autonomy, promoting a view of the legal subject in its ideal form as individualistic, rationalistic and atomised. Yet this model of autonomy is impoverished, creating one of the main conceptual impediments to securing effective resources to improve the agency and equality of people with psychosocial disability. Proponents of the CRPD support framework highlight the interdependent and relational nature of autonomy and decision-making. This relational emphasis, while not without complications,[77] places a high priority on the constitutive relationships through which people exercise rights.

This last point deserves special consideration. Early on, the concept of 'supported decision-making', contested as it may be, developed from supportive relationships between people with disabilities and their typically informal

also T Carney, 'Globalisation and Guardianship: Harmonisation or (Postmodern) Diversity?' (2001) 24 *International Journal of Law and Psychiatry* 95.

73 See, e.g., B Davar and TK Ravindran (eds), *Gendering Mental Health: Knowledges, Identities, and Institutions* (Oxford University Press, 2015); Pathare and Shields, above n 53.

74 B Davar, 'Legal Capacity and Civil Political Rights for People with Psychosocial Disabilities' in A Hans (ed), *Disability, Gender and the Trajectories of Power* (Sage, 2015) ch 11.

75 Ibid.

76 Ibid.

77 See L Series, 'Relationships, Autonomy and Legal Capacity: Mental Capacity and Support Paradigms' (2015) 40 *International Journal of Law and Psychiatry* 80.

support networks.[78] Perhaps more accurately, those practices have developed within peer groups, families and communities, often alongside the development of theory – and often *prior* to being formalised in law or policy. Even as these ideas and practices were drawn into CRPD negotiations and elevated into international human rights law, they are likely to continue developing in spaces quite outside the formal domains of service provision, scholarship and policymaking, particularly where individuals and families deal with the day-to-day issues of mental distress and disorder. Acknowledging these informal contributions can help to guard against the 'juridification' of concepts such as supported decision-making or their 'professionalisation' by any one group – and helps to promote support 'on the ground' in the lives of those it is meant, ultimately, to assist.

C AUDIENCE

In terms of audience, the book is aimed at those who have an interest in mental health, disability and human rights. It is directed at researchers, but I have sought to make it accessible to policymakers, people with lived experience of mental health crises, family members and organisations working to incorporate the CRPD into domestic systems. The book is also aimed at judges, mental health professionals, lawyers, activists, social workers and others who engage daily with the puzzles of mental health and who are seeking ways to address what they view as the crucial concerns of their work. It is also written to reach the general public, and particularly those who may seek formal language to describe their sense of fairness due to people with psychosocial disability.

The book is also directed at those who may have long viewed mental health issues from a 'human rights perspective' yet may lack the formal language to describe it. A major shift has occurred in debates about mental health issues in recent decades, particularly given the increasing contributions of persons with lived experience of mental health crises and those who have used – or felt abused by – mental health services.[79] Difficulties arise where

78 See R Gordon, 'The Emergence of Assisted (Supported) Decision-Making in the Canadian Law of Adult Guardianship and Substitute Decision-Making' (2000) 23(1) *International Journal of Law and Psychiatry* 61, 64. For an example of early theory to inform supported decision-making, see W Wolfensberger, *A Brief Introduction to Social Role Valorization: A High-Order Concept for Addressing the Plight of Societally Devalued People, and for Structuring Human Services* (Training Institute for Human Service Planning, Leadership and Change Agentry, 3rd ed, 1998).

79 While the contribution of this group to contemporary debate – as policymakers, professional support providers and human rights lawyers, among others – has increased in scale over recent decades, it would be misleading to suggest that this is an entirely new phenomenon. For a historical overview of contributions from people with lived experience in asylums, and under

people's reference points in debates do not fit with dominant frameworks. Some people may feel inarticulate or marginalised. Diana Rose states that 'service users cannot avoid emotional language when presenting their experience but worry that it will disrupt dialogue with professionals in contexts' such as conferences, university classrooms or workplace meetings'.[80] This generalisation – and it is a generalisation, given the increase in formal contributions by people with psychosocial disabilities[81] – may extend to others seeking inroads to debates, including family members, allied health professionals and social workers. Applying formal language to intuitively held viewpoints can improve chances for deliberative participation—though it is also true that making space for unconventional contributions can have the same effect.

Throughout, I have sought to engage with such groups to offer tools for undertaking a human rights analysis and to see whether it is of use – which, of course, I believe it will be. Among the diverse views of commentators, from those who look sceptically upon the CRPD to those who herald its potential to 'shift paradigms', there is a shared desire to see the law used to strengthen people's agency, reduce suffering and improve equality in the mental health context. This is not to ignore the real and potentially intractable differences at certain points in the debate, particularly where questions of coercion arise. Instead, by focusing on common values articulated in widely ratified human rights instruments and teasing out important differences, it is possible to advance debates and reveal potential solutions. This book is premised on the belief that an organised public can create space to express authentic concern for human rights, and that a human rights analysis can effect institutional change.

Finally, the book is designed for students. I have written with undergraduate and postgraduate reading requirements in mind, which are typically chapter-based. As such, minor points of repetition occur between chapters. In aiming for such a broad audience, the book was designed so that readers can skip certain sections to suit their knowledge and interests.

lunacy laws and policies in nineteenth-century England, for example, see S Wise, *Inconvenient People: Lunacy, Liberty and the Mad-Doctors in Victorian England* (Bodley Head, 2012).

80 T Burns and D Rose, 'How Can the Service User Voice Be Best Heard at Psychiatric Meetings?' (2013) 203(2) *The British Journal of Psychiatry* 88.

81 See, e.g., Spandler, Anderson and Sapey, above n 40; A Dhanda, 'Legal Capacity in the Disability Rights Convention: Stranglehold of the Past or Lodestar for the Future?' (2007) 34 *Syracuse Journal of International Law and Commerce* 429.

D CONCLUSION

The various approaches adopted in this book to the competing values at stake in mental health law will be contested (as well they should be). Yet I argue that mental health law and those it authorises to act are de facto making choices among competing values now. Such decisions, whether regarding policymaking or individual instances of coercion, are often presented as practical interventions based on neutral expert knowledge. However, such decisions are based on moral judgements (often unstated) and potentially spurious scientific claims. A CRPD-based approach would bring choices about competing values into the open and provide a frame for pursuing principled, evidence-based responses, whether in policy or in other forms of social organisation among civil society. When courts, tribunals and other bodies that administer justice make judgements about legal interpretations, an approach that was cognisant of the CRPD support framework could facilitate greater self-awareness and thus improve the quality of those judgements.

In the face of major concerns with mental health policy and practice worldwide, this book is offered as a contribution to the ongoing quest to identify and develop persuasive and workable alternatives. It builds on the initial enthusiasm for the CRPD, but aims to give it firmer grounds in law, policy and practice.

PART I

WHAT DO HUMAN RIGHTS MEAN FOR MENTAL HEALTH LAW?

1

Mental Health Law: Purpose and Procedures

A INTRODUCTION

Mental health legislation faces an uncertain future. The UN Convention on the Rights of Persons with Disabilities ('CRPD')[1] has bolstered calls to repeal or fundamentally alter laws that allow for involuntary psychiatric intervention. The CRPD also strengthens calls to provide support for people in mental health crises in ways that uphold self-determination, liberty, mental and physical integrity, the right to health, and so on. In order to isolate the questions and dilemmas raised by these proposals, it is useful to identify the function, purpose and procedures of mental health law today.

Elizabeth Farr's account of her own mental health crisis helps to illustrate the broad aims of mental health law. After years of aural and visual hallucinations, Farr experienced an urgent need to undertake a dangerous act:

> I thought the voices came from other worlds. I believed I was approaching an Enlightened State. The voices told me that in order to reach this Enlightened state I would have, at the appropriate moment, to jump from the seventh floor of a building and land on my head in a certain way. This would put me in a cosmic junction whereupon … I would be able to enlighten all mankind.[2]

The dilemma that arises when people appear to be putting themselves (or others) in grave risk without apparent knowledge of that risk produces no easy answers. At present, mental health legislation provides the principal grounds in law for finding these answers.

1 Convention on the Rights of Persons with Disabilities, opened for signature 30 March 2007, Doc.A/61/611 (entered into force 3 May 2008).

2 E Farr, 'A Personal Account of Schizophrenia', in M Tsuang (ed), *Schizophrenia: The Facts* (Oxford University Press, 1982) 1–2.

Brenda Hale has observed that mental health law perpetually struggles to 'reconcile three overlapping but often competing goals: protecting the public, obtaining access to the services people need, and safeguarding users' civil rights'.[3] The regulatory role of mental health law places detention in hospital and compulsory treatment in a different category to deprivation of liberty and assault. Monitoring and procedural protections then allow those subject to involuntary interventions to challenge their commitment. From this view, if emergency powers are needed in *some* circumstances for *some* mental health crises – which, it can be reasonably assumed, the majority of people agree should be the case – then these powers need to be clearly authorised and regulated. Mental health legislation currently provides this function. It offers procedural protection and safeguards to prevent paternalistic overreach, negligence or inconsistent application of the law.

However, this view has been sharply criticised by a range of commentators, including the UN Committee on the Rights of Persons with Disabilities,[4] the Office of the High Commissioner and UN Special Rapporteurs for Torture, Disability and Health.[5] In order to contextualise these criticisms, this chapter will chart the historical development of 'rights-based' mental health law. It will ask how an area of law that was widely held to be liberal, humanist and compassionate came to be seen by major UN agencies and human rights commentators today as its opposite – illiberal, cruel and a violation of human rights.

B THE ORIGINS OF MENTAL HEALTH LEGISLATION IN COMMON LAW

English statutes from the era of the reign of Edward I in the late thirteenth century form the basis of modern mental health law.[6] Those early laws permitted

[3] B Hale, 'Justice and Equality in Mental Health Law: The European Experience' (2007) 30(1) *International Journal of Law and Psychiatry* 18, 19. See also G Richardson, 'Reforming Mental Health Laws: Principle or Pragmatism?' (2001) 54 *Current Legal Problems* 415; G Richardson, 'Involuntary Treatment: Search for Principles' in K Diesfeld and I Freckelton (eds), *Involuntary Detention and Therapeutic Jurisprudence* (Aldershot, 2003) 54.

[4] Committee on the Rights of Persons with Disabilities, *General Comment No 1: Article 12: Equal Recognition Before the Law*, 11th sess, UN Doc CRPD/C/GC/1 (19 May 2014) 11 [42].

[5] Office of the High Commissioner for Human Rights, '"Dignity Must Prevail" – An Appeal to Do Away with Non-consensual Psychiatric Treatment World Mental Health Day – Saturday 10 October 2015', Geneva, 8 October 2015.

[6] The medieval origins of mental health law are often traced back to the *Statute De Prerogativa Regis* 1324, 17 Edw 2, st 1, c IX and XP Fennell, 'Mental Health Law: History, Policy, and Regulation' in L Gostin et al. (eds), *Principles of Mental Health Law and Policy* (Oxford University Press, 2010) 1.05.

the sovereign to intervene in order to protect the private property of those deemed 'unsound of mind', on the legal basis of *parens patriae*.[7] The *parens patriae* power, translating literally as 'parent of the country', justified detaining and/or treating a person compulsorily on the basis that the person was not able to look after his or her own interests.[8] Today, *parens patriae* is typically identified with guardianship and family law, where state interventions address abusive or negligent parents or legal guardians, and the state acts as the 'parent' of any child or individual needing protection.[9]

Another important legal doctrine underpinning mental health law concerns the 'police powers' of the state. In the eighteenth century, powers of this nature were introduced into common law by the Vagrancy Act 1744.[10] Such laws were mostly designed to protect private property from the interference of 'mad' people.[11] The 'police powers' doctrine justifies intervention to protect other people from the person deemed 'mad', typically from physical violence. As with *parens patriae*, subjects became wards of the sovereign.

The entwinement of the legal doctrines of *parens patriae* and the police powers of the state have remained an important feature of mental health law. Indeed, the basis for non-consensual treatment and detention today, of posing 'risk of harm to self or others', reflects the entwinement of these dual legal doctrines.

The eighteenth and nineteenth centuries saw the development of a new role for the state in relation to treatment and welfare.[12] Laws began to reflect what was ostensibly a greater protective impulse. Theobald argues that, in the nineteenth century, two major professional groups propelled the development of 'lunacy laws' from then on: '[M]edical men ... desired early and easy treatment of persons afflicted with mental disease, and at the same time demanded protection against the risks they ran in certifying persons as lunatics; lawyers ... attached more weight to the liberty of the person than to the possibility of a cure by facility for compulsory confinement'.[13] Theobald's observation captures a recurring tension between the medical and legal professional frameworks along the theoretical lines of the paternalist and libertarian. (However, commentators may have overstated this case, as will be discussed shortly.)

7 Ibid. 1.06.

8 M Cavadino, *Mental Health Law in Context: Doctors' Orders?* (Aldershot, 1989) 132.

9 Cavadino distinguishes three types of paternalism which underpin *parens patriae* powers: physical (preventing physical harm), psychological (safeguarding mental health) and moral (preventing the individual from coming to 'moral harm'). Ibid.

10 Vagrancy Act 1744, 17 Geo 2, c 5.

11 For Cavadino's elaboration on 'police powers', see Cavadino, above n 8, 132.

12 See, generally, Fennell, above n 6 [1.89]–[1.103].

13 H Theobald, *The Law Relating to Lunacy* (Oxford University Press, 1987 [original publication, 1924]) 78.

Patricia Allderidge has characterised the history of mental health law as a pendulum swinging between the preference for legal regulation, on the one hand, and a greater emphasis on clinical discretion to treat and detain, on the other.[14] Thus viewed, the middle of the twentieth century saw a swing from legalism towards clinical discretion in mental health law.[15] An indication of the decisive endorsement of the medical approach is captured in the titles of the new statues – for example, the Mental Treatment Act 1930 (UK) and later the Mental Health Act 1959 (UK),[16] which were replicated in most common-law countries.[17]

The Mental Health Act 1959 (UK) saw the abolition of legal proceedings heard by magistrates in matters of detainment and detention upon which clinicians decided.[18] Detention was justified on the basis that mental illness so affected a person as to warrant his or her detention in the interests of his or her (or others') health and safety. Lunacy laws granted consulting psychiatrists plenary powers and the authority to impose detention. Once an individual had been admitted, the Mental Health Review Tribunal, a quasi-judicial body constituted under the Mental Health Act 1959 (UK), provided periodic review of the detention following the first twenty-eight-day period after certification.[19]

However, to suggest that the Mental Health Act 1959 (UK) represented a wholesale medicalisation of mental health law would be misleading. After all, social workers gained increased powers at the commitment stage, and family members were vested with equal power to apply for certification.[20] Further, the Royal Medico-Psychological Association and the British Medical Association did not entirely support the extent of the discretionary powers granted under the Mental Health Act 1959 (UK); both expressed concern that the discretionary power would delegitimise the profession.[21]

[14] P Allderidge, 'Hospitals, Madhouses and Asylums: Cycles in the Care of the Insane' (1979) 134 *British Journal of Psychiatry* 321.

[15] Fennell, above n 6, s H[37].

[16] Mental Health Act 1959 7 & 8 Eliz. 2.

[17] In Australia, for example, the Mental Health Act 1958 (NSW) and the Mental Health Act 1959 (Vic) consolidated laws for the treatment and care of people described in the Victorian legislation as 'the mentally ill and the intellectually defective' – understood in contemporary terms as people with psychosocial and intellectual disabilities.

[18] There was, however, limited recourse for protection of patients in the form of a tribunal system. See Mental Health Act 1959 (UK) 7 & 8 Eliz. 2 s 2(1), 2(2), 2(3), and s 3(1).

[19] Mental Health Act 1959 (UK) 7 & 8 Eliz. 2 s 3(1).

[20] P Fennell, 'Institutionalising the Community: The Codification of Clinical Authority and the Limits of Rights-Based Approaches' in B McSherry and P Weller (eds), *Rethinking Rights-Based Mental Health Law* (Hart, 2010) 13, 38.

[21] In particular, the British Medical Association and the Royal Medico-Psychological Association resisted the devolution of the power to detain from the super-intendant physician

It is debatable as to why legislation expanded clinical powers. Clive Unsworth has argued that the Mental Health Act 1959 (UK) reflects the state's ideological departure from the classical liberal emphasis on autonomy that drove the Lunacy Act 1890 and its reorientation towards the collectivist and interventionist objectives of the post-war welfare state.[22]

Regardless, the legislation expanded the scope and importance of the term 'health' in the justification of detention and treatment. Fennell argues that the term 'health' was broadened to include mental health and the justification for detention and involuntary treatment was moved further along a continuum from 'negative paternalism', where intervention was justified if it brought benefit to the subject, and not necessarily just to prevent immediate harm.[23] This new health framework in law helped establish a medical model as the dominant model of disability. The United Kingdom Mental Health Act 1959 brought both 'mental illness' and 'mental handicap' (the latter referring, in contemporary terms, to intellectual disability) under the one statute.[24]

The Mental Health Act 1959 continued authorising non-consensual treatment following admission, as had been the case since the Lunacy Act 1845.[25] Even as mainstream hospitals began to replace asylums as the main sites of state psychiatric intervention, it was still assumed that once a person was admitted, consent was not required. It is worth noting that the very *notion* of informed consent more generally was new to medical practice at this time, and was by no means predominant in general medical care.[26] Tom Beauchamp details the emerging acceptance in the 1970s among physicians and biomedical researchers that informed consent was a moral and legal duty for certain procedures.[27] Yet even then, in Beauchamp's terms, '[t]hese developments prompted an

to all consulting psychiatrists. See C Unsworth, *The Politics of Mental Health Legislation* (Clarendon Press, 1987).

22 Ibid.

23 Fennell, above n 20, 38–39.

24 It provided a guardianship regime under which appointed guardians were granted the powers of a father over a child younger than fourteen. Even at its peak, guardianship power was used infrequently, given that psychiatric institutions could readily compel people without consent and access to courts to confer guardianship powers was limited. Coverage of both disability categories under one statute becomes relevant decades later, when separate and parallel substituted decision-making legislation (guardianship and mental health statutes) emerges in developed Western jurisdictions.

25 Fennell, above n 20, 41.

26 R Faden and T Beauchamp, *A History and Theory of Informed Consent* (Oxford University Press, 1986) 86–90.

27 T Beauchamp, 'Informed Consent: Its History, Meaning, and Present Challenges' (2011) 20(4) *Cambridge Quarterly of Healthcare Ethics*, The International Journal of Healthcare Ethics Committees 515.

explosion of largely negative commentary on informed consent in the medical literature of the mid-1970s', in which '[p]hysicians saw the demands of informed consent as impossible to fulfill and, at least in some cases, inconsistent with good patient care'.[28] This seems to be an important (and oft-overlooked) feature of medical history and, interestingly, echoes contemporary controversies provoked by the CRPD.[29] Beauchamp's characterisation of clinicians who viewed the 'demands of informed consent as impossible to fulfill and, at least in some cases, inconsistent with good patient care' could well summarise the response to the CRPD by some prominent commentators today.[30]

Overall, the medicalising shift of early and mid-twentieth-century mental health legislation took place in the context of increasing state intervention and social welfare in health policy, one in which the biomedical model of mental health issues was strongly endorsed.

C DEINSTITUTIONALISATION AND 'RIGHTS-BASED' LEGALISM

From the late 1970s, mental health laws began shifting towards so-called legalism, which saw the development of greater procedural protections over involuntary treatment and detention.[31] In the second half of the twentieth century, deinstutitionalisation saw the dismantling of the stand-alone psychiatric hospital system, a transition tied inextricably to the evolution of modern mental health law. The reforms established a diverse range of mental health services that included general hospital, residential, community and other support services. The number of psychiatric hospital beds gradually declined. In the United Kingdom, for example, the number of psychiatric beds diminished from 150,000 in 1954[32] to 30,533 in 2010, as recorded in the 2010 census count,[33] which is considerable given the associated population increase during that time. Governments introduced new statutes in the policy context of reforming liberal states in the 1980s, which included the language of rights.[34] Under

28 Ibid.

29 See Chapter 7.

30 See, e.g., M Freeman et al., 'Reversing Hard Won Victories in the Name of Human Rights: A Critique of the General Comment on Article 12 of the UN Convention on the Rights of Persons with Disabilities' (2015) 2 *Lancet Psychiatry* 844; J Dute, 'Should Substituted Decision-Making Be Abolished?' (2015) 22 *European Journal of Health Law* 315.

31 See, generally, McSherry and Weller, above n 20.

32 N Rose, 'Historical Changes in Mental Health Practice' in G Thornicroft and G Szmukler (eds), *Textbook of Community Psychiatry* (Oxford University Press, 2001) 13.

33 A Molodynski, J Rugkasa and T Burns, 'Coercion and Compulsion in Community Mental Health Care' (2010) 95 *British Medical Bulletin* 107.

34 McSherry and Weller, above n 20, 5.

the Mental Health Act 1986 (Vic), for example, section 4(1)(ac) states that one objective of the act is to 'Protect the rights of people with a mental disorder'.[35] Section 4(2)(b) states that interpretations of the act should consider that: 'Any restriction upon the liberty of patients and other people with a mental disorder and any interference with their rights, privacy, dignity and self-respect are kept to the minimum necessary in the circumstances'.[36]

This trend of using rights vocabularies in mental health law can be seen across common-law countries and other Western, high-income jurisdictions and is characterised by the expanded review process through mental health review tribunals or similar bodies.[37] Such courts or tribunals today continue to operate within parameters detailed in mental health laws, including review periods and requirements for procedural fairness.[38] Statutory duties introduced under mental health law include those designed to secure individual rights, including rights to access services, refuse medical treatment, and review detention and imposed treatment decisions.[39]

Bernadette McSherry and Penelope Weller characterise mental health law from this time as 'rights-based legalism' given the precedence granted to the language of rights.[40] Such laws formulated both defensive claims (rights not to be interfered with; for example, ensuring 'least possible restrictive' interventions) and positive demands (rights to be provided with quality care; for example, 'effective giving of … care and treatment').[41] Case law, as illustrated by the US case of *Rogers v Okin* (1979),[42] affords the right to refuse medication in non-emergency conditions. One reason for the introduction of new mental health statutes, typified in common-law jurisdictions by the Mental Health Act 1983 (England and Wales), was to constrain professional power and bring greater accountability to clinical discretion through the regulation of decision-making processes, combined with quasi-judicial review. There is some evidence to suggest that this change resulted in lower rates of involuntary psychiatric intervention. For example, a multistate study across the European

35 Mental Health Act 1986 (Vic) s 4 (1)(ac).

36 Ibid. (2)(b).

37 Under the Mental Health Act 1986 (Vic), for example, the Mental Health Review Board was established to review and hear appeals by or on behalf of involuntary or security patients, with expanded powers to discharge. Ibid. s 22 (1a), (2).

38 D Tait and T Carney, *Australian Mental Health Tribunals: Space for Fairness, Freedom, Protection and Treatment?* (Themis, 2011).

39 L Gostin, 'The Ideology of Entitlement: The Application of Contemporary Legal Approaches to Psychiatry' in P Bean (ed), *Mental Illness: Changes and Trends* (Wiley, 1983) 50.

40 See, generally, McSherry and Weller, above n 20.

41 Ibid. 4–5.

42 *Rogers v Okin*, 478 F Supp 1342 (1979).

Union found significantly lower compulsory admission rates in member states that mandated an independent counsel, tribunal or court process.[43]

Importantly, these 'legalist' reformers introduced new criteria for involuntary treatment and detention. Section two of the Mental Health Act 1983 (England and Wales) is typical; applications for assessment of eligibility for involuntary treatment and detention can be made where:

> (a) [the person] is suffering from mental disorder of a nature or degree which warrants the detention of the patient in a hospital for assessment (or for assessment followed by medical treatment) for at least a limited period; and
> (b) [the person] ought to be so detained in the interests of his [or her] own health or safety or with a view to the protection of other persons.[44]

Although the added procedural protections of rights-based mental health law moved involuntary treatment closer to of the kind of procedural protections found in criminal proceedings, laws remained couched in the language of care and treatment. A paternalistic framework endured, expressed in the 'best interests' standard which guided interventions – either implicitly or explicitly – in mental health law in Canada, New Zealand, Australia, Ireland, the United Kingdom and elsewhere.[45] The power to detain was reframed to occur, as exemplified by the terms of the Mental Health Act 1986 (Vic), 'in the least possible restrictive environment and least possible intrusive manner consistent with the effective giving of that care and treatment'.[46]

Such legislation exists, in part, to provide a statutory basis for treatment and detention as a health issue, which might otherwise warrant a charge of assault and detention.[47] Under most contemporary mental health laws, the principal persons granted power to treat and detain involuntarily are psychiatrists.[48]

43 H J Salize and H Dressing, 'Epidemiology of Involuntary Placement of Mentally Ill People Across the European Union' (2004) 184(2) *The British Journal of Psychiatry* 163.

44 Mental Health Act 1983 (England and Wales) c 20, s 2(a)(b).

45 See, e.g., Mental Capacity Act 2005 (England and Wales) c 9. Chapter 1, Sections 4 and 6 of the Mental Health Act 2007 refer to the 'appropriate treatment test' for responding to those subject to the Act. Mental Health Act 2007 (UK) c 12, ch 1 ss 4, 6; See, e.g., Ontario Mental Health Act, RSO. 1990, c M.7., s 20(1.1); Mental Health (Care and Treatment) (Scotland) Act 2003 (Scot) asp 13 s 276(3); Mental Health Act 2001 (Ireland) s 4(1); Mental Health (Northern Ireland) Order 1986 No 595 (N.I. 4) s 3(1); Mental Capacity Bill 2014 (NI) s 1(7); Mental Health (Compulsory Assessment and Treatment) Act 1992 (NZ) s 2(1). In Australia, see, e.g., Mental Health Act 2014 (WA) pt 2 div 3.

46 Mental Health Act 1983 (England and Wales) c 20, s 5(a).

47 Fennell, above n 20, 24–5.

48 B Burdekin, 'Human Rights and Mental Illness: Report of the National Inquiry into the Human Rights of People with Mental Illness, Human Rights and Equal Opportunity Commission', vol 1 (Australian Government Publishing, 1993) 40.

In its 1993 'Report of the National Inquiry into the Human Rights of People with Mental Illness', the Australian Human Rights and Equal Opportunity Commission describes psychiatrists as being granted 'effective decision-making power under the legislation'.[49] Under the Mental Health Act (1986) (Vic), for example, the following applies: 'If an involuntary patient refuses to consent to necessary treatment or is unable to consent to treatment for his or her mental illness, consent in writing may be given by the authorised psychiatrist'.[50]

Neil Rees has characterised this power as a form of 'clinical guardianship' because 'the treating doctor becomes the substitute decision-maker for psychiatric treatment'.[51] Decisions under mental health law may regard matters of detention (in seclusion or otherwise) and in some cases may relate to accommodation and other lifestyle choices, such as driving.[52] However, clinical decisions generally regard medical treatment, typically psychiatric medication, as well as electroconvulsive therapy ('ECT'), which is commonly known as electric shock treatment, and psychosurgery. ECT refers to an intervention in which clinicians pass an electric current through a person's brain, stimulating an epileptic fit. ECT and psychosurgery treatments are administered infrequently compared to other involuntary interventions and typically require authorisation by a mental health tribunal or similar statutory body given their invasive nature.[53] Mental health tribunals and similar statutory bodies also have effective substituted decision-making power.[54] In the case

49 Ibid.

50 Mental Health Act 1986 (Vic) s 12AD(2).

51 N Rees, 'Learning From the Past, Looking to the Future: Is Victorian Mental Health Law Ripe for Reform?' (Mental Health Review Board of Victoria's 20th Anniversary Conference, Melbourne, 6 December 2007).

52 The term 'treatment' is interpreted widely in legislation and in practice. It is understood by some to encompass matters beyond the explicitly medical, including, for example, accommodation or driving. Carney has identified this as a semantic issue that causes confusion where clinical imperatives for 'treatment' may veer towards 'behavioural management'. See T Carney, 'Mental Health Law in Postmodern Society: Time for New Paradigms?' (2003) 10(1) *Psychiatry, Psychology and Law* 12.

53 For example, there is some evidence indicating that the numbers are relatively low. See, e.g., W Chanpattana, 'A Questionnaire Survey of ECT Practice in Australia' (2007) 23 *Journal of ECT* 89.The same conclusion may be drawn about psychosurgery. In Victoria, for example, the Victorian Psychosurgery Review Board, which must grant permission for any psychosurgery measure, dealt with no operations between 2001 and 2006, and 12 applications between 2007 and 2012 (all of them for 'deep brain stimulation'). Mental Health Review Board of Victoria and Psychosurgery Review Board of Victoria, *2012/2013 Annual Report* (2013) 30 <www.mht.vic.gov.au/forms-and-publication/annual-reports>.

54 There is some controversy as to whether this is the case, as mental health tribunals are meant to be a regulatory safeguard. See, generally, E Perkins, *Decision-Making in Mental Health Review Tribunals* (Policy Studies Institute, 2003); see also W Obomanu and H Kennedy,

of *MH2 v Mental Health Review Board*,[55] for example, the Victorian Mental Health Review Board was described as having 'all the functions of the decision maker … that are relevant to the decision under review'.[56]

1 *Involuntary Interventions Outside Hospital: The Rise of Compulsory Psychiatric Interventions in the 'Community'*

Another important development in recent decades is the introduction of non-consensual psychiatric interventions outside the hospital, in people's residences. These measures are typically referred to as 'assisted outpatient treatment' ('AOT') in the United States and 'community treatment orders' ('CTOs') in jurisdictions like England, Wales, Canada, Australia and New Zealand,[57] and have been introduced in multiple jurisdictions over the past three decades (with the notable exception of jurisdictions like Northern Ireland and the Republic of Ireland). An AOT or CTO authorises the imposition of conditions on a former inpatient following hospital discharge. Conditions typically relate to medication. However, depending on the jurisdiction, conditions can also relate to where the person must live and other lifestyle matters, such as how much alcohol he or she can consume.[58] If individuals breach conditions, clinicians can recall them to involuntary hospitalisation.

Early on, reformers portrayed AOT and CTOs as middle options on a spectrum between voluntary community support and involuntary hospitalisation.[59] This claim forms the basis for an account of compulsory outpatient treatment as enhancing autonomy. According to the Australian Human Rights and Equal Opportunity Commission in 1993, for example, CTOs 'encouraged' community-based treatment by providing an alternative to detention and involuntary inpatient treatment.[60] John Dawson conducted interviews

'"Juridogenic" Harm: Statutory Principles for the New Mental Health Tribunals' (2005) 21 *Psychiatric Bulletin* 331.

55 MH2 v Mental Health Review Board (Human Rights) [2013] VCAT 734 (8 May 2013).

56 Ibid. para 2(d).

57 For example, England and Wales saw the introduction of supervised community treatment orders in 2008 through amendments to the 1983 Mental Health Act. See Mental Health Act 1983 (England and Wales) ss 3, 37. See also E Light et al., 'Community Treatment Orders in Australia: Rates and Patterns of Use' (2012) 20(6) *Australasian Psychiatry* 478. In Canada, all jurisdictions, with the exception of New Brunswick and the Territories, use CTOs or comparable legislation.

58 See, generally, SR Kisely, LA Campbell and NJ Preston, 'Compulsory Community and Involuntary Outpatient Treatment for People with Severe Mental Disorders' (2011) (2) *Cochrane Database Systematic Review* CD004408.

59 E McDonnell and T Bartholomew, 'Community Treatment Orders in Victoria: Emergent Issues and Anomalies' (1997) 4(1) *Psychiatry, Psychology, and Law* 25, 26.

60 Burdekin, above n 48, 67.

with clinical professionals in Victoria, Australia, who tended to see CTOs as being instrumental to the rapid pace of deinstitutionalisation and the associated shift of resources from hospitals to 'community-based' services.[61] This hypothesis may be true with respect to CTOs having a *role* in moving resources. However, the cause is unlikely to be the efficacy of CTOs (and Dawson's findings are perhaps more indicative of psychiatrists' increased comfort in allowing patients to leave hospital knowing that they were subject to compulsory treatment in the community). Indeed, since the introduction of CTOs, three large-scale randomised controlled trials and their meta-analyses have failed to support the view that they are effective in achieving their principal aim; that is, lowering hospitalisation rates or protecting individuals subject to them.[62] Given these results, some prominent early supporters of CTOs in England and Wales, including senior figures in the United Kingdom's Royal College of Psychiatrists, have called for their repeal;[63] human rights bodies today are unlikely to endorse CTOs, particularly given the prohibition of disability-based restrictions on rights in the CRPD (as shall be discussed in detail in the next chapter).

CTOs reflect a paradox in the era of 'rights-based legalism', one that might give pause for us to consider whether 'rights-based legalism' is the best way to characterise developments in mental health law around the turn of the twenty-first century. Despite the increasing focus on procedural protections in mental health law, the coercive 'powers' of clinicians have expanded in certain respects. Roughly one-quarter of US states, and most common-law high-income countries, have adopted outpatient commitment statutes in the past three decades, leading to increased clinical powers for the supervision and non-consensual intervention of people outside hospital.[64] In the United States, Paul Appelbaum observes that the increase in forced outpatient treatment

[61] J Dawson, *Community Treatment Orders: International Comparisons* (University of Otago, 2005).

[62] T Burns et al., 'Community Treatment Orders for Patients with Psychosis (OCTET): A Randomised Controlled Trial' (2013) 381(9878) *The Lancet* 1627; S Kisely and L Campbell, 'Compulsory Community and Involuntary Outpatient Treatment for People with Severe Mental Disorders' (2015) 41 *Schizophrenia Bulletin* 542; S Kisely and K Hall, 'An Updated Meta-analysis of Randomized Controlled Evidence for the Effectiveness of Community Treatment Orders' (2014) 59 *Canadian Journal of Psychiatry* 561; M Swartz et al., 'Can Involuntary Outpatient Commitment Reduce Hospital Recidivism? Findings from a Randomized Trial with Severely Mentally Ill Individuals' (1999) 156 *American Journal of Psychiatry* 1968.

[63] R Heun, S Dave and P Rowlands, 'Little Evidence for Community Treatment Orders – A Battle Fought with Heavy Weapons' (2016) 40 *BJPsych Bulletin* 115; S Manning, '"Psychiatric Asbos" Were an Error Says Key Advisor', *The Independent*, 14 April 2013.

[64] See P Appelbaum, 'Ambivalence Codified: California's New Outpatient Commitment Statute' (2003) 54 *Psychiatric Services* 26.

over the past twenty-five years has meant that legal oversight of clinical activity has diminished, which 'almost always' makes it easier for clinical authorities to enforce civil commitment and involuntary treatment.[65] Reflecting on this period of mental health law, Appelbaum observes that '[c]riteria for involuntary hospitalization have been expanded gradually in many jurisdictions, and procedural rigor has been somewhat relaxed'.[66] Similarly, in England and Wales, according to Molodynski and colleagues, the use of CTOs has 'substantially outstripped' official expectations since their introduction in 2008.[67] In Victoria, Australia, which was one of the first non-US jurisdictions to introduce CTOs, rates of use are the highest per capita in the world.[68] It also appears likely that a number of jurisdictions, at least in the US, allow preventive compulsory community treatment, even if this is not explicitly promoted in law; that is, if the person is *at risk* of becoming eligible for civil commitment.[69]

2 *Separating Mental Health and Capacity/Guardianship Laws*

The separation of adult guardianship laws and mental health legislation is relevant here. Adult guardianship laws (which are sometimes referred to as mental capacity laws)[70] provide for substituted decision-making for adults deemed to lack mental capacity. Typical legislation attributes mental incapacity to 'an impairment of, or a disturbance in the functioning of, the mind or brain'.[71] As early as the 1980s, Australia,[72] New Zealand[73] and Canada[74] saw substantial reform of adult guardianship laws along a different but parallel trajectory to

65 P Appelbaum, 'Law and Psychiatry: Twenty-Five Years of Law and Psychiatry' (2006) 57(1) *Psychiatric Services* 18.

66 Ibid.

67 Molodynski, Rugkasa and Burns, above n 33.

68 E Light et al., 'Community Treatment Orders in Australia: Rates and Patterns of Use' (2012) 20(6) *Australasian Psychiatry* 478.

69 P Clark Robbins et al., 'Regional Differences in New York's Assisted Outpatient Treatment Program' (2010) 61(10) *Psychiatric Services* 970; E Saks, 'Involuntary Outpatient Commitment' (2003) 9(1–2) *Psychology, Public Policy, and Law* 94, 97; Treatment Advocacy Center, 'State Standards for Assisted Treatment: Civil Commitment Criteria for Inpatient or Outpatient Psychiatric Services' (2014) <www.treatmentadvocacycenter.org>.

70 See, e.g., Mental Capacity Act 2005 (England and Wales) c 9.

71 Ibid. s 2(1).

72 See, e.g., Guardianship and Administration Board Act 1986 (Vic); Disability Services and Guardianship Act 1987 (NSW).

73 See WR Atkin, 'Adult Guardianship Reforms – Reflections on the New Zealand Model' (1997) 20(1) *International Journal of Law and Psychiatry* 77.

74 R Gordon, 'The Emergence of Assisted (Supported) Decision-Making in the Canadian Law of Adult Guardianship and Substitute Decision-Making' (2000) 23(1) *International Journal of Law and Psychiatry* 61.

mental health law.[75] These new statutes created a substituted decision-making regime in step with the transition from large-scale institutions to 'community-based' services. Guardianship laws were typically designed for persons with cognitive and intellectual disabilities (who no longer fell under mental health law)[76] but could apply to anyone found to lack mental capacity, including some persons with psychosocial disabilities.[77] Typically, guardianship/mental capacity laws authorise a tribunal to appoint a guardian or a 'deputy', potentially a relative or close friend, to make decisions regarding healthcare or 'lifestyle' choices, or to appoint an administrator to manage financial matters. Public officials may serve as substituted decision-makers and/or financial administrators. Neil Rees has argued that the new wave of guardianship/mental capacity laws from the 1980s onward aimed to 'operate as a "last resort" option under legislation which promoted autonomy and self-sufficiency, encouraged the appointment of family members rather than representatives of the state as substituted decision-makers, and resulted in limited and reviewable orders'.[78]

To state the differences clearly, mental health legislation is typically concerned with the following:

a) people with psychiatric diagnoses or apparent mental disorder – mental incapacity is not used as a grounds for involuntary psychiatric intervention;[79]
b) crisis intervention, involuntary treatment and detention; and
c) the authorisation of a treating clinician, who is granted primary substituted decision-making power on matters of healthcare and detention.[80]

By contrast, a guardianship/mental capacity law, such as the Mental Capacity Act (2005) (England and Wales), is characterised by the following:

a) it is meant for those with a range of impairments that affect cognitive functioning;
b) it relies on assessing mental capacity to determine where 'deficits' are relevant to decisions that need to be made; and

[75] For example, in Victoria, Australia, the Guardianship and Administration Act 1986 (Vic) was introduced alongside the Mental Health Act 1986 (Vic) as a cluster of substituted decision-making statutes, with a view to reforming the Mental Health Act 1959 (Vic).

[76] N Rees, 'The Fusion Proposal: A Next Step?' in McSherry and Weller, above n 20, 73.

[77] Ibid. 80.

[78] Ibid. 79–80.

[79] Notable exceptions include laws introduced since the CRPD came into force, which have integrated a mental capacity assessment into criteria for involuntary interventions. See in Mental Health Law (2016) 39(2) *University of New South Wales Law Journal* 596.

[80] Burdekin, above n 48, 40.

c) the substituted decision-maker is (in ideal circumstances) a trusted person appointed according to the preference of the person, potentially a family member, but also a public official such as a 'deputy', public advocate, financial administrator or public trustee.

The idea of 'supported decision-making' evolved, in large part, from changes to adult guardianship law. British Columbia in Canada, for example, adopted one of the first legislative models for decision-making assistance from as early as 1996.[81] In the Republic of Ireland, the Assisted Decision-Making (Capacity) Act 2015 is a mental capacity law emerged from reform to the country's 'wardship' system, which may have taken the British Columbian model a step further by providing multiple statutory support options for citizens who may require support to make decisions and exercise legal capacity.[82] Specific guardianship/mental capacity laws, as well as the general literature on adult capacity law and other mental capacity-related laws, will provide a useful resource throughout this book when examining key issues in the mental health context. The differences and overlap between mental health law and guardianship law will become important later in the book, in the discussion about possible legal frameworks for mental health support in line with the CRPD.

D DISCUSSION: CHANGE AND CONTINUITY IN MENTAL HEALTH LAW

Before proceeding to outline the implications of the CRPD for mental health law, it is useful to ask what the background in this chapter means for this book. First, it is noteworthy that the function, justification and (to a lesser extent) procedures of mental health laws over time have remained largely the same. Mental health law continues to authorise the restriction of liberty and the right to refuse medical treatment through interventions that would otherwise be unlawful.

The legal basis for mental health law continues to be to prevent harm to individuals and the community by entwining the doctrine of *parens patriae* with the police powers of the state. Protection remains a major driver, in terms of addressing risk (whether real or imagined) both to the broader public and to unwell individuals.[83] So, too, there remains an unchanging premise in all domestic mental health statutes that special legal treatment is required for people with apparent or diagnosed mental disorder. This position is justified on two grounds: such persons are less responsible causally and, hence, legally

[81] Representation Agreement Act, RSBC 1996, c 405 (British Columbia).

[82] Assisted Decision-Making (Capacity) Act 2015 (Ireland).

[83] See Fennell, above n 20, 13.

for their actions,[84] and they are more dangerous than others.[85] (The veracity of these claims will be scrutinised in Chapter 3.) Overall, then, mental health laws retain the decades-long tension between the principles of autonomy and protection. In William Bingley and Chris Heginbotham's terms, these dual objectives seek 'to recognise, preserve and enhance the self-determination of individual patients whilst at the same time providing a framework for the care and treatment of those who are genuinely disabled as a result of mental illness'.[86]

This latter point – which is deeply contested, as shall be discussed in later chapters – raises another important issue regarding language. As a general comment, language around mental health law is greatly contested.[87] In particular, ongoing debates in this field have centred around two fluid and disputed topics, namely 'mental illness' and 'self-determination' (or, in earlier terminology, 'insanity' and 'liberty'). Spaulding has argued that the extent to which 'legalistic' mental health laws are seen to be libertarian 'depends on one's understanding of the relationship between liberty and mental disorder'.[88] One person may view untreated mental disorder as a *denial* of liberty; while another might see forced treatment in the same way. Using terms such as 'mental illness' and 'autonomy' without acknowledging their intended meaning, or without noting their fluidity and relationship, can result in commentators cloaking the underlying purposes of their use, which remain, at best, only vaguely stated. In analysing how the support framework of the CRPD might reshape the law's response to mental distress, disorder and disablement, it will be interesting to consider whether the 'human rights model of disability' and associated concepts can more satisfactorily address some of these persistent conceptual challenges.[89]

In terms of change, the following points are noteworthy. By the end of the twentieth century, and still today, the picture of mental health law in Western,

84 WJ Spaulding, 'Mapping the "New Legalism" of English Mental Health Law' (1989) 17(2) *The Journal of Law, Medicine and Ethics* 187.

85 See, e.g., G Szmukler, 'A New Mental Health (and Public Protection) Act: Risk Wins in the Balance Between Providing Care and Controlling Risk' (2001) 322(7277) *British Medical Journal* 2.

86 W Bingley and C Heginbotham, 'Mental Health Law: Objectives and Principles' in N Eastman and J Peay (eds), *Law Without Enforcement: Integrating Mental Health and Justice* (Hart, 1999) 39, 40.

87 In many ways, this difficulty is inherent to the entire mental health law project, as Peay has pointed out. See J Peay, *Seminal Issues in Mental Health Law* (Ashgate, 2005) xvi.

88 For example, alleviation of psychosis might be seen as a restoration of liberty by re-establishing reason; involuntary treatment would, from this view, enhance autonomy and ostensibly minimise state intervention. If, on the other hand, involuntary treatment is viewed as an incursion by the state into the individual sphere and into legitimate ways of thinking and being, such an act becomes a paternalistic state intrusion. Spaulding, above n 84, 187.

89 I will directly consider these issues in Chapter 5.

high-income countries has become more complex. While large-scale stand-alone institutions have largely closed, the scope of substituted decision-making powers has expanded outside hospitals and into the 'community'. Compulsory psychiatric intervention today occurs in people's residences. An apparent contradiction emerges: despite the move to rights-based legislation, rates of non-consensual psychiatric intervention appear to be increasing in some respects, particularly regarding involuntary outpatient treatment.

A number of reviews have commented upon the lack of substantive rights brought about by rights-based mental health law. For example, the Irish Department of Health's 'Interim Report of the Steering Group on the Review of the Mental Health Act' found that, although it 'was anticipated that the introduction in the [Mental Health Act 2001 (Republic of Ireland)] of the statutory "best interests" principle would lead to a new emphasis on the rights of the patient … the reality is that the principle has been interpreted by the Courts in a paternalistic manner'.[90] According to the Steering Group, this interpretation is 'undermining the significant advances in mental health law which the Act was intended to enshrine, and has given rise to concerns that the human rights aspects of the legislation have been diluted and diminished'.[91] Alternatively, consider the comment of the Australian Human Rights and Equal Opportunity Commission in 1993, which found that legislative formulations in Australian states are 'marked by circularity of reasoning and apparently designed to intrude to a minimal degree upon the territory of psychiatrists'.[92] On the other hand, as noted previously, there is some evidence to show that jurisdictions which mandate tribunal or court processes have significantly lower compulsory admission rates compared to those that do not.[93]

These paradoxes suggest that, just as mental health 'systems' have become more complex, so too have configurations of mental health laws around the world. While general principles are shared, considerable variation occurs in specificities; for example, as relates to compulsory treatment in the community, the role of family and informal carers, and the relationship between detention and non-consensual treatment. To provide one example, the Ontario Mental Health Act 1990 includes powers to detain which do not

[90] Department of Health (Ireland), Interim Report of the Steering Group on the Review of the Mental Health Act 2001 (2012) 11 <www.dohc.ie>.

[91] Ibid.

[92] Burdekin, above n 48, 40.

[93] HJ Salize and H Dressing, 'Epidemiology of Involuntary Placement of Mentally Ill People Across the European Union' (2004) 184(2) *The British Journal of Psychiatry* 163.

necessarily extend to powers for involuntary treatment.[94] Instead, Ontario's Health Care Consent Act 1996 governs rules of capacity to consent to medical treatment.[95] In contrast, all Australian states and territories (each with its own distinct mental health statute) entwine detention and involuntary treatment, whereby people detained under mental health law are automatically subject to involuntary treatment powers.[96] This is just one example highlighting the diversity of mental health laws, which adds an extra layer of complexity when discussing cross-jurisdictional trends.

Some changes in commentary on mental health law are noteworthy. The first is the increasing push to use assessments of mental capacity to activate involuntary psychiatric intervention. Peter Bartlett has argued that the idea of using mental capacity–based tests for involuntary treatment has characterised progressive mental health law reform in recent years.[97] This priority partly arises from the question of whether mental capacity should be a central criterion for involuntary treatment in all medical contexts, regardless of whether they relate to 'mental' or 'physical' health.[98] In the past, most libertarian concerns with protecting autonomy and non-interference were directed to those 'falsely accused of mental disorder', whereas recent years have seen an emphasis on equality and non-discrimination in the exercise of patient choice *regardless of diagnosis* – especially for those who retain mental capacity.[99] These concerns centre on the question, Should we respect the right of competent patients to refuse psychiatric treatment, given that we respect their right to refuse physical medical care (such as chemotherapy), even if they die?[100] This fraught line of enquiry will become particularly relevant later in Chapter 4 when considering the potential benefits and drawbacks of the support framework of the CRPD.

94 Ontario Mental Health Act, RSO 1990, c M.7.

95 Health Care Consent Act, SO 1996, c 2, sch A. This approach relates, in part, to ethical questions around detaining someone due to an apparent or diagnosed mental disorder, without imposing medical treatment that might alleviate the disorder. See JE Gray and RL O'Reilly, 'Supreme Court of Canada's "Beautiful Mind" Case' (2009) 32(5) *International Journal of Law and Psychiatry* 315.

96 JE Gray et al., 'Australian and Canadian Mental Health Acts Compared' (2010) 44(12) *Australian and New Zealand Journal of Psychiatry* 1126.

97 P Bartlett, '"The Necessity Must Be Convincingly Shown to Exist": Standards for Compulsory Treatment for Mental Disorder Under the Mental Health Act 1983' (2011) 19 *Medical Law Review* 514, 541.

98 J Dawson and G Szmukler, 'Fusion of Mental Health and Incapacity Legislation' (2006) 188 *The British Journal of Psychiatry* 504.

99 Ibid.

100 J Dawson and G Szmukler, 'Compulsory Treatment and the Patient's Capacity to Consent' (Paper presented at the Australasian Institute of Judicial Administration Conference, Auckland, 2010).

For now, it is important to note that, despite mental capacity becoming a key concern in mental health law reform trends in mental health law are shifting still, particularly since the coming into force of the CRPD.[101] Indeed, Bartlett follows his appraisal of mental capacity as a major concern of recent mental health law reform by noting that the CRPD has created a 'significant shift in the legal landscape' away from mental capacity tests and towards evaluating a person's support requirements, and particularly his or her decision-making support needs.[102]

A second major change concerning the mental health field in recent decades is the existence of an expanded range of commentators. In particular, mental health service users and others with psychosocial disability are increasingly contributing to debates and developments in mental health law, policy and practice.[103] The fall of the asylum era in the West brought with it a rise in the 'global disability movement'. This diverse group of people with disabilities and their allies have helped change social responses to disability (including mental health) at the local, national and international level. The CRPD reflects this shift in international human rights law, as the next chapter outlines.[104] This broad social movement included persons with psychosocial disability who made a significant contribution to the development of the CRPD.[105] Sheila Wildeman describes the 'radical challenges to global mental health policy that have gained new legitimacy and momentum through the participation of [disabled people's organisations] in the CRPD process'.[106] This influence is also evident at the domestic level, where the increasing influence of persons with psychosocial disabilities, as well as family members of this group, is evident on a small and large scale across law, policy and programming.[107]

101 See, generally, B McSherry (ed), *International Trends in Mental Health Laws* (Federation Press, 2008).

102 Bartlett, above n 97, 541. I will discuss this shift in detail in Part II of the book.

103 See P Weller, *New Law and Ethics in Mental Health Advance Directives: The Convention on the Rights of Persons with Disabilities and the Right to Choose* (Routledge, 2013) 53–60.

104 See, generally, S Bagenstos, *Law and the Contradictions of the Disability Rights Movement* (Yale University Press, 2009); D Fleischer and F Zames, *The Disability Rights Movement: From Charity to Confrontation* (Temple University Press, 2nd ed, 2011).

105 Weller, above n 103, 55.

106 S Wildeman, 'Protecting Rights and Building Capacities: Challenges to Global Mental Health Policy in Light of the Convention on the Rights of Persons with Disabilities' (2013) 41(1) *The Journal of Law, Medicine and Ethics* 48, 49.

107 See, generally, J Wallcraft et al., 'Partnerships for Better Mental Health Worldwide: WPA Recommendations on Best Practices in Working with Service Users and Family Carers' (2011) 10(3) *World Psychiatry* 229.

E CONCLUSION

This chapter has looked to the past to clarify the purposes and objectives of mental health law, providing grounds to interrogate the major issues that the CRPD might address today. Since the latter decades of the twentieth century, mental health law has struggled to balance the dual prerogatives of self-determination and protection. Mental health law outwardly seeks to uphold the Western legal doctrine of autonomy and other rights of the individual, while also imposing protective measures that mediate collective concern and fear about the danger and vulnerability (whether real or imagined) that are associated with mental illness. Historic and contemporary debates centre on a critical issue at the heart of mental health law: should 'unsoundness of mind' operate as a criterion for special exception to normative rights? Is this special exception an acceptable cost for the opportunities it affords in protecting other rights (such as the right to life, to dignity and so on)? Mental health law has retained the long-held assumption that profound distress, mental illness, extreme states of consciousness and so on, compromise human agency and volition in such a way that the law cannot operate under the same rules as it does for non-affected persons in conferring legal responsibility and competency.

The CRPD challenges this proposition on a fundamental level. It challenges the long-established sense that mental health issues constitute a special exception that allows for the suspension of principles of equality and non-discrimination. Bernadette McSherry has distilled this challenge into two major questions:

(a) whether mental health laws that enable involuntary detention and treatment should be abolished on the basis that they unjustifiably breach human rights; as well as
(b) whether such laws can be reformed in the light of human rights principles to ensure respect for individual choices in relation to treatment.[108]

Having set out the main function, purpose and procedures of mental health law, it is now useful to turn to the CRPD, to examine in detail the challenges it raises for rules on involuntary psychiatric intervention.

[108] B McSherry, 'Mental Health Law: Where To from Here?' (2014) 40(1) *Monash University Law Review* 175.

2

Mental Health, Law and the United Nations Convention on the Rights of Persons with Disabilities: New Tools or New Paradigm?

A INTRODUCTION

From the late 1970s, international human rights law increasingly influenced mental health legislation.[1] For example, the Convention for the Protection of Human Rights and Fundamental Freedoms (commonly known as the European Convention on Human Rights) was being used for the judicial review of involuntary psychiatric intervention as early as 1983.[2] However, Michael Perlin and Éva Szeli argue that movement in the mental health context towards human rights was slow and hindered by pervasive discrimination against people with 'mental disabilities', whose human rights were progressively 'ignored for decades by the international agencies vested with the protection of human rights on a global scale'.[3] The CRPD[4] has challenged this exclusion and builds on earlier efforts to bring mental health into the fold of international human rights law.

[1] See TW Harding, 'The Application of the European Convention of Human Rights to the Field of Psychiatry', (1989) *International Journal of Law and Psychiatry* 245.

[2] L Gostin, 'The Ideology of Entitlement: The Application of Contemporary Legal Approaches to Psychiatry' in P Bean (ed), *Mental Illness: Changes and Trends* (Wiley, 1983) 27–54.

[3] Perlin and Szeli write that 'it appears that the first time disability rights was conceptualized as a human rights issue was as recently as 1993'. M Perlin and E Szeli, 'Mental Health Law and Human Rights: Evolution and Contemporary Challenges' in M Dudley, D Silove and F Gale (eds), *Mental Health and Human Rights: Vision, Praxis, and Courage* (Oxford University Press, 2013) 80.

[4] Convention on the Rights of Persons with Disabilities, opened for signature 30 March 2007, Doc.A/61/611 (entered into force 3 May 2008).

B THE LONG ROAD TO INCLUSION OF DISABILITY AND MENTAL HEALTH IN HUMAN RIGHTS LAW

Theresia Degener has observed that in the early development of international human rights law, people with disabilities were not viewed 'as a distinct group vulnerable to human rights violations'.[5] In contrast, categories such as race and gender were explicitly incorporated into foundational human rights instruments. Yet, '[n]one of the equality clauses of any of the three instruments of (the International Bill of Human Rights), the Universal Declaration of Human Rights (1948), the International Covenant on Civil and Political Rights (1966), and the International Covenant on Economic, Social and Cultural Rights (1966), mention disability as a protected category'.[6] This exclusion is particularly prominent for people with psychosocial disability. Clarence Sundram highlights that during the twentieth century in Western, high-income countries, people with psychosocial disabilities were subject to arbitrary detention without legal process (sometimes for life); endured forced sterilisation; were chained and caged; and were subjected to cruel, inhuman and degrading treatment, including confinement to squalid conditions in institutions and subjection to medical experimentation and the use of painful medicines and unmodified electroconvulsive treatment without anaesthesia.[7]

This is not to say, of course, that state, professional and societal interventions have failed at every turn. Stories of success and humanity in services to support those in mental health crises are well represented in the literature, as they ought to be.[8] However, it is also true that when widespread practices occurred which are generally considered today to have been abusive and prejudicial, interference of this nature was often lawful.

Throughout the twentieth century, instances of grievous wrongs against persons with disability occurred despite the creation of twenty-four international human rights conventions. Under these conventions, which the global community adopted, in large part it appears that mental health law, policy and practice were regarded as a well-established anomaly to normative human

5 T Degener, 'International Disability Law – A New Legal Subject on the Rise: The Interregional Experts Meeting in Hong Kong, December 13–17, 1999' (2000) 18 *Berkeley Journal of International Law* 180, 187.

6 Ibid., cited in M Perlin, *International Human Rights Law and Mental Disability Law: When the Silenced Are Heard* (Oxford University Press, 2012) 60.

7 CJ Sundram, 'Lost in the Shadows: Willowbrook and the Era of Institutionalization' (Paper presented at Albany Law School, 22 March 2013) 4 <www.justicecenter.ny.gov>.

8 See, e.g., T Burns, *Our Necessary Shadow: The Nature and Meaning of Psychiatry* (Penguin, 2014).

rights.[9] Consider Article 7 of the International Covenant on Civil and Political Rights, which is binding international law for state signatories and states: 'No one shall be subjected to torture or cruel, inhuman or degrading treatment or punishment. In particular, no one shall be subjected without his free consent to medical or scientific experimentation'.[10] According to Sundram, researchers simply viewed this rule as inapplicable to persons diagnosed as mentally ill.[11] Human experimentation occurred without consent, even where experiments had no intended benefit for the individual[12] (though, as noted in the previous chapter, obtaining informed consent was generally not considered to be the moral and legal duty of doctors performing many procedures across medicine, even up to the 1980s).[13] Researchers published their methods and findings in professional journals with no requirement to regard the human rights of their subjects.[14] Sundram articulates this systemic exclusion in the following terms:

> Generic recognition of human rights for *all* people has been insufficient to bring people with mental disabilities under the same umbrella because there had been a long history in society of regarding them as a separate class, with separate and lesser rights. Worse, the abuses to which people with mental disabilities have been exposed have generally not been recognized as violations of human rights even by organizations that are engaged in human rights work.[15]

The legal text of human rights instruments provides some insight as to why this might be the case. For example, the Universal Declaration of Human Rights confers rights and legal status because humans are endowed with 'reason' and 'conscience'.[16] The European Convention on Human Rights, which prohibits discrimination on 'any ground such as sex, race, colour, language, religion,

9 CJ Sundram, 'A Discussion of Legal Capacity in the Draft Convention on Disability' (Issue Paper, National Disability Authority, Ireland, 15 June 2006) 6 <www.mdri.org>. See also Perlin, above n 6.

10 International Covenant on Civil and Political Rights, opened for signature 19 December 1966, 999 UNTS 171 (entered into force 23 March 1976), ratified by Australia on 13 November 1980, art 7 (emphasis added).

11 CJ Sundram, 'In Harm's Way: Research Subjects Who Are Decisionally Impaired' (1998) 1 *Journal of Health Care Law and Policy* 36.

12 Ibid.

13 R Faden and T Beauchamp, A *History and Theory of Informed Consent* (Oxford University Press, 1986) 86–90. See Chapter 1, Section B.

14 Sundram, above n 9, 6.

15 Ibid. (emphasis in original).

16 Universal Declaration of Human Rights, GA Res 217A (III), UN GAOR, 3rd sess, 183rd plen mtg, UN Doc A/810 (entered into force 10 December 1948) art 1.

political or other opinion',[17] does not prohibit disability-based discrimination; it makes an exception for those of 'unsound mind' – which it equates with 'alcoholics ... drug addicts or vagrants' and 'persons [detained] for the prevention of the spreading of infectious diseases' – to the right to liberty and security of the person.[18] It could be argued that this exception, which is set out in article 5(1)(e), is anachronistically worded and that the European Court of Human Rights has evolved over time. Contrariwise, Lisa Waddington and Bernadette McSherry argue that this is not the case.[19] In their view, Article 5(1)(e)'s provisions – and other 'exceptions and exclusions' that appear throughout European human rights law, including those in the Council of Europe Convention on Human Rights and Biomedicine – have meant that only '"weak" protection has been afforded to people with psychosocial disabilities by the European Convention on Human Rights and the European Court of Human Rights' in relation to informed consent for medical treatment.[20]

In the last two decades of the twentieth century, a range of people began to challenge the marginalisation of persons with psychosocial disability from the substance of international human rights law.[21] The shift became evident with the UN announcement that 1981 would be the International Year of Disabled Persons. Significant UN initiatives followed, including the World Programme of Action Concerning Disabled Persons and the Decade of Rights of People with Disability, which culminated in 1993 with the publication of the Standard Rules on the Equalization of Opportunities for Persons with Disabilities.[22]

Notably, in 1991, the General Assembly adopted the Principles for the Protection of Persons with Mental Illness and for the Improvement of Mental

[17] Convention for the Protection of Human Rights and Fundamental Freedoms ('ECHR'), opened for signature 4 November 1950, 213 UNTS 221 (entered into force 3 September 1953) art 14.

[18] ECHR art 5(1)(e).

[19] L Waddington and B McSherry, 'Exceptions and Exclusions: The Right to Informed Consent for Medical Treatment of People with Psychosocial Disabilities in Europe' (2016) 23(3) *European Journal of Health Law* 279.

[20] Ibid.

[21] Perlin, above n 6, 60.

[22] UN General Assembly, standard rules on the equalization of opportunities for persons with disabilities: resolution, adopted by the General Assembly, 48th sess UN Doc A/RES/48/96, 20 December 1993. Other significant legal instruments in the history of disability and human rights law include the Declaration of the Rights of Mentally Retarded Persons (1975) and the Declaration on the Rights of Disabled Persons (1975), both of which are non-binding documents focusing on mental and physical disability. See UN General Assembly, Declaration on the Rights of Disabled Persons, GA Res 3447 (XXX), UN GAOR, 30th sess, 2433rd plen mtg, Supp No 34, UN Doc A/Res/3447/(XXX) (9 December 1975); UN General Assembly, Universal Declaration of Human Rights, GA Res 217A (III), UN GAOR, 3rd sess, 183rd plen mtg, UN Doc A/810 (entered into force 10 December 1948).

Health Care (or the 'MI Principles', as they became widely known).[23] Perlin and Szeli have argued that the 'MI Principles established the most comprehensive international human rights standards for persons with mental disabilities, and their adoption was a critical global step in recognizing mental disability rights issues within the human rights arena'.[24] The MI Principles require the delivery of services in the least restrictive manner, using individualised planning, and under the independent and impartial authority of mental health tribunals.[25] Under the MI Principles, the principle of autonomy is elevated,[26] medication is restricted to therapeutic use[27] and clinicians must ensure that '[n]o treatment shall be given to a patient without his or her informed consent'.[28] However, the principle of informed consent is qualified extensively, and involuntary medical treatment is decisively endorsed when a person 'by reason of his or her mental illness ... lacks legal capacity'.[29] This formulation of legal capacity, as I shall discuss, diverges sharply from the conceptualisation of legal capacity in the CRPD.

Meanwhile, domestic human rights and equal opportunity laws brought mental health policy and law in domestic courts closer to the rights advanced in the MI Principles. In the United States, under the Americans with Disabilities Act of 1990, Congress clearly identified the isolation and segregation of persons with disabilities as a serious and widespread form of discrimination.[30] In 2011, the US Supreme Court ruled (by majority) in *Brown v Plata* that failure to provide adequate health conditions for persons in custodial confinement, and particularly for persons with mental disorder, constituted an abuse of human rights.[31] Elsewhere, the increased use of regional courts like the European Court of Human Rights in mental health-related matters[32] reflected the increasing influence of human rights, and also signalled a shift away (at least nominally)

23 UN General Assembly, Principles for the Protection of Persons with Mental Illness and for the Improvement of Mental Health Care, UN Doc A/RES/46/119 (17 December 1991).

24 Perlin and Szeli, above n 3, 80.

25 The MI Principles helped clarify the role of tribunals by mandating periodic review and the right of judicial appeal. P Weller, 'Lost in Translation: Human Rights and Mental Health Law' in B McSherry and P Weller (eds), *Rethinking Rights-Based Mental Health Law* (Hart, 2010) 64.

26 UN General Assembly, above n 23, Principle 9.

27 Ibid., Principle 10.

28 Ibid., Principle 11.

29 Ibid., Principle 1(6).

30 42 USC 12101 (A)(2), (5).

31 *Brown v Plata* 563 US 493 (2011). See also, I Freckelton, 'Cruel and Unusual Punishment of Prisoners with Mental Illnesses: from Oates to Plata' (2011) 18(3) Psychiatry, *Psychology and Law* 329.

32 L Gostin, 'Human Rights of Persons with Mental Disabilities: The European Convention on Human Rights' (2000) 23(2) *International Journal of Law and Psychiatry* 125.

from framing people diagnosed with mental disorders as being – in some way – anomalous to human rights law. (There are also signs that regional human rights bodies in Africa and the Americas are increasingly linking mental health with human rights.)[33] However, the effectiveness of some of these human rights instruments in protecting the rights of people with psychosocial disability is questionable.[34] For example, Brenda Hale was reluctant to describe the use of human rights in mental health law in Europe as successful,[35] while others have raised concerns that rights-based laws have codified medical discretion rather than upholding the rights of those subject to them.[36] The MI Principles provide a good example of why this might be the case.

The authors of the MI Principles aimed to provide a coherent human rights framework for mental health care. At face value, they achieve this task. Commentators around the turn of the twenty-first century echoed Timothy Harding, who viewed the MI Principles as the '"centrepiece" of international human rights law in the field of mental health'.[37] However, the MI Principles have been strongly criticised on several points. Harding has argued that the MI Principles do not have the status of a formal international treaty; states have no obligation to adopt them as 'minimum standards' and there are no implementation mechanisms, thus raising questions about their efficacy.[38] Second, as Caroline Gendreau has argued, the MI Principles uncritically endorse a disease model approach to mental health, which particularly affects provisions regarding consent to treatment, including the removal of patient rights.[39] Disabled people's organisations, such as the World Network of Users and Survivors of Psychiatry, have criticised the MI Principles on the basis that the instrument was negotiated to the complete exclusion of service users and other people with psychosocial disabilities and their representative organisations.[40]

[33] See M Dudley, D Silove and F Gale, *Mental Health and Human Rights – Vision, Praxis, and Courage* (Oxford University Press, 2012) 84.

[34] Ibid. See Perlin and Szeli, above n 3.

[35] B Hale, 'Justice and Equality in Mental Health Law: The European Experience' (2007) 30(1) *International Journal of Law and Psychiatry* 18.

[36] See P Fennell, 'Institutionalising the Community: The Codification of Clinical Authority and the Limits of Rights-Based Approaches' in McSherry and Weller, above n 25, 13. See Chapter 3, Section C(4).

[37] TW Harding, 'Human Rights Law in the Field of Mental Health: A Critical Review' (2000) 399 *Acta Psychiatric Scandinavica Supplement* 24.

[38] Ibid.

[39] C Gendreau, 'The Rights of Psychiatric Patients in the Light of the Principles Announced by the United Nations: A Recognition of the Right to Consent to Treatment?' (1997) 20(2) *International Journal of Law and Psychiatry* 259, 272.

[40] World Network of Users and Survivors of Psychiatry, 'World Network of Users and Survivors of Psychiatry Preliminary Statement on the United Nations Principles for the Protection of

Finally, perhaps the strongest criticism is that the MI Principles offer weaker protection than other pre-existing human rights instruments in key respects, particularly on the issue of consent to treatment; according to Harding, 'the Principles remove patients' rights rather than reinforce them'.[41]

1 *The CRPD and Mental Health Law*

Broader disability groups, including people with physical, sensory and intellectual disabilities, identified a shared sense of being marginalised from international human rights law.[42] Cross-disability alliances were formed, which led to a successful campaign to create a distinct international human rights treaty for people with disabilities.[43] The CRPD represents the culmination of two and a half decades of development in international human rights law aimed at addressing human rights violations experienced by people with disabilities. The purpose of the CRPD is to 'promote, protect and ensure the full and equal enjoyment of all human rights and fundamental freedoms by all persons with disabilities, and to promote respect for their inherent dignity'.[44] The CRPD can be seen as a recent addition to the 'pluralization of human rights', in Frédéric Mégret's terms, to describe the recognition of particular categories within humanity as being worthy of specific human rights protection.[45]

As noted previously, the CRPD offers a de facto definition of persons with disabilities that 'include[s] those who have long-term physical, *mental*, intellectual or sensory impairments which in interaction with various barriers may hinder their full and effective participation in society on an equal basis with others'.[46] The emphasis placed on the interaction between a person's impairment with attitudinal and environmental barriers draws attention to disabling social and physical factors.[47] Mike Oliver has described the harms caused by such barriers as the 'politics of disablement'.[48] Oliver is a major proponent

Persons with Mental Illness to the United Nations Commission on Human Rights' (2000) <www.wnusp.org>.

41 Harding, above n 37.

42 F Mégret, 'The Disabilities Convention: Human Rights of Persons with Disabilities or Disability Rights?' (2008) 30 *Human Rights Quarterly* 494.

43 Ibid.

44 CRPD art 1.

45 This trend is most evident in international covenants against racial discrimination, and discrimination against women, children, migrant workers and indigenous people. Mégret, above n 42, 495.

46 CRPD art 1 (emphasis added).

47 CRPD Preamble (e).

48 M Oliver, *The Politics of Disablement* (Macmillan, 1990).

of the 'social model of disability', which greatly influenced CRPD negotiations.[49] The social model view of disability aims to shift the emphasis away from the individual deficits in persons with disabilities and towards identifying external barriers to their participation on an equal basis with others.[50] In contrast, the 'medical model of disability', which dominated disability law, policy and practice throughout the twentieth century, uses biomedical explanations that locate disability within the individual, in terms of pathology.[51] The social model is premised on a view of disability as arising, once again, from 'the interaction *between persons with impairments and attitudinal and environmental barriers* that hinders their full and effective participation in society on an equal basis with others'.[52] Clearly, the distinction between 'impairment' and 'disability' is not always clear. The social context is always up for debate. Nevertheless, the social model and, indeed, the CRPD advance an inclusive view of disability, which seeks to avoid diagnostic categorisation and instead shine a spotlight on the external barriers to human flourishing.[53]

The CRPD potentially introduces a new model of disability, which Gerard Quinn and Theresia Degener have termed the 'human rights model of disability'.[54] The human rights model, according to Degener, builds upon the social model in key ways; for example, although the social model holds strong explanatory power in identifying the formation of disability, it does not affirm the inherent human dignity of persons with disabilities and attribute them with the capacity to hold human rights regardless of impairment.[55] As well as this affirmation, the human rights model offers a more comprehensive framework for achieving social justice, offering not just an explanation, but also

49 R Kayess and P French, 'Out of Darkness into Light? Introducing the Convention on the Rights of Persons with Disabilities' (2008) 8(1) *Human Rights Law Review* 1.

50 M Prince, 'Canadian Disability Policy: Still a Hit and Miss Affair' (2004) 29 *Canadian Journal of Sociology* 59.

51 Ibid.

52 CRPD Preamble (e) (emphasis added). See, generally, C Thomas, 'How Is Disability Understood? An Examination of Sociological Approaches' (2004) 19(6) *Disability and Society* 569. For a critique of the social model, see T Shakespeare, *Disability Rights and Wrongs* (Routledge, 2006).

53 See generally, Kayess and French, above n 49.

54 Theresia Degener and Gerard Quinn were early proponents of the term 'human rights model of disability'. See T Degener and G Quinn, 'A Survey of International, Comparative and Regional Disability Law Reform' in ML Breslin and S Yee (eds), *Disability Rights Law and Policy* (Transnational Publishers, 2002) 14. More contemporary, post-CRPD explications of the term have recently emerged. See, e.g., T Degener, 'A Human Rights Model of Disability' in P Blanck and E Flynn (eds), *Routledge Handbook of Disability Law and Human Rights* (Routledge, 2017).

55 Degener, above n 54.

a prescription for change.[56] After all, the CRPD is among the longest and most detailed of all UN human rights conventions, elucidating human rights in the disability context in a wide range of areas of life, including employment, education, health services and transportation, access to justice and access to the physical environment.[57]

For the mental health context, the human rights model raises questions about the relationship and differences between 'impairment' and the external barriers which give rise to 'disability'. Brendan Kelly has queried the extent to which 'mental disorder' or 'mental illness' falls within the definition of 'disability' according to the CRPD.[58] He writes: 'it appears likely that some people with mental disorder meet this definition at least some of the time (e.g., a person with chronic schizophrenia) but others do not (e.g., a person with a single phobia)'.[59] Kelly argues that the question of whether mental health legislation in its current form violates the CRPD 'depends critically on whether or not the CRPD's definition of disability includes mental disorder'.[60] Tina Minkowitz has countered that

> While the provision refers only to people with 'long term' impairments and does not mention imputed impairment or disability, it is non-exhaustive and should not limit coverage of the Convention where such a result would be counterproductive. In particular, the obligations of non-discrimination cannot be properly implemented if they are to depend on the details of a person's experience with disability; the mere fact that a person is perceived as having a disability, and accorded adverse treatment as a result, is enough to invoke these provisions.[61]

From this view, the question of who is disabled hinges upon adverse treatment on the basis of impairment or disability, thus shifting the emphasis to the substance of mental health law (or any other process) and whether or not it constitutes adverse treatment – which the CRPD Committee, the OHCHR, the Special Rapporteur on Torture and others have indicated it does. Setting aside these concerns, which will be discussed in detail in Chapter 3, it is clear that negotiators of the CRPD agreed that it was unnecessary to spell out a detailed

56 Ibid.

57 CRPD arts 9, 13, 24, 25, 28.

58 B Kelly, *Dignity, Mental Health and Human Rights: Coercion and the Law* (Ashgate, 2015) 95–105.

59 Ibid. 95.

60 Ibid. 105.

61 T Minkowitz, 'The United Nations Convention on The Rights of Persons with Disabilities and the Right to Be Free from Non-consensual Psychiatric Interventions' (2007) 34(2) *Syracuse Journal of International Law and Commerce* 405, 407–8.

definition of who constitutes a disabled person, and that there are distinct advantages in leaving the application of the definition to be worked out, as far as necessary, on a case-by-case basis.

In its prohibition of all discrimination based on disability, the CRPD requires that States Parties take all reasonable steps to accommodate mental and physical impairments and sets out several rights for people with disabilities, including rights relating to employment, education, health services, transportation, access to justice and accessibility to the physical environment.[62] In setting out these rights, the CRPD is said by diverse commentators to have affirmed or restated existing human rights, or modified certain rights in a manner specific to the experience of people with disabilities, and even to have extended rights into new areas of life.[63]

In contrast to the MI Principles, commentators generally agree that the CRPD was the most participatory international legal instrument in history, where those typically subject to the human rights violations in question took a leading role in its development. This included people with psychosocial disabilities, as well as their representative organisations – although, in recent years, some commentators have raised concerns that only a narrow group of persons with psychosocial disability, service users and so on were involved.[64] Nevertheless, as Perlin and Szeli have stated, the CRPD brought mental health issues more forcefully into the fold of human rights law than ever before.[65]

C THE SCOPE OF PROTECTED RIGHTS

The preamble of the CRPD affirms 'the inherent dignity and worth and the equal and inalienable rights of all members of the human family as the foundation of freedom, justice and peace in the world'.[66] Acknowledging the 'inherent dignity' of people with disabilities emphasises from the outset that

62 CRPD arts 9, 13, 24, 25, 28.

63 Mégret, above n 42, 498.

64 See, e.g., A Plumb, 'UN Convention on the Rights of Persons with Disabilities: Out of the Frying Pan and into the Fire? Mental Health Service Users and Survivors Aligning with the Disability Movement' in H Spandler, J Anderson and B Sapey (eds), *Madness, Distress and the Politics of Disablement* (Policy Press, 2015) 183–98; M Freeman et al., 'Reversing Hard Won Victories in the Name of Human Rights: A Critique of the General Comment On Article 12 of the UN Convention on the Rights of Persons with Disabilities' (2015) 2 *Lancet Psychiatry* 844.

65 Perlin and Szeli, above n 3. See also, P Weller, 'Supported Decision-Making and the Achievement of Non-Discrimination: The Promise and Paradox of the Disabilities Convention' (2008) 26(2) *Law in Context* 85.

66 CRPD Preamble (h).

people with disabilities are the holders of inherent rights, rather than needing to meet a certain standard – for example, as a rational agent – in order to lay claim to rights. (In contrast, consider Moore's claim that 'one is a moral agent only if one is a rational agent'.)[67] Louise Arbour, the UN High Commissioner for Human Rights when the CRPD was adopted, stated that Article 1 of the CRPD establishes an authoritative challenge to the 'view of persons with disabilities as objects of charity, medical treatment and social protection',[68] instead affirming that they are 'subjects of rights, able to claim those rights as active members of society'.[69]

The preamble also affirms previous UN instruments, such as the Universal Declaration of Human Rights, which have 'proclaimed and agreed that everyone is entitled to all the rights and freedoms set forth therein, without distinction of any kind'.[70] Yet the preamble also notes the failure of previous human rights instruments to prevent, for people with disabilities, 'barriers in their participation as equal members of society and violations of their human rights in all parts of the world'.[71] The 'universality, indivisibility, interdependence and interrelatedness of all human rights and fundamental freedoms' is observed, to which persons with disabilities should be 'guaranteed their full enjoyment without discrimination'.[72]

International cooperation is called for to improve 'the living conditions of persons with disabilities in every country, particularly in developing countries' – an important point, given that low- and middle-income countries are home to the majority of people with disabilities globally. The preamble highlights material inequality, acknowledging 'that the majority of persons with disabilities live in conditions of poverty' and emphasising 'the critical need to address the negative impact of poverty on persons with disabilities'.[73] This point is especially relevant in the mental health context, where the cyclical relationship between poverty and profound mental distress and disorder is well-established.[74]

[67] MS Moore, *Law and Psychiatry: Rethinking the Relationship* (Cambridge University Press, 1984) 244.

[68] Statement by Louise Arbour, UN High Commissioner for Human Rights, on the Ad Hoc Committee's Adoption of the International Convention on the Rights of Persons with Disabilities, 5 December 2006, available at <www.un.org>

[69] Ibid.

[70] CRPD Preamble (a).

[71] Ibid., Preamble (k).

[72] Ibid., Preamble (c).

[73] Ibid., Preamble (t).

[74] R Poole, R Higgo and C Robinson, *Mental Health and Poverty* (Cambridge University Press, 2013).

1 *Framing Rights*

Articles 1 through 9 establish 'framing' rights, offering obligations and principles of general application. Equality, non-discrimination, accessibility and autonomy are key themes, with specific attention paid to women and girls with disabilities.[75] 'Disability-based discrimination' is defined in Article 2 as any distinction, exclusion or restriction on the basis of disability which has the 'purpose or effect of impairing or nullifying the recognition, enjoyment or exercise, on an equal basis with others, of all human rights and fundamental freedoms in the political, economic, social, cultural, civil or any other field'. Importantly, this 'includes all forms of discrimination, including denial of reasonable accommodation'.[76]

'Reasonable accommodation' is an important tool for achieving the equality demands of the CRPD and refers to 'necessary and appropriate modification and adjustments not imposing a disproportionate or undue burden, where needed in a particular case, to ensure to persons with disabilities the enjoyment or exercise on an equal basis with others of all human rights and fundamental freedoms'.[77] According to Rosemary Kayess and Phillip French, reasonable accommodation is 'the most fundamental instrumental element of the convention'.[78] The provision effectively introduces a duty on states to ensure 'reasonable' adjustments as a matter of equality and non-discrimination. This duty creates a positive obligation on States Parties to provide the resources that individuals need in order to exercise their rights (rather than simply a duty to refrain from intruding on individuals' lives). Almost all national disability discrimination laws have adopted this concept, which has remained a central demand of the global disability movement for many decades.[79]

Article 5 addresses equality and non-discrimination specifically, and directs States Parties to 'recognize that all persons are equal before and under the law and are entitled without any discrimination to the equal protection and equal benefit of the law'. Article 5 also prohibits disability-based discrimination (paragraph 2); directs States Parties to provide reasonable accommodation (paragraph 3); and permits special measures that are not discriminatory in nature under the terms of the CRPD but are intended to accelerate or achieve de facto equality of persons with disabilities (paragraph 4).[80]

75 CRPD art 6.
76 Ibid., art 2.
77 Ibid.
78 Kayess and French, above n 49, 27.
79 Ibid.
80 CRPD art 5(2)(3)(4).

Article 6 recognises 'that women and girls with disabilities are subject to multiple discrimination', which may be a useful frame for addressing the consistent patterns of difference between the experiences of men and women with psychosocial disabilities relating to impairment, service use and the application of involuntary psychiatric intervention.[81]

Similarly, Article 7 obligates States Parties to 'take all necessary measures to ensure the full enjoyment by children with disabilities of all human rights and fundamental freedoms on an equal basis with other children'.

Article 8 sets out awareness raising obligations on States Parties 'regarding persons with disabilities, [including] foster[ing] respect for the rights and dignity of persons with disabilities'. Themes include combating 'stereotypes, prejudices and harmful practices relating to persons with disabilities'[82] and promoting 'awareness of the capabilities and contributions of persons with disabilities'.[83] Measures involve '[i]nitiating and maintaining effective public awareness campaigns' that 'nurture receptiveness to the rights of persons with disabilities', including through education systems and the media and in workplaces.[84] Awareness raising is likely to be particularly relevant to the mental health context. Populist fears and stereotypes perpetuate prejudice and discrimination against persons with psychosocial disability throughout the world (and may underpin key justifications for having separate mental health legislation, as the next chapter explores).

Finally, Article 9 requires States Parties to 'take appropriate measures to ensure to persons with disabilities access, on an equal basis with others, to the physical environment, to transportation, to information and communications, including information and communications technologies and systems, and to other facilities and services open or provided to the public, both in urban and in rural areas'. This includes 'identification and elimination of obstacles and barriers to accessibility'.[85] While this article generally appears to relate to physical accessibility measures for persons with physical and sensory disabilities, the reference to 'other facilities and services open or provided to the public'[86] could reasonably include mental health services, but could also schools and universities, banks, utility companies and so on. What it means to 'take

[81] See, e.g., P Prior, *Gender and Mental Health* (New York University Press, 1999); B Audini and P Lelliott, 'Age, Gender and Ethnicity of Those Detained under Part II of the Mental Health Act 1983' (2002) 180 *British Journal of Psychiatry* 222.

[82] CRPD art 8(1)(a).

[83] Ibid., art 8(1)(b).

[84] Ibid., art 8(2).

[85] Ibid., art 9(1).

[86] Ibid.

appropriate measures' to ensure accessibility is debatable, and is likely to be refined with reference to specific operative rights, for example, related to education (Article 24), health (Article 25) or employment (Article 27). Measures could reasonably include mental health services improving accessibility for people with intellectual disabilities,[87] banks or utility companies establishing procedures to work with a person's preferred supporter, or workplaces allowing flexible working hours where medications affect morning alertness. Article 9 seems to reiterate the call for 'universalism', which eschews separate services and facilities for persons with disabilities in favour of accommodation and accessibility measures being built into mainstream services and facilities. Rosemary Kayess and Phillip French define 'universalism' as the 'radical modification of the social norm to reflect human diversity'.[88]

2 *Operative Rights*

Articles 10 to 30 refer to operative rights, each of which has a more specific focus. Some articles are more relevant to the mental health context than others.

One of the most significant of these is the right to equal recognition before the law set out in Article 12. Article 12(1) establishes that persons with disabilities have the right to be recognised everywhere as persons before the law.[89] Article 12(2) directs that 'States Parties shall recognize that persons with disabilities enjoy legal capacity on an equal basis with others in all aspects of life'. The meaning of 'legal capacity' and its enjoyment 'in all aspects of life' has been the subject of considerable debate (which I will discuss in detail in Chapter 4). The right to enjoy legal capacity on an equal basis in Article 12(2) draws upon a formulation of legal capacity comprising two elements: a person's legal standing (legal personality), but also his or her ability to act on such legal standing (legal agency).[90] On this point, an immediate issue arises with mental health legislation which clearly restricts a person's legal capacity, and specifically his or her legal agency.

87 See, e.g., Department of Developmental Disability Neuropsychiatry, *Accessible Mental Health Services for People with an Intellectual Disability: A Guide for Providers* (University of New South Wales, 2014).

88 Kayess and French, above n 49, 10.

89 CRPD art 12(1). See UN Office of the High Commissioner for Human Rights, 'Background Conference Document Prepared by the Office of the United Nations High Commissioner for Human Rights: Legal Capacity' (2005) <www.un.org>.

90 Ibid.

Article 12(3) sets out States Parties' obligation to 'take appropriate measures to provide access by persons with disabilities to the support they may require in exercising their legal capacity'[91] and is often regarded as the *locus situ* for the obligation on states to provide 'supported decision-making'.[92] Article 12(4) sets out safeguards required for all measures related to the exercise of legal capacity.[93] These include the principle of proportionality, freedom from conflict of interest, and undue influence on and respect for the rights, will and preference of the person. These safeguards should ensure that the provision of legal capacity support measures 'apply for the shortest time possible and are subject to regular review by a competent, independent and impartial authority or judicial body'.[94] Finally, Article 12(5) contains explicit recognition of the importance of the right to legal capacity for persons with disabilities in respect of financial and property matters.[95] Overall, Article 12 sets out a commitment by States Parties to uphold the legal standing of people with disabilities and to ensure that they act in this respect on an equal basis with others. (I will discuss the implications of Article 12 for mental health law in detail in Chapter 4 and 5.)

Article 14 sets out provisions on the liberty and security of the person, which are among the most important and controversial for the mental health context. Article 14(1)(b) requires States Parties to ensure that people with disabilities, on an equal basis with others, '[a]re not deprived of their liberty unlawfully or arbitrarily, and that any deprivation of liberty is in conformity with the law, and *that the existence of a disability shall in no case justify a deprivation of liberty*'. This subsection of Article 14(1) was the subject of considerable debate during the drafting negotiations.[96] Some States Parties, including Australia, advocated strongly for the narrow view that Article 14 forbade detention solely based on disability, but not detention based on disability *in combination with another justification or multiple justifications*.[97] On this view, detention

[91] CRPD art 12(3).

[92] G Quinn, 'Personhood and Legal Capacity: Perspectives on the Paradigm Shift of Article 12 CRPD' (Paper presented at the Conference on Disability and Legal Capacity under the CRPD, Harvard Law School, Boston, 20 February 2010) 16 <www.nuigalway.ie>.

[93] CRPD art 12(4).

[94] Ibid.

[95] Ibid., art 12(5).

[96] Daily Summaries of the Fifth Session of the Ad Hoc Committee, 26 January 2005, afternoon session; Daily Summaries of the Fifth Session of the Ad Hoc Committee, 27 January 2005, afternoon session; Daily Summaries of Discussion at the Seventh Session of the Ad Hoc Committee, 18 January 2006, afternoon session; and Daily Summaries of Discussion at the Seventh Session of the Ad Hoc Committee, 19 January 2006, morning session <www.un.org>.

[97] Daily Summaries of the Fifth Session of the Ad Hoc Committee, 26 January 2005, afternoon session.

because of disability along with other factors is justifiable; this would include, for example, preventing harm to self or others, as per mental health legislation. However, the CRPD Committee adopted a broader interpretation, stating that Article 14 'prohibits the deprivation of liberty on the basis of actual or perceived impairment *even if* additional factors or criteria are also used to justify the deprivation of liberty'.[98] It states that:

> legislation of several states party, including mental health laws, still provide instances in which persons may be detained on the grounds of their actual or perceived disability, provided there are other reasons for their detention, including that they are dangerous to themselves or to others. *This practice is incompatible with article 14 as interpreted by the jurisprudence of the* CRPD Committee.[99]

This reading may come as a surprise to governments that have signed and ratified the CRPD, especially those that explicitly stated reservations, understandings and interpretative declarations,[100] such as Canada and Australia, which interpret Article 14(1) to permit substituted decision-making under mental health law.[101] Interestingly, the UN Human Rights Committee issued a General Comment that contradicts the view of the CRPD Committee on this point.[102] The Human Rights Committee stated that 'the existence of a disability shall not in itself justify a deprivation of liberty', but must be combined with 'the purpose of protecting the individual in question from serious harm or preventing injury to others'.[103] This tension, even within human rights treaty bodies, is perhaps indicative of tensions between the CRPD and approaches

[98] Committee on the Rights of Persons with Disabilities, 'Guidelines on Article 14 of the Convention on the Rights of Persons with Disabilities: The Right to Liberty and Security of Persons with Disabilities' (2015) [7] <www.ohchr.org> (emphasis added).

[99] Ibid. [1] (emphasis added).

[100] An 'interpretative declaration' is a unilateral statement made by states or international organisations by which they specify or clarify the meaning or scope of a treaty or of certain of its provisions, outlining the state's understanding of obligations under the CRPD, without purporting to exclude or modify its legal effects. International Law Commission, *Guide to Practice on Reservations to Treaties* (2011) [1.1–3].

[101] See, e.g., Convention on the Rights of Persons with Disabilities: Declarations and Reservations (Canada), opened for signature 30 March 2007, 999 UNTS 3 (entered into force 3 May 2008). Australia declared 'its understanding that the Convention allows for compulsory assistance or treatment of persons, including measures taken for the treatment of mental disability, where such treatment is necessary, as a last resort and subject to safeguards'. Convention on the Rights of Persons with Disabilities: Declarations and Reservations (Australia), opened for signature 30 March 2007, 999 UNTS 3 (entered into force 3 May 2008).

[102] Human Rights Committee, *General Comment No 35: Article 9: Liberty and Security of Person*, 112th sess, UN Doc CCPR/C/GC/35 (16 December 2014) [19] (emphasis added).

[103] Ibid.

to disability in previous human rights instruments. Alternatively, the relative youth of the CRPD may mean that normative interpretations and theoretical coherence are still being established.

Article 15 directs that 'no one shall be subjected to torture or cruel, inhuman or degrading treatment or punishment', and Article 16 promotes 'freedom from exploitation, violence and abuse'. Article 16(3) includes a provision for monitoring, whereby 'States Parties shall ensure that all facilities and programmes designed to serve persons with disabilities are effectively monitored by independent authorities', and directs States Parties to 'take all appropriate measures to promote the physical, cognitive and psychological recovery, rehabilitation and social reintegration of persons with disabilities who become victims of any form of exploitation, violence or abuse, including through the provision of protection services'. Recovery and reintegration practices 'shall take place in an environment that fosters the health, welfare, self-respect, dignity and autonomy of the person and takes into account gender- and age-specific needs'.[104] Effective remedies must be created by States Parties, 'to ensure that instances of exploitation, violence and abuse against persons with disabilities are identified, investigated and, where appropriate, prosecuted'.[105]

Article 17 states: 'Every person with disabilities has a right to respect for his or her physical and mental integrity on an equal basis with others'. Those subject to involuntary psychiatric intervention clearly face interference with their mental and physical integrity. Again, commentators are likely to contest definitions. Proponents of compulsory, non-consensual treatment could argue that involuntary intervention *restores* mental and physical integrity in certain circumstances, which is an argument made by some people who have personally experienced such interventions.[106] Australia, upon ratification of the CRPD, made an interpretative declaration in respect of Article 17 that explicitly positions mental health legislation as complying with the CRPD.[107] In contrast, the UN Special Rapporteur on Torture, with reference to Articles 15, 16 and 17, stated that 'the more intrusive and irreversible the treatment, the greater the obligation on States to ensure that health professionals provide

[104] CRPD art 16(4).

[105] Ibid., art 16(5).

[106] See, e.g., European Union Agency for Fundamental Rights, *Involuntary Placement and Involuntary Treatment of Persons with Mental Health Problems* (Publication Office of the European Union, 2012) 3.2.1. *Contra* D Webb, 'Is Involuntary Psychiatric Treatment — Reasonable, Necessary, Justified and Proportionate?' (Paper presented at the Victorian Mental Health Legal Centre Forum: 'Victorian Charter of Human Rights and Responsibilities and Mental Health Rights', 20 May 2008, 9–10 <www.thinkingaboutsuicide.org>.

[107] CRPD: Reservations and Declarations (Australia) UNHCR 2008 <www.treaties.un.org>.

care to persons with disabilities only on the basis of their free and informed consent'.[108] This comment was directed at the use of forced psychosurgery and electroconvulsive therapy (ECT), but the rapporteur also stated that forced intervention, including psychiatric medication, 'needs to be closely scrutinised' and 'warrants greater attention', as it may constitute 'a form of torture or ill-treatment'.[109]

Article 19 regards 'living independently and being included in the community' and 'recognize[s] the equal right of all persons with disabilities to live in the community, with choices equal to others, and shall take effective and appropriate measures to facilitate full enjoyment by persons with disabilities of this right and their full inclusion and participation in the community'.[110] Article 19 is one of the few articles with no real precedent in pre-CRPD human rights law. Its genesis appears to be the harm caused by institutionalisation and other forms of exclusion, which is clearly relevant to the mental health context. Thomas Hammarberg, Council of Europe Commissioner for Human Rights, has highlighted the positive obligation on States Parties to provide resources to persons with disabilities for securing independent living and community inclusion:

> Article 19 of the CRPD embodies a positive philosophy, which is about enabling people to live their lives to their fullest, within society. The core of the right, which is not covered by the sum of the other rights, is about neutralising the devastating isolation and loss of control over one's life, wrought on people with disabilities because of their need for support against the background of an inaccessible society. 'Neutralising' is understood as both removing the barriers to community access in housing and other domains, and providing access to individualised disability-related supports on which enjoyment of this right depends for many individuals.[111]

Measures for achieving these aims are set out in the Article 19 subsections. These include 'the opportunity to choose … where and with whom [persons with disabilities] live on an equal basis with others' and 'access to a range of in-home, residential and other community support services, including personal assistance necessary to support living and inclusion in the community,

[108] M Nowak, Special Rapporteur, Interim Report of the Special Rapporteur on Torture and Other Cruel, Inhuman or Degrading Treatment or Punishment, 63rd sess, UN Doc A/63/175 (28 July 2008) 14.

[109] Ibid. 16.

[110] CRPD art 19.

[111] T Hammarberg, 'The Right of People with Disabilities to Live Independently and Be Included in the Community' (Issue Paper, Council of Europe Commissioner for Human Rights, June 2012) 8.

and to prevent isolation or segregation from the community'.[112] These provisions remain highly relevant in the mental health context, given that 'persons with mental health conditions or psychosocial disabilities, in particular persons using mental health services, may be subject to, inter alia, widespread ... social exclusion and segregation, unlawful or arbitrary institutionalization'.[113]

Article 25 sets out the right to health, directing that States Parties shall '[r]equire health professionals to provide care of the same quality to persons with disabilities as to others, including on the basis of free and informed consent'. Such services must be available to 'persons with disabilities with the same range, quality and standard of free or affordable health care and programmes as provided to other persons'.[114] This provision may be useful for those wishing to challenge unequal fiscal spending between physical and mental health services. Article 25(b) directs States Parties to provide health services 'needed by persons with disabilities specifically because of their disabilities, including early identification and intervention as appropriate, and services designed to minimize and prevent further disabilities'. The governments considered in this book have, at times, emphasised early-stage support for people experiencing mental health issues.[115] For example, the Australian Mental Health Commission promotes policy that 'shifts groups of people towards "upstream" services (population health, prevention, early intervention, recovery and participation) and thereby reduces "downstream", costly services ([emergency department] presentations, acute admissions, avoidable readmissions and income support payments)'.[116] This 'downstream' list could also include involuntary psychiatric intervention. Article 25(d) broadens the promotion of free and informed consent to include an obligation on States Parties to raise 'awareness of the human rights, dignity, autonomy and needs of persons with disabilities through training and the promulgation of ethical

[112] CRPD art 19(a)(b).

[113] UN Human Rights Committee, 'Promotion and Protection of All Human Rights, Civil, Political, Economic, Social and Cultural Rights, Including the Right to Development', adopted 29 June 2016, A/HRC/32/L.26, 2.

[114] CRPD art 19(a).

[115] See, e.g., Ministry of Health (New Zealand), *Office of the Director of Mental Health Annual Report* 2014 (2015) 16; Department of Health (Australia), 'National Mental Health Reform 2011–12: Early intervention and prevention, and mental health services for children and young people' (6 June 2011) <www.health.gov.au>; Department of Health, National Health Service (England), *Achieving Better Access to Mental Health Services by 2020* (8 October 2014) 1 <www.gov.uk>.

[116] National Mental Health Commission (Australia), 'Report of the National Review of Mental Health Programmes and Services: Summary', 30 November 2014, 12 <www.mentalhealthcommission.gov.au>. The National Mental Health Commission is an independent statutory body tasked with providing independent reports and advice on effective service provision.

standards for … health care', which links to obligations set out in Article 8, and to prominent proposals for the integration of a human rights perspective in mental health law and policy.

Other articles are relevant to the mental health context, even as they may not be directly relevant to civil commitment legislation. For example, justice-related provisions remain relevant. Article 13 obliges States Parties to ensure that persons with disabilities 'enjoy access to justice on an equal basis with all others', which includes 'the provision of procedural and age-appropriate accommodations' and training for judicial staff.[117] Article 13 may help address the reported overrepresentation of persons with psychosocial disability as victims of crimes, in imprisonment rates and so on, and in creating justice systems that are more responsive to disability-related need; for example, in policing practices, courtroom modifications or prison reform.[118] Particular areas of criminal law which are more closely related to mental health legislation include laws on unfitness to plead and the 'insanity defence'. Such 'special defences' create disability-based exceptions to typical legal processes. Justifications for mental health legislation – such as the view that 'there really is something special about mental illness'[119] – reappear where laws are predicated on the view that impairment can compromise legal capacity to the extent that a person cannot have representative capacity (unfitness to plead laws) or be held culpable for a particular act (the 'insanity defence'/defence of mental impairment). As with mental health legislation, this view is seemingly challenged by the CRPD directive guaranteeing the legal capacity of all people, regardless of disability, in all areas of life. After all, in order to enforce a person's legal rights against another, or for the person to defend himself or herself in legal proceedings, the individual must be recognised as the holder of legal rights, with the associated legal agency to exercise those rights.[120]

[117] Ibid., art 13(1).

[118] See E Flynn, *Disabled Justice? Access to Justice and the UN Convention on the Rights of Persons with Disabilities* (Ashgate, 2015).

[119] T Burns and D Rose, 'How Can the Service User Voice Be Best Heard at Psychiatric Meetings?' (2013) 203(2) *The British Journal of Psychiatry* 88.

[120] Perhaps for this reason, the CRPD Committee has stated that 'the recognition of the right to legal capacity is essential for access to justice in many respects'. Committee on the Rights of Persons with Disabilities, *General Comment No 1: Article 12: Equal Recognition before the Law*, 11th sess, UN Doc CRPD/C/GC/1 (19 May 2014) 10 [38]. For CRPD-based analyses of 'special defences', such as unfitness to plead and the insanity defence, see A Arstein-Kerslake et al., 'Human Rights and Unfitness to Plead: The Demands of the Convention on the Rights of Persons with Disabilities', *Human Rights Law Review* (accepted for publication); T Minkowitz, 'Rethinking Criminal Responsibility from a Critical Perspective: The Abolition of Insanity/Incapacity Acquittals and Unfitness to Plead, and Beyond' (2014) 23 *Griffith Law Review* 434; C Slobogin, 'Eliminating Mental Disability as a Legal Criterion in Deprivation of Liberty Cases: The Impact of the Convention on the Rights of Persons with Disability on the

Other CRPD articles relevant to mental health issues include those related to 'comprehensive habilitation and rehabilitation services and programmes, particularly in the areas of health, employment and social services';[121] employment and the right 'to work on an equal basis with others';[122] an 'adequate standard of living and social protection';[123] 'political rights and the opportunity to enjoy them on an equal basis with others';[124] and the rights of 'participation in cultural life, recreation, leisure and sport'.[125] Anyone with an interest in mental health policy and practice is likely to see the immediate relevance of these rights, particularly given the widespread social, political and economic marginalisation of persons with psychosocial disability.

3 *Implementation, Monitoring and the Optional Protocol*

Articles 31 to 40 are concerned with implementation and monitoring, where States Parties are required to establish monitoring bodies both inside and independent of the government.[126] Michael Stein and Janet Lord have argued that the monitoring mechanisms of the CRPD make it one of the strongest in international human rights, given the 'breadth of reporting and investigative procedures' it mandates.[127] These provisions are designed to help translate CRPD provisions into hard domestic laws, policies and good practices.

Article 33 provides for the operation of independent national-level monitoring mechanisms. According to the Office of the UN High Commissioner for Human Rights, the CRPD 'is the first human rights treaty that contains detailed provisions on the establishment and functioning of national monitoring and implementation frameworks'.[128] The incorporation of such provisions

Insanity Defense, Civil Commitment, and Competency Law' (2015) 15 *Vanderbilt University Law School Public Law and Legal Theory* 1. *Contra* A Plumb, 'UN Convention on the Rights of Persons with Disabilities: Out of the Frying Pan into the Fire? Mental Health Service Users and Survivors Aligning with the Disability Movement' in H Spandler, J Anderson and B Sapey (eds), *Madness, Distress and the Politics of Disablement* (Policy Press, 2015).

121 CRPD art 26.

122 Ibid., art 27.

123 Ibid., art 28.

124 Ibid., art 29.

125 Ibid., art 30.

126 Ibid., art 33.

127 M Stein and J Lord, 'Monitoring the Convention on the Rights of Persons with Disabilities: Innovations, Lost Opportunities, and Future Potential' (2010) 32 *Human Rights Quarterly* 689. See also JE Bickenbach, 'Monitoring the United Nation's Convention on the Rights of Persons with Disabilities: Data and the International Classification of Functioning, Disability and Health' (2011) 11(4) *BMC Public Health* 8.

128 UN Office of the High Commissioner for Human Rights, 'Thematic Study by the Office of the United Nations High Commissioner for Human Rights on Enhancing Awareness and

moves beyond merely offering specific remedies for what ought to be, to developing the institutional preconditions necessary to ensure realisation of the rights of the CRPD.[129]

The CRPD does not contain a judicial enforcement system. However, Article 34 establishes a committee of experts, the CRPD Committee, to monitor implementation at the international level. Article 34 authorises the CRPD Committee to review the compliance reports of States Parties.[130]

The CRPD also has an 'Optional Protocol', which can be signed and ratified separately. The Optional Protocol allows the CRPD Committee to 'receive and consider communications from or on behalf of individuals or groups of individuals subject to its jurisdiction who claim to be victims of a violation by that State Party of the provisions of the Convention'.[131] The Optional Protocol remains an important avenue for individuals or groups wishing to claim that a rights violation has taken place.

D NEW TOOLS OR NEW PARADIGM?

Key concepts of the CRPD, such as 'supported decision-making', 'support to exercise legal capacity' and independent living and being included in the community, hold promise for addressing major issues in the mental health context. Do they herald a new paradigm or simply offer more tools for responding to these issues? Penelope Weller has argued that the main promise of the CRPD for people with psychosocial disability is the development of supported decision-making processes in mental health-related laws, policies and programming.[132] Brendan Kelly more cautiously forecasts 'significant issues regarding the CRPD's implications for systems of supported decision-making in national mental health legislation, among other areas'.[133] Taking a somewhat different approach, McSherry and Andrew Butler caution against a narrow focus on supported decision-making,

Understanding of the Convention on the Rights of Persons with Disabilities', UN Doc A/HRC/10/48 (26 January 2009) [59].

129 G Quinn, 'Resisting the "Temptation of Elegance": Can the Convention on the Rights of Persons with Disabilities Socialise States to Right Behaviour?' in OM Arnardóttir and G Quinn (eds), *The UN Convention on the Rights of Persons with Disabilities: European and Scandinavian Perspectives* (Martinus Nijhoff Publishers, 2009) 215.

130 CRPD art 34.

131 CRPD Optional Protocol, art 1(1).

132 P Weller, 'Supported Decision-Making and the Achievement of Non-Discrimination: The Promise and Paradox of the Disabilities Convention' (2008) 26(2) *Law in Context* 85.

133 Kelly, above n 58, 93.

because it risks pushing debate back to the vexing issue of involuntary psychiatric intervention.[134] Instead, they argue, the focus could turn to what it means to ensure voluntary access to the highest attainable standard of mental health services and community care, or what it means to be supported to 'exercise legal capacity', which goes beyond decision-making.[135] McSherry and Butler write:

> Endeavours to provide both informal and more formal supports for those with mental and intellectual impairments to make their own decisions should be welcomed. However, in the mental health field, the major drawback to the current law reform focus on Article 12 and matters of capacity is that it serves to keep attention on compulsory detention and treatment, rather than viewing the CRPD as an opportunity to find new ways of ensuring voluntary access to the highest attainable standard of mental health services and community care.[136]

These concerns about the role of supported decision-making and support to exercise legal capacity highlight the intertwined demands of the CRPD for civil and political rights on the one hand, and social, economic and cultural rights on the other. Civil and political rights (or so-called first-generation rights) typically emphasise non-interference by the state, such as the freedom to associate, the right to free speech and so on. In contrast, social, economic and cultural rights (so-called second-generation rights) tend to require material resources to enjoy; for example, resources for education, employment opportunities or cultural observance. The CRPD as a whole combines these two categories of rights.[137] This is a point to which I will return throughout the book, particularly regarding the duties and responsibilities of States Parties to provide resources for persons with disabilities to *exercise* their rights.

Yet as McSherry and Butler observe, recent debates about mental health and human rights have tended to revert to a focus on whether compulsory interventions should be abolished. As noted, UN treaty bodies have tended to fall on the side of abolition. The OHCHR, for example, has expressed the view that mental health legislation is unjustly discriminatory against people with psychosocial disability, because it systematically uses mental illness/

[134] B McSherry and A Butler, 'Support for the Exercise of Legal Capacity: The Role of the Law' (2015) 22(4) *Journal of Law and Medicine* 739.

[135] Ibid.

[136] Ibid.

[137] P Bartlett, 'The United Nations Convention on the Rights of Persons with Disabilities and Mental Health Law' (2012) 75(5) *The Modern Law Review* 752, 757.

disorder as a criterion to limit legal capacity.[138] In 2009, the OHCHR made the following statement:

> Legislation authorizing the institutionalization of persons with disabilities on the grounds of their disability without their free and informed consent must be abolished. This must include the repeal of provisions authorizing institutionalization of persons with disabilities for their care and treatment without their free and informed consent, as well as provisions authorizing the preventive detention of persons with disabilities on grounds such as the likelihood of them posing a danger to themselves or others, in all cases in which such grounds of care, treatment and public security are linked in legislation to an apparent or diagnosed mental illness.[139]

The CRPD Committee echoed this view. In 'concluding observations' made to China, the CRPD Committee recommended 'the abolishment of the practice of involuntary civil commitment based on actual or perceived impairment'.[140] In 'concluding observations' to Australia, the CRPD Committee called for the repeal of 'legal provisions that authorize commitment of individuals to detention in mental health services, or the imposition of compulsory treatment either in institutions or in the community via Community Treatment Orders'.[141] It is worth citing in full Paragraph 42 of the General Comment 1 of the CRPD Committee, which states:

> As has been stated by the Committee in several concluding observations, forced treatment by psychiatric and other health and medical professionals is a violation of the right to equal recognition before the law and an infringement of the rights to personal integrity (art. 17); freedom from torture (art. 15); and freedom from violence, exploitation and abuse (art. 16). This practice denies the legal capacity of a person to choose medical treatment and, is therefore, a violation of article 12 of the Convention. States parties must, instead, respect the legal capacity of persons with disabilities to

[138] UN General Assembly, OHCHR, 10th sess, agenda item 2, 'Annual Report of the United Nations High Commissioner for Human Rights and Reports of the Office of the High Commissioner and the Secretary-General: Thematic Study by the Office of the United Nations High Commissioner for Human Rights on Enhancing Awareness and Understanding of the Convention on the Rights of Persons with Disabilities', UN Doc A/HRC/10/48 (26 January 2009).

[139] Ibid. para 49.

[140] Committee on the Rights of Persons with Disabilities, *Concluding Observations on the Initial Report of China*, 8th sess, UN Doc CRPD/C/CHN/CO/1 (27 September 2012) [26]. 'Concluding observations' essentially refers to a review of a States Party's compliance with the CRPD.

[141] Committee on the Rights of Persons with Disabilities, *Concluding Observations on the Initial Report of Australia*, 10th sess, UN Doc CRPD/C/AUS/CO/1 (4 October 2013) [34].

> make decisions at all times, including in crisis situations; must ensure that accurate and accessible information is provided about service options and that non-medical approaches are made available; and must provide access to independent support. States parties have an obligation to provide access to support for decisions regarding psychiatric and other medical treatment. Forced treatment is a particular problem for persons with psychosocial, intellectual and other cognitive disabilities. *States parties must abolish policies and legislative provisions that allow or perpetrate forced treatment, as it is an ongoing violation found in mental health laws across the globe, despite empirical evidence indicating its lack of effectiveness and the views of people using mental health systems who have experienced deep pain and trauma as a result of forced treatment.* The Committee recommends that States parties ensure that decisions relating to a person's physical or mental integrity can only be taken with the free and informed consent of the person concerned.[142]

The CRPD Committee directs States Parties to replace mental health law with a 'supported decision-making regime'.[143]

Similarly, the UN Special Rapporteur on the rights of persons with disabilities, Catalina Devandas-Aguilar, and on the right of everyone to the enjoyment of the highest attainable standard of health, Dainius Pûras, made an appeal in 2016 for states to 'do away with all forms of non-consensual psychiatric treatment':

> Locked in institutions, tied down with restraints, often in solitary confinement, forcibly injected with drugs and overmedicated, are only few illustrations of the ways in which persons with disabilities, or those perceived to be so, are treated without their consent, with severe consequences for their physical and mental integrity.
>
> Globally, persons with developmental and psychosocial disabilities face discrimination, stigma and marginalization and are subject to emotional and physical abuse in both mental health facilities and the community. And every year, the rights and dignity of hundreds of thousands of people across the world are violated as a consequence of non-consensual psychiatry [sic] interventions.[144]

I will discuss the views of UN treaty bodies and the implications of the CRPD for mental health law in detail in Chapter 3.[145]

[142] Committee on the Rights of Persons with Disabilities, above n 120, 11 [42] (emphasis added).

[143] Ibid. 6 [26].

[144] Office of the High Commissioner for Human Rights, '"Dignity Must Prevail" – An Appeal to Do Away with Non-consensual Psychiatric Treatment World Mental Health Day – Saturday 10 October 2015', Geneva, 8 October 2015.

[145] See Chapter 3, Section B; Chapters 4 and 5.

No government appears willing – at least at this stage – to adhere to the directive to abolish 'mental health laws that permit forced treatment',[146] and some, such as Canada and Australia, have even refuted that the CRPD requires as such.[147] Nevertheless, in the short time since coming into force, the CRPD can be seen to have affected the development of domestic law, including mental health law.[148] For example, the judiciary in England and Wales appear increasingly mindful of the state's CRPD obligations and the philosophy that underpins them. Lady Hale stated in *P v Cheshire West* [2014]:

> The rights set out in the European Convention are to be guaranteed to 'everyone' (article 1). They are premised on the inherent dignity of all human beings whatever their frailty or flaws. The same philosophy underpins the *United Nations Convention on the Rights of Persons with Disabilities* (CRPD), ratified by the United Kingdom in 2009. Although not directly incorporated into our domestic law, the CRPD is recognised by the Strasbourg court as part of the international law context within which the guarantees of the European Convention are to be interpreted.[149]

The focus of governments has typically turned to reforming mental health legislation in efforts to secure CRPD compliance. The CRPD appears to have informed a number of mental health law reform initiatives at the domestic level. For example, two states in Germany have seen certain powers under mental health legislation invalidated for violating the country's obligations under the CRPD.[150] In Argentina, public officials have interpreted the National Mental Health Law 2010[151] with reference to the CRPD to provide

[146] Committee on the Rights of Persons with Disabilities, above n 120, 2 [7].

[147] See, e.g., CRPD: Reservations and Declarations (Canada), (Australia) UNHCR 2008 <www.treaties.un.org>.

[148] See, e.g., D Sachan, 'Mental Health Bill Set to Revolutionise Care in India' (2013) 382(9889) *The Lancet* 296; FJ Bariffi and MS Smith, 'Same Old Game but with Some New Players: Assessing Argentina's National Mental Health Law in Light of the Rights to Liberty and Legal Capacity under the United Nations Convention on the Rights of the Persons with Disabilities' (2013) 31(3) *Nordic Journal of Human Rights* 325; Department of Health, *Exposure Draft Mental Health Bill 2010, Explanatory Guide* (2010) Victorian Government, Australia; E Flynn, 'Mental (In)capacity or Legal Capacity? A Human Rights Analysis of the Proposed Fusion of Mental Health and Mental Capacity in Northern Ireland' (2013) 64(4) *Northern Ireland Legal Quarterly* 485; see also Chapter 5, Section 3.

[149] P (by his litigation friend, the Official Solicitor) v Cheshire West and Chester Council and another; P and Q (by their litigation friend, the Official Solicitor) v Surrey County Council [2014] UKSC 19.

[150] Federal Constitutional Court (Germany), 'Press Office – Press Release No 28/2011 of 15 April 2011, Order of 23 March 2011', 2 BvR 882/09 <www.bverfg.de>.

[151] Law No 26657, 3 December 2010 [32041] BO 1 (Argentina); 'Mental Health Regime', House of Representatives, Res D-276/07, (7 March 2007) art 1.

support measures for people in mental health crises, including with consideration of the harm caused by involuntary treatment.[152] In Australia, as Sascha Callaghan and Chris Ryan note, 'all but one of eight Australian jurisdictions have undertaken substantial reviews of their mental health laws', wherein all 'reviewing authorities have acknowledged the impact of the CRPD and, to varying degrees, have sought to make amendments that would improve compliance with human rights obligations, and particularly the central challenge established in article 12'.[153] To provide one example from Australia, the Mental Health Act 2015 of the Australian Capital Territory contains a clear reference to the CRPD.[154] Section 6(d) states: 'a person with a mental disorder or mental illness has the right to have the person's *will and preferences*, to the extent that they are known or able to be known, taken into account in decisions made about treatment, care or support'.[155] Internationally, key concepts behind the CRPD have appeared in policy documents and law reform processes, contributing to new ideas and practices, including rethinking mental health law altogether.

However, the influence of the CRPD on legislative reform varies considerably and is difficult at this early stage to generalise. (Arguably, it is easier to see the impact of the MI Principles, with which typical mental health legislation appears to comply; this is surprising given the MI Principles are a non-binding international legal instrument.)

In summary, the major implications of the CRPD for mental health law relate to the potential to bolster calls for more responsive support, and additional support where required, as well as calls to restrict coercive intervention. In some areas, such as strengthening demands for access to services, CRPD provisions will be uncontroversial. In other areas, namely involuntary psychiatric intervention, controversy will continue for the foreseeable future. Kelly argues that certain provisions of the CRPD 'appear to be incompatible with certain aspects of mental health legislation in England, Wales, Scotland, Northern Ireland and Ireland [to which could be added Canada, Australia, New Zealand and so on], and certain other provisions are, at best, unclear'.[156] In certain respects, he writes, these laws 'diverge clearly and significantly from the CRPD'.[157] Key challenges in mental health law, policy and practice, which are relevant here, centre upon questions that require clarification, namely:

[152] Bariffi and Smith, above n 148, 325.

[153] SM Callaghan and C Ryan, 'An Evolving Revolution: Evaluating Australia's Compliance with the Convention on the Rights of Persons with Disabilities in Mental Health Law' (2016) 39(2) *University of New South Wales Law Journal* 596, 597.

[154] Mental Health Act 2015 (ACT) A2015-38. Republication No 4.

[155] Ibid. Republication No 4 s 6(d).

[156] Kelly, above n 58, 111.

[157] Ibid.

- What does the positive obligation of the CRPD to provide 'support to exercise legal capacity' (Article 12) or the right to highest attainable health (Article 25) or the right to 'live independently and be included in the community' (Article 19) require? What is the relationship between these provisions, and what do 'community-based' services that secure human rights look like?
- How can mental health legislation be reconciled with the CRPD, particularly the directive that the 'existence of disability shall in no case justify a deprivation of liberty'? At present, mental health legislation clearly links detention and involuntary treatment with a diagnosis of mental disorder/illness and risk.
- How can current approaches to non-consensual psychiatric interventions be reconciled with the CRPD directive to replace a 'best interests' approach to substituted decision-making (not including children)[158] with supported decision-making based on a person's 'will, preference and rights'? Under typical mental health legislation, the 'best interests' formulation governs clinical substituted decision-making. This formulation appears either explicitly or implicitly in relevant legislation in England and Wales,[159] Canada,[160] Scotland,[161] Ireland,[162] Northern Ireland,[163] New Zealand,[164] Australia[165] and so on.

These are among the major questions relevant here which remain unanswered, and which form the basis for the investigations conducted throughout the rest of the book.

E CONCLUSION

New ideas have emerged in the 'post-carceral era' about mental health law and the issues it is meant to address. According to Gerard Quinn, the CRPD offers a means to escape the 'imprisoning logic' in debates about rights-based

158 CRPD art 7(2).

159 Mental Capacity Act 2005 (c 9) (England and Wales). Chapter 1, Sections 4 and 6 of the Mental Health Act 2007 refer to the 'appropriate treatment test' for responding to those subject to the act. Mental Health Act 2007 (c 12) (England and Wales) ch 1 ss 4, 6.

160 See, e.g., Ontario Mental Health Act R.S.O. 1990 ch M.7. s 20(1.1).

161 Mental Health (Care and Treatment) (Scotland) Act 2003 (Scot) asp 13 s 276(3).

162 Mental Health Act 2001 s 4(1).

163 Mental Health (Northern Ireland) Order 1986 No 595 (N.I. 4) s 3(1); Mental Capacity Bill (2014) s 1(7).

164 Mental Health (Compulsory Assessment and Treatment) Act 1992 No 46 s 2(1).

165 See, e.g., Mental Health Act 2014 (WA) pt 2 div 3.

legalism in mental health law, which led to a breakdown of meaningful dialogue:

> Some civil libertarians would hesitate to use an argument for a legal right to treatment (no matter how meritorious) lest the need for treatment might be used to justify an undue encroachment on liberty. Contrariwise, some professionals in the field who have the responsibility to deliver services, would hesitate to embrace liberty-enhancing arguments lest it interfere too much with their capacity to deliver a substantive right to treatment – with their professional prerogatives.[166]

The extent to which the CRPD might offer a way out of this impasse may depend on how far States Parties are willing to go to meet their positive obligations to provide support. The 'expressive, educational and proactive' role of the CRPD, to use Oliver Lewis's terms, can also help change mindsets.[167] Importantly for mental health law, policy and practice, the support framework set out in the CRPD seeks to change the long-standing status of medical expert from one that is *tutelary* to one in which experts *facilitate* access to support resources in ways that secure a range of human rights. The CRPD may also encourage people to request and provide accommodations, to reconfigure existing services to promote participation, to seek ways to alter communities to improve 'accessibility' or to use the law to claim rights. The CRPD appears to propose a 'middle-path' notion of freedom, one determined in close collaboration with persons with disability in which abuse is seen to span from excessive state intervention and protectionism at one end to neglect and relinquishment of government duties to support those in need at the other.

166 G Quinn, 'The United Nations Convention on the Rights of Persons wth [sic] Disabilities – Towards a Unified Field Theory of Disability' (presentation paper) Indian Law Society, G. V. Pandit Memorial Oration, Pune, India, 10 October 2009, 11 <www.nuigalway.ie/cdlp>.

167 O Lewis, 'The Expressive, Educational and Proactive Roles of Human Rights' in McSherry and Weller, above n 25, 96.

3

Major Criticisms of Mental Health Law

A INTRODUCTION

Mental health laws codify non-consensual psychiatric treatment and involuntary hospitalisation, and regulate the powers of those given charge to do so. This function is largely unchanged since the nineteenth century, when private 'madhouses' and asylums began proliferating in the West.[1] Contemporary mental health laws in high-income common-law jurisdictions appear to reflect concerns associated with deinstitutionalisation; that is, the shift from large-scale stand-alone psychiatric institutions to a more diffuse set of 'community-' and hospital-based services. Today, according to Bernadette McSherry, the law is integral to the functioning of mental health systems.[2] Such systems exert a powerful influence over people's lives. Lawrence Gostin catalogues some of the effects in legal terms.[3] He writes that the law continues to empower the medical profession to 'limit individual liberty ... bodily integrity ... privacy ... and capacity to act', as well as to arbitrate special rules of citizenship.[4] These limitations primarily take the form of compulsory admission and involuntary treatment.

By imposing such restrictions, it can be argued that mental health law operates to protect individuals and create opportunities for social justice[5]; they

1 J Ellard, 'The Madness of Mental Health Acts' (1990) 24 *Australian and New Zealand Journal of Psychiatry* 167, 174.

2 B McSherry (ed), *International Trends in Mental Health Laws* (Federation Press, 2008) 1.

3 L Gostin, *Public Health Law and Ethics: A Reader* (University of California Press, 2nd ed, 2010) v.

4 Ibid. An example of arbitrating special rules of citizenship is with regard to the right to drive a car, which can be restricted under certain mental health statutes. Another relates to restrictions on where to live. See, e.g., Mental Health Act 1986 (Vic) s 14(3)(b).

5 HK Jagodic et al., 'Involuntary Treatment Is Better than No Treatment' (2008)18(4) *European Neuropsychopharmacol* 568.

provide a framework for civil rights protection and procedural due process for those subject to civil commitment. Such laws have undoubtedly achieved a great deal of good: helping individuals avoid harm, providing much-needed access to assistance, creating procedures to prevent arbitrary incarceration and raising standards by which governments (and public officials) use coercive measures to prevent injury to individuals and communities. Certainly, the rights-based legalistic approaches that shaped contemporary mental health legislation were advanced by well-meaning legal and medical professionals who were humanist, liberal and compassionate.

However, there are other ways of seeing mental health law. Despite the hard-won gains and achievements of reformers seeking to improve upon earlier legislation, mental health law has been the subject of wide-ranging criticism, with some commentators charging that it creates more problems in today's world than it solves.[6] Various commentators have described mental health law as counter-therapeutic, ineffective on its own terms and discriminatory. In this sense, mental health law can be seen as an emancipatory tool to protect communities and individuals affected by extreme mental health crises, or a veil to legitimise the prejudicial control and exclusion of a confusing and objectionable minority.

These concerns reflect deep and lasting tensions in debates about mental health law. Deep political convictions about how the individual should be valued in relation to the collective give rise to competing answers to the question, How wide should the individual sphere of liberty be before the collective will can impose upon that sphere, whether for public safety or for the safety of the individual? This is essentially a question of political science and moral philosophy. Its consideration in law draws attention to the complex interplay between important and frequently competing principles of freedom, protection and fairness. This dynamic is complicated further by disputed premises regarding the impact of mental disorder upon a person's ability to make 'autonomous' decisions. Willis Spaulding has described this conceptual controversy as arising from competing 'understanding(s) of the relationship between liberty and mental disorder'.[7] These concerns populate the background of current mental

6 See A Nilsson, 'Objective and Reasonable? Scrutinising Compulsory Mental Health Interventions from a Non-discrimination Perspective' (2014) 14 *Human Rights Law Review* 459; T Minkowitz, 'The United Nations Convention on the Rights of Persons with Disabilities and the Right to Be Free from Non-consensual Psychiatric Interventions' (2007) 34(2) *Syracuse Journal of International Law and Commerce* 405; Juan E Méndez, Special Rapporteur, *Report of the Special Rapporteur on Torture and Other Cruel, Inhuman or Degrading Treatment or Punishment*, 22nd sess, UN Doc A/HRC/22/53 (1 February 2013) para 64.

7 WJ Spaulding, 'Mapping the "New Legalism" of English Mental Health Law' (1989) 17(2) *The Journal of Law, Medicine and Ethics* 187.

health law, which this chapter seeks to bring to the fore. The CRPD has offered an opportunity to navigate an alternative path through long-standing debates.[8] Before focusing on the corrective potential of the CRPD support framework, it is useful to list the major practical and conceptual dilemmas in mental health law today.

In her meta-analysis of mental health law, Jill Peay noted that it is difficult to locate key issues, as there are so many,[9] a view echoed by the Health and Consumer Protection Directorate-General of the European Commission.[10] Nonetheless, a diverse array of commentators view the current era of mental health law as wanting in key respects, and have identified specific concerns.[11] The strident directives of the CRPD Committee and other UN agencies have amplified these concerns.

Although the theoretical lens of this book is human rights-based, pragmatic arguments are also relevant and include matters of resourcing, the internal coherence of mental health law and comparative analysis of evidence regarding its success and shortcomings. The purpose of articulating these issues is to assist in weighing the costs and harms of specific civil commitment laws, and to tease out some of the major practical and conceptual concerns relevant to a human rights analysis. In assessing these costs and benefits, it is perhaps as easy to give mental health law too much blame for the costs as too much credit for the benefits. One possibility is that the potential downsides of mental health law arise when it is distorted or misapplied. Another possibility is that any benefits of mental health law are overwhelmed by other powerful forces in society,[12] such as wealth inequality and resource distribution.[13]

8 Convention on the Rights of Persons with Disabilities, opened for signature 30 March 2007, Doc.A/61/611 (entered into force 3 May 2008).

9 J Peay (ed), *Seminal Issues in Mental Health Law* (Ashgate, 2005) xvi.

10 In 2002, the Health and Consumer Protection Directorate-General of the European Commission cited an earlier study to describe involuntary commitment in the following terms: '[a] complex set of still poorly understood legal, political, economic, social, medical and multiple other factors seems to interact in the process of involuntary placement'. European Commission, Health and Consumer Protection Directorate-General, 'Compulsory Admission and Involuntary Treatment of Mentally Ill Patients – Legislation and Practice in EU Member States' (Central Institute of Mental Health, Mannheim, Germany, 15 May 2002).

11 See, generally, Peay above n 9.

12 M Jones and LA Basser-Marks, 'The Limitations on the Use of Law to Promote Rights: An Assessment of the Disability Discrimination Act 1992' in M Haurit, C Sampford and S Blencowe (eds), *Justice for People with Disabilities – Legal and Institutional Issues* (Federation Press, 1998).

13 See, e.g., M Maroto and D Pettinicchio, 'The Limitations of Disability Antidiscrimination Legislation: Policymaking and the Economic Well-being of People with Disabilities' (2014) 36(4) *Law & Policy* 370.

In evaluating the main issues in mental health law, therefore, researchers must isolate and assess these causes and effects as carefully as possible. For the purposes of this chapter, it should be noted that most of the arguments are listed as concisely as possible, even at the risk of seeming overly polemical. The intention here is to explore a range of critical issues in order to evaluate which issues the CRPD support framework may *or may not* address, as the case may be. Finally, even if the costs of mental health law were established, it would still be necessary to evaluate them alongside the very real accomplishments of mental health law reform in recent decades.

B RIGHTS-BASED ARGUMENTS

1 *Mental Health Law Is Discriminatory*

Mental health law can be seen to be unjustly discriminatory, as it only applies to people with apparent or diagnosed mental illness/mental disorder. Mental health law constitutes an entrenched anomaly in a legal system that traditionally privileges and protects individual autonomy and routinely upholds the right to refuse treatment in general healthcare.[14] Core Western legal values of equality and non-discrimination are compromised where powers of mandatory detention and compulsory medical intervention only apply to those with an apparent or diagnosed mental illness in certain circumstances.[15] The authorisation of powers that circumscribe the right to refuse medical treatment, even when individuals retain mental capacity, remains an exception to ethical standards in general medicine. Judy Laing argues that '[c]oercive care remains predominant in the treatment of mental ill health', making it 'distinctive as one of the very few areas of medical practice where overtly paternalistic traditions still dominate, and patients can be admitted compulsorily to hospital and forcibly treated, irrespective of their mental capacity or individual autonomy'.[16] There are some exceptions to this broad observation; for example, a number of Australian jurisdictions have authorised competent

[14] M Donnelly, 'From Autonomy to Dignity: Treatment for Mental Disorders and the Focus for Patient Rights', in McSherry (ed), above n 2, 38.

[15] Some mental health legislation refers to mental 'disorder' for the purposes of the legislation. See, e.g., Mental Health Act 2007 (England and Wales) c 12, Ch. 1 s (1)(2). For the sake of simplicity, when referring to relevant criteria for mental health law, I will refer to 'mental illness'.

[16] J Laing, 'Coercive Care: Rights, Law and Policy' (2015) *Medical Law Review* (online) <https://academic.oup.com/medlaw/article-abstract/24/2/297/2413144/Coercive-Care-Rights-Law-and-Policy?redirectedFrom=PDF>.

refusal of psychiatric treatment, as is generally the case with other medical treatments.[17] However, these remain largely the exception and, as Chapter 4 will detail, continue to fall shy of 'harder' readings of the CRPD, where a number of UN agencies have called for the abandonment of mental capacity assessments because they discriminate *in effect* (even as they remain formally non-discriminatory) against persons with disabilities.

General medical law has seen a major shift in the past fifty years towards patient autonomy and away from traditional medical paternalism.[18] Medico-legal standards today provide that doctors who treat patients contrary to their expressed wishes breach the following principle: 'An adult patient … has an absolute right to choose whether to consent to medical treatment, to refuse it or to choose one rather than another of the treatments being offered …'[19] To breach this principle leaves doctors liable for battery under tort law and defies ethical codes of practice.[20] This liability applies throughout the common-law world.[21] Again, mental health law remains an exception to this principle.

It is true that even medical law has limits to respecting patient autonomy when weighed against majoritarian interests and competing human rights. Exceptions include matters of public risk (for example, when epidemics require quarantining and treatment), immediate crises (for example, emergency intervention following severe physical trauma) and specific restricted

17 See Mental Health Act 2016 (Qld) s 12(1)(b); Mental Health Act 2013 (Tas) s 40(e); Mental Health Act 2014 (WA) ss 25(1)(c), (2)(c). For analysis of these laws in light of the CRPD, see SM Callaghan and C Ryan, 'An Evolving Revolution: Evaluating Australia's Compliance with the Convention on the Rights of Persons with Disabilities in Mental Health Law' (2016) 39(2) *University of New South Wales Law Journal* 596.

18 RE Ashcroft, A Dawson, H Draper and JR McMillan (eds), *Principles of Health Care Ethics* (Wiley, 2nd ed, 2007) 347. See also, generally, P Appelbaum, CW Lidz and A Meisel, *Informed Consent: Legal Theory and Clinical Practice* (Oxford University Press, 1987). A large body of evidence supports the view that autonomous choice is a valued ideal. See R Young, 'The Value of Autonomy' (1982) 32(126) *The Philosophical Quarterly* 35; J Christman, 'Autonomy, Self-Knowledge, and Liberal Legitimacy' in J Christman and J Anderson (eds), *Autonomy and the Challenges to Liberalism: New Essays* (Cambridge University Press, 2005) 330.

19 *Re T* [1993] Fam 95, 102–3 (Lord Donaldson).

20 See, e.g., General Medical Council, 'GMC Consent Guidance: Patients and Doctors Making Decisions Together' (2008) <www.gmc-uk.org>.

21 For Canada, see *Nancy B v HôtelDieu Québec* (1992) 86 DLR (4th) 385, 390–2 (Dufour J) (Quebec Superior Court); *Malette v Shulman* (1990) 67 DLR (4th) 321, 328 (Robins JA) (Ontario Court of Appeal). For English and Welsh law, see *Airedale NHS Trust v Bland* [1993] AC 789, 857 (Lord Keith), 864 (Lord Goff); *Re T* [1993] Fam 95, 102–3 (Lord Donaldson); *Re MB* [1997] 2 FLR 426, 432 (Butler-Sloss LJ); *Re B* [2002] 2 All ER 449, 455–6 [16]–[21] (Dame Butler-Sloss P). In Australia, see *H Ltd v J* (2010) 107 SASR 352, 364–9 [33]–[46] (Kourakis J); *Hunter and New England Area Health Service v A* (2009) 74 NSWLR 88, 91–2 [9]–[15] (McDougall J). In New Zealand, see *Auckland Area Health Board v Attorney General* [1993] 1 NZLR 235, 245 (Thomas J).

decisions (such as the selling of organs, or end-of-life treatment when patients express the wish to die). However, these exceptions at the ethical boundaries of medical law, even as they differ between jurisdictions, are *generally* applicable. By contrast, mental health law applies on an unequal basis to a specific group of people in both principle and application. Even as mental health law applies specifically in certain circumstances, particularly where risk to self or others exists, it is *only* applicable to those with an apparent or diagnosed mental illness. This creates inconsistency with other areas of medicine where patients deemed 'mentally capable' are entitled to make personal health choices, even where such choices result in a risk of death.

The criticism that mental health law is unjustly discriminatory is not new. In 1977, Stephen Morse concluded a journal article with what remains a powerful argument today:

> Mental disorder is not an efficient and adequate threshold criterion for social and legal regulation of the behaviours regulated by mental health law. Mental health laws often deprive citizens of liberty, autonomy, and dignity without sufficient justification for doing so. Justifications based on disease or on the differences of crazy persons are terribly over- and under-inclusive. Most people with mental disorders, even severe ones, are not different enough from normal persons to warrant special treatment … Conversely, for example, many normal persons behave dangerously or incompetently, and there is good reason to believe they have as little or as much control over their behaviour as crazy persons.[22]

Tom Campbell has argued that mental health law leads to 'institutional discrimination' by establishing, at law, 'the idea that there is something about "mental illness" itself which invites a system of control and coercion'.[23] As a result, he suggests, medical treatment and social control become dangerously entangled, promoting stereotyped prejudice and compromising therapeutic support.[24] George Szmukler and John Dawson have even intimated that separate mental health legislation is discriminatory against mental health professionals by virtue of their being obliged under law to intervene on prejudicial grounds,[25] a view consonant with Joanna Moncrieff's argument that mental

22 SJ Morse, 'Crazy Behavior, Morals, and Science: An Analysis of Mental Health Law' (1997) 51 *Southern California Law Review* 653. Peay describes Morse's argument as a 'powerful case for the abolition of mental health law'. Peay, above n 9, xvii.

23 T Campbell, 'Mental Health Law: Institutionalised Discrimination' (1994) 28 *Australian and New Zealand Journal of Psychiatry* 554, 556.

24 Ibid. 555.

25 J Dawson and G Szmukler, 'Fusion of Mental Health and Incapacity Legislation' (2006) 188 *The British Journal of Psychiatry* 504.

health law unfairly positions psychiatrists as agents of social control at the cost of therapeutic duty.[26]

The imposition of involuntary psychiatric intervention and restrictions on legal capacity can have secondary effects, some of which are counter to therapeutic support. Stephen Rosenman has argued:

> Once they have qualified for compulsory hospitalisation, patients lose their autonomy and personal standing. Not only treatment but all facets of the patient's personal life fall completely under the power of the hospital staff. However benevolent the staff may be, patients resent staff who are at once their custodians and carers. Such resentment discourages the development of collaboration in treatment.[27]

Abridging or restricting fundamental rights can inflict profound psychic damage, arguably undermining the healing benefits those restrictions seek to bring about. Bruce Winick has argued that labelling someone as 'incompetent' induces feelings of helplessness and leads to non-participation in decisions that are central to living a full life.[28] Incompetency labelling can impede the basic human need for self-determination and self-actualisation.[29] Michael Bach, Jane Anweiler and Cameron Crawford have argued that placing limitations on legal capacity – in the sense of restricting a person from making decisions based on values and a reasonable availability of meaningful choices – diminishes personhood and citizenship.[30] This, in turn, reduces a person's status in society, contributing to social exclusion and potentially increasing powerlessness and vulnerability to abuse.[31]

[26] J Moncrieff, 'The Politics of a New Mental Health Act' (2003) 183 *The British Journal of Psychiatry* 8.

[27] S Rosenman, 'Mental Health Law: An Idea Whose Time Has Passed' (1994) 28 *Australian and New Zealand Journal of Psychiatry* 561, 562.

[28] B Winick, 'The Side Effects of Incompetency Labelling and the Implications for Mental Health' (1995) 1 *Psychology Public Policy and Law* 6.

[29] Ibid.

[30] M Bach, J Anweiler and C Crawford, *Coming Home – Staying Home, Legal Research: Supported Decision-making and the Restriction of Guardianship* (The Roeher Institute, 1994).

[31] F Morrissey, 'The United Nations Convention on the Rights of Persons with Disabilities: A New Approach to Decision-Making in Mental Health Law' (2012) 19 *European Journal of Health Law* 423, 428. The notion of social inclusion and integration was established at the World Summit for Social Development in March 1995, and was designed with the aim of creating an inclusive society. An inclusive society was stated as being 'based on respect for all human rights and fundamental freedoms, cultural and religious diversity, social justice and the special needs of vulnerable and disadvantaged groups, democratic participation and the rule of law'. UN, *Report of the World Summit for Social Development*, UN Doc A/CONF.166/9 (19 April 1995) 68 [66].

2 *Mental Health Law Violates International Human Rights Law*

As the previous chapter outlined, the CRPD has added weight to arguments that mental health legislation violates a range of human rights.[32] Particular sections of the CRPD will create ongoing challenges to the operation of mental health legislation. Laws that discriminate on the grounds of disability can be seen to violate fundamental principles of the CRPD, particularly with regard to '[r]espect for inherent dignity, individual autonomy including the freedom to make one's own choices, and independence of persons', 'non-discrimination' and 'equality of opportunity'.[33] Article 5(2) prohibits all forms of discrimination based on disability, while Article 14 specifically states that 'the existence of a disability shall in no case justify a deprivation of liberty'.[34] Article 17 states that '[e]very person with disabilities has a right to respect for his or her physical and mental integrity on an equal basis with others'.[35] Article 25 directs that States Parties shall '[r]equire health professionals to provide care of the same quality to persons with disabilities as to others, including on the basis of free and informed consent'.[36] Finally, Article 12 directs that States Parties shall not place restrictions on legal capacity based on disability,[37] which mental health legislation clearly does. (I will discuss Article 12 in detail in Chapters 4 and 5.)

As noted previously, UN treaty bodies have elaborated on legal arguments that involuntary psychiatric intervention under current mental health legislation violates the CRPD.[38] For example, the CRPD Committee commented:

> As has been established in numerous concluding observations, forced treatment by psychiatric and other health and medical professionals is a violation of the right to equal recognition before the law and an infringement upon the rights to personal integrity (Article 17), freedom from torture (Article 15), and freedom from violence, exploitation and abuse (Article 16). This practice denies the right to legal capacity to choose medical treatment and is therefore

[32] See Chapter 2, Section D. See, generally, M Dudley, D Silove and F Gale, *Mental Health and Human Rights – Vision, Praxis, and Courage* (Oxford University Press, 2012); P Bartlett, O Lewis and O Thorold, *Mental Disability and the European Convention on Human Rights* (Martinus Nijhoff, 2007) vol 10. B McSherry and P Weller (eds), *Rethinking Rights-Based Mental Health Laws* (Hart, 2010); Morrissey, above n 31, 423.

[33] CRPD art 3.

[34] Ibid., art 14(1)(b).

[35] Ibid., art 17. See, generally, A Kämpf, 'Involuntary Treatment Decisions: Using Negotiated Silence to Facilitate Change?' in McSherry and Weller, above n 32, 141.

[36] CRPD art 25(d).

[37] Ibid., art 12(2). See Chapter 2, Section C(2).

[38] See Chapter 2, Section D.

> a violation of Article 12. States Parties must, instead, provide access to support for decisions about psychiatric and other medical treatment. Forced treatment has been a particular problem for persons with psycho-social, intellectual, and other cognitive disabilities. Policies and legislative provisions that allow or perpetrate forced treatment must be abolished. This is an on-going violation in mental health laws across the globe, despite empirical evidence indicating its lack of effectiveness as well as views of people using mental health systems who have expressed deep pain and trauma as a result of forced treatment. The Committee recommends that State parties should ensure that decisions that involve a person's physical or mental integrity can only be taken with the free and informed consent of the person with disability concerned.[39]

Setting aside the veracity of these claims, which I will discuss throughout this chapter, the CRPD Committee directs States Parties to replace mental health law with a 'supported decision-making regime'.[40] The nature and feasibility of this directive will be the subject of Part II of this book.

3 *Mental Health Law May Lead to Cruel, Inhuman or Degrading Treatment or Punishment*

The UN Special Rapporteur on torture and other cruel, inhuman or degrading treatment or punishment, Juan Méndez, reported in 2013 'that involuntary treatment and other psychiatric interventions in health-care facilities are forms of torture and ill-treatment', and urged the 'revision of domestic legislation allowing for forced interventions'.[41] Méndez submitted his report to the UN Human Rights Council, which examined the nexus between the torture prevention mandate, the CRPD and the right to health. Concerns about the detention and treatment of persons with psychosocial disabilities formed the majority of the report. Controversially, recommendation 89(b) directed states to:

> Impose an absolute ban on all forced and non-consensual medical interventions against persons with disabilities, including the non-consensual administration of psychosurgery, electroshock and mind-altering drugs such as neuroleptics, the use of restraint and solitary confinement, for both long- and short-term application. The obligation to end forced psychiatric interventions

[39] Committee on the Rights of Persons with Disabilities, *General Comment No 1: Article 12: Equal Recognition Before the Law*, 11th sess, UN Doc CRPD/C/GC/1 (19 May 2014) 11 [42].
[40] Ibid. 4 [22].
[41] Méndez, above n 6, para 64; see also Minkowitz, above n 6, 405.

> based solely on grounds of disability is of immediate application and scarce financial resources cannot justify postponement of its implementation.[42]

Likewise, Minkowitz calls for the 'immediate cessation of forced psychiatric interventions' and the abolition of mental health law.[43] While Minkowitz does not identify the exceptions to substituted decision-making, Méndez makes exceptions for life-threatening emergencies 'in which there is no disagreement regarding absence of legal capacity', at which point 'a health-care provider [may] proceed without informed consent to perform a life-saving procedure'.[44]

As this last comment indicates, the report is somewhat conflicted, here endorsing what appears to be a functional mental capacity approach (which accepts that an absence of legal capacity can be agreed upon), although elsewhere in the report suggesting that legal capacity is held by all people regardless of impairment.[45] The special rapporteur's comments on risk of harm also appear to be inconsistent. Earlier in the report, he comments that 'the State must ... show that detention (based on mental illness) is necessary to protect the safety of the person or of others'.[46] Interestingly, however, Méndez revised this position in a statement accompanying the submission of the report to the Human Rights Council, in which he stated, 'I believe the severity of the mental illness cannot justify detention nor can it be justified by a motivation to protect the safety of the person or of others'.[47] While the UN Special Rapporteur on Torture directed that the treatment of those with psychosocial disabilities must only be consensual, his inconsistent commentary does leave open an argument that some form of coercive intervention may be justified in some circumstances, namely where interventions are based on a sufficient risk of harm or the 'absence of legal capacity'. Some countries will endorse the focus of the special rapporteur on mistreatment in healthcare settings, while others may charge that the statement fell outside his mandate, or that the statement did little to provide alternative solutions or concrete recommendations, such as alternative models for 'supporting legal capacity'. Clearly, as

[42] Elsewhere in the report, Méndez states that 'involuntary treatment and other psychiatric interventions in health-care facilities are forms of torture and ill-treatment' and urges the 'revision of domestic legislation allowing for forced interventions. Mendez, above n 6, para 64.

[43] Minkowitz, above n 6.

[44] Méndez, above n 6, para 66.

[45] For more on the differentiation between the universal and functional view of legal capacity, see Chapter 4, Section B(1); Chapter 5, Section B.

[46] Méndez, above n 6, para 69.

[47] Juan E Méndez, Special Rapporteur, 'Statement by Mr Juan E Méndez Special Rapporteur on Torture and Other Cruel, Inhuman or Degrading Treatment or Punishment', 22nd sess (4 March 2013) 5 <www.ohchr.org>.

with the views of the CRPD Committee, the task of developing alternatives is left up to States Parties. What is also clear is that an emerging consensus has formed within parts of the UN that the discriminatory nature of mental health legislation justifies its abolition rather than reform, with some notable exceptions.[48] The special rapporteur endorses what he describes as the 'very explicit' directive of the CRPD Committee, which 'call[s] for the prohibition of disability-based detention, i.e. civil commitment and compulsory institutionalization or confinement based on disability'.[49]

4 *'Special Measures': Can Lawmakers Justify Differential Treatment?*

Both proponents and opponents of mental health law acknowledge that it subjects people with psychosocial disabilities to different rights – or, at the very least, a substantially different calculus for applying competing rights. Where controversy does arise is in whether such restrictions constitute discrimination in the sense of unjust prejudicial treatment of one group, or whether 'special measures' are justified due to the unusual nature of mental illness and the distinct issues it raises.[50] 'Special measures' are typically understood to refer to an acceptable departure from the principle that people are entitled to equal protection of the law and should not be subject to discrimination on the grounds of a certain attribute.[51] Tom Burns writes: 'Coercion in psychiatry is only justified if you accept that there really is something special about mental illness, that people are not their normal selves when acutely ill. Without such a view, compulsory treatment is indefensible and any analysis of the experience of coercion without acknowledging it strikes me as incomplete'.[52] The special-case argument rests on a number of critical claims. Jillian Craigie and Lisa Bortolotti summarise the many justifications for the use of psychiatric diagnosis as grounds for involuntary intervention, which range from claims about

> impaired insight in mental disorder; to mental disorder removing autonomous control; to the association of mental illness with global irrationality; and

48 Human Rights Committee, above n 48, [19]; World Health Organisation, above n 48.

49 Méndez, above n 6, para 68.

50 See, e.g., N Rose, 'Unreasonable Rights: Mental Illness and the Limits of the Law' (1985) 12(2) *Journal of Law and Society* 210; DA Treffert, 'Dying With Your Rights On', Paper presented at the 127th annual APA meeting, 1974.

51 This definition was drawn from the Victorian Law Reform Commission. See Victorian Law Reform Commission, *Guardianship: Final Report* 24 (2012) 540 n115 <www.lawreform.vic.gov.au>. For statutory definitions of 'special measures', see, e.g., Charter of Human Rights and Responsibilities Act 2006 (Vic) s 8(4); Equal Opportunity Act 2010 (Vic) s 12.

52 T Burns and D Rose, 'How Can the Service User Voice Be Best Heard at Psychiatric Meetings?' (2013) 203(2) *The British Journal of Psychiatry* 88.

> to the idea that mental disorder undermines personal identity or diachronic agency. Whatever the underlying assumptions, law that bases interference on the presence of mental disorder – the so-called 'status' approach – holds that a psychiatric diagnosis eliminates the need to assess the person's decision-making ability. The diagnosis alone is taken to mean that the person is not in a position to decide for themselves, at least in relation to psychiatric treatment ...[53]

Three major justifications for distinct legal rules for persons with an apparent or diagnosed mental illness emerge. First, such persons are unusual legal actors who may be unable to make decisions and thus require unique laws in certain circumstances. Second, certain types of mental illness create public risks that necessitate involuntary interventions. Third, emergency interventions in mental health crises require specific regulations and safeguards, which is substantively different from other forms of emergency intervention. I will consider these justifications in turn.

a The Incompetence Claim

The first claim holds that persons with psychosocial disabilities are less responsible causally, and therefore legally, for their actions. Hence, their ability to give or withhold consent for treatment cannot occur to the same extent or in the same manner as for persons with physical disorders.[54] This view, according to Paul Appelbaum and Thomas Grisso, rests on 'premises concerning the degree to which persons with mental illness manifest impairment of their decision-making abilities'.[55] Perhaps the most significant of these premises is the widely held assumption that people who meet the criteria for civil commitment under mental health law generally lack mental capacity.

However, the MacArthur Treatment Competence Study (MAC Study), the largest study to compare the mental capacity of patients admitted to psychiatric institutions with that of general medical patients, found that the majority

[53] J Craigie and L Bortolotti, 'Rationality, Diagnosis, and Patient Autonomy in Psychiatry' in JZ Sadler, K Fulford and C Werendly van Staden (eds), *Oxford Handbook of Psychiatric Ethics* (Oxford University Press, 2015).

[54] This question has been the subject of considerable controversy in courts throughout the world. See T Grisso and PS Appelbaum, 'The MacArthur Treatment Competence Study. III: Abilities of Patients to Consent to Psychiatric and Medical Treatments' (2005) 19(2) *Law and Human Behavior* 149, 171.

[55] PS Appelbaum and T Grisso, 'The MacArthur Treatment Competence Study: I. Mental Illness and Competence to Consent to Treatment' (1995) 19 *Law and Human Behavior* 105.

of research subjects admitted to psychiatric institutions had the mental capacity to make decisions.[56] Further, more than half of the inpatients in the study were found to have similar mental capacity levels to their counterparts in physical health care.[57] The study did identify significant differences in 'decision-making abilities' between people 'with and without mental illness, especially when the comparisons focus on patients with schizophrenia'.[58] The authors caution that such variance 'may justify differences in the ways in which consent to treatment for mental illness and for [physical] illness are handled'.[59] They refer to practices for gaining informed consent that accommodate the needs of mental health inpatients as compared to general health inpatients and conclude that overall, the findings disprove the commonly held assumption that people with severe mental health conditions automatically lack mental capacity.[60] On this basis, mental health law that enables treatment without consent should not be based on a presumption of mental incapacity. While mental capacity is not typically used as a criterion for civil commitment,[61] with an increasing number of exceptions,[62] the commonly held correlation between mental illness and incompetence may premise claims that mental health law ought to be viewed as a special measure.

[56] Appelbaum and Grisso found that 'half of the schizophrenia group and 76% of the depression group performed in the "adequate" range ... across all decision-making measures, and a significant portion performed at or above the mean for persons without mental illness. When performance on a single measure is examined, as may be relevant, for example, in jurisdictions that have adopted only an understanding standard for legal competence, the rate of adequate performance rose to roughly 75% for patients with schizophrenia and to approximately 90% or more for patients with depression. Thus, the justification for a blanket denial of the right to consent to or refuse treatment for persons hospitalized because of mental illness cannot be based on the assumption that they uniformly lack decision-making capacity'. Ibid. 171.

[57] It was even found that some individuals accepting treatment voluntarily did not have the mental capacity to consent to it. However, Appelbaum and Grisso did argue that the higher frequency of 'deficiencies in decision-making abilities in patients with schizophrenia, and to a lesser extent in patients with depression, may justify differences in the ways in which consent to treatment for mental illness and for medical illness *are handled*'. Grisso and Appelbaum, above n 56, 149, 171 (emphasis added).

[58] Ibid. 171.

[59] Ibid.

[60] The same conclusion was drawn in similar studies. For example, Okai and colleagues undertook a meta-analysis and found that 'the majority of psychiatric in-patients are capable of making treatment decisions', although 'psychosis, severity of symptoms, involuntary admission and treatment refusal were the strongest risk factors for incapacity'. D Okai et al., 'Mental Capacity in Psychiatric Patients: A Systematic View' (2007) 191 *The British Journal of Psychiatry* 291.

[61] See Chapter 1, Section C(2).

[62] See Chapter 4, fn 271.

b The Public Risk Claim

Another major premise behind seeing persons with psychosocial disabilities as sufficiently unique to justify separate mental health laws is that they pose a significantly higher risk to others than those without such disabilities.[63] Indeed, preventing public risk is posed in authoritative accounts as a principal justification for the unusual powers of mental health law; that is, police powers are required in the interest of protecting the community.[64] (The issue of 'risk to self' will be discussed in the section on efficacy, where it is noted that a significant body of research has brought into question the ability of clinicians to predict the likelihood of self-harm.)[65] However, the risk-of-harm criterion can be criticised as being discriminatory in its application to only those with psychosocial disabilities, whilst other groups at high risk of harming others do not face involuntary treatment and preventive detention.[66]

In part, this special treatment is based on the hypothesis that untreated symptoms of mental illness are the main source of criminal behaviour for offenders with psychosocial disability, and that linkage with psychiatric services is the solution.[67] However, Jillian Peterson and colleagues have argued that a growing body of evidence is challenging this 'widely embraced explanation' which 'drives much contemporary policy related to offenders with mental illness'.[68] Their own study analysed the offence patterns of 220 parolees in the United States, 111 of whom had a 'serious mental illness' and 109 of whom did not. The findings suggest that substance abuse has a much stronger

[63] For example, the white paper that preceded significant reforms to the Mental Health Act 1983 (England and Wales) described a new era of mental health law in which 'concerns of risk will always take precedence, but care and treatment provided under formal powers should otherwise reflect the best interests of the patient'. Department of Health (United Kingdom), *Reforming the Mental Health Act* (Stationery Office, 2000). As Szmukler noted, the foreword to the white paper, which promised the '"biggest shake up in mental health legislation for four decades" is signed by both the health and the home secretaries, and half the paper is devoted to "high risk patients"'. G Szmukler, 'A New Mental Health (and Public Protection) Act: Risk Wins in the Balance between Providing Care and Controlling Risk' (2001) 322(7277) *British Medical Journal* 2.

[64] P Fennell, 'Institutionalising the Community: The Codification of Clinical Authority and the Limits of Rights-Based Approaches' in McSherry and Weller, above n 32, 13, 19.

[65] See Chapter 3, Section C(1).

[66] G Szmukler and F Holloway, 'Mental Health Legislation Is Now a Harmful Anachronism' (1998) 22 *Psychiatric Bulletin* 662, 663–4.

[67] MF Abramson, 'The Criminalization of Mentally Disordered Behavior: Possible Side Effect of a New Mental Health Law' (1972) 23 *Hospital and Community Psychiatry* 101.

[68] J Peterson et al., 'Analyzing Offense Patterns as a Function of Mental Illness to Test the Criminalization Hypothesis' (2010) 61(12) *Psychiatric Services* 324, nn 11, 12 and 13.

correlation with violence than solely mental health problems.[69] A series of American studies support the view that a small subgroup of those diagnosed with severe mental illness may be arrested because their hallucinations or delusions lead to violence or they may cause public disturbances.[70] Yet Mary Donnelly argues that the correlation between psychosocial disability and acts of violence is less significant than is widely perceived, especially when compared to other factors such as age, history of violence, gender, substance abuse and family breakdown.[71] The broad perception of a connection between mental illness and violence is likely to have been reinforced consistently by the media in the countries considered in this book.

In a series of studies, Paul Mullen and colleagues found that the highest rates of violence occurred where substance abuse coexisted with mental illness.[72] Mullen has argued that, while most people with a diagnosis of mental illness will never commit an act of violence, people with untreated psychotic illness (and particularly those involved in substance abuse) are more likely than the average person on the street to be seriously violent.[73] However, Mullen has argued that 'there is a correlation between having a schizophrenic syndrome and increased rates of antisocial behaviour in general and violence in particular', and that 'the evidence that such associations are not just statistically but clinically and socially significant is now overwhelming'.[74] Mullen qualifies this assertion by noting that this small fraction of at-risk individuals (about 10

69 Ibid. See also WH Fisher, E Silver and N Wolff, 'Beyond Criminalization: Toward a Criminologically Informed Framework for Mental Health Policy and Services Research' (2006) 33 *Administration and Policy in Mental Health and Mental Health Services Research* 544; J Bonta, M Law and K Hanson, 'The Prediction of Criminal and Violent Recidivism among Mentally Disordered Offenders: A Meta-analysis' (1998) 123 *Psychological Bulletin* 123; J Junginger, K Claypoole and R Laygo, 'Effects of Serious Mental Illness and Substance Abuse on Criminal Offense' (2006) 57 *Psychiatric Services* 879.

70 B McSherry, *Managing Fear: The Law and Ethics of Preventive Detention and Risk Assessment* (Routledge, 2013) 55; see Junginger et al., above n 69; JK Peterson et al., 'Comparing the Offense Patterns of Offenders with and without Mental Disorder: Exploring the Criminalization Hypothesis' (2012) 61(12) *Psychiatric Services* 1217.

71 For epidemiological data from the United Kingdom, see Donnelly, above n 14. See also, J Swanson et al., 'Violence and Psychiatric Disorder in the Community: Evidence from the Epidemiologic Catchment Area Surveys' in *Violent Behaviour and Mental Illness* (American Psychiatric Association, 1990) 20; E Walsh and T Fahy, 'Violence in Society: Contribution of Mental Illness Is Low' (2002) 325(7363) *British Medical Journal* 507.

72 C Wallace, PE Mullen and P Burgess, 'Criminal Offending in Schizophrenia over a 25 Year Period Marked by Deinstitutionalisation and Increasing Prevalence of Comorbid Substance Use Disorders' (2004) 172(6) *American Journal of Psychiatry* 477; C Wallace et al., 'Serious Criminal Offending and Mental Disorder' (1998) 172(6) *British Journal of Psychiatry* 477.

73 P Mullen, 'Schizophrenia and Violence: From Correlations to Preventive Strategies' (2006) 12 *Advances in Psychiatric Treatment* 239.

74 Ibid.

per cent of those with the schizophrenia diagnosis, who themselves are only one portion of those placed under civil commitment orders) are identifiable and can be assisted with a 'structured programme in which the ... behavioural factors, substance misuse and social dislocation are managed together with the active symptoms of the disorder [to] prevent the progress to violence'.[75]

In what appears to be the largest study to date on the correlation between schizophrenia diagnosis and rates of violent crime, 8,003 people diagnosed with schizophrenia were compared with general population controls (n = 80,025) in respect of criminal convictions for violent crimes.[76] For the vast majority of those with a diagnosis who had committed a violent crime, the acts were attributed to drug use.[77] Where other factors were controlled, those diagnosed with schizophrenia who had not abused drugs were only 1.2 times more likely to have committed at least one violent crime than the control group.[78] However, where drug use was a contributing factor, and where unaffected siblings were used as controls, the comparison showed that the subject's 'substance abuse comorbidity was significantly less pronounced ... suggesting significant familial (genetic or early environmental) confounding of the association between schizophrenia and violence'.[79]

Nonetheless, 'risk of harm to others' has remained a strong focus of mental health law despite the modest correlation of psychosocial disability causing violent crime, particularly when compared to other factors such as drug and alcohol abuse. This skewed focus has arguably contributed to prejudice and discrimination towards people with psychosocial disabilities. There have been long-standing calls to abandon the risk criterion in mental health legislation, which have been reiterated in recent years.[80] These concerns stem from claims that the test is prejudicial (as it only applies to people with psychosocial disability), misguided (as a diagnosis of mental illness per se is a marginally significant indicator of the likelihood of violence being perpetrated) and largely ineffective, as discussed in the next section. Having considered the two major premises behind the claim that people diagnosed with mental illness require certain exceptions from human rights and non-discrimination standards,

75 Ibid.

76 S Fazel et al., 'Schizophrenia, Substance Abuse, and Violent Crime' (2009) 301(19) *Journal of the American Medical Association* 2016.

77 Ibid.

78 Ibid.

79 Ibid.

80 C Ryan, 'Capacity as a Determinant of Non-consensual Treatment of the Mentally Ill in Australia' (2011) 18(2) *Psychiatry, Psychology and Law* 248; C Ryan and S Callaghan, 'Rising to the Human Rights Challenge in Compulsory Treatment – New Approaches to Mental Health Law in Australia' (2012) 46(7) *Australian and New Zealand Journal of Psychiatry* 611.

I will now examine the second major justification for the unique suspension of rights in mental health law.

c Regulating Treatment and Emergency Powers

Another major claim justifying separate mental health law as a 'special measure' (and perhaps the most compelling) is its power to respond to extreme mental crises with urgency, and to regulate those responses. Even some critics of separate mental health legislation acknowledge this benefit. George Szmukler, Rowena Daw and John Dawson, for example, have appraised emergency powers under civil commitment in the following terms:

> A major strength of non-consensual treatment schemes that are based on incapacity principles [as compared to civil commitment schemes] is the respect shown for the autonomy of those patients who retain their capacity; but these schemes are, nevertheless, often weak on the regulation of emergency treatment powers, detention in hospital, and forced treatment. These are the areas, in contrast, in which civil commitment schemes are strong. The use of force, and the detention and involuntary treatment of objecting patients, is clearly authorised and regulated by mental health legislation.[81]

Regulation through mental health legislation ensures that such interventions can be authorised and monitored. In other words, if emergency powers are needed for some mental health crises, then these powers need to be clearly authorised and regulated – a function that is best provided by mental health legislation.

Michael Perlin has argued that comprehensive mental health legislation can serve the dual function of ensuring that (1) individuals can access independent counsel and judicial review mechanisms,[82] and (2) their treatment and living conditions, especially those in highly marginalised settings, can be regulated and monitored.[83] Perlin points to examples of states that have failed to regulate mental health services and address inhumane treatment in institutional settings.[84] Mental health legislation can assist by establishing legal protection to persons with psychosocial disability in order to prevent such abuse, as exemplified in the MI Principles.[85]

[81] G Szmukler, R Daw and J Dawson, 'A Model Law Fusing Incapacity and Mental Health Legislation' (2010) 20 *Journal of Mental Health Law* 11, 12.

[82] ML Perlin, 'International Human Rights Law and Comparative Mental Disability Law: The Universal Factors' (2007) 34(2) *Syracuse Journal of International Law and Commerce* 333, 337.

[83] Ibid. 343.

[84] Ibid.

[85] See Chapter 2, Section B.

Procedural mechanisms in mental health law arguably safeguard those subject to intervention powers. The Victorian Law Reform Commission ('VLRC') evaluated mental health law in its review of guardianship laws and commended its accountability processes, noting that '[t]here is clearly a great need for transparent decision-making processes and appropriate external review when the law authorises public officers to deprive people of their liberty and to provide them with compulsory psychiatric treatment'.[86] The VLRC was responding to a proposal to 'fuse' mental health law with guardianship law in order to create one overarching substituted decision-making law. In its report, the VLRC argued that (Victorian) mental health legislation accommodates the aforementioned transparency, while guardianship law, in contrast, has few mechanisms to 'review a decision to deprive someone of their liberty and provide treatment without consent'.[87] Under Victoria's Guardianship and Administration Act 1986, for example, there is no review process for individual decisions made by either tribunal-appointed or personally appointed guardians.[88]

Another added procedural protection in mental health law is the external review process, which is a central feature of contemporary mental health laws.[89] Mental health tribunals and other bodies empowered under mental health law have a range of powers to review clinical decisions. Under typical guardianship laws, the delegation of decision-making powers to single individuals does not afford as much oversight. Again, on this view, if intervention in some mental health crises is going to occur without the consent of the individual, then it must be appropriately regulated with adequate procedural protection and safeguards against paternalistic overreach.

However, it could also be argued that earlier access to services and support might prevent the very crises for which involuntary intervention is lawfully required. On the need for coercive powers, a wide range of commentators agree that mental health law has failed most specifically in its function to provide access to support services.[90] (I will discuss this apparent failure shortly.) If this is indeed the case, then the push for improved procedural protections

[86] Victorian Law Reform Commission, *Guardianship: Final Report 24* (2012) para 24.40 <www.lawreform.vic.gov.au>.

[87] Ibid.

[88] Ibid.

[89] See above Chapter 1, Section C.

[90] McSherry and Weller, above n 32, 6; G Quinn, 'The United Nations Convention on the Rights of Persons wth [sic] Disabilities – Towards a Unified Field Theory of Disability' (presentation paper) Indian Law Society, G. V. Pandit Memorial Oration, Pune, India, October 2009) 11 <www.nuigalway.ie>.

may be the outcome of a troubling circular logic; that is, mental health law increases the need for involuntary treatment by contributing to the failure to address access to voluntary support at an early stage of the crisis. As a consequence of this failure, increased procedural protections are required for those treated involuntarily. The focus on procedural protections dominates debates on mental health justice, and therefore commands disproportionate institutional attention and resources. While the procedural protections under current mental health law are the result of hard-won gains by reformers, the question remains as to whether this institutional and political focus occupies commentators in the mental health field to the point of making other, more constructive, strategies less available.

It is also worth noting that although policymakers designed mental health laws to safeguard the rights of people subject to involuntary treatment, this very cohort was excluded from the development of these laws. The term 'cohort' here refers to people subject to involuntary treatment and detention, but this would also reasonably include all persons with psychosocial disability whose rights to liberty and consent in (mental) healthcare are, according to the terms of mental health law, held to a different standard to other citizens. Yet, as Perlin has commented, '[t]here is little evidence that these groups are taken seriously either by lawyers or academics'.[91] If it were the case that safeguarding users' civil rights was the most compelling function of mental health law, it would seem logical that the development of such safeguards and rights protections should occur with input from those subject to them. For this reason, perhaps, existing procedural mechanisms do not appear to satisfy prominent disabled people's organisations[92] or UN human rights agencies[93] that

[91] ML Perlin, '"You Have Discussed Lepers and Crooks": Sanism in Clinical Teaching' (2003) 9(2) *Clinical Law Review* 683, 699. See also G Browne and M Hemsley, 'Consumer Participation in Mental Health in Australia: What Progress Is Being Made?' (2008) 16(6) *Australasian Psychiatry* 446.

[92] For example, the World Network of Users and Survivors of Psychiatry made the following argument in the early development of the CRPD, rejecting the mitigating value of procedural protections in mental health legislation: 'We reject any suggestion that procedural safeguards may suffice to mitigate the human rights violations consisting of deprivation of liberty based on disability or forced interventions'. World Network of Users and Survivors of Psychiatry, 'Position Paper for the 3rd Meeting of the Ad Hoc Committee' <www.un.org>; see also M O'Hagan, 'Legal coercion: the elephant in the recovery room', Scottish Recovery Network, 2002 <www.scottishrecovery.net>; Minkowitz, above n 6; D Webb, 'A New Era in Disability Rights; A New Human Rights Charter Plus a New United Nations Convention', Insane Australia <www.thinkingaboutsuicide.org>.

[93] See Chapter 2, Section D. Cf World Health Organisation, Comprehensive Mental Health Action Plan 2013–2020 (2013) 6; Human Rights Committee, Promotion and protection of all human rights, civil, political, economic, social and cultural rights, including the right to development, 32nd sess, UN Doc A/HRC/32/L.26 (adopted 29 June 2016) [2].

have commented on the issue, even as the mechanisms appear to satisfy most policymakers and professional bodies.

Having discussed the principal human rights concerns relating to mental health law, as well as some of the principal justifications for its 'special measure' status as an exception to certain human rights standards, it is now appropriate to consider the effectiveness of mental health law.

C EFFICACY ARGUMENTS: THAT MENTAL HEALTH LAW IS INEFFECTIVE ON ITS OWN TERMS

Mental health law is ineffective on its own terms; there is limited evidence to support its success in relation to three of its primary functions. This is essentially a utilitarian line of enquiry. While the human rights-based criticisms of mental health law might provide sufficient grounds for law reform efforts, it is the aim of this book to consider the full range of major conceptual and practical issues arising from mental health law. Further, efficacy concerns are particularly relevant to policymakers given the limited resources facing any government.

The purposes of mental health law are well summarised by Hale, who has observed that civil commitment legislation perpetually struggles to 'reconcile three overlapping but often competing goals: protecting the public, obtaining access to the services people need, and safeguarding users' civil rights'.[94] I will consider the evidentiary basis of each of these functions in turn.

1 *Lawmakers Cannot Show Mental Health Law Reduces the Risk of Self-Harm*

I have already discussed the use of risk-of-harm criteria in relation to the minimal correlative significance of the public risk associated with a diagnosis of mental illness compared to other factors. Perhaps unsurprisingly then, there is limited evidence to support the view that risk assessments conducted

[94] B Hale, 'Justice and Equality in Mental Health Law: The European Experience' (2007) 30(1) *International Journal of Law and Psychiatry* 18, 19. Richardson has observed that '[t]he priority afforded to each of these goals will vary between jurisdictions and across time, but they are all likely to play some part in the design of most mental health legislation'. G Richardson, 'Balancing Autonomy and Risk: A Failure of Nerve in England and Wales?' (2007) 30 *International Journal of Law and Psychiatry* 72; see also, G Richardson, 'Reforming Mental Health Laws: Principle or Pragmatism?' (2001) 54 *Current Legal Problems* 415; G Richardson, 'Involuntary Treatment: Search for Principles' in K Diesfeld and I Freckelton (eds), *Involuntary Detention and Therapeutic Jurisprudence* (Aldershot, 2003) 54.

under mental health law reduce violent crimes and other risks to the public.[95] Predicting who will be at risk of harming others is extremely difficult, given the low rate of violence among people with psychosocial disabilities compared with other groups.

Douglas Mossman conducted a meta-analysis of studies looking retrospectively at risk-categorisation criteria in the lead-up to violent acts.[96] Mossman argued that there was no way to find a satisfactory balance between specificity and sensitivity in identifying risk.[97] 'Hindsight', Mossman concludes, 'makes "warning signs" clear, but before violent tragedies occur we cannot efficiently distinguish the signs that point to violence from those that will turn out to be false positive signals'.[98] Indeed, it remains an open question in the literature on legal psychiatric coercion and violence as to whether the range of civil commitment and legal involuntary treatment measures – including those applied by mental health courts, terms of sentencing, and inpatient and outpatient commitment orders – is effective in reducing the risk of violence.[99]

Similarly, there is limited evidence to support the hypothesis that mental health legislation prevents self-harm and suicide. Alex Pokorny's large-scale study of 4,800 people admitted to a psychiatric hospital in the United States found that there are no reliable methods to predict particular suicides 'before the fact'.[100] In a case-control study of ninety-two suicides of people who were inpatients, Jimmy Dong, Ting-Pong Ho and Chui-Kwan Kan found that the '[m]ajority of in-patient suicides occurred at a time of perceived low risk'.[101] More recently, Matthew Large and colleagues conducted a meta-analysis of longitudinal cohort studies where 'psychiatric patients or people who had made suicide attempts were stratified into high-risk and lower-risk groups for suicide' and found the following: 'The strength of suicide risk categorizations based on the presence of multiple risk factors does not greatly exceed the association between individual suicide risk factors and suicide. A statistically strong and reliable method to usefully distinguish patients with a high-risk of

95 See, e.g., D Mossman, 'The Imperfection of Protection through Detection and Intervention. Lessons from Three Decades of Research on the Psychiatric Assessment of Violence Risk' (2009) 30 *Journal of Legal Medicine* 109, 139–40; P Appelbaum, 'Violence and Mental Disorders: Data and Public Policy' (2006) 163 *American Journal of Psychiatry* 1319.

96 Mossman, above n 95.

97 Ibid.

98 Ibid. 139–40.

99 Appelbaum, above n 95.

100 AD Pokorny, 'Prediction of Suicide in Psychiatric Patients' (1983) 40 *Archives of General Psychiatry* 249.

101 JY Dong, TP Ho and CK Kan, 'A Case-Control Study of 92 Cases of In-Patient Suicides' (2005) 87(1) *Journal of Affective Disorder* 91.

suicide remains elusive'.[102] The fact that limited evidence exists to prove the effectiveness of tests assessing risk of harm to self or others brings into question the justification for their use as a criterion for civil commitment.

David Webb even argues that mental health law has the perverse consequence of *increasing* suicides by compelling patients who seek discharge or fear involuntary commitment to conceal their suicidal thoughts, hence cutting off the potential for supportive intervention.[103] Darian Leader summarises this line of argument and assigns blame to the culture of risk-aversion in mental health services when he writes: 'Risk management means lives cannot be lost, and patients learn to hide suicidal thoughts to facilitate discharge ... The more you insist that the person can't kill themselves the more the chances of a suicidal act increase'.[104] While Webb's and Leader's argument remains a hypothesis, and one which seems difficult to validate, a number of other commentators have raised similar concerns. David Jobes reportedly stated that '[m]uch of what was done in the name of clinical suicide prevention was actually coercive, shaming and controlling'[105] – a conclusion that speaks to the potentially traumatising and *disabling* responses of services. Susan Stefan, after interviewing and surveying 244 suicide-attempt survivors for her 2016 study on suicide law and policy, concluded that

> our policies and practices regarding suicide create an irrational incentive structure where people understand that they have to attempt suicide to get help, help which is of questionable utility, while community-based approaches that are less expensive and work are underfunded. We have a system that doesn't work for anyone – neither the people who are supposed to be providing help, nor the people who are supposed to be receiving it.[106]

Stefan (writing in the US context) notes the resulting frustration of mental health professionals: 'Mental health professionals in my interviews also sounded powerless and hopeless: asked to do the impossible with

[102] M Large et al., 'Meta-Analysis of Longitudinal Cohort Studies of Suicide Risk Assessment among Psychiatric Patients: Heterogeneity in Results and Lack of Improvement Over Time' (2016) 11(6) *PLoS ONE*.

[103] D Webb, *Thinking About Suicide: Contemplating and comprehending the urge to die* (PCCS, 2010) 170.

[104] D Leader, 'How Psychiatry Became a Damage Limitation Exercise' (op-ed) *The Guardian* 22 June 2011 <www.theguardian.com>. Cf L Appleby and H Griffiths, 'Our Mental Health Service Is Far from Crisis, It's a World Leader' (op-ed) *The Guardian* 29 June 2011 <www.theguardian.com>.

[105] J Chen, 'A Handful of Doctors Are Working to Revolutionize How We Think About Self-Harm', *GOOD*, 20 April 2016 <www.good.is>.

[106] S Stefan, *Rational Suicide, Irrational Laws: Examining Current Approaches to Suicide in Policy and Law* (Oxford University Press, 2016) xxi.

ever-dwindling resources, profoundly anxious about liability, genuinely baffled about how to help some of their patients, plagued by insurance demands and paperwork'.[107]

Stefan's view that 'we have a system that doesn't work' is debatable.[108] However, it is generally agreed that there is a remarkable absence of empirical evidence, which demonstrates the effectiveness of involuntary psychiatric intervention in achieving one of its core objectives, reducing self-harm. On the contrary, according to Stefan, her study suggests that 'involuntary psychiatric detention *increases* rather than decreases the risk of suicide for many people, while evidence-based treatments that actually reduce suicidality are all community-based'.[109] She concludes: '[W]e focus enormous amounts of resources and inflict substantial pain in the form of involuntary commitment and treatment on people who, statistically speaking, are actually at a fairly low risk of suicide'.[110]

2 *Mental Health Law Fails to Facilitate Access to Treatment*

Mental health legislation fails to facilitate access to voluntary support during times of crisis. From a rights perspective, mental health law fails to secure substantive rights for people with psychosocial disabilities. The claim that mental health law fails to facilitate access to treatment forms a major critique of the pre-CRPD human rights approaches to mental health law, which have involved a strong focus on negative liberties or so-called first-generation rights. This cluster of rights is based around non-interference and finds expression in mental health law around the 'rights to liberty and autonomy in relation to the involuntary commitment of individuals with very serious mental illnesses'.[111] This libertarian push, captured particularly in Gostin's concept of a 'new legalism' in mental health law, saw procedural safeguards increased to regulate the control of psychiatrists and address the misuse of medical power.[112]

It is true, however, that the legalistic approach also sought to provide for the right to treatment. However, this goal was arguably the least successful of the 'new legalism' framework, a shortcoming which, according to Gerard Quinn,

[107] Ibid.
[108] See Appleby and Griffiths, above n 104.
[109] Stefan, above n 108, 119 (emphasis added).
[110] Ibid. 335.
[111] McSherry and Weller, above n 32, 6.
[112] See LO Gostin, 'Perspectives on Mental Health Reforms' (1983) 10 *Journal of Law and Society* 47; LO Gostin, 'The Ideology of Entitlement: The Application of Contemporary Legal Approaches to Psychiatry' in P Bean (ed), *Mental Illness: Changes and Trends* (Wiley, 1983) 27.

has drawn mental health debates into an 'imprisoning logic' and caused a breakdown of meaningful dialogue:

> Some civil libertarians would hesitate to use an argument for a legal right to treatment (no matter how meritorious) lest the need for treatment might be used to justify an undue encroachment on liberty. Contrariwise, some professionals in the field who have the responsibility to deliver services, would hesitate to embrace liberty-enhancing arguments lest it interfere too much with their capacity to deliver a substantive right to treatment – with their professional prerogatives.[113]

The impasse forms a conceptual tension in mental health law linked to a common critique of 'new legalism': it has typically struggled to provide substantive rights to persons with mental impairments in the form of access to healthcare and support. Peay describes the lopsided emphasis on negative rights as the 'problematic nexus of mental health and law', where the law has taken a historical role of restraining rather than facilitating access to services.[114]

Numerous commentators have raised the concern that mental health law exacerbates the inaccessibility of services, especially for individuals in crisis.[115] As early as 1985, Nikolas Rose criticised the rights-based approach to mental health law on the basis that it is 'impotent when it comes to debating or securing positive policy alternatives'.[116] Rose argued against a rights-based strategy of mental health reform from the perspective that 'new legalism' simply transfers the involuntary powers from doctors to lawyers.[117] This transfer occurred somewhat misleadingly, according to Rose, cloaked in the language of a vaguely defined notion of human rights: 'There might be an argument for the tactical use of the language of rights because of its consonance with the common sense of western social and political thought. But it is clear that such language provides no means of formulating objectives for substantive reforms or for implementing such reforms'.[118]

Rose was prescient in identifying the difficulty with which a 'new legalism' approach could garner appropriate social provisions, conceive and defend 'freedom',[119] and appraise and alter the powers of expertise over subjects of

113 Quinn, above n 90, 11.

114 J Peay (ed), *Seminal Issues in Mental Health Law* (Ashgate, 2005) xvii.

115 M Maj, 'Physical Health Care in Persons with Severe Mental Illness: A Public Health and Ethical Priority' (2009) 8 *World Psychiatry* 1.

116 N Rose, 'Unreasonable Rights: Mental Illness and the Limits of the Law' (1985) 12(2) *Journal of Law and Society* 199.

117 Ibid.

118 Ibid. 214.

119 Spaulding has argued that the conceptual confusion arising from competing 'understanding(s) of the relationship between liberty and mental disorder' introduces an added complexity to the

mental health law.[120] Rose's argument is located in a broader critique of the trend to pursue sociopolitical objectives in legal terms[121] – an argument he and others have made against human rights more generally.[122] Rose's proposition that a rights vocabulary provides 'no means of formulating objectives for substantive reforms' is arguably less prescient in the light of conceptual advances in human rights in the twenty-first century,[123] although some commentators remain sceptical of the power of CRPD-based strategies to garner necessary resources (as shall be discussed in Chapter 7).

According to the International Disability Alliance, the narrow focus on civil and political liberties in mental health and adult mental capacity law has often left people with disabilities in a 'binary system of self-sufficiency versus enforced dependence'.[124] The tension, then, between the protection of individual rights and the discretionary powers of non-consensual treatment means that mental health law has struggled to address the matter of access to supportive services, except by authorising coercive treatment. As such, there remains a strong call to bolster state duties to provide resources to enhance a range of human rights (for example, the right to enjoy the highest attainable physical and mental health, and the right to autonomy and self-determination), rather than simply inviting non-interference.

3 *'Involuntary Outpatient Treatment' Is Ineffective*

It is worth considering the efficacy of legal frameworks for involuntary psychiatric intervention outside the hospital, in people's residences. As noted in Chapter 1, involuntary outpatient treatment, often referred to as community treatment orders ('CTOs'), was partly designed to promote adherence

already nuanced field of mental health law. WJ Spaulding, 'Mapping the "New Legalism" of English Mental Health Law' (1989) 17(2) *The Journal of Law, Medicine and Ethics* 187.

120 P Weller, 'Lost in Translation: Human Rights and Mental Health Law' in McSherry and Weller, above n 32, 51.

121 Rose, above n 116, 215.

122 See D Kennedy, 'The International Human Rights Movement: Part of the Problem?' (2002) 14 *Harvard Human Rights Law Journal* 101.

123 Rose, above n 116, 215. Weller has argued that the CRPD represents a 'quiet revolution' in international human rights law, which does more than any other UN Convention before it to recognise 'the indivisible and interdependent nature of all human rights', with particularly strong provisions for substantive rights. P Weller, 'Human Rights and Social Justice: The Convention on the Rights of Persons with Disabilities and the Quiet Revolution in International Law' (2009) 4 *Public Space: The Journal of Law and Social Justice* 74.

124 International Disability Alliance, 'Letter on Functional Capacity to the CRPD Committee' (2010) <www.internationaldisabilityalliance.org>.

to medication regimes and reduce rates of hospitalisation.[125] However, of the three large-scale randomised controlled trials to consider its success in achieving these aims, according to Steve Kisely and Leslie Campbell, none could demonstrate that CTOs were effective.[126] For example, the largest randomised trial of CTOs in England and Wales to date found that 'the imposition of compulsory supervision does not reduce the rate of readmission of psychotic patients'.[127] The authors of the study, Tom Burns and colleagues, 'found no support in terms of any reduction in overall hospital admission to justify the significant curtailment of patients' personal liberty'.[128] Following the study, Burns, formerly a major proponent of CTOs, reportedly stated simply that CTOs 'don't work'.[129]

Similarly, a 2011 Cochrane Review by Steve Kisely, Linda Campbell and Nick Preston examined the 'effectiveness of compulsory community treatment for people with severe mental illness' by systematically reviewing all relevant randomised controlled clinical trials.[130] Overall, they concluded that the trials 'provided little evidence of efficacy on any outcomes such as health service use, social functioning, mental state, quality of life or satisfaction with care'.[131] According to the authors, the studies faced challenges of data availability: there were no reliable data for assessing cost and 'unclear presentation of data made it impossible to assess the effect on mental state and most aspects of satisfaction with care'.[132] However, the findings generally supported an earlier review by the same researchers that could not demonstrate that CTOs achieved their aims.[133] Likewise, Andrew Molodynski and colleagues reported on the general 'absence of convincing evidence that [CTOs] improve clinical or social outcomes or reduce hospital use'.[134] Pointing out a troubling

[125] See Chapter 1, Section C(1). See also S Khurmi and M Curtice 'The supervised community treatment order and the Human Rights Act 1998' (2010) 16 *Advances in Psychiatric Treatment* 263.

[126] S Kisely and L Campbell, 'Compulsory community and involuntary outpatient treatment for people with severe mental disorders' (2015) 41 *Schizophrenia Bulletin* 542.

[127] T Burns et al., 'Community Treatment Orders for Patients with Psychosis (OCTET): A Randomised Controlled Trial' (2013) 381(9878) *The Lancet* 1627.

[128] Ibid.

[129] Cited in S Manning, '"Psychiatric Asbos" Were an Error Says Key Advisor', *The Independent*, 14 April 2013.

[130] SR Kisely, LA Campbell LA and NJ Preston, 'Compulsory Community and Involuntary Outpatient Treatment for People with Severe Mental Disorders' (2011) 2 *Cochrane Database Systematic Review*.

[131] Ibid.

[132] Ibid.

[133] Ibid.

[134] A Molodynski, J Rugkasa and T Burns, 'Coercion and Compulsion in Community Mental Health Care' (2010) 95 *British Medical Bulletin* 117.

methodological issue in assessing CTOs more generally, Light and colleagues observe that *even if* CTOs were found to be effective, 'it is not clear whether any benefit is due to their compulsory nature or simply a result of the intensity of treatment that they facilitate'.[135]

Steven Segal and Phillip Burgess have challenged claims that the current evidence base provides grounds to dismiss the utility of CTOs. Segal and Burgess undertook two studies which found that in certain circumstances, CTOs were associated with reductions in bed-days[136] and mortality rates.[137] But despite these claims, Sonia Johnson has argued that 'the case for urgent review' of legislation permitting involuntary outpatient treatment, 'both at government level and within the professions involved in CTO use, is now strong'.[138] Reinhard Heun, Subodh Dave and Paul Rowlands, who are members of the Executive Committee of the Faculty of General Adult Psychiatry of the Royal College of Psychiatrists in the United Kingdom, went a step further, calling for an end to the use of CTOs in their current form.[139] The authors referred to the existing evidence base and argued that '[u]nder these circumstances, no clinical procedure would have any support from any regulatory institution. The use of coercion without or even against scientific evidence may be seen as unethical and might violate the patients' human rights. These circumstances may increase the stigma against psychiatry'.[140]

4 *Mental Health Law Codifies Medical Discretion, Control and Regulation*

Phil Fennell has argued that mental health law's rights-based rhetoric contradicts the lack of substantive rights protection that the law offers in practice, and

[135] E Light et al., 'Out of Sight, Out of Mind: Making Involuntary Community Treatment Visible in the Mental Health System' (2012) 196(9) *Medical Journal of Australia* 591. See also, R Churchill et al., *International Experiences of Using Community Treatment Orders* (Department of Health and Institute of Psychiatry, King's College London, 2007) <www.dh.gov.uk>; AJ O'Brien, BG McKenna and RR Kydd, 'Compulsory Community Mental Health Treatment: Literature Review' (2009) 46 *International Journal of Nursing Studies* 1245; Kisely, Campbell and Preston, above n 130.

[136] SP Segal and P Burgess, 'Conditional Release: A Less Restrictive Alternative to Hospitalization?' (2006) 57(11) *Psychiatric Services* 1600.

[137] SP Segal and P Burgess, 'Effect of Conditional Release from Hospitalization on Mortality Risk' (2006) 57(11) *Psychiatric Services* 1607.

[138] S Johnson, 'Can We Reverse the Rising Tide of Compulsory Admissions?' (2013) 381(9878) *The Lancet* 1603.

[139] R Heun, S Dave and P Rowlands, 'Little Evidence for Community Treatment Orders – a Battle Fought with Heavy Weapons' (2016) 40 *BJPsych Bulletin* 115.

[140] Ibid 117.

instead codifies medical authority to treat and detain.[141] This is despite policymakers designing mental health law to provide special rights and improve the freedom of a group whose rights to liberty and healthcare decision-making were previously subject to almost unfettered medical discretion. Despite the rights-based framework of mental health law, coercive 'powers' held by clinicians have increased in certain respects.[142] Weller queries whether rights-based legalism better protects substantive rights, given that discretionary power remains with medical authorities who retain a privileged status as expert witnesses.[143] Similarly, Appelbaum concluded his 1994 treatise on mental health law in the United States thus:

> Although patients' right to refuse treatment in general is frequently endorsed, it is rare for courts to uphold the refusal of any given patient. The nearly uniform consequence of a court hearing is treatment against the patient's will. The levels at which discretion can be applied to thwart the narrow limits of mental health law are manifold. In civil commitment, for example, family members and mental health professionals have considerable scope in framing their allegations of a patient's committability; attorneys appointed to represent respondents can vary the vigor with which they contest commitment petitions; and judges can elect to apply broader or narrower interpretations of commitment standards … The effectiveness of mental health law in most contexts depends on the willingness of those who gather information and make decisions – often operating with low visibility – to conform to the dictates of the law. When the law seems wrong-headed, however, unless incentives can be provided for their cooperation or sanctions imposed for their resistance, they will often respond according to their own lights.[144]

In Australia, the Human Rights and Equal Opportunity Commission Report of 1993, which was influential in the development of Australian mental health policy, found that legislative formulations in Australian states are 'marked by circularity of reasoning and apparently designed to intrude to a minimal degree upon the territory of psychiatrists'.[145]

[141] Fennell, above n 64.
[142] See Chapter 1, fn 14.
[143] Weller, above n 120, 51.
[144] PS Appelbaum, *Almost a Revolution: Mental Health Law and the Limits of Change* (Oxford University Press, 1994) 212.
[145] Australian Human Rights and Equal Opportunity Commission, Human Rights and Mental Illness: Report of the National Inquiry into the Human Rights of People with Mental Illness (Australian Government Publishing, 1993) vol 1, 40.

D PRAGMATIC CONCERNS

A number of pragmatic issues arise in mental health law relevant to this investigation. While many of the issues identified below are corollary to human rights and efficacy concerns, they warrant separate consideration for the sake of a clearer and more complete analysis.

1 *Mental Health Law Fails to Protect against the 'Tyranny of the Majority'*

Mental health legislation provides poor protection for people with psychosocial disabilities (and potentially even medical practitioners) in the face of malign public attitudes. Given the discretionary power of typical mental health legislation, and in the absence of strong laws against mental health- or disability-based discrimination, the majority of public fears concerning mental health, no matter how irrational their basis, could pressure policymakers, mental health tribunals and professionals to broaden the operation of mental health laws. Abuse of the authority to treat may occur, particularly when powerful sources apply sporadic pressure (for example, politicians or media who tap populist fears and push for greater control of feared groups).

Moncrieff has argued that mental health legislation allows broader society to abrogate responsibility for people in distress and crisis, and instead wield authority over a marginalised population.[146] She argues that governments aim to contain and isolate problematic groups by compelling clinicians to use their unusual powers to 'treat'.[147] Appelbaum points to involuntary outpatient treatment laws in almost half of US states as an example of public scandals resulting in laws with questionable effectiveness (and constitutionality).[148] A more recent example is US gun control law reform. Following extreme acts of gun violence, reform proposals have resulted in expanded criteria for involuntary treatment and additional duties on psychiatrists to report suspect persons.[149] Peay discusses the potential for such scandals to generate public pressure on legislators and clinicians, particularly where violent crimes have

[146] Moncrieff, above n 26.

[147] Ibid.

[148] PS Appelbaum, 'Assessing Kendra's Law: Five Years of Outpatient Commitment in New York' (2005) 56 *Psychiatric Services* 791.

[149] See E Goode and J Healy, 'Focus on Mental Health Laws to Curb Violence Is Unfair, Some Say', *The New York Times* 31 January 2013 <www.nytimes.com>; Bazelon Center, 'Wrong Focus: Mental Health in the Gun Safety Debate' (Press Release, 17 April 2013) <www.bazelon.org>.

been committed by persons with a diagnosis of mental illness, in this case personality disorder:

> The existence of a vocal and seriously injured section of the public may in turn combine with a further significant proportion of the wider public who may live in fear, justified or not, of becoming victims. And this fear may be inappropriately fed by … common lay misunderstanding … This can create a momentum for those very legislators and policymakers to act, and for clinicians to respond.[150]

Peay's observation was specific to personality disorder and particular political issues in England and Wales at the time. Yet her observations seem applicable more broadly. Crimes committed by people with a psychiatric diagnosis often act as a precursor to greater incursions upon the civil rights of persons with psychosocial disabilities – mental health law, despite ostensibly being aimed at upholding the rights of people with psychosocial disability, seemingly offers little to prevent such systemic discrimination, and can even be seen to facilitate such incursions.

These concerns bring to the forefront the tension between the majoritarian principle of democratic rule and the humanitarian principle of protecting excluded and marginalised minorities. In seeking to achieve that fine balance, it is questionable whether mental health law is currently achieving this aim.

2 *'Voluntarism' in the Shadow of Compulsion*

Mental health law creates a 'gap' between voluntary admission and involuntary psychiatric intervention in which compulsion becomes a threat. The threat of being placed on an involuntary order means voluntary service users can be coerced into agreeing to unwanted treatment, in order to avoid legal compulsion and the associated stigma, discrimination and loss of rights.[151] Consider the following illustrative case:

> A man voluntarily admitted himself to a hospital's psychiatric inpatient unit. At no time was the man given information regarding his rights as a voluntary patient, and there was a failure to provide him with services for his pre-existing diabetes. The man became concerned that his 'treatment' involved only medication and not a referral to a social worker, psychologist,

[150] J Peay, 'Personality Disorder and the Law: Some Awkward Questions' (2011) 18(3) *Philosophy, Psychiatry, and Psychology* 231, 235.

[151] See Donnelly, above n 14, 41; see also A Zigmond and AJ Holland, 'Unethical Mental Health Law: History Repeats Itself' (2000) 49 *Journal of Mental Health Law* 53.

> or community counselling service, despite the psychiatrist recommending this. Although the issue was raised with hospital staff, no action was taken. The man notified staff of his intention to discharge himself (which was within his rights as a voluntary patient), however he was warned his status would be changed to 'involuntary' should he attempt to discharge himself. The man then attempted to leave the ward, and was subsequently reclassified as an involuntary patient and put into seclusion for 6½ hours, and stripped of his clothing. The man was not provided with an explanation of his change of patient status to involuntary or the reason for being placed in seclusion.[152]

This case was presented in Australia's 2012 'shadow report' to the CRPD Committee, which was compiled by People with Disabilities Australia in partnership with multiple law and human rights organisations.[153]

The issue of unregulated coercion via threats of civil commitment was raised as far back as 1964.[154] Rachel Bingham has argued that the issue is systemic rather than an unusual instance of distorted process or 'bad' practice.[155] Bingham refers to the 'common clinical scenario' in which a person 'acquiesces to continued admission to a mental health unit primarily because he or she believes he or she will otherwise be formally detained'.[156] Some mental health services have produced guidelines and patient information materials addressing informal patients.[157] For example, the 2015 Mental Health Act Code of Practice for England and Wales makes clear that '[t]he threat of detention must not be used to coerce a patient to consent to admission to hospital or to treatment (and is likely to invalidate any apparent consent)'.[158] However, according to Bingham, '[u]nfortunately, in many ways this sort of information simply makes explicit the original predicament: you will be "allowed" to

[152] Disability Representative, Advocacy, Legal and Human Rights Organisations Australia, *Disability Rights Now: Civil Society Report to the United Nations Committee on the Rights of Persons with Disability* (2012) 15 <www.disabilityrightsnow.org.au>.

[153] Ibid. The 'shadow report' refers to a compliance report submitted to the Committee on the Rights of Persons with Disabilities under the terms of the CRPD. The shadow report is compiled by civil society representatives, particularly disability people's organisations, and submitted alongside a government's report.

[154] PR Breggin, 'Coercion of Voluntary Patients in an Open Hospital' (1964) 10 *Archives of General Psychiatry* 173.

[155] R Bingham, 'The Gap Between Voluntary Admission and Detention In Mental Health Units' (2012) 38 *Journal of Medical Ethics* 281.

[156] Ibid.

[157] Ibid. 281.

[158] Department of Health, *Code of Practice, Mental Health Act 1983* (The Stationery Office, 2015) 116.

exercise your rights, "unless …"' with the implication being that treatment refusal or leaving a hospital will be sufficient to activate coercive powers.[159]

Anne Rogers has examined coercion in British psychiatric inpatients settings, including surveying in 1990 412 psychiatric patients who had experienced at least one period of hospitalisation.[160] Her research suggested that 'a substantial number of nominally voluntary patients reported coercive aspects of their hospitalisation',[161] which 'was found to produce a more rejecting attitude towards psychiatric services'.[162] Certainly, there is evidence that clinicians have explicitly drawn on the threat of coercion. Consider the following quite extraordinary statement from Tim Lambert, Bruce Singh and Maxine Patel about people subject to CTOs:

> Arguably, CTOs are most successful when patients perceive (if erroneously) that they can be treated against their wishes outside the hospital setting. This remains a form of coercion over and above the legislation itself. Hence, CTOs may serve to 'persuade the persuadable', in the hope that the patient does not test the resolve of the community teams to rescind the CTO for breaches relating to non-adherence.[163]

Even as certain methods have been introduced to address this issue (transparency about the legal situation of voluntary patients, clearer information for voluntary patients and so on), the gap between genuine consent and legal safeguards will always exist where there is recourse to detention and involuntary treatment on the partial basis of a diagnosis of mental disorder. This is more likely where the threshold for intervention is lower than for life-threatening emergencies.

3 *Coercion Interrupts the Development of Decision-Making Skills*

Where legal coercion takes away decision-making control from individuals, the development of their decision-making skills is potentially disrupted. Webb has argued that mental health legislation can lead to disempowerment when the decision of a psychiatrist with substituted decision-making power conflicts with the relevant person's views about treatment.[164] His argument echoes those

159 Bingham, above n 157, 281.

160 A Rogers, 'Coercion and "Voluntary" Admission: An Examination of Psychiatric Patient Views' (1993) 11(3) *Behavioral Sciences and the Law* 259.

161 Ibid.

162 Ibid.

163 T Lambert, B Singh and M Patel, 'Community Treatment Orders and Antipsychotic Long-Acting Injections' (2009) 52 *British Journal of Psychiatry Supplement* s57.

164 D Webb, 'An New Era in Disability Rights; A New Human Rights Charter Plus a New United Nations Convention' Insane Australia, n.d. <www.thinkingaboutsuicide.org>.

of intellectual disability advocates, who suggest that substituted decision-making can stifle decision-making learning, which, in turn, gives the false impression that a person's decision-making difficulties are 'natural'.[165]

In the mental health context, Gunvant Patel has argued that the widespread use of CTOs in Victoria, Australia, which reportedly has the highest rate of CTO use per capita in the world,[166] produces a similar effect: '[W]ith CTOs, learning and growth through experiencing the adverse consequences of one's actions is sabotaged (developmentally a particularly crucial step for young adults). Relapse prevention and risk management (often poorly assessed and addressed by use of ad hoc untested locally developed measures) are reified instead'.[167] Patel continues to argue that the 'over-emphasis on positive symptom control over longer term concerns' prevents clinical staff from being able to 'engage in a long term relational-based approach to enhancing compliance and engagement'.[168] He argues that clinical staff are negatively affected by the ease with which they have recourse to CTOs, where the

> [a]brogation of responsibility for finding alternative and creative solutions is too easily supported. Pejorative terms come into being to both exclude undesirable elements and evade responsibility for tackling difficult to hold patients or parts of them that are difficult to manage. The classic example is the re-labelling of challenging behaviours as 'behavioural' or 'personality' and thus legitimizing rejection, particularly when resources are limited.[169]

Patel further argues that the coercive aspect of CTOs leads to clinicians having 'the unconscious and at times conscious tendency ... to perceive the client as having less human value than ourselves'.[170] Concerns that psychiatric coercion diminishes the ability of individuals to exercise autonomy are especially relevant in the light of mounting evidence that CTOs are ineffective.[171]

Patel's arguments are reminiscent of service-user activist Peter Campbell's description of the effect of stand-alone psychiatric institutions in the United Kingdom. He argues that the old asylums fostered a 'double

[165] S Herr, 'Self-determination, Autonomy, and Alternatives to Guardianship', in S Herr, LO Gostin and H Hong-Ju Koh (eds), *The Human Rights of Persons with Intellectual Disabilities* (Oxford University Press, 2003) 432.

[166] E Light et al., 'Community Treatment Orders in Australia: Rates and Patterns of Use' (2012) 20(6) *Australasian Psychiatry* 478–82.

[167] G Patel, 'Community Treatment Orders in Victoria: A Clinico-ethical Perspective' (2008) 16(5) *Australasian Psychiatry* 340, 341.

[168] Ibid.

[169] Ibid.

[170] Ibid. 341.

[171] See Chapter 3, Section C(3).

dependency': 'On the one hand the users of existing services [were] bred to accept dependency as a characteristic of relationships. On the other, the caring team based their operations on this inequality'.[172] He noted the dehumanising result of long-term institutionalisation, and the constant iterations of difference: '[a]t times, it is hard work not to believe we are a separate branch of humanity'.[173]

There is some empirical support for the view that coercive powers undermine the development of effective voluntary services during emergency mental health crises. In Germany in 2011 and 2012, several landmark decisions by the Constitutional Court and Federal Supreme Court restricted the imposition of involuntary psychiatric treatment.[174] The restriction narrowed the grounds for intervention to 'life-threatening emergencies' only.[175] The court restrictions were based on Germany's constitutional obligations as a signatory to the CRPD. According to Martin Zinkler, the resulting legal provisions led to 'examples where clinicians put an even greater emphasis on consensual treatment and did not return to coercive treatment'.[176] There is some evidence that the changes resulted in lower rates of coercive treatment, although the study was small-scale.[177] Despite these findings, some adverse effects were reported, including a possible increase in 'violent incidents' at some services, which potentially increased the use of physical and mechanical restraint.[178] There is current evidence from mental health services that substituted decision-making by clinical staff occurs in general services, even outside the context of civil commitment. A study by Marion Freidl and colleagues, for example, examined how 588 patients experience decision making in community-based mental health services in six European countries.[179] The study investigated the 'relationship between decision topic and involvement in the decision, satisfaction with it, and its subsequent implementation

172 P Campbell, 'Peter Campbell's story', in A Brackx and C Grimshaw (eds), *Mental Health Care in Crisis* (Pluto Press, 1989) 13.

173 Ibid. 15.

174 Federal Constitutional Court (Germany), Press Office – Press Release No 28/2011 of 15 April 2011, Order of 23 March 2011, 2 BvR 882/09.

175 Ibid.

176 M Zinkler, 'Germany without Coercive Treatment in Psychiatry: A 15 Month Real World Experience' (2016) 5(1) *Laws* 15.

177 E Flammer and T Steinert, 'Involuntary Medication, Seclusion, and Restraint in German Psychiatric Hospitals after the Adoption of Legislation in 2013' (2015) 6 *Frontiers in Psychiatry* 153.

178 Zinkler, above n 176.

179 M Freidl et al., 'Effects of Clinical Decision Topic on Patients' Involvement In and Satisfaction with Decisions and Their Subsequent Implementation' (2016) 67(6) *Psychiatric Services* 658.

from both staff and patient perspectives'.[180] The researchers stated that service users 'reported poorer involvement, satisfaction, and implementation in regard to treatment-related decisions', and concluded that 'clinicians may need to employ different interactional styles for different types of decisions to maximize satisfaction and decision implementation'.[181] It is not clear whether lawful coercion in inpatient and outpatient settings contributes to a broader culture of informal substituted decision-making in service provision. Yet civil commitment law could reasonably be seen to have numerous flow-on effects and consequences for individuals, including stymied decision-making skills, delayed recovery, passivity, learned helplessness and an increased dependence on services, all of which have significant individual and public implications.

4 *The Competing Aims of Mental Health Law Blurs Decision-Making Processes*

Mental health law is an unsound mechanism for distinguishing the reasons for and processes of substituted decision-making following emergency mental health crises. According to Moncrieff, the entwinement of the legal doctrines of police powers and *parens patriae* in mental health law, which have distinct ends, creates a destructive tension – the policing mandate presents a conflict of interest against the therapeutic role of the clinician.[182] The competing aims may also create confusion as to the rationale for substituted decision-making. The punitive or protective role of the authorised clinician or mental health tribunal adds yet another aim (preventive detention) to an already confusing decision-making process, where clinicians must make single decisions that also include consideration of resource constraints, access needs, treatment advice and individuals' rights. For clinicians, the constituent motives for clinical decision-making can be exceedingly complex. John Brayley has argued that this motivational confusion often results in clinicians (and other service providers) prioritising risk-reduction for the service above the interests of the individual.[183] Decision-making processes become unclear with the blurring of resource concerns and support needs, thus generating confusion about which decisions are being made

[180] Ibid.

[181] Ibid.

[182] Moncrieff, above n 26.

[183] J Brayley, 'Supported Decision Making in Australia: Presentation Notes' (Presentation to the Victorian Offices of the Public Advocate and the Law Reform Commission, Melbourne, 14 December 2009) 9 <www.opa.sa.gov.au>.

and for what reasons. In the guardianship context, Brayley argues that the confusion of decision-making motives creates a gap at the point where law meets policy, and the interests of the individual are potentially undermined because decision-makers are limited by the narrow set of service delivery options open to them.[184] This argument could be reasonably applied to mental health law.

5 *The Medical Model Dominates in Mental Health Law*

Mental health law gives precedence to the neurobiological model of mental health at the expense of other strategies for addressing mental health issues. The competing epistemological (and professional) responses to mental illness are important to consider. Throughout history, differing approaches to regulating coercive measures have related not just to cultural or legal traditions, but also to the variety of concepts and structures of professional intervention.[185] The medical model tends to view the problems facing people in crisis in individual, medicalised terms, rather than from a 'systems perspective', including where a person sits in the social context. A strong medical focus thus tends to concentrate attention upon isolated individuals, rather than on social and economic policies that enhance the capacity of communities, families and individuals to respond to mental health crises.

This is illustrated by the rise in the use of psychopharmacological treatment, which is an important feature of the curtailment of legal capacity in mental health law.[186] In Australian mental health law, Ian Freckelton and John Lesser have identified a 'heavy emphasis on pharmacological management of serious mental illnesses'.[187] In relation to CTO use in the United States, Simon Stefan has characterised forced medication as the 'core of outpatient commitment',[188] and Marvin Schwartz and Chris Constanzo propose that outpatient commitment 'already has or will become synonymous with forced medications'.[189] The side effects of neuroleptic drugs are

184 Ibid. 7.

185 European Commission Health and Consumer Protection Directorate-General, *Compulsory Admission and Involuntary Treatment of Mentally Ill Patients – Legislation and Practice in EU Member States* (Central Institute of Mental Health, 2002) 2.

186 H Verdoux, M Tournier and B Bégaud, 'Antipsychotic Prescribing Trends: A Review of Pharmaco-epidemiological Studies' (2010) 121 *Acta Psychiatrica Scandanavica* 4.

187 I Freckelton and J Lesser, 'Detention, Decisions and Dilemmas: Reviewing Involuntary Detention and Treatment into the 21st Century' (2003) 10(1) *Psychiatry, Psychology and Law* v.

188 S Stefan, 'Preventative Commitment: The Concepts and the Pitfalls' (1987) 11(4) *Mental and Physical Disability Law Reporter* 288.

189 SJ Schwartz and CE Costanzo, 'Compelling Treatment in the Community: Distorted Doctrines and Violated Values' (1987) 20 *Loyola of Los Angeles Law Review* 1329.

well-documented.[190] Research indicates that side effects range from anticholinergic and antiadrenergic to neurologic (including endocrine disturbances), all of which can have serious and negative impacts on a person's quality of life.[191] Many neuroleptic medications have permanent and serious possible side effects, including docility, passivity, diabetes, Parkinson's-type symptoms, dental pathology, weight gain, and salivation and elocution problems.[192]

The vocabulary of the medical model has implications for realising justice. As noted previously, it can draw the focus from collective responsibility by individualising issues of disability. The centrality of diagnosis in the operation of mental health law is important to consider, particularly given expanding categories of diagnosis in the past century. In 1952, the original American Psychiatric Association *Diagnostic and Statistical Manual* ('DSM') had 106 diagnoses.[193] The second edition of the DSM-IV in 2000 included 360.[194] Controversy surrounding the creation of the DSM-IV went beyond the

[190] See, generally, J Ballesteros, A Gonzales-Pinto and A Bulbena, 'Tardive Dyskinesia Associated with Higher Mortality in Psychiatric Patients: Results of a Meta-analysis of Seven Independent Studies' (2000) 20(2) *Journal of Clinical Psychopharmacology* 188; JL Waddington, 'Cognitive Dysfunction, Negative Symptoms, and Tardive Dyskinesia in Schizophrenia' (1987) 44 *Archives of General Psychiatry* 907. Waddington found that neuroleptic drug treatment is one reason that people diagnosed with schizophrenia have a shorter life expectancy. Waddington JL, HA Youssef and A Kinsella, 'Mortality in Schizophrenia: Antipsychotic Polypharmacy and Absence of Adjunctive Anticholinergics Over the Course of a 10-Year Prospective Study' (1998) 173 *British Journal of Psychiatry* 325; JB Wade, 'Cognitive Changes Associated with Tardive Dyskinesia' (1989) 1 *Neuropsychiatry, Neuropsychology, and Behavioral Neurology* 217. R Yassa, 'Functional Impairment in Tardive Dyskinesia: Medical and Psychosocial Dimensions' (1989) 80 *Acta Psychiatrica Scandinavica* 64. MS Myslobodsky, 'Central Determinants of Attention and Mood Disorder in Tardive Dyskinesia (Tardive Dysmentia)' (1993) 23 *Brain and Cognition* 88; H Spohn, 'The Effect of Attention/Information Processing Impairment of Tardive Dyskinesia and Neuroleptics in Chronic Schizophrenics' (1993) 23 *Brain and Cognition* 28; J Baribeau, 'Tardive Dyskinesia and Associated Cognitive Disorders: A Convergent Neuropsychological and Neurophysiological Approach' (1993) 23 *Brain and Cognition* 40; J Waddington, 'Cognitive Dysfunction in Schizophrenia: Organic Vulnerability Factor or State Marker for Tardive Dyskinesia?' (1993) 23 *Brain and Cognition* 56; P Sachdev, 'Negative Symptoms, Cognitive Dysfunction, Tardive Akathisia and Tardive Dyskinesia' (1996) 93 *Acta Psychiatrica Scandinavica* 451; R McShane, 'Do Neuroleptic Drugs Hasten Cognitive Decline in Dementia? Prospective Study with Necropsy Follow Up' (1997) [314] *British Medical Journal* 266; A Madsen, 'Neuroleptics in Progressive Structural Brain Abnormalities in Psychiatric Illness' (1998) [352] *The Lancet* 784.

[191] Ibid.

[192] Ibid.

[193] *Diagnostic and Statistical Manual of Mental Disorders* (American Psychiatric Association, 1952).

[194] *Diagnostic and Statistical Manual of Mental Disorders, Fourth Edition* (American Psychiatric Association, 1994), *Diagnostic and Statistical Manual of Mental Disorders, Fourth Edition, Text Revision* (American Psychiatric Association, 2000).

expansion of diagnostic categorisation and included the well-documented influence of pharmaceutical corporations.[195] The latest iteration, DSM-5, has faced similar criticisms.[196] For example, the British Psychological Society's division of clinical psychology has criticised the manual and called for abandoning its diagnostic categories altogether.[197] Lucy Johnstone, who co-authored the response by the division of clinical psychology, argued that '[t]here is now overwhelming evidence that people break down as a result of a complex mix of social and psychological circumstances – bereavement and loss, poverty and discrimination, trauma and abuse'.[198]

The implications of a biomedical conceptualisation of extreme mental stress affect the operation of law. In a 2007 World Health Organisation study into mental health policy and practice across Europe, the authors argued that '[f]ar too much confidence has been placed in the brain disease model, which may compound rather than challenge the stereotypes of dangerousness and, particularly, incompetence'.[199] When the focus is narrowed to 'risk' at an individual level, the emphasis turns to personal responsibility and individual behavioural change, and relies on traditional coercive powers of public and mental health. Bernadette McSherry has written that 'a simplistic, reductionist account of the causes of mental impairments brings with it the dangers of sanism and discrimination'.[200] Endorsement of a strong biological account of mental distress in mental health law may therefore impose further legal barriers to effective support.

6 *Family, Friends, Partners and Other Informal Supporters Are Sidelined*

Although there is a general lack of research into the effects of mental health law on interpersonal relationships,[201] there is some evidence to suggest that

[195] BC Pilecki, JW Clegg and D McKay, 'The Influence of Corporate and Political Interests on Models of Illness in the Evolution of the DSM' (2011) 26(3) *European Psychiatry* 194, s 4.1.

[196] Ibid. s 4.2; A Frances, 'Diagnosing the DSM', *The New York Times*, 11 May 2012.

[197] Division of Clinical Psychology, Position Statement on the Classification of Behaviour and Experience in Relation to Functional Psychiatric Diagnoses: Time for a Paradigm Shift (British Psychological Society, 2013).

[198] J Doward, 'Psychiatrists Under Fire in Mental Health Battle', *The Observer*, 12 May 2012.

[199] L Sayce and C Curran, 'Tackling Social Exclusion Across Europe' in M Knapp et al. (eds), *Mental Health Policy and Practice Across Europe* (World Health Organisation, 2007) 34, 51.

[200] B McSherry, 'Decision-Making, Legal Capacity and Neuroscience: Implications for Mental Health Laws' (2015) 4 *Laws* 125, 134.

[201] See F Beaupert and A Vernon, 'Odyssey of Hope': The Role of Carers in Mental Health Tribunal Processes and Systems of Mental Health Care' (2011) 18(1) *Psychiatry, Psychology and the Law* 44; V Yeates, 'Ambivalence, Contradiction, and Symbiosis: Carers' and Mental Health Users' Rights' (2007) 29 *Law and Policy* 435; J lesser, 'All Care and Whose Responsibility?' (2004) 11 *Psychiatry, Psychology, and Law* 236.

current legal and policy frameworks effectively exclude family members and other supporters. Most of the literature on families is medical in nature and centres on assessing the 'burden of care' placed on families, as well as the effectiveness of family interventions for treating mental illness.[202] In contrast, literature on contact between family and clinicians and on the effects of mental health law on informal supporters is limited. Notable exceptions suggest that families and other informal supporters often experience mental health law within a more general sense of being devalued and ignored in the mental health 'system'.[203] Fleur Beaupert and Alikki Vernon examined the 'role of carers in mental health tribunal processes and systems of mental health care' in different Australian jurisdictions.[204] They found that '[f]oremost among concerns expressed by carers was the experience of being marginalized in the mental health care system' as a whole.[205]

Provisions in mental health law relating to families and other supporters differ in each jurisdiction and can have a significant impact on the supporter and service-user relationship.[206] For example, Lesser argued in 2004 that the Victorian Mental Health Review Boards were under no obligation to provide information to informal supporters of those subject to its decisions, and he identified a number of legal and practical barriers that prevent the board from involving supporters in hearings in meaningful ways.[207] The Victorian Law Reform Commission's review of Victorian guardianship law noted that 'some families have felt forced to apply for Guardianship Orders in order not to have mental health services exclude them from the treatment and care of their family member, and to have their role as advocates recognised'.[208]

202 See, e.g., AJ Shah, O Wadoo and J Latoo, 'Psychological Distress in Carers of People with Mental Disorders' (2010) 3(3) *BJMP* 327; L Magliano et al., 'Carers and Families of People with Mental Health Problems' in M Knapp et al. (eds), *Mental Health Policy and Practice Across Europe* (World Health Organisation, 2007) 374; M Ostman and L Hansson, 'Stigma by Association' (2002) 181 *BJP* 494–8; C Lauber, A Eichenberger and P Luginbuhl, 'Determinants of Burden in Caregivers of Patients with Exacerbating Schizophrenia' (2003) 18 *European Psychiatry* 285; B Schulze and W Rössler, 'Caregiver Burden in Mental Illness: Review of Measurement, Findings and Interventions, 2004–2005' (2005) 18(6) *Current Opinion in Psychiatry* 684; S Andren and S Elmstahl, 'The Relationship between Caregiver Burden, Caregivers' Perceived Health and Their Sense of Coherence in Caring for Elders with Dementia' (2008) 17(6) *Journal of Clinical Nursing* 1365–2702; J Hoenig and M Hamilton, 'The Schizophrenic Patient and His Effect on the Household' (1966) 12 *International Journal of Social Psychiatry* 165–76.

203 Beaupert and Vernon, above n 201, 46.

204 Ibid.

205 Ibid.

206 Ibid.

207 Lesser, above n 201, 239–41.

208 See, generally, Carers Australia, 'Carers Australia Victoria submission to the Victorian Law Reform Commission's Guardianship Review' 6, 12 <www.lawreform.vic.gov.au>.

On the other hand, there remain legitimate concerns that individuals may require legal protection to prevent the unwanted involvement of family members and other informal supporters through, for example, provisions relating to privacy and confidentiality. The rights of those subject to mental health law may sometimes give rise to tension with the interests (and even rights) of families and other supporters.[209] However, in general, reports from people with psychosocial disabilities, and families and supporters, indicate that informal support networks are often overlooked by clinical substituted decision-makers who may not seek their counsel in decision-making processes or take into account the effect of particular treatment decisions upon those relationships.[210] Relationships are compromised between individuals and those in their support network where significant psychiatric interventions, regulated by mental health law, are decided upon without consideration of those relationships. Further, these relationships can be significantly affected where supporters are placed in coercive roles which effectively impose legal obligations on them to assist in implementing involuntary orders and engage in substituted decision-making.[211]

7 *Perverse Incentives to Use Coercive Mechanisms*

Mental health law may inadvertently skew the distribution of institutional resources towards coercive mechanisms by focusing solely on the parameters for involuntary detention. This can result in compulsion becoming synonymous with much-needed access to support in a sector often beset by resource shortages. Clinicians may be faced with situations in which compulsion becomes the quickest avenue for necessary resource allocation. This has been a particular concern regarding the use of CTOs.[212]

Community service providers and support agencies that wish clients to receive acute care services may also be inclined to exaggerate reporting to improve their chances for involuntary admission. Family, friends and other supporters may also be presented with similar incentives, where compulsion enables the supported person to access resources that would otherwise be unavailable to voluntary service users. Accounts such as the following appear

[209] Yeates, above n 201.

[210] See K Baker, 'Families: A Help or Hindrance in Recovery?' in P Stastny and P Lehmann (eds), *Alternatives Beyond Psychiatry* (Peter Lehman Publishing, 2007) 254; see also New South Wales Consumer Advisory Group, 'Privacy and Confidentiality' (Issue Paper, 1 June 2004) 25.

[211] Beaupert and Vernon, above n 201.

[212] See AM and S Fox, 'Opening Pandora's Box: The Practical and Legal Dangers of Involuntary Outpatient Commitment' (2001) 52 *Psychiatric Services* 342.

regularly in the literature on family and other supporters concerned with civil commitment:

> We weren't so worried about actually making an order against D, we were wanting to make an order against the system. We wanted them to say: 'The system must provide this man with some help'. And that was the major outcome we were after ... You can't just keep on letting this guy out of jail, not provide him with any supports and services, and not expect a bad thing to happen.[213]

Where voluntary services are not available, interpersonal problems may arise when informal supporters seek out coercive care for their parent, friend, sibling, partner, adult son or daughter, and so on. Possibly this is an issue to be resolved by policy (and particularly budgetary considerations) and not law. Yet it could be argued that the law is creating an unintended negative consequence, which undermines its original intention to provide responses to worst-case scenarios.

E CONCLUSION

As previously noted, the listing of issues in this chapter is not exhaustive. Other concerns that could be listed include the increasing number of first-person accounts of trauma caused by coercive interventions; reports of sexual assault, harassment and other forms of abuse that people, especially women, experience in acute settings;[214] the situations of those who admit themselves who lack the 'mental capacity' to consent to admission and treatment and thus become de facto detained without procedural oversight (the so-called Bournewood gap);[215] and the overrepresentation of persons with psychosocial disabilities as *victims* of violence and abuse, for which mental health law offers little protection.[216] Instead, I have chosen to discuss major issues along the

[213] Cited in Beaupert and Vernon, above n 201, 53.

[214] See Victorian Mental Illness Awareness Council, Zero Tolerance for Sexual Assault: A Safe Admission for Women (2013).

[215] The 'Bournewood gap' refers to those who admit themselves to hospital who lack the 'mental capacity' to consent to admission and treatment. Hence they remain voluntary patients, not because they have consented to admission, but rather because they have not objected. Although they are then de facto detained, they are not afforded the safeguards of formally detained patients. See N Eastman and J Peay, 'Bournewood: An Indefensible Gap in Mental Health Law, Capacity Is Set to Become a Major Clinicolegal Issue' (1998) 317 (7151) *British Medical Journal* 94; Department of Health (Ireland), *Interim Report of the Steering Group on the Review of the Mental Health Act 2001* (2012) s 3.4 <www.dohc.ie>.

[216] See LA Teplin et al., 'Crime Victimization in Adults with Severe Mental Illness: Comparison with the National Crime Victimization Survey' (2005) 62(8) *Archives of General Psychiatry* 911.

lines of rights, efficacy and other pragmatic matters, in order to investigate the potential contribution of the CRPD support framework.

The notion of 'wise constraints' has long been advanced by liberal philosophers such as John Locke as a means to enhance human freedom.[217] Locke's idea captures the essential logic of those who defend the unusual coercive powers of mental health legislation: civil commitment can augment autonomy through prudent intervention to restore people to their normal selves, or it can restrict autonomy rights in order to uphold other rights – the right to life, to health, to physical and mental integrity. Where interventions are undertaken for public safety purposes, mental health law provides the 'best of the worst' ways to reduce harm caused by the peculiar consequences of mental illness, mental impairment, 'madness' and so on.

In other words, for doctors and lawmakers who endorse the need for separate, mental health-specific legislation, the ends of mental health law appear to justify the means. On this view, the suspension of principles of autonomy and non-discrimination are viewed as acceptable costs in the pursuit of timely treatment, procedural safeguards and public protection. Mental health law provides for the emergency powers needed to intervene during extreme mental health crises – emergency powers that have been refined over decades of trial and error, and developed through entrenched infrastructure for the regulation and oversight of coercive intervention. This view has been adopted by governments in all jurisdictions considered by this book, irrespective of the apparent divergence between the CRPD and mental health law.

However, even if the human rights issues identified in this chapter are set aside, can it be said that society as a whole is better served by the powers of mental health law? Is greater protection for citizens achieved by restrictions under mental health law on the movement and decisions of certain individuals who may pose harm to others? The claim that such powers are necessary appears to rest on justifications that have been challenged by a growing body of evidence. Indeed, the literature suggests that the public protection measures contained in mental health law are overblown, ineffective and unreasonable, particularly when tied to a diagnosis of mental disorder. This would suggest that the 'risk of harm to others' justification is informed by

[217] 'Freedom of men under government', writes Locke, 'is to have a standing rule to live by, common to every one of that society, and made by the legislative power vested in it; a liberty to follow my own will in all things, when the rule prescribes not, and not to be subject to the inconstant, uncertain, unknown, arbitrary will of another man'. J Locke, *Second Treatise of Civil Government* (1690) ch 4 s 22(a).

disability-based prejudice, or 'sanism' as Perlin has termed it.[218] As for the protection of people from themselves, can it be said that the present legal system is actually protecting people with psychosocial disability from harming themselves, even in acute crisis?[219] Again, the literature does not support this view. Therefore, even if one accepts that at least some crises warrant coercive intervention of some kind, the aim of preventing the risk of harm to self or others appears to be ill-served by mental health legislation.

The second primary function of mental health law identified at the beginning of this chapter, ensuring access to support, returns even more troubling results. On this point, the literature is unequivocal: mental health law does not effectively ensure timely voluntary access to support for those in crisis. The lopsided focus on 'negative rights' in rights-based legalism – or the narrow application of 'positive rights' to involuntary intervention only – appears to hinder this function of mental health law. The impasse then contributes significantly to the common experience of people with psychosocial disabilities, who see themselves as being stuck in a 'binary system of self-sufficiency versus enforced dependence'.[220] This 'binary system' can be explained not just by a lack of resources, but by the design of mental health legislation itself.

The third and final major function of mental health law discussed here is the need to ensure procedural safeguards for persons subject to civil commitment. Arguably, the push for improved procedural protections is compromised from the outset by the apparent failure of the first two major functions of mental health law. Such safeguards appear to command disproportionate attention and resources, and detract from a focus on substantive rights and the provision of (voluntary) treatment and support more generally. Consider the significant costs of administering and regulating CTOs, a cost that could be reinvested in achieving positive rights, for example, via personal advocacy services.[221] Nevertheless, the regulatory function of mental health law continues to provide perhaps the most compelling case to a range of academics, service providers, lawyers, government agencies and others on the need to retain it.

[218] The term 'sanism' was coined by Perlin, who defines the term as '(d)iscrimination and oppression against people who have, or who are labelled or perceived as having, a mental illness'. See ML Perlin, 'Things Have Changed: Looking at Non-institutional Mental Disability Law Through the Sanism Filter' (2002–2003) 46 *New York Law School Review* 535, 539; see also ML Perlin and DA Dorfman, 'Sanism, Social Science, and the Development of Mental Disability Jurisprudence' (1993) 11(1) *Behavioral Sciences and the Law* 47.

[219] Freckelton and Lesser, above n 189.

[220] International Disability Alliance, 'Letter on Functional Capacity to the CRPD Committee' (2010) <www.internationaldisabilityalliance.org>.

[221] See Chapter 6, Section B(3).

It is noteworthy that this justification does not appear to be shared by prominent commentators with lived experience of mental health issues or by representative service user and survivor organisations,[222] as well as prominent UN human rights agencies. Indeed, existing safeguards and rights protections were not developed with the active participation of those whose rights are deemed to need safeguarding. Instead, it appears that in all of the jurisdictions considered by this book, it is clinicians, lawyers and service providers who have taken a more prominent role in developing procedural safeguards than service users themselves.[223]

The concerns outlined above paint a general picture of some of the drawbacks to current mental health law. It seems obvious, when reflecting on the major issues in mental health law overall, that there is clearly a need for a practical and conceptual evaluation of any proposed change to such law, with as much consideration as possible given to the full range of potential downsides or negative flow on effects. Appelbaum concluded his treatise on the history of mental health law reform in the second half of the twentieth century by observing that '[i]f generalization is possible across these very disparate areas of law, our conclusion must be that the consequences of reform were much more limited than partisans on either side anticipated'.[224] In a similar vein, Brendan Kelly observed that many of the deficits in securing the rights of persons with disabilities

> relate not to the *content* of declarations of rights (such as the CRPD) or to the *specific provisions* of legislation (such as mental health and capacity legislation), but to a profound failure to *observe* laws, *implement* policy and *realise* agreed principles in the day-to-day lives of persons with disabilities and mental disorder, resulting in systematic denial of rights, social exclusion and political disempowerment.[225]

[222] See, e.g., above n 94 and 95.

[223] Arguably, with the increasing involvement of service users in the development of mental health law, policy and practice, this is beginning to change. There is evidence of increasing public consultation in the development of mental health and related legislation, including those concerned with mental capacity law. In Ireland, for example, Eilionóir Flynn describes the deliberative process behind the development of the Assisted Decision-Making (Capacity) Bill 2013. E Flynn, 'Assisted Decision-Making (Capacity) Bill 2013 Finally Published' on *Human Rights in Ireland* (17 July 2013) <www.humanrights.ie>. In Northern Ireland, the development of the Draft Mental Capacity Bill involved significant public consultation, including with mental health service-user groups. See Minister of the Department of Health, Social Services and Public Safety in Northern Ireland, Northern Ireland Department of Justice, Government of Northern Ireland, 'Draft Mental Capacity Bill (NI) Consultation Document' (May 2014).

[224] Appelbaum, above n 146, 210.

[225] B Kelly, *Dignity, Mental Health and Human Rights: Coercion and the Law* (Ashgate, 2015) 119 (emphasis in original).

Or consider Tom Burns's (quite extraordinary) statement about the way practicing psychiatrists engage with mental health law: '[F]ew, if any, clinicians ever read the details of legislation. Most familiarise themselves "on the job" with the mechanics of those parts of the Act they regularly use. They learn what they have to sign and complete in order to achieve what they have already clinically decided on'.[226] This is not to disparage law reform efforts. Instead, these observations suggest that it is important to be circumspect about our expectations of what law reform can deliver, or to consider the mechanisms required to ensure the effective implementation of law. Further, acknowledging the limitations of past reform efforts encourages the careful evaluation of new ideas for promoting substantive equality for persons with psychosocial disability, including the support framework of the CRPD itself.

[226] T Burns, 'Mental Illness Is Different and Ignoring Its Differences Profits Nobody' (2010) Special Issue, *Journal of Mental Health Law* 34.

PART II

THE CRPD SUPPORT FRAMEWORK AND MENTAL HEALTH: NEW TOOLS OR NEW PARADIGM?

4

The CRPD Support Framework

There are as many preferences as there are people.

– Horace[1]

A INTRODUCTION

Part II of this book will focus on how the support framework of the CRPD[2] might address the major conceptual and practical issues of mental health law. The 'CRPD support framework' is here used to refer to CRPD provisions relevant to claiming and exercising human rights in the mental health context, particularly concerning strengthening self-determination, ensuring support and affirming equal recognition before the law. Domestic laws and policies within this frame include those governing involuntary psychiatric intervention. Also at stake are policies and practices that have the capacity to strengthen agency; for example, in achieving rights to the highest attainable physical and mental health, independent living and community participation (for example, related to housing policy), and freedom from abuse, violence and exploitation (relevant to, for example, criminal laws or expanded civil powers for preventing abuse).

Critical here is Article 12 of the CRPD, over which much 'ink has been spilled'. Commentators have paid particular attention to Article 12 (3), which requires that States Parties provide access for persons with disabilities to 'the support they may require in exercising their legal capacity'.[3] For many,

1 Horace, *Sermones*, 2.1.247–8, cited in A Sen, *Development as Freedom* (Oxford University Press, 1999) 68.

2 Convention on the Rights of Persons with Disabilities, opened for signature 30 March 2007, Doc.A/61/611 (entered into force 3 May 2008).

3 Ibid., art 12(3).

Article 12 (3) is the *locus situ* of 'supported decision-making' in international human rights law.[4] A quick glance at the range of 'supported decision-making' resources created in the wake of the CRPD (a quick online search at the time of writing returns over 26,000 results[5]) indicates that the concept refers to a collection of various demands rather than having a single fixed meaning. Broadly, these demands centre on tools and resources to make choices between good options about how to live.

Early on in the CRPD negotiations, according to Amita Dhanda, it became clear that 'supported decision-making' was going to be used by negotiators as a shorthand designation for the CRPD mandate to promote 'autonomy with support'.[6] Prominent disabled people's organisations quickly positioned 'supported decision-making' as a concept to describe the innovation of the CRPD. For example, the International Disability Alliance, a global alliance of 1,100 organisations of persons with disabilities and their families, stated that 'by devising the supported decision making model of legal capacity [the CRPD] has made an innovative effort to recognise the aspirations of all persons with disabilities'.[7]

In this chapter, I will seek to refine the conceptual foundations of the CRPD support framework, of which supported decision-making is a key component. I will do so with reference to the major issues outlined in the previous chapter. (Readers more interested in practical examples of CRPD-based mental health services and other practices may wish to skip forward to Chapter 6.) At the outset, it is important to note the indivisibility of Article 12 from other articles in the CRPD. Peter Bartlett highlights that the CRPD has changed the traditional relationship between civil/political and socioeconomic rights, making it far more 'nebulous' than ever before.[8] The range of rights across the CRPD

4 G Quinn, 'Personhood and Legal Capacity: Perspectives on the Paradigm Shift of Article 12 CRPD' (Paper presented at the Conference on Disability and Legal Capacity under the CRPD, Harvard Law School, Boston, 20 February 2010, 16 <www.nuigalway.ie>.

5 Using the search terms '"supported decision-making" AND "mental health"'. Around 37,000 results were yielded from the search terms '"supported decision-making" AND "disability"'.

6 A Dhanda, 'Constructing a New Human Rights Lexicon: Convention on the Rights of Persons with Disabilities' (2008) 5(8) *Sur – International Journal on Human Rights* 45.

7 Legal Capacity Taskforce, International Disability Alliance, 'Legal Opinion on Article 12' (IDA Position Papers and Statements, 2008) 2 <www.internationaldisabilityalliance.org>. Inclusion Europe, a representative group for Europeans with intellectual disability, stated that 'a paradigm shift in international and national law [has occurred] with the concept of "supported decision-making"'. Inclusion Europe, *Key Elements of a System for Supported Decision-Making: Position Paper of Inclusion Europe: Adopted at the General Assembly 2008* (2008) <www.inclusion-europe.org>.

8 P Bartlett, 'The United Nations Convention on the Rights of Persons with Disabilities and Mental Health Law' (2012) 75(5) *The Modern Law Review* 752, 757.

should be seen as 'building blocks' for the enjoyment of equal recognition before the law, including rights concerned with independent living and community participation (Article 19), the highest attainable physical and mental health (Article 25), habilitation and rehabilitation (Article 26), housing (Articles 9 and 28), access to justice (Article 13), and freedom from abuse, neglect and exploitation (Article 16). Reinforcing the indivisibility and interdependent character of rights in this way ensures that discussions about mental health and human rights move beyond a mere focus on decision-making, which, although important, may unduly narrow the frame of debate and interfere with efforts to achieve a full range of human rights.

B ARTICLE 12: EQUAL RECOGNITION BEFORE THE LAW

ARTICLE 12 – EQUAL RECOGNITION BEFORE THE LAW

1. States Parties reaffirm that persons with disabilities have the right to recognition everywhere as persons before the law.
2. States Parties shall recognize that persons with disabilities enjoy legal capacity on an equal basis with others in all aspects of life.
3. States Parties shall take appropriate measures to provide access by persons with disabilities to the support they may require in exercising their legal capacity.
4. States Parties shall ensure that all measures that relate to the exercise of legal capacity provide for appropriate and effective safeguards to prevent abuse in accordance with international human rights law. Such safeguards shall ensure that measures relating to the exercise of legal capacity respect the rights, will and preferences of the person, are free of conflict of interest and undue influence, are proportional and tailored to the person's circumstances, apply for the shortest time possible and are subject to regular review by a competent, independent and impartial authority or judicial body. The safeguards shall be proportional to the degree to which such measures affect the person's rights and interests.
5. Subject to the provisions of this article, States Parties shall take all appropriate and effective measures to ensure the equal right of persons with disabilities to own or inherit property, to control their own financial affairs and to have equal access to bank loans, mortgages and other forms of financial credit, and shall ensure that persons with disabilities are not arbitrarily deprived of their property.

Article 12 of the CRPD sets out the right to enjoy legal capacity on an equal basis with others as a subsidiary to the right to equal recognition before the law.[9] The right to equal recognition before the law appears in the Universal Declaration of Human Rights[10] and the International Covenant on Civil and Political Rights.[11] A right to 'exercise legal capacity' on an equal basis with others was first established in 1979 in the Convention to Eliminate All Forms of Discrimination Against Women.[12] This right in international law draws on a formulation of legal capacity constituted by two things: a person's legal standing (legal personality) and his or her ability to act on such legal standing (legal agency).[13] A practical example to distinguish the two elements is that a person may be granted a formal right to vote, but may be unable to exercise that right, for example where the person's town lacks voting infrastructure, or electoral staff refuse him or her entry to the polling booth.

Article 12 of the CRPD applies the existing right to equal recognition before the law to the specific context of persons with disabilities. Article 12 (1) establishes that persons with disabilities have the right to recognition everywhere as persons before the law,[14] and 12(2) emphasises the right to *enjoy* legal capacity on an equal basis, indicating that states must provide the resources needed to make use of that recognition. Article 12(3) reinforces this obligation on States Parties, which must 'take appropriate measures to provide access by persons with disabilities to the support they may require in exercising their legal capacity'.[15] Subsection 12(4) sets out safeguards required for all measures related to the exercise of legal capacity,[16] while 12(5) explicitly recognises the importance of the right of persons with disability to exercise legal capacity in respect of financial and property matters.[17]

9 CRPD art 12.

10 Universal Declaration of Human Rights, GA Res 217A (III), UN GAOR, 3rd sess, 183rd plen mtg, UN Doc A/810 (entered into force 10 December 1948) art 6.

11 International Covenant on Civil and Political Rights, opened for signature 19 December 1966, 999 UNTS 171 (entered into force 23 March 1976) art 16(1).

12 Convention on the Elimination of All Forms of Discrimination Against Women, GA Res 34/180, A/34/46 (entered into force 3 September 1981) arts 15(2)(3).

13 UN Office of the High Commissioner for Human Rights, 'Background Conference Document Prepared by the Office of the United Nations High Commissioner for Human Rights: Legal Capacity' (2005) <www.un.org>.

14 CRPD art 12(1). See UN Office of the High Commissioner for Human Rights, 'Legal Capacity', (Background Conference Document for the Sixth Session of the Ad Hoc Committee on a Comprehensive and Integral International Convention on Protection and Promotion of the Rights and Dignity of Persons with Disabilities, 1–12 August 2005).

15 CRPD art 12(3).

16 Ibid., art 12(4).

17 Ibid., art 12(5).

Overall, Article 12 sets out a commitment by States Parties to uphold the legal standing of people with disabilities on an equal basis with others, and to ensure that they may *act* on such legal standing.

C THE CRPD SUPPORT FRAMEWORK: KEY CONCEPTS

In recent decades, literature on disability and equal recognition before the law has proliferated. Studies include the challenges posed by cognitive disability to moral philosophy,[18] the way in which constructions of legal capacity 'regulate personhood',[19] the evolution of legal capacity in international human rights law,[20] typologies of CRPD-based support,[21] and the application of issues raised in Article 12 to a wide range of laws, including mental health law,[22] elder law[23] and mental capacity law,[24] and in response to extreme self-harm and suicide.[25] To sift through this material, and to better identify the legal and political implications of the CRPD support framework today, it is useful to clearly articulate the key concepts of the framework.

On 19 May 2014, the CRPD Committee provided interpretive guidance on Article 12 in a General Comment.[26] A General Comment is a quasi-legal

[18] E Kittay and L Carlson (eds), *Cognitive Disability and Its Challenge to Moral Philosophy* (Wiley-Blackwell, 2010).

[19] Quinn, above n 4, 16.

[20] B McSherry, 'Legal Capacity under the Convention on the Rights of Persons with Disabilities' (2012) 20(1) *Journal of Law and Medicine* 22.

[21] M Browning, C Bigby and J Douglas, 'Supported Decision Making: Understanding How Its Conceptual Link to Legal Capacity Is Influencing the Development of Practice' (2014) 1 *Research and Practice in Intellectual and Developmental Disabilities* 34.

[22] See P Weller, 'Supported Decision-Making and the Achievement of Non-Discrimination: The Promise and Paradox of the Disabilities Convention' (2008) 26(2) *Law in Context* 85; P Gooding, 'Navigating the "Flashing Amber Lights" of the Right to Legal Capacity in the *United Nations Convention on the Rights of Persons with Disabilities*: Responding to Major Concerns' (2015) 15(1) *Human Rights Law Review* 45.

[23] T Carney, 'Guardianship, Citizenship, and Theorizing Substitute-Decision-Making Law' in I Doron and AM Soden (eds), *Beyond Elder Law: New Directions in Law and Ageing* (Springer, 2012) 11.

[24] W Martin et al., 'The Essex Autonomy Project Three Jurisdictions Report: Towards Compliance with CRPD Art. 12 in Capacity/Incapacity Legislation across the UK' (University of Essex, 6 June 2016) <www.autonomy.essex.ac.uk>.

[25] G Richardson, 'Mental Capacity in the Shadow of Suicide' (2013) 9(1) *International Journal of Law in Context* 87.

[26] Committee on the Rights of Persons with Disabilities, *General Comment No 1: Article 12: Equal Recognition before the Law,* 11th sess, UN Doc CRPD/C/GC/1 (19 May 2014). The CRPD Committee is authorised under Article 34 to review the compliance reports of States Parties. CRPD art 34.

document published by a UN committee that provides a detailed interpretation of an article or issue relating to its respective human rights treaty or treaties. Together with documents such as 'concluding observations', which report on States Parties' treaty compliance, General Comments provide guidance on the actions required by governments to ensure implementation. Helen Keller and Leena Grover have described General Comments as 'non-binding norms that interpret and add detail to the rights and obligations contained in the respective human rights treaties'.[27] The CRPD Committee, which is made up of members elected by States Parties[28] (nearly all of whom are persons with disabilities), is a meaningful conduit through which the views of persons with disabilities may engage with international human rights law. While there is some disagreement about the positive legal significance of General Comments,[29] there is a general 'presumption in favour of substantive correctness of such views', even as those views can be challenged by States Parties and contested with good counter-arguments.[30] The CRPD Committee's first General Comment, although controversial,[31] helps to identify key concepts of the CRPD support framework.

Defining core terms helps avoid situations where participants in debates misunderstand one another and offer arguments that do not meet.[32] The analytical distinctions set out in this chapter are not meant to be conclusive, nor will they provide a falsifiable judgement dictating the 'right' or 'true' approach to all conceptual questions. But they can help avoid confusion, and help indicate when an analysis – for the purposes of this book, a human rights analysis – is good, or comparably better, for a particular purpose.[33]

1 *Support to Exercise Legal Capacity*

As noted earlier, international human rights law conceptualises *legal* capacity in a particular way; it refers to a person's legal standing and his or her power

[27] H Keller and L Grover, 'General Comments of the Human Rights Committee and Their Legitimacy' in H Keller and G Ulfstein (eds), *UN Human Rights Treaty Bodies: Law and Legitimacy* (Cambridge University Press, 2012) 116, 129.

[28] CRPD art 34.

[29] S Michalowski and W Martin, 'MoJ/EAP UNCRPD Project Research Note: The Legal Status of General Comments' (The Essex Autonomy Project, 23 May 2014) <www.autonomy.essex.ac.uk>.

[30] C Tomuschat, *Human Rights: Between Idealism and Realism* (Oxford University Press, 2008) 220

[31] Prominent critiques of the General Comment will be addressed in Chapter 7.

[32] B Bix, *Jurisprudence: Theory and Context* (Sweet and Maxwell, 3rd ed, 2006) 29.

[33] Ibid.

to act on that standing.[34] Article 16 of the International Covenant on Civil and Political Rights upholds legal standing and refers to the right to be recognised as a person before the law and as someone subject to rights and entitlements.[35] Legal *agency*, on the other hand, refers to the 'capacity and power to engage' in a legal undertaking, to use the terms of the UN Office of the High Commissioner for Human Rights (OHCHR).[36]

Mental health legislation restricts legal capacity most clearly, insofar as it restricts a person's legal *agency*.[37] That is, the person arguably maintains a formal standing in law: he or she is recognised as a rights-holder, and procedural mechanisms to appeal civil commitment are available to him or her. Yet the law clearly restricts legal agency in relation to particular rights, and does so on the basis of disability, in violation of Article 12(2).

The idea of providing *support* to exercise legal capacity builds on the fundamental principle in international human rights law of the right to autonomy, free from paternalistic intervention by others.[38] Michael Bach and Lara Kerzner describe the significance of this principle in the following terms:

> The ability to make one's own decisions based on personal values and in the context of meaningful choices is a defining feature of what it means to be a person and a full citizen. A basic tenet of liberal democratic philosophy is that the state has a primary role in protecting autonomy or the right of individuals to choose and pursue their own life path, and all the decisions that entails along the way.[39]

Article 12(3) does not define 'support'. However, according to the CRPD Committee, support 'encompasses both informal and formal support arrangements, of varying types and intensity'.[40] Hence, 'support to exercise legal capacity' includes a broad spectrum of support, some of which may engage legal mechanisms, some of which may not. Such support in the mental health context might include personal advocacy, plain-language aids, decision-making assistance and, in exceptional circumstances – when it is necessary to make a decision where a person's will and preference are unknown or unclear – using

34 UN Office of the High Commissioner for Human Rights, above n 14.

35 Article 16 of the International Covenant on Civil and Political Rights simply states: 'Everyone shall have the right to recognition everywhere as a person before the law'. International Covenant on Civil and Political Rights, above n 11.

36 UN Office of the High Commissioner for Human Rights, above n 13, para 37.

37 McSherry, above n 20, 22.

38 See International Covenant on Civil and Political Rights, above n 11, art 1(1), (3).

39 M Bach and L Kerzner, *A New Paradigm for Protecting Autonomy and the Right to Legal Capacity* (Report to the Law Commission of Ontario, 2010) 6 <www.lco-cdo.org>.

40 Committee on the Rights of Persons with Disabilities, above n 26, para 15.

the 'best interpretation of a person's will and preference' to guide decisions.[41] I will discuss this 'best interpretation' standard shortly.

Bach and Kerzner propose three main types of support required to meet the provisions of Article 12(3) which help refine the broad possibilities of the CRPD support framework. These are:

- Supports to assist in formulating one's purposes, to explore the range of choices and to make a decision;
- Supports to engage in the decision-making process with other parties to make agreements that give effect to one's decision, where one's decisions requires this; and
- Supports to act on the decisions that one has made, and to meet one's obligations under any agreements made for that purpose.[42]

Bach and Kerzner break this down further into six main types of support services that should be provided: life-planning supports; advocacy; communication and interpretive supports; representational supports with people who know the person well; relationship-building supports; and administrative supports.[43]

Elaborating on these categories illuminates the range of supports that can strengthen self-determination. Life-planning supports can help people consider their values, priorities and goals, and to think about ways of achieving them. In practice, services may refer to 'person-centred planning' to describe this approach, although this practice appears to be used to refer to a wide range of different practices, some of which appear to place more emphasis on self-determination than others.[44] 'Personalised' supports can be especially important for people who have not had the opportunity to make decisions for themselves and/or have experienced long-term institutional living. Often the long-term effects of being deemed incapable of making decisions has meant that people lack decision-making skills and chances to develop them.[45] Independent advocacy (such as that used by the PO Skåne model,[46] local

[41] Ibid. para 21. I will discuss the 'best interpretation' standard in Chapter 7, Section B(1).

[42] Bach and Kerzner, above n 39, 73.

[43] Ibid. 74–82.

[44] 'Person-centred planning' typically describes a model of service provision for boosting the self-determination and independence of individuals with disabilities or others who require support. The service grew out of a critique of the 'facility-based services' approach that provided group-based services. See J Mansell and J Beadle-Brown, 'Person-Centred Planning or Person-Centred Action? Policy and Practice in Intellectual Disability Services' (2004) 17(1) *Journal of Applied Research in Intellectual Disabilities* 1.

[45] Bach and Kerzner, above n 39, 75.

[46] See Chapter 6, Section B(3).

area coordination[47] and Independent Mental Health Advocates)[48] may help support people to assert their rights and challenge assumptions about their ability to make decisions. Advocacy can be especially useful when negotiating the sometimes complex nature of multidisciplinary, multiagency service provision.[49]

Specific communication and interpretive support tools may help people to provide information, discuss options and communicate decisions.[50] Such supports may include signing, computer-assisted devices or interpreters, but may also include the assistance of an informal supporter who is in a trusting relationship with the person. They may also include individualised plain-language assistance as well as assisted communication.[51]

Representational supports can assist in instances where planning, advocacy and communication supports are insufficient.[52] A trusted or close associate of the person, or possibly a network of supporters, can help convey a sense of who the person is, and to communicate what is known of his or her identity, intentions and yearnings. This may include using the 'best interpretation of a person's will and preference'. Gordon and others have articulated the value of statutory recognition of trusted others within a person's support network.[53] The registering of previously informal supporters has occurred in British Columbia, through the non-governmental organisation Nidus,[54] which helps provide recognition and guidance to relationships of support.[55]

Relationship-building support can be necessary, given the social isolation that can disproportionately impact those subject to involuntary psychiatric intervention or other restrictions on legal capacity, such as guardianship.[56] Social exclusion often undermine a person's ability to develop trust and

47 R Broad, *People, Place, Possibilities* (Centre for Welfare Reform, United Kingdom, 2015).

48 Mental Health Act 1983 (England and Wales) c 20 s 30.

49 Bach and Kerzner, above n 39, 76–7.

50 Ibid. 77–8.

51 Ibid.

52 Ibid. 79.

53 R Gordon, 'The Emergence of Assisted (Supported) Decision-Making in the Canadian Law of Adult Guardianship and Substitute Decision-Making' (2000) 23(1) *International Journal of Law and Psychiatry* 61; see also Victorian Law Reform Commission, 'Chapter 16: A New Registration Scheme' in *Guardianship: Final Report* 24 (2012) 349 <www.lawreform.vic.gov.au>.

54 The Nidus homepage indicates that the organisation has between two and four staff members, and registers approximately 600 agreements per year; 5000 agreements are currently registered. Links to the website are provided on the Guardian and Trustee of British Columbia website. See Public Guardian and Trustee of British Columbia, *It's Your Choice – A Guide to Making a Representation Agreement* (PGT BC, 6th ed, 2007) <www.trustee.bc.ca>.

55 Gordon, above n 53.

56 Bach and Kerzner, above n 39, 79.

support networks. On the other hand, many people retain strong family relationships and social networks. These relationships may benefit from resources to prevent informal substituted decision-making and to encourage practices that strengthen the agency of the relevant person. (I will discuss such practices in Chapter 6, including Open Dialogue and intentional peer support practices.)[57] Finally, administrative support may assist people with matters ranging from completing forms and paying bills to managing complex personal budgets.

Dianne Chartres and John Brayley reiterate the importance of the supports listed above, adding that a 'systemic approach to support is required given the longstanding disadvantage people with disabilities face in having their right to legal capacity recognized, protected and promoted'.[58] These include assisting third parties to understand the relevant individuals and how they can meet their duty to provide accessibility and reasonable accommodation.[59] As part of this 'systemic approach to support' Chartres and Brayley also recommend the development of practice guidelines which are readily accessible to all parties.[60] They also suggest a move towards community support systems that provide individualised, flexible and responsive disability-related supports.[61] This would include practical assistance for people with disability, their families and supporters to make supported decision-making agreements, including a register of such agreements.[62]

The supports listed above are just some examples of the forms of support that might fall under the broad term 'support to exercise legal capacity'.

Finally, it is self-evident that there will be some persons for whom no amount of support can evince their directly expressed wishes. As previously noted, the CRPD Committee directs that in such cases decisions should be made about a person based on the 'best interpretation' of his or her will and preferences, and that this standard falls *within* the scope of 'support to exercise legal capacity'. This 'best interpretation' standard is defined by the CRPD Committee in the following terms:

57 See Chapter 6, Section C(2).

58 D Chartres and J Brayley, 'Office of the Public Advocate South Australia: Submission to the Productivity Commission Inquiry into Disability Care and Support' (submission) Office of the Public Advocate (SA) (2010) 27 <www.pc.gov.au>.

59 Chartres and Brayley emphasise that such efforts are 'also likely to take time – to communicate, to understand and to meet', so regular meetings may be required. Ibid. 28.

60 Ibid.

61 Ibid.

62 Ibid.

> Where, after significant efforts have been made, it is not practicable to determine the will and preferences of an individual, the 'best interpretation of will and preferences' must replace the 'best interests' determinations. This respects the rights, will and preferences of the individual, in accordance with article 12, paragraph 4. The 'best interests' principle is not a safeguard which complies with article 12 in relation to adults. The 'will and preferences' paradigm must replace the 'best interests' paradigm to ensure that persons with disabilities enjoy the right to legal capacity on an equal basis with others.[63]

I will discuss this proposed standard in Chapter 7, focusing on critiques and possible pitfalls of the 'will, preference and rights' standards, and exploring ways to address the concerns raised.[64] For the purposes of this section, it is important to emphasise that support to exercise legal capacity goes *beyond* the narrow scope of 'decision-making', to include a wide range of measures aimed at securing equal recognition before the law – an aim inevitably entwined with the many human rights elucidated in the CRPD.

2 *Substituted Decision-Making*

According to the CRPD Committee, support to exercise legal capacity is meant to replace 'substituted decision-making' in law, policy and practice. Some States Parties to the CRPD, and other commentators, have contested the view that Article 12 prohibits substituted decision-making, concluding instead that Article 12 (4) implies an endorsement of substituted decision-making in certain circumstances, subject to the safeguards it sets out.[65] Others, including the CRPD Committee, propose that these terms have simply been retained from the 'old paradigm'.[66] Although the terms may echo provisions for safeguarding substituted decision-making, the safeguards described in Article 12 (4) refer only to state interventions to *support* the exercise of legal capacity.[67]

63 Committee on the Rights of Persons with Disabilities, above n 26, 5 [21].

64 See Chapter 7, Section B.

65 See A Ward, 'Adults with Incapacity: Freedom and Liberty, Rights and Status: Part 1' (2011) 5 *Scots Law Times* 21; CRPD: Reservations and Declarations (Canada), (Australia) UNHCR 2008 <treaties.un.org>. The text of Article 12 (4) and (5) does not explicitly prohibit substituted decision-making, and there is language that could even be used to justify substituted decision-making. Indeed, Article 12 (4) includes terminology that appears in various existing adult capacity laws which establish safeguards for substituted decision-making arrangements. However, this is rejected by the CRPD Committee, as I will discuss shortly.

66 Committee on the Rights of Persons with Disabilities, above n 26, para 20. See also A Dhanda, 'Legal Capacity in the Disability Rights Convention: Stranglehold of the Past or Lodestar for the Future?' (2007) 34 *Syracuse Journal of International Law and Commerce* 429, 450.

67 Committee on the Rights of Persons with Disabilities, above n 26, 5 [20].

The General Comment states that support to exercise legal capacity 'must respect the rights, will and preferences of persons with disabilities and should never amount to substitute decision-making'.[68]

The term 'substitute decision-making' is defined by the CRPD Committee with reference to 'certain common characteristics' of systems in which:

> (i) legal capacity is removed from a person, even if this is just in respect of a single decision; (ii) a substitute decision-maker can be appointed by someone other than the person concerned, and this can be done against his or her will or (iii) any decision made by a substitute decision-maker is based on what is believed to be in the objective 'best interests' of the person concerned, as opposed to being based on the person's own will and preferences.[69]

This definition seemingly encompasses both formal and informal encounters, include the type of informal substituted decision-making that occurs in families and elsewhere, such as in unregulated encounters with service providers. As the South Australian Office of the Public Advocate noted in its final review, '[w]hile formal substitute decision-making is clearly recognisable (for example, a guardianship order), more commonly, substitute decision making can be "informal" when decisions are made for a person by family, friends or professionals'.[70] Low expectations may be held by some parents of adult children with psychosocial disability who may make regular, informal substituted-decisions on their behalf, including in relation to housing, healthcare, finances and lifestyle.

3 *Replacing 'Best Interests' with 'Will, Preference and Rights'*

'Best interests' standards are applied under mental health legislation where the relevant person appears to pose or be subject to an unacceptable level of risk. The standard also seems pervasive in clinical and community mental health policy and practice, and in public attitudes to what is required during dilemmas raised by profound distress or mental health crises. Yet, despite its widespread use in law in particular, according to Mary Donnelly the 'best interests' standard has received little detailed analysis in scholarship.[71]

Despite this gap, a number of prominent critiques have emerged, and the standard clearly contradicts the 'rights, will and preference' approach

68 Ibid.

69 Ibid. para 23.

70 South Australian Office of the Public Advocate, 'Promoting Rights and Interests: Office of the Public Advocate Annual Report 2011–2012' (2013).

71 M Donnelly, 'Best Interests, Patient Participation and the Mental Capacity Act 2005' (2009) 17(1) *Medical Law Review* 1.

advanced in Article 12. Robert Gordon has argued that the right to assume moral risks is an essential component of decision-making, and is crucial to the expression of personhood.[72] The 'best interests' approach, often leads to denial of this so-called 'dignity of risk' for persons with disabilities.[73] To this end, CRPD negotiators sought to shift the state's protective impulse away from policing the actions of the individual purportedly at risk (for example, by restricting his or her power to choose) and towards ensuring adequate information and assistance, and striving for an environment (pursuant to Article 16 of the CRPD) that is free from abuse, exploitation and neglect (by policing others who may abuse, exploit or neglect).[74] Critics could reasonably point out that some types of risk, whether during mental health crises or otherwise, carry no dignity whatsoever. I will return to this challenging issue in Chapter 7 when considering major critiques of the CRPD support framework.

Graeme Laurie and Ken Mason summarise a major concern with the 'best interests' standard, arguing that the 'essentially paternalistic [standard is] inappropriate when applied to adults'.[75] Courts have criticised the concept for being vague and seemingly relying on an outcome based on the values of the person applying the test.[76] The Victorian Law Reform Commission endorsed the view of the Victorian Public Advocate, who noted that the term 'has come to constitute somewhat of a euphemism for overriding free will': 'In common usage, 'best interests' has come to be associated negatively with paternalism, which itself is perceived negatively as being antithetical to individual rights. Whilst this may be a misinterpretation of the Act, it creates a problem in community understanding and acceptance of the legislation'.[77]

In a similar vein, Donnelly argues that policymakers, professionals and laypeople often regard the standard as though it is applied based on the good will of the decision-maker, a good will that is both ill-defined and open to abuse[78] (which has been the case in the past). Ian Kennedy, writing in the context of

72 Gordon, above n 53.

73 The term 'dignity of risk' has been defined by Hommel as the placement 'of greater value on respecting the individual's right to decide – even when a person's choices may seem foolish to others – than on protecting the "best interests" of the individual'. Ibid. n15.

74 See Chapter 2.

75 GM Laurie and JK Mason, 'Negative Treatment of Vulnerable Patients: Euthanasia by Any Other Name' (2000) 3 *The Juridical Review* 176.

76 *Department of Health and Community Services (NT) v JWB* (Marion's case) (1992) 175 CLR 218, 2770–71 (Brennan J) [14].

77 The public advocate is a statutorily appointed advocate for Victorians with disabilities.

78 M Donnelly, 'Decision-making for Mentally Incompetent People: The Empty Formula of Best Interests?' (2001) 20(1) *Medicine and Law* 405.

family law, offered the following critique of the 'best interests' standard, even in the context of children:

> To decide any case by reference to the formula of the best interests of the child must be suspect … The best interests formula may be beloved of family lawyers but a moment's reflection will indicate that although it is said to be a test, indeed the legal test for deciding matters relating to children, it is not really a test at all. Instead, it is a somewhat crude conclusion of social policy. It allows lawyers and courts to persuade themselves and others that theirs is a principled approach to law. Meanwhile, they engage in what to others is clearly a form of 'ad hocery'. The best interests approach of family law allows the courts to atomise the law, to claim that each case depends on its own facts. The court can then respond intuitively to each case while seeking to legitimate its conclusion by asserting that it is derived from the general principle contained in the best interests formula. In fact, of course, there is no general principle other than the empty rhetoric of best interests; or rather, there is some principle (or principles) but the court is not telling. Obviously the court must be following some principles, otherwise a toss of a coin could decide cases. But these principles, which serve as pointers to what amounts to the best interests, are not articulated by the court. Only the conclusion is set out. The opportunity for reasoned analysis and scrutiny is lost.[79]

Some reformers have sought to transform the 'best interests' standard to discard its negative connotations. For example, considerable work has been undertaken to clarify and regulate the 'best interests' standard under the Mental Capacity Act 2005 (England and Wales).[80] Other law reform efforts have sought to discard it altogether. The Australian Law Reform Commission, with reference to the CRPD and the General Comment in particular, recommended replacing the 'best interests' standard with the Article 12(4) standard of adhering to the 'rights, will and preference' of the individual concerned.[81] The application of this standard in practice remains largely theoretical, and it is unclear whether courts and others would apply it in a way that is substantially different to existing formulations of 'best interests' standards. Nevertheless, this aspect of the CRPD support framework provides an important point of

[79] I Kennedy, 'Patients, Doctors and Human Rights', in R Blackburn and J Taylor (eds), *Human Rights for the 1990s: Legal, Political and Ethical Issues* (Mansell, 1991) 81, 90–1.

[80] See Department of Constitutional Affairs, 'Mental Capacity Act: Code of Practice', the Stationary Office, 2005, 33–44; M Donnelly, 'Best Interests, Patient Participation and the Mental Capacity Act 2005' (2009) 17(1) *Medical Law Review* 1, 11. For criticisms of how the 'best interest' provisions are working in practice, see House of Lords, 'Select Committee on the Mental Capacity Act 2005 Report of Session 2013–14 Mental Capacity Act 2005: post-legislative scrutiny', HL Paper 139, the Stationery Office Limited, 13 March 2014, paras 90–101.

[81] Australian Law Reform Commission, Equality, Capacity and Disability in Commonwealth Laws (2014) rec 3–1.

conceptual departure – at least at first glance – wherein 'will and preference' is elevated higher than in typical 'best interests' formulations. Using this standard, ambiguities about a person's will and preference could be mediated with reference to his or her rights. Although the 'hard cases' are unlikely to be any less fraught – for example, how would the law uphold the will, preference and rights of a person who expresses the will to live but a preference not to eat food? – the use of 'will, preference and rights' may narrow the focus to a more explicit consideration of the legal and moral issues at stake.[82]

4 *Supported Decision-Making*

'Supported decision-making' is the broad alternative to substituted decision-making posed by the CRPD Committee and others.[83] The OHCHR defines supported decision-making as simply 'the process whereby a person with a disability is enabled to make and communicate decisions with respect to personal or legal matters'.[84] The OHCHR, in its *Handbook for Parliamentarians on the Convention on the Rights of Persons with Disabilities*, elaborates in the following terms:

> With supported decision-making, the presumption is always in favour of the person with a disability who will be affected by the decision. The individual is the decision maker; the support person(s) explain(s) the issues, when necessary, and interpret(s) the signs and preferences of the individual. Even when an individual with a disability requires total support, the support person(s) should enable the individual to exercise his/her legal capacity to the greatest extent possible, according to the wishes of the individual.[85]

Soumitra Pathare and Laura Shields define supported decision-making for the mental health context thus:

> Supported decision-making … can consist of organisations, networks, provisions or agreements with the aim of supporting and assisting an individual

[82] See Chapter 7.

[83] UN Office of the High Commissioner for Human Rights, 'Tenth Session Agenda item 2, Annual Report of the United Nations High Commissioner for Human Rights and Reports of the Office of the High Commissioner and the Secretary-General: Thematic Study by the Office of the United Nations High Commissioner for Human Rights on Enhancing Awareness and Understanding of the Convention on the Rights of Persons with Disabilities', UN Doc A/HRC/10/48, 26 January 2009.

[84] Committee on the Rights of Persons with Disabilities, above n 26; UN Office of the High Commissioner for Human Rights, above n 83.

[85] UN Office of the High Commissioner for Human Rights, 'Chapter Six: From Provisions to Practice: Implementing the Convention, Legal Capacity and Supported Decision-Making' in *United Nations Handbook for Parliamentarians on the Convention on the Rights of Persons with Disabilities* (Geneva, 2007) 89 <www.un.org>.

> with a mental illness to make and communicate decisions. In supported decision-making, the individual is always the primary decision maker, but it is acknowledged that autonomy can be communicated in a number of ways, thus provision of support in different forms and intervals can assist in the expression of autonomous decisions.[86]

The OHCHR acknowledges the wide range of needs of persons with disabilities to which supported decision-making must respond: 'Supported decision-making can take many forms. Those assisting a person may communicate the individual's intentions to others or help him/her understand the choices at hand. They may help others to realize that a person with significant disabilities is also a person with a history, interests and aims in life, and is someone capable of exercising his/her capacity'.[87] It is important to reiterate the implicit point of the General Comment that 'supported decision-making' refers to *one type* of support to exercise legal capacity. Support to exercise legal capacity is broader. A narrow focus on decision-making and directly expressed wishes can easily steer discussions back to the libertarian/paternalist impasse associated with mental health law. Such a narrow focus can easily ignore the experience of persons in profound distress or mental health crises whose will and preferences are unclear or unknown. For the purposes of this section, containing the definition of supported decision-making to 'the process whereby a person with a disability is enabled to make and communicate decisions with respect to personal or legal matters' prevents the concept from becoming too broad, and thus of limited practical value.

Some commentators have used 'supported decision-making' to refer to statutory arrangements alone.[88] An example of such a formal arrangement can be found in British Columbia's Representation Agreement Act 1986, which provides informal supporters (referred to as 'associates') with specific legal powers.[89] Others use the term 'supported decision-making' to refer to both formal and informal support arrangements for decision-making (to which I will subscribe here).[90] For example, the South Australian Office of the Public Advocate completed a small-scale trial of 'non-statutory supported decision-making' for people with intellectual and cognitive disabilities, in order to assist

86 S Pathare and LS Shields, 'Supported Decision-making for Persons with Mental Illness: A Review' (2012) 34(2) *Public Health Reviews* 1, 4.

87 UN Office of the High Commissioner for Human Rights, above n 85, 89.

88 Bach and Kerzner, above n 39, 84.

89 Representation Agreement Act BC 1996 (Canada) c 405.

90 M Wallace, 'Evaluation of the Supported Decision Making Project Office of the Public Advocate' (Muirgen Nominees, 2012) 4 <www.opa.sa.gov.au>.

them with avoiding statutory *substituted* decision-making arrangements for which they were otherwise eligible.[91]

Amita Dhanda has argued that ideas like 'supported decision-making' address the paradox inherent in substituted decision-making laws, such as mental health legislation and adult (in)capacity laws, a paradox that lies between their purported 'ends' (to protect the rights of the individual and to preserve the legal notion of autonomy) and the 'means' through which these are notionally achieved (restricting rights by appointing substitutes).[92] Terry Carney and David Tait observe that mental (in)capacity laws often draw on the language of personal rights and the promotion of autonomy, independence and social inclusion, even as their principal function is 'to strip citizens of rights, entrust proxies with the exercise of legal decision-making, and sometimes authorise incarceration through physical and chemical means'[93] – a description that could well describe mental health law. However, Carney takes issue with the view that supported decision-making is a panacea for this paradox, whether in mental capacity or mental health law,[94] as I shall discuss in Chapter 7.

Michelle Browning and colleagues argue that 'decision-making *assistance*' provides a further conceptual distinction to supported decision-making, where decision-making assistance refers to a range of measures aimed at strengthening self-determination without directly assisting a person to exercise legal capacity.[95] 'Decision-making assistance' of this kind could include, for example, providing plain-language information, allowing more time in clincal meetings to explain matters or providing self-advocacy training to individuals.[96] Such efforts may *indirectly* influence the exercise of legal capacity, for example by giving people the confidence and skills to engage in legal transactions or the knowledge to do so independently. This form of assistance could also be understood with reference to the CRPD, as measures for ensuring accessibility and providing reasonable accommodation.[97] According to the CRPD Committee:

> The right to reasonable accommodation in the exercise of legal capacity is separate from, and complementary to, the right to support in the exercise of

91 Ibid. 4.

92 See Dhanda, above n 66.

93 T Carney and D Tait, *The Adult Guardianship Experiment: Tribunals and Popular Justice* (Federation Press, 1997) 47.

94 See T Carney, 'Guardianship, Citizenship, and Theorizing Substitute-Decision-Making Law' in I Doron and A Soden (eds), *Beyond Elder Law: New Directions in Law and Ageing* (Springer, 2012).

95 Browning, Bigby and Douglas, above n 21.

96 Ibid.

97 CRPD arts 5, 9.

> legal capacity. States parties are required to make any necessary modifications or adjustments … [which] may include, but are not limited to, access to essential buildings such as courts, banks, social benefit offices and voting venues; accessible information regarding decisions which have legal effect; and personal assistance.[98]

Distinguishing between obligations to make systems accessible, and those directed to specific supports for individuals, or between statutory and non-statutory schemes for supporting decision-making, will be useful when converting the generalities of the CRPD into specific forms of policy, practice and other forms of social organisation.

5 *Supported Decision-Making Regime*

General Comment No 1 uses the term 'supported decision-making regime' as a short-hand designation to describe an overarching framework for achieving equal recognition before the law across domestic legislation, policy and practice.[99] Elements of the regime include giving 'primacy to a person's will and preferences and respect[ing] human rights norms'; and providing 'protection for all rights', including 'those related to autonomy (right to legal capacity, right to equal recognition before the law, right to choose where to live, etc.) and rights related to freedom from abuse and ill-treatment (right to life, right to physical integrity, etc.)'.[100] Systems of supported decision-making 'should not overregulate the lives of persons with disabilities'; should be 'available to all', even those with complex communication and intensive support needs; and should be 'based on the will and preference of the person, not on what is perceived as being in his or her objective best interests'.[101] The regime should include readily available and accessible supports, including those facilitating support for 'people who are isolated and may not have access to naturally occurring supports in the community', as well as upholding the right to refuse such supports.[102]

Based on this definition, a supported decision-making regime includes *supported decision-making*, reasonable accommodations and accessibility measures, as well as broader *support to exercise legal capacity* across a range of areas in law, policy and practice.

98 Committee on the Rights of Persons with Disabilities, above n 26, 8–9 [34].
99 Ibid., 6–7 [29].
100 Ibid.
101 Ibid. 7 [29](d).
102 Ibid.

The term 'supported decision-making regime' arguably causes confusion by giving the impression that the CRPD Committee interprets Article 12 to *preclude* some decisions being 'made for' a person. Instead, the CRPD Committee invites States Parties to rethink how decisions are 'made for' people in exceptional circumstances, such as when a person's will and preferences are unclear or unknown,[103] as previously noted. (To avoid such confusion, I use the term 'CRPD support framework' rather than supported decision-making regime to describe this over-arching regime advanced by the CRPD, particularly in the mental health context.)

6 *Interdependence and Relational Autonomy*

The CRPD support framework places greater emphasis on the role of interdependence in autonomy compared with mental health legislation and other substituted decision-making laws. The Canadian Association for Community Living commented that 'supported decision-making gives legal recognition to a process for self-determination that is communal and interdependent'.[104] Robert Gordon identifies the implications of this recognition in law and policy when he writes: '[s]ome people require more in the way of support and assistance than others, and with respect to more areas of decision-making than others; it is a matter of degree, rather than a case of absolutes'.[105]

This emphasis challenges the traditional liberal view of decision-making where individuals are seen to make judgements independently, in isolation, as free and liberal subjects.[106] This standpoint fails to recognise that, in fact, individuals rely to a greater or lesser extent on relations with others – from informal supporters such as family members and friends to experts such as accountants and teachers.[107] John Christman writes that the idea of relational autonomy has 'importantly shifted attention concerning autonomy to the social and interpersonal dynamics that shape its enjoyment, connecting ideas about autonomy with broader issues of social justice, recognition, and social practices'.[108] From

[103] Ibid. 5 [21].

[104] Canadian Association of Community Living, 'Report of the C.A.C.L. Task Force on Alternatives to Guardianship' (1992) <www.worldenable.net>.

[105] Ibid. 65.

[106] An oft-cited definition of the 'understand and appreciate' approach comes from Beauchamp and Childress, who argue that competent decision-making occurs when an individual has the capacity to understand relevant information, and can cast judgement on the information according to his or her values, envisage an outcome and freely communicate her or his ultimate wishes. See TL Beauchamp and JF Childress, *Principles of Biomedical Ethics* (Oxford University Press, 4th ed, 1994) 135.

[107] Gordon, above n 53, 61.

[108] J Christman, 'Autonomy in Moral and Political Philosophy' in EN Zalta (ed), *The Stanford Encyclopaedia of Philosophy* (Spring 2011 ed) <www.plato.stanford.edu>.

a disability rights perspective, the 'broader issues' to which Christman refers could include enjoying the right to independent living and being included in the community (Article 19), or the importance of safe and accessible housing in providing stronger grounds to live a self-directed life (Article 28). In the mental health context, reformers might consider the interpersonal dynamics that shape the enjoyment of autonomy in mental health services, for example by seeking to address power imbalances between staff members and service users.

The notion of interdependence recognises the vital role that community and family have in decision-making in many cultures. This is the case in a number of indigenous cultures, for example. According to Ian Anderson, 'many, if not all' Indigenous Australian commentators reject the philosophical proposition of an idealised rational subject at the heart of self-determination according to liberalism[109] – an observation that is particularly relevant to settler democracies such as Canada, Australia and New Zealand. Instead, Anderson writes, indigenous cultures tend to advance 'constructions of personhood that emphasise relationality – wherein individual autonomy lies in contingent balance with reciprocal relations to kin, country or cosmology'.[110] Some Māori cultures share a similar worldview, as expressed in 'tikanga Māori' (which roughly refers to 'Māori customary values and practices'), which have been recognised in the legislation and evolving common law of New Zealand.[111] Alison Douglass has written that '[t]he positive obligation in the CRPD to recognise supportive relationships has synergies with tikanga Māori, where values of individual autonomy and collective decision-making work alongside each other'.[112] Relational cultural priorities in accord with tikanga Māori have informed some New Zealand mental health services, particularly with respect to identifying and working with persons in their social network.[113] Nick Drury and Te Ata Munro have argued for the need to 'engag[e] more frequently with the social network' as a means to realise a cultural priority of Māori, whose sense of respect 'would make it sacrilegious to overpower the Other in most situations'.[114] In considering briefly how indigenous cultures may advance a view of relational autonomy, it is important to acknowledge Anderson's

109 I Anderson, 'Indigenous Australia and Health Rights' (2008) 15(5) *Journal of Law and Medicine* 760.

110 Ibid.

111 Te Ture Whenua Maori Act 1993 (New Zealand) s 3/93.

112 A Douglass, 'Mental Capacity: Updating New Zealand's Law and Practice' (Report for the New Zealand Law Foundation, Dunedin, July 2016) xii <www.aspenltd.co.nz/mc/assets/Full_Report.pdf>.

113 N Drury and TA Munro, 'Crisis Engagement in Mental Health: A New Zealand Maori Contribution' (2008) 17(5) *International Journal of Mental Health Nursing* 317.

114 Ibid.

warning that 'indigenous cultures are diverse and not a simple inverse of "Western" cultural values',[115] a cautionary note also sounded by Douglass.[116]

Even within 'Western' moral philosophy, the notion of relational autonomy has a strong presence, particularly in theories of communitarianism.[117] Marilyn Friedman argues that 'although the language of autonomy in popular culture might still suggest asocial atomistic images of the self-made man, academic philosophers now seldom share this view'.[118] Further, 'many contemporary philosophers of autonomy have ... tended to gravitate toward relational or intersubjective accounts of autonomy'.[119] This does not necessarily mean that relational autonomy is 'deeply integrated into popular culture, political theory, or law', as Jennifer Nedelsky points out.[120] Yet the CRPD support framework appears to be an important step towards such integration, and seems particularly well suited to the mental health context. Further, a number of commentators have explored the practical implications of applying such a model in law, policy and practice in the mental health context, including the potential drawbacks that result,[121] which I will consider in Chapters 6 and 7.

7 *'Disability-Neutral' Criteria for Intervention*

The CRPD expressly prohibits disability-based discrimination (Articles 2 and 5), which, in relation to Article 12, means legal capacity cannot be restricted based on disability. Arlene Kanter uses the term 'disability-neutral' to refer to that which avoids discriminating on the basis of disability.[122] 'Disability-neutral' grounds for determining the 'limits' of legal capacity exist in law, including restricting legal capacity; examples include when a person claims bankruptcy (which may restrict him or her from serving as a board director) or receives a criminal conviction (which can lead to restrictions on the right to vote). As long as the denial occurs on the same basis for all persons, and not in

[115] Anderson, above n 109.

[116] Douglass, above n 112, 61 [2.67].

[117] Christman, above n 108.

[118] M Friedman, *Autonomy, Gender, Politics* (Oxford University Press, 2003) 103.

[119] Ibid. 104.

[120] J Nedelsky, *Law's Relations: A Relational Theory of Self, Autonomy, and Law* (Oxford University Press, 2011). As Lucy Series has argued, the concept of 'functional mental capacity' – which is distilled from a view of legal personality and legal capacity that emphasises rationality and the 'responsible subject' – is used in an enormous range of laws. L Series, 'Relationships, Autonomy and Legal Capacity: Mental Capacity and Support Paradigms' (2015) 40 *International Journal of Law and Psychiatry* 80.

[121] Series, above n 120; Richardson, above n 25.

[122] AS Kanter, *The Development of Disability Rights Under International Law: From Charity to Human Rights* (Routledge, 2014) 151.

relation to a personal trait such as disability, then the standard remains non-discriminatory. Seeking disability-neutral grounds for setting the limits of legal capacity may then become important in in creating a CRPD support framework.

Indirect discrimination must also be avoided, so that apparently neutral grounds for limiting legal capacity do not disproportionately affect disabled people. Article 2 clearly defines disability-based discrimination as 'any distinction, exclusion or restriction on the basis of disability which has the purpose *or effect* of impairing or nullifying the recognition, enjoyment or exercise, on an equal basis with others, of all human rights and fundamental freedoms'.[123] This could pose issues where a restriction on the voting rights of convicted felons, for example, might disproportionately affect persons with disabilities if they are over-represented in the criminal justice system.

Some commentators have argued that replacing the 'diagnostic threshold' of mental health law with generic mental capacity assessments – that is, replacing a criterion that a person has a psychiatric diagnosis with the requirement that the person lacks mental capacity – satisfies the quest for non-discrimination. This view has been rejected most notably by the CRPD Committee, which views such a move as doing little to stem indirect discrimination, including against people with intellectual and cognitive disabilities.[124] Significant questions then arise about ways to intervene and assist people in certain emergency crises (for example, where an adult is walking toward a busy highway with no apparent understanding of the danger involved, or a person is about to jump from a building because they wrongly believe doing so will save the world). In such cases, coercive elements are likely to be used, and indeed may be expected by a broader public and required by law, which will result in what appears to be a clear restriction of legal capacity. I will investigate this issue of establishing the limits of legal capacity in ways that are disability-neutral in subsequent chapters.

8 *Safeguarding*

The support framework of the CRPD appears to require two broad categories of safeguarding. The first involves safeguards to uphold the person's self-determination, by preventing substituted decision-making. The second is to safeguard against abuse, exploitation and neglect perpetrated by others. These categories can be conflated under current law, such that the rights of the safeguarded person are restricted in order to prevent harm caused by *others*. An

[123] CRPD art 2 (emphasis added).

[124] Committee on the Rights of Persons with Disabilities, above n 26, 4 [15].

example of this conflation was raised in interviews with psychiatrists concerning their views of 'supported decision-making' in Victoria, Australia.[125] One interviewee described using the threat of guardianship to address a potentially abusive relationship, whereby a mother of a young adult man was withholding her son's disability support pension money and forbidding him from taking prescribed medication, which he wished to take:

> When she said 'I won't let him have the antipsychotic medication'. I said, 'I will pursue an administration order application if you don't, with a guardianship application as well,' because he wasn't getting his basic healthcare needs met and at that point she decided she'd let him be treated [...] He was having time where he was hungry because she wouldn't feed him and the like ... [S]he decided financially, that I don't want them putting in an administration order. And the decision I've made as his consultant – because he's still to some degree dependent on her in different ways – is that we're going to work over time to increase his independence without going in with an admin order. So you'd still have those resorts if you believed that someone was being exploited or if their decisions and their relationships were artificially influenced by them ... there'd still be protective measures you could take to make sure that someone didn't have undue influence – I guess, I'd be concerned about that in the case of someone who is vulnerable.[126]

The interviewee used the threat of a guardianship and administration order ostensibly to defend the young man from abusive, informal substituted decision-making. It seems reasonable to assume that this is not an isolated incident and that formal substituted decision-making occurs for a significant number of people as an effort to address abuse and exploitation in the private sphere. Hence, it is important to decouple safeguards to uphold support to exercise legal capacity from those to prevent abuse and exploitation, particularly given the common concern that supported decision-making practices increase the potential for manipulation by so-called supporters.[127]

Within the rights articulated in the CRPD, this distinction occurs along the lines of Articles 12 and 16. Of the safeguards set out in Article 12 (4), the CRPD Committee commented that 'Article 12, paragraph 4, must be read in conjunction with the rest of article 12 and the whole Convention. It requires States parties to create appropriate and effective safeguards for the exercise of legal capacity. *The primary purpose of these safeguards must be to ensure the*

[125] P Gooding, 'Psychiatrists' Perceptions of Supported Decision-Making: A Victorian Empirical Study' (2014) 22(5) *Psychiatry, Psychology and Law* 701.
[126] Ibid. 711.
[127] I will engage directly with this concern in Chapter 7, Section B(2).

respect of the person's rights, will and preferences'.[128] Proposals for such safeguards include increased training for people in support roles, statutory duties placed on formal supporters and the appointment of 'monitors' or even those in a coaching and mentoring role to observe support relationships and prevent incursions on a person's will, preference and rights.[129]

In contrast, Article 16 guides the establishment of safeguards to achieve freedom from exploitation, violence and abuse, whether by support persons or anyone else. Article 16(5) directs that 'States Parties shall put in place effective legislation and policies, including women- and children-focused legislation and policies, to ensure that instances of exploitation, violence and abuse against persons with disabilities are identified, investigated and, where appropriate, prosecuted'.[130] Proposals to apply such safeguards include expanding criminal powers to prosecute perpetrators,[131] broadening the investigative role and civil powers of statutory advocacy bodies,[132] providing information and education to identify and report such abuse,[133] and creating a monitoring role for independent authorities over programs, services and community resources.[134] The authors of the South Australian Office of the Public Advocate supported decision-making pilot program explicitly refer to Article 16 as the basis upon which they recommend stronger domestic adult protection laws, especially for the elderly, by policing those who may perpetrate abuse or discrimination.[135] Brayley argued that such laws could complement efforts to strengthen the self-determination of persons with cognitive disabilities by disentangling abuse-prevention measures from decision-making support measures.[136] Similarly, the Victorian Law Reform Commission ('VLRC') promoted a transition to a 'supported decision-making approach' to adult guardianship law, which would ideally include the introduction of 'a new public wrong of abusing, neglecting or exploiting a person with impaired decision-making ability … enforceable

128 Committee on the Rights of Persons with Disabilities, above n 26, 5 [20] (emphasis added).

129 For example, a 'monitor' was appointed in the South Australian Office of the Public Advocate supported decision-making trial to facilitate the relationship between decision-maker and supporter. See Chartres and Brayley, above n 58, 48.

130 CRPD art 16(5).

131 Victorian Law Reform Commission, *Guardianship: Final Report 24* (2012) 460, rec 336 <www.lawreform.vic.gov.au>.

132 Ibid. 460, rec 337.

133 CRPD art 16(2).

134 Ibid., art 16(3).

135 J Brayley, *Supported Decision Making: A Case for Change* (Presentation to the Supported Decision Making Forum, Queensland Advocacy Inc and the Queensland University of Technology Health Law Research Centre, Brisbane, June 2013) 9–10 <www.qai.org.au>.

136 Ibid.

by civil penalty'.[137] The proposed law would function to 'complement existing criminal laws … [to] be used where criminal proceedings would be unlikely to succeed or might not be appropriate'.[138] The VLRC also recommended broadening the role and powers of statutory advocacy bodies to investigate alleged instances of exploitation, abuse and neglect.[139] Law reformers in the mental health context could make similar recommendations.

The notion of 'informal safeguards' is also relevant, particularly for socially isolated people. Informal safeguards could include relationships with family, friends, personal networks and members of the wider community. Such 'natural' safeguards can be seen as one aspect of the taken-for-granted features of self-determination enjoyed by most (for example, friends warning each other about exploitative or risky financial decisions, or neighbours 'looking out' for older people vulnerable to accidents). The General Comment directs states to 'facilitate the creation of support and particularly for people who are isolated and may not have access to naturally occurring support in the community'.[140] Recommendations include creating 'mechanisms for third parties to verify the identity of a support person and … to challenge the action of a support person if they believe [he or she] is not acting in accordance with the will and preferences of the person concerned'.[141]

Relationships and connections may need to be intentionally developed. Intentional informal safeguards are being built into some policy and programming, particularly following the push towards 'personalised' and 'self-directed' support in mental health services in recent years.[142] For example, the Western Australian Mental Health Commission has promoted informal safeguards, which it defines as 'individualised precautions and safety measures that are put in place to protect individuals from exploitation, and harm, and provide protection against foreseeable unintended events, while at the same time enabling the person to make choices, take considered risks and live a life that reflects [his or her] personal preferences'.[143] These broader aims must be considered when imagining safeguards under a CRPD support framework with reference to other rights, such as the right to live independently

[137] Victorian Law Reform Commission, *Guardianship: Final Report 24* (2012) xxix <www.lawreform.vic.gov.au>.
[138] Ibid.
[139] Ibid. 456.
[140] Committee on the Rights of Persons with Disabilities, above n 26, 5 [29(d)].
[141] Ibid.
[142] See, e.g., Government of Western Australia, Mental Health Commission, 'Draft Safeguards Framework for Individualised Support and Funding', May 2013, 7 <www.mentalhealth.wa.gov.au>.
[143] Ibid.

and participate in community (Article 19) and to receive an 'adequate standard of living and social protection' (Article 28). Any law or policy must be viewed in its social context, including formal and informal governance.[144] Developing family-based supports will be important in this respect, including for those who are not isolated but whose family circumstances might benefit from mentoring, guidance and other forms of support. Although the development of intentional informal safeguards and accountability mechanisms remains a 'work in progress',[145] such measures are important, given that the autonomy and social inclusion of people with disabilities have been historically restricted by so-called safeguards and protective measures. (I will discuss practical examples of intentionally developed informal safeguards in a mental health context in Chapter 6.)[146]

Tensions will arise in some circumstances between the right to '*enjoy* legal capacity on an equal basis with others' (Article 12) and the right to be free from exploitation, abuse and neglect (Article 16). Consider a person in an abusive relationship whose enjoyment of legal agency might be restricted (for example, when he is bullied into not having a personal bank account) but whose preference is to stay in that relationship. Some psychoses and other mental health crises might also be said to intrude upon the *enjoyment* of legal capacity to the extent that a person becomes 'uncommunicative and unmoving', deeply confused or unclear as to his or her will and preferences.

Setting aside for a moment the unique issues concerning mental health, it is important to note that these tensions relate to intractable ambiguities about the content of human freedom. Long-standing debates about liberalism have considered these tensions. For example, John Rawls criticised John Stuart Mill for not allowing people to choose *not* to endorse autonomy and freedom as central tenets of a good life.[147] Those who identified with an authoritarian religion, for example, would not identify autonomy as desirable – Mill's approach was to denigrate those people.[148] Rawls argued that Mill's view failed to show respect for a reasonable pluralism of different comprehensions of the good life. Martha Nussbaum has echoed Rawls's call to respect pluralism, arguing that '[w]e should respect people who prefer a life within an authoritarian religion (or personal relationship), so long as certain

[144] T Carney and F Beaupert, 'Public and Private Bricolage – Challenges Balancing Law, Services and Civil Society in Advancing CRPD Supported Decision-Making' 2013 36(1) *UNSW Law Journal* 175, 177.
[145] Ibid. 179.
[146] See Chapter 6, Section C(3).
[147] J Rawls, *Political Liberalism* (Columbia University Press, 1993) 199.
[148] See JS Mill, *On Liberty and Other Essays* (Oxford University Press, 2008) ch 3.

basic opportunities and exit options are firmly guaranteed'.[149] This latter view has been characterised as that of a 'political' liberal, in contrast to the Millean view, which has been characterised as the 'comprehensive' liberal view.[150] A political liberal view of safeguards in the mental health context, which the CRPD appears to promote, would direct attention to the different comprehensions of the good life. This would seemingly pay 'respect for difference and acceptance of persons with disabilities as part of human diversity and humanity',[151] leaving greater scope for respecting people who prefer a life with mental distress, disorder, 'madness', unusual states of consciousness and any associated risks and dangers, and resisting the urge to intervene against the person's wishes. What this means in practice is likely to differ considerably, as abstract theorising about human freedom can so easily belie the infinite variables at play in real-world situations that are bound in place and time. The question of whether to respect a hoarder's wish to live in decrepit conditions is substantively different to the decision to hold back a person who is about to jump off a building based on the belief that doing so will save the world.

Suffice to say that the CRPD support approach invites a shift towards establishing 'basic opportunities and exit options', to use Nussbaum's terms, and not applying differential standards restricting the rights of persons with disabilities. This is by no means an easy task. The challenge posed by the CRPD is for states to develop safeguards for those experiencing mental health crises, and to ensure that the boundaries of 'legal capacity' are determined and negotiated in a disability-neutral way only.

Under current substituted decision-making schemes, safeguards vary from being seen as too heavy-handed to too 'light touch',[152] and balancing autonomy rights with protection remains one of the greatest challenges facing policymakers, service providers, families and disabled people's organisations today. There is nothing to suggest that creating safeguards under a CRPD support framework will be any less challenging. The standard of adhering to the 'best interpretation of a person's will, preference and rights', to take just one example, is likely to occupy entire treatises into the future. Addressing matters of risk is likely to be equally challenging.

[149] M Nussbaum, 'Capabilities as Fundamental Entitlements: Sen and Social Justice' in E Kaufman (ed), *Capabilities and Equality: Basic Issues and Problems* (Routledge, 2006) 44, 60.

[150] Ibid.

[151] CRPD art 3(d).

[152] Ibid. xxviii, rec 70. The safeguards recommended by the VLRC, in its comprehensive review of Victorian adult guardianship law, are discussed in detail in Chapter 18 of the report. See Ibid. 405.

9 *Risk*

Phil Fennell describes risk management as the 'prime driver of social policy and the *raison d'être* of mental health legislation'.[153] He suggests that public concerns are related to 'risk to the health and safety of mentally disordered people themselves, but also risk to public safety'.[154] In contrast, the support framework would assign a relatively low priority to risk. Nevertheless, the CRPD is an enunciation of all human rights, including those associated with social protection, the right to health, freedom from abuse, exploitation and neglect, for which issues of risk are important to consider. Equally, the dominance of risk as a driver for mental health legislation, makes it unavoidable as a point of deliberation in considering the application of the CRPD to the mental health context.

a Addressing Risk to Self

A common anxiety provoked by elevating liberty rights in debates about coercive psychiatric intervention is that people with serious mental health issues will be left to 'die with their rights on', as Darold Traffert famously put it.[155] Nothing within the text of the CRPD itself, or the interpretation of the CRPD Committee, for that matter, suggests that States Parties should turn away from people in mental health crises or that duties to citizens end with a blind adherence to their expressed wishes. The numerous positive obligations in the CRPD (relating to social protection, independent living, the highest attainable physical and mental health, and so on) should dispel any such glib interpretations. Accordingly, States Parties must provide a sufficient 'protective cloak' of rights to such persons, with any intrusions upon liberty rights occurring on an equal basis with others.[156] Such rights protections have been explored throughout this chapter, and include ensuring a range of supports related to housing, health and social protection; strong provision for anti-discrimination to prevent unfair prejudicial treatment by others; strong mechanisms to address abuse, violence and exploitation by others; and non-discriminatory

[153] P Fennell, 'Institutionalising the Community: The Codification of Clinical Authority and the Limits of Rights-Based Approaches' in B McSherry and P Weller (eds), *Rethinking Rights-Based Mental Health Law* (Hart, 2010) 13, 15.

[154] Ibid.

[155] DA Treffert, 'Dying With Your Rights On' (Paper presented at the 127th Annual APA Meeting, 1974) 39.

[156] Clearly, the term 'equal basis with others' is ambiguous in regard to applying rules that mediate individual and collective concerns. I will engage criticisms of this ambiguity in Chapter 7.

grounds for emergency interventions. (I will explore the search for such non-discriminatory grounds in Chapters 5, 6 and 7.) As noted in the previous section on safeguarding, liberal democracies perennially struggle to balance the autonomy rights of the individual, with collectivist, paternalistic agendas (whether related to the wearing of seatbelts, cigarette advertising or the regulation of pharmaceutical drugs, for example). The CRPD directs that any rules to arbitrate these intractable tensions must apply to persons with disabilities 'on an equal basis with others'. As Chapter 3 highlights, current mental health legislation does not comply with this requirement because it subjects persons with mental health diagnoses to risk assessments (and subsequent restrictions) on prejudicial grounds, which seems particularly egregious given the lack of empirical evidence to support the accuracy of risk assessment tools.

The relatively low priority given to risk in the CRPD compared to current mental health law may challenge public and private institutions that maintain a strong focus on risk aversion. However, it may also be that clarifying ways in which risk can be respected will provide institutions with greater 'room to move' in providing support and assistance, while also respecting a person's sphere of freedom to pursue his or her will and preference. Mental health professionals who currently feel restricted in the range of choices they can offer people may benefit from this clarification, particularly those who (rightly or wrongly) fear liability when adverse events occur. An example of policy which aimed to 'shift … the balance away from risk-aversion towards supported decision-making' was developed by the United Kingdom, Department of Health.[157] This effort included the creation of resources 'for providers to extend choices and practical support for people who use mental health services and their carers',[158] although it is difficult to assess the effectiveness of such resources.

Many clinicians and other professionals are already likely to seek ways to respect the dignity of risk of those they support. Consider Elyn Saks's personal account:

157 See National Health Service, *Independence, Choice and Risk: A Guide to Best Practice in Supported Decision-Making* (UK Department of Health, 2007) 5. See also National Health Service, *Best Practice in Managing Risk: Principles and Evidence for Best Practice in the Assessment and Management of Risk to Self and Others in Mental Health Services* (UK Department of Health for Mental Health Services, 2007).

158 National Health Service, *Independence, Choice and Risk*, 29 [2.58]. See Care Services Improvement Partnership, 'Our Choices in Mental Health: A Framework for Improving Choice for People Who Use Mental Health Services and Their Carers', Department of Health <www.londonhp.nhs.uk>.

> In addition to frequent delusions, I experienced violent ideation. To protect myself, at one point I carried a serrated kitchen knife and a box cutter to therapy sessions – which I told my analyst about, but never brandished. Thus, setting a precedent that all my subsequent analysts adopted – being willing to sit with a certain amount of anxiety about my safety for the sake of respecting my wishes not to be hospitalized.[159]

Respecting risk also involves living with the consequences when things go wrong. Lisa Rosenbaum recounts a story by an internist at a US homelessness program who adopted a permissive approach to respecting the risky choices of people in the program compared to other professionals:

> [His] willingness to honor patients' wishes has also backfired. One woman lived on a stoop for 2½ years but wouldn't allow the outreach team to give her a sandwich or socks, screaming incessantly whenever they approached. One day she became so unmoored that the police brought her to the emergency department for psychiatric evaluation – an intervention authorized [under mental health law] … Three years later, [the internist] ran into her at a meeting of a nonprofit organization. She was a board member, all dressed up, totally transformed. 'You look fabulous,' he told her. 'And she said, "Screw you. You left me out there for all those years and didn't help me,"' [he] recalls. 'And she walked away.'[160]

Grave catastrophe was seemingly avoided in both instances noted above (regardless of whether one views the individuals' decisions as right or wrong). Countless other examples presumably show the opposite, where people have died or come to terrible harm in instances in which risk was tolerated to avoid coercive interventions. These narratives should inform the search for non-discriminatory ways of balancing individual and collectivist concerns, as should instances in which risk was negotiated 'successfully'. Rosenbaum's account highlights that although a decision to impose involuntary psychiatric intervention would have fallen foul of the CRPD Committee, the same might be said of the initial impulse to simply 'leave her be'. This is not an indictment of the individual internist; instead, it is to suggest that the service framework could well have been designed in such a way to better promote the person's agency, and secure other rights for her (such as the right to the highest attainable physical and mental health (Article 25), or the right to an adequate standard of living and social protection (Article 28), or even sufficient accessibility and

[159] E Saks, 'Mental Health Law and the Americans with Disabilities Act: One Consumer's Journey' (2016) 4(1) *Inclusion* 39, 40.

[160] L Rosenbaum, 'Liberty versus Need – Our Struggle to Care for People with Serious Mental Illness' (2016) 375(15) *New England Journal of Medicine* 1490.

reasonable accommodations to ensure that she could avail herself of existing services). In Chapter 6, I will describe programs that have sought to negotiate risk and achieve these aims by creating voluntary outreach and advocacy programs which have sought to transcend the binary between involuntary intervention on the one hand, and neglect and abandonment on the other.

b Addressing Risk to Others

The public safety prerogative of mental health law appears to stand at cross-purposes with the broad aims of the CRPD support framework. The CRPD was not conceived to perform the function of public protection, except insofar as it ensures that people with disabilities enjoy public protection rights (on an equal basis with others). This is not to suggest that the CRPD fails to account for persons with disabilities who are criminal offenders or who may be dangerous to others. Instead, it directs that any efforts to address these matters remain disability-neutral in the restrictions imposed. In the words of Article 13, States Parties must 'ensure effective access to justice for persons with disabilities on an equal basis with others, including through the provision of procedural and age-appropriate accommodations'.[161] In contrast, the unequal application of risk assessments to people with a psychiatric diagnosis under mental health law could be said to criminalise disability.

Some commentators have advanced possible solutions to the discriminatory application of risk assessments under mental health law. For example, Jill Peay has suggested that laws maintain behavioural intervention principles to prevent dangerous criminal acts without specific reference to a psychiatric diagnosis; that is, 'intervening on dangerous behaviour but not on persons with a diagnosis of mental illness who *may* be dangerous'.[162] Peay's proposal may raise other rights-based concerns, although, from a CRPD perspective, it seemingly avoids formal disability-based discrimination. As Chapter 3 indicates, there is negligible or low correlation between violence and various psychiatric diagnoses – and certainly not when compared to other groups who do not face similar rights restrictions.[163] Any such correlation only implicates a very small subset of people with psychiatric diagnoses, with other variables appearing far more relevant in assessing dangerousness.[164] Bach and Kerzner have advanced

[161] See, e.g., E Flynn, *Disabled Justice? Access to Justice and the UN Convention on the Rights of Persons with Disabilities* (Ashgate, 2015).

[162] See J Peay (ed), *Seminal Issues in Mental Health Law* (Ashgate, 2005) xvii.

[163] See Chapter 3, Section B.

[164] See Chapter 3, Section B(4).

a threshold of 'serious adverse effects' to activate 'facilitated decision-making' interventions, as I will discuss in Chapter 5, which could also be applied in efforts to prevent harm against others.[165]

Thus, where States Parties insist on some grounds to restrict the liberty of those acting dangerously (some of whom might be persons with psychosocial disability), it seems *possible* to create disability-neutral grounds for 'civil' detention. It is doubtful that CRPD negotiators would have envisaged such a shift (or would necessarily support it today). However, such laws already exist in relation to, for example, dangerous sex offenders and those with infectious diseases – although these measures are not without their own rights issues.[166] A challenge that is likely to prove harder to overcome is preventing indirect discrimination when implementing such a scheme. Formally 'neutral' deprivation of liberty measures could easily disproportionately affect persons with disabilities. The apparent over-representation of people with disabilities in the criminal justice system, in and of itself, suggests that indirect discrimination is occurring writ large in criminal law.[167] It is outside the scope of this book to engage with the CRPD requirements for criminal law, although certain matters, such as the insanity defence, laws related to 'dangerous persons', unfitness to plead laws and so on, are clearly relevant to applying the support framework to the mental health context.

D CONCLUSION

There appears to be broad agreement regarding the apparent benefits of the CRPD support framework, even as specific issues remain unclear or controversial. According to Gerard Quinn, the approach to equal recognition before the law harnessed a wide range of discontents.[168] Three groups in particular emerged:

[165] See Chapter 5, Section C(1).

[166] See, generally, B McSherry, 'Sex, Drugs and "Evil" Souls: The Growing Reliance on Preventive Detention Regimes' (2006) 32 *Monash University Law Review* 237; B McSherry, *Managing Fear: The Law and Ethics of Preventive Detention and Risk Assessment* (Routledge, 2014).

[167] After all, people with intellectual, cognitive and psychosocial disabilities are typically over-represented in the criminal justice systems of the jurisdictions considered by this book. See, e.g., S Hayes et al., 'The Prevalence of Intellectual Disability in a Major UK Prison' (2007) 35(3) *British Journal of Learning Disabilities* 162; Disability Representative, Advocacy, Legal and Human Rights Organisations Australia, *Disability Rights Now: Civil Society Report to the United Nations Committee on the Rights of Persons with Disability* (2012) [216–7] <www.disabilityrightsnow.org.au>.

[168] G Quinn, 'European Foundation Centre and European Disability Forum: Symposium on the Legal Capacity of Persons with Disabilities in Light of the United Nations Convention on the Rights of Persons with Disabilities: An Ideas Paper', 4 June 2009, 7 <www.nuigalway.ie>.

those 'trained on the philosophy of equal opportunities';
those concerned with 'traditional civil liberties issues especially with respect to mental health law and the civil commitment of persons with mental disabilities'; and
those who focus on intellectual disability and associated issues like legal capacity and deinstitutionalization'.[169]

'If the Convention has done one thing', Quinn noted shortly after the CRPD came into force, 'it has enabled a common language to emerge across all three fields – producing a unified field theory, if you will, of disability law'.[170] While the ensuing controversies about Article 12, particularly in relation to involuntary treatment, raise questions about just how 'unified' such a field theory really is,[171] there appear to be enough consiliences, irrespective of disagreements, to achieve what Cass Sunstein has described as 'an imperfectly theorized agreement'.[172] In other words, a wide range of actors with various heterodox approaches appear to have endorsed the CRPD support framework. This type of 'overlapping consensus' can help break an impasse when the theory is not entirely explicated or agreed upon.[173] From this view, the core ideas of the CRPD support framework have breathed new life into long-standing debates about legal and policy responses to mental distress, disorder and disablement, even as precise conceptual agreement remains elusive.

The framework appears to address a number of the conceptual issues with mental health law discussed in Chapter 3, including:

- shifting attention to the material resources required for a person to exercise a range of human rights, thus avoiding a narrow focus on involuntary psychiatric intervention as the defining measure of statutory support and crisis intervention;
- incorporating a more realistic account of decision-making and autonomy that recognises the social context in which decisions are made;
- focusing on assistance for a person to develop decision-making skills (which would seem especially significant for children, teenagers and young adults who may enter mental health services at a crucial developmental stage of life);

[169] Ibid.
[170] Ibid.
[171] See Chapter 7.
[172] C Sunstein, 'Incompletely Theorized Agreements' (1995) 108 *Harvard Law Review* 1733.
[173] See Rawls, above n 147, 15.

- providing a countervailing approach to risk-averse mental health law, which currently draws on scientifically unfounded risk assessments applied on a seemingly prejudicial basis;
- providing stronger grounds to exercise rights compared to the 'best interests' approach by moving attention to 'will, preference and rights' as a guiding standard in hard cases; and
- providing a framework for achieving equal recognition before the law, with a strong emphasis, once again, on the positive rights associated with ensuring accessibility and reasonable accommodations to exercise rights on an 'equal basis with others'.

These interim conclusions are certainly promising, but many questions remain. For example, does the 'will, preference and rights' standard really provide stronger grounds to claim rights, or is it as ambiguous as the 'best interest' standard – and does it need to be? What is meant by 'support to exercise legal capacity' in practice and what role (if any) should mental capacity assessments play in providing it? Finally, any analysis of the potential for the CRPD support framework to address persistent issues in mental health law would be limited without considering matters of implementation and other issues to do with the practical politics. The potential pitfalls of applying the support framework in practice, need to be carefully considered. Prominent implementation strategies and other efforts to guarantee the legal capacity of *all* persons raise a host of issues, to which the next chapter will turn.

5

Applying the CRPD Support Framework in Law

A INTRODUCTION

The CRPD Committee promotes the view that 'all persons, regardless of disability or decision-making skills, *inherently possess* legal capacity'.[1] Accordingly, States Parties 'must abolish denials of legal capacity that are discriminatory on the basis of disability in purpose or effect',[2] which includes 'policies and legislative provisions that allow or perpetrate forced treatment … [as] found in mental health laws across the globe'.[3] For some, the sheer divergence of this view from what seems to be the majority-held view, that some mental health crises, in some cases, warrant coercive intervention, will be enough to dismiss the view of the CRPD Committee out of hand.

However, given the issues with mental health law set out in Part I of this book, including the major gaps in human rights coverage for persons with psychosocial disabilities throughout the twentieth century, it is clear that such arguments should not be dismissed outright. In the terms of Thomas Hammarberg, the Council of Europe Commissioner for Human Rights:

> A basic principle of human rights is that the agreed norms apply to every human being, without distinction. However, the international human rights norms have been denied to persons with disabilities. It was this failure which prompted member States of the United Nations to adopt the Convention on the Rights of Persons with Disabilities, which emphasises that people with all types of disabilities are entitled to the full range of human rights on an

1 Committee on the Rights of Persons with Disabilities, *General Comment No 1: Article 12: Equal Recognition Before the Law*, 11th sess, UN Doc CRPD/C/GC/1 (19 May 2014) 6 [25] (citations omitted) (emphasis added).

2 Ibid. 6 [25].

3 Ibid. 11 [42].

> equal basis with others ... When we deprive some individuals of their right to represent themselves we contradict these standards.[4]

Hammarberg insisted that European Union members must dismantle any laws that unequally restrict the legal capacity of people with disabilities in the name of 'so-called protection'.[5] Instead, '[p]ersons with mental disabilities should be assisted [with] but not deprived' of their right to exercise legal capacity.[6] Yet, the implications of guaranteeing legal capacity to all are potentially legion, extending beyond mental health laws to a raft of laws concerned with disability and legal capacity, such as guardianship law, tort laws related to contractual incapacity, health law regarding consent, criminal laws governing unfitness to stand trial and the insanity defence, and so on. In order to critically engage with the call to repeal mental health law in particular, it is useful to elaborate on what is meant by the directive of Article 12 to secure 'support to exercise legal capacity'. What are the purported benefits and potential pitfalls of this directive? Why does the seemingly 'common-sense' solution to make decisions for someone who lacks mental capacity fall foul of the CRPD Committee? This chapter will explore such questions, looking to major proposals for implementation in domestic law to help link practical and theoretical concerns about the CRPD and mental health law.

B UNTANGLING 'LEGAL CAPACITY' AND 'MENTAL CAPACITY'

'Capacity' is a fundamental concept in law – it is essential to the notion of autonomy and helps distinguish between decisions that are legally recognised and those that are not. Laws in Western common-law systems rest upon respect for the autonomy of individuals in accordance with John Stuart Mill's proposition that one has the right to make choices to be respected so long as they do not harm others.[7] 'Capacity', broadly understood, is fundamental to the evaluation and validation of those choices before the law.

In domestic laws, the term 'capacity' typically refers to 'mental capacity' (which is distinct from legal capacity, as I will discuss shortly). 'Mental capacity' has as many working definitions as there are jurisdictions that use it.[8]

4 T Hammarberg, 'Persons with Mental Disabilities Should Be Assisted but Not Deprived of Their Individual Human Rights' (Council of Europe 2009) <www.coe.int>.

5 Ibid.

6 Ibid.

7 See JS Mill, *On Liberty* (Ticknor and Fields, 1863).

8 Capacity Assessment Office, *Guidelines for Conducting Assessments of Capacity* (Ministry of the Attorney General of Ontario, May 2005) s II.1 <www.attorneygeneral.jus.gov.on.ca>.

Assessments of mental capacity typically require the demonstration of particular cognitive tasks.[9] For example, Section 3(1) of the Mental Capacity Act 2005 (England and Wales) defines mental incapacity with reference to a person being unable, 'because of an impairment of, or a disturbance in the functioning of, the mind or brain':[10]

> (a) to understand the information relevant to the decision,
> (b) to retain that information,
> (c) to use or weigh that information as part of the process of making the decision, or
> (d) to communicate his decision (whether by talking, using sign language or any other means).[11]

I will return to this assessment of functioning shortly. Before doing so, it is important to emphasise, again, the difference between mental capacity and legal capacity. As noted in Chapter 4, 'legal capacity' refers to a person's legal standing (being able to hold a right) and his or her ability to act on such legal standing (having the 'legal agency' to exercise that right).[12] The CRPD Committee elaborates on this distinction:

> Legal capacity and mental capacity are distinct concepts. Legal capacity is the ability to hold rights and duties (legal standing) and to exercise those rights and duties (legal agency). It is the key to accessing meaningful participation in society. Mental capacity refers to the decision-making skills of a person, which naturally vary from one person to another and may be different for a given person depending on many factors, including environmental and social factors.[13]

To avoid confusion, I will refer to 'decision-making ability' instead of 'mental capacity' whenever doing so improves clarity.[14] In most jurisdictions, those found to lack decision-making ability will not enjoy *legal* capacity, as their

[9] Traditional incapacity tests may address the apparent risk-management needs of service providers rather than protect the person against risk. J Brayley, 'Supported Decision Making in Australia: Presentation Notes', (2009) Presented to the Victorian Offices of the Public Advocate and the Law Reform Commission (Vic), Melbourne 9 <www.opa.sa.gov.au>.

[10] Mental Capacity Act 2005 (c 9) (England and Wales) s 2(1)(a).

[11] Mental Capacity Act 2005 (c 9) (England and Wales) s 3(1).

[12] UN Office of the High Commissioner for Human Rights, 'Background Conference Document Prepared by the Office of the United Nations High Commissioner for Human Rights: Legal Capacity' (2005) para 37.

[13] Committee on the Rights of Persons with Disabilities, above n 1, 3 [13].

[14] Australian Law Reform Commission, *Equality, Capacity and Disability in Commonwealth Laws* (2014) [2.50].

decisions will not be recognised as autonomous under the law. Yet decision-making ability and legal capacity need not be conflated, as I will discuss below.

Charles Sabatino and Erica Wood describe legal capacity as a 'legal fiction'.[15] They argue that '[l]egal capacity' is necessary as an idea 'to tell us when a state legitimately may intrude into an individual's affairs and take action to limit an individual's rights to make decisions about his or her own person or property'.[16] Further:

> Legal incapacity, so conceived, is important precisely because a [legal] fiction is determined by prevailing values, knowledge, and even the economic and political spirit of the time … [T]he criteria or elements needed to establish legal incapacity are the products of society's prevailing beliefs concerning individual autonomy and social order, tempered by the restraint of legal precedent. Just as societal values and needs have evolved over time, so will the legal criteria for capacity and incapacity.[17]

Historically, legal capacity has been extended or denied to various groups. At one point in every jurisdiction considered by this book, married women were not entitled to enter into legal contracts.[18] Similarly, indigenous people in some nineteenth-century British colonies had their legal 'personality' denied under systems of wardship – 'protection boards' held complete statutory power over their lives.[19] Those subject to denials of legal capacity have been described as suffering 'civil death' due to their complete (or near-complete) lack of legal personality.[20]

Scholars have sought to distinguish various approaches to regulating legal capacity throughout history.[21] The earliest approach was a 'status-based' understanding of capacity. Jurists viewed incapacity as residing in individual

[15] CP Sabatino and E Wood, 'The Conceptualization of Capacity of Older Persons in Western Law' in I Doron and A Snoden (eds), *Beyond Elder Law: New Directions in Law and Aging* (Springer, 2012) 35, 36.

[16] Ibid. 36.

[17] Ibid.

[18] ML Shelley, *Feminism, Marriage, and the Law in Victorian England* (Princeton University Press, 1989) 22.

[19] See, e.g., Aboriginal Protection Act 1869 (Vic) No 349. This act was the first of its kind in the Australian colony to provide grounds for the systematic regulation of Aboriginal people's lives, including the regulation of residence, employment, marriage and other aspects of daily life.

[20] Shelley, above n 18, 10. See, e.g., ML Perlin, '"Striking for the Guardians and Protectors of the Mind": The Convention on the Rights of Persons with Mental Disabilities and the Future of Guardianship Law' (2013) 117 *Pennsylvania State Law Review* 1159, 1162.

[21] See, e.g., A Dhanda, 'Legal Capacity in the Disability Rights Convention: Stranglehold of the Past or Lodestar for the Future?' (2007) 34 *Syracuse Journal of International Law and Commerce* 429; Sabatino and Wood, above n 15.

characteristics, which restricted an individual who exhibited such characteristics from making legally recognised choices. Typical status designations included 'idiots' or 'lunatics'[22] (or, indeed, 'Aborigine' or 'married woman', as the case may have been).

Later, incapacity law aligned with the medicalising shift of the twentieth century in relation to which diagnostic classifications became the deciding factor. Laws such as the Mental Health Act 1959 (UK) were typical, providing as it did for plenary guardianship.[23] Today, as outlined in Chapters 1 and 2, typical mental health legislation essentially retains a diagnostic status approach to restrictions on legal capacity. The view that a psychiatric diagnosis means a person cannot decide for himself or herself has been widely criticised, particularly as a justification for laws suspending the liberal values of equality and the freedom to choose how to live one's life.[24] Others argue that mental illness, madness and so on serve as a special exception requiring distinct rules of citizenship.[25]

The latest formulation of mental capacity, which prevails in almost all areas of law, uses the medicolegal concept of 'functional mental capacity' – that is, decision-making ability. This formulation emerged from developments in science, psychology and ideas about civil rights. A 'presumption of mental capacity' is often included in legislation as a means to counteract the status-based approach, whereby public officials must presume that all adults have sufficient decision-making ability until a functional 'understand and appreciate test' (as noted previously) demonstrates otherwise.[26]

A functional approach aims to serve as the 'least restrictive means available' to interfere with a person's rights. Identifying 'functional limitations' ostensibly narrows the scope for substituted decision-making, and a host of procedural safeguards can follow. This 'tailored' or 'limited' form of guardianship helps avoid a situation in which the person is viewed as globally capable or incapable. Instead, he or she is seen as comprising a 'bundle of capacities'.[27] Some capacities require a 'substitute' to step in and make decisions, while

22 See, e.g., P Fennell, 'Mental Health Law: History, Policy, and Regulation' in L Gostin, P Bartlett, P Fennell, J McHale and R Mackay (eds), *Principles of Mental Health Law and Policy* (Oxford University Press, 2010) 1.05.

23 See Chapter 1, Section B.

24 See Chapter 3, Section B.

25 See Ibid.

26 See, e.g., Guardianship and Administration Act 2000 (Qld) Schedule 1 – Principles s270.

27 KB Glen, 'Changing Paradigms: Mental Capacity, Legal Capacity, Guardianship, and Beyond' (2012) 44(93) *Columbia Human Rights Law Review* 115.

the remaining abilities can be propped up to promote the independence and autonomy of the person, as far as possible.

Lawmakers promoted functional mental capacity assessments as a way to move disability-related laws from welfare rights to liberty rights.[28] This new approach discarded the strict paternalistic principle (where substituted decision-makers were often informed quite literally to act *in loco parentis*) in favour of 'best interests', which included giving consideration to a person's will and preference.

The definition of 'best interests' under the Mental Capacity Act 2005 (England and Wales), as noted previously, exemplifies this trend.[29] Several provisions of this definition require consideration of the will and preferences of the person. The appointed decision-maker is obliged, 'so far as reasonably practicable, [to] permit and encourage the person to participate, or to improve his ability to participate, as fully as possible in any act done for him and any decision affecting him'.[30] Further, he or she must 'consider, so far as is reasonably ascertainable the person's past and present wishes and feelings (and, in particular, any relevant written statement made by him when he had capacity), the beliefs and values that would be likely to influence his decision if he had capacity, and the other factors that he would be likely to consider if he were able to do so'.[31] In the United States, the New York Mental Hygiene Law captures this effort in Section 81.01:

> [I]t is desirable for and beneficial to persons with incapacities to make available to them the least restrictive form of intervention which assists them in meeting their needs but, at the same time, permits them to exercise the independence and self-determination of which they are capable.
>
> [We thus establish a guardianship system] which takes into account the personal wishes, preferences and desires of the person, and which affords the person the greatest amount of independence and self determination and participation in all the decisions affecting such person's life.[32]

According to Terry Carney and Fleur Beaupert, by promoting the person's wishes and preferences, and carefully circumscribing the grounds for substituted decision-making, guardianship law reformers 'valiantly sought to shake off its paternalist philosophy from Roman law and 13th century prerogatives of

[28] See, e.g., N.Y. Mental Hygiene Law S.81 (McKinney, 2012).
[29] See above n 11.
[30] Mental Capacity Act 2005 (England and Wales) c 9, s 4(4).
[31] Mental Capacity Act 2005 (England and Wales) c 9, s 4(6)(a)–(c).
[32] See N.Y. Mental Hygiene Law S.81 (McKinney 2012).

chancery'.[33] Perhaps unsurprisingly, a number of commentators have sought to apply this liberalising trend to mental health law.

1 *Decision-Making Ability Assessments in Mental Health Law*

Prominent commentators in the field of mental health law have called for decision-making ability tests to replace the diagnostic criterion of mental health law.[34] One reform option in this direction would be to 'fuse' mental health law and mental capacity law (the so-called fusion approach).[35] A second option is merely to replace the diagnostic threshold of mental health law with a mental capacity assessment.[36] According to Sascha Callaghan and Christopher Ryan, the latter approach would not only provide a more ethical basis for involuntary psychiatric intervention, it would also help align mental health law more closely with the CRPD.[37]

Purported benefits of this approach include harmonising mental healthcare with ethical and legal standards in general healthcare.[38] The justification for overriding autonomy would be standardised for a range of non-consensual interventions (whether concerning concussion, delirium or mental health crises). Professionals could avoid the discriminatory application of risk-based assessments to people with psychosocial disability, and tolerate decisions with possibly grave outcomes, so long as the person retained mental capacity. This could help avoid the subjective judgement of authorised clinicians about the outcome of a person's choice. Instead, the focus could turn to whether the person comprehends a particular matter requiring urgent attention. In this way, the person could maintain the right to live according to his or her own wishes, no matter how eccentric he or she was. A range of professionals (not simply psychiatrists) could achieve greater impartiality by applying a long-standing test for securing informed consent in general health settings. Where

33 T Carney and F Beaupert, 'Public and Private Bricolage – Challenges Balancing Law, Services and Civil Society in Advancing CRPD Supported Decision-Making' (2013) 36(1) *UNSW Law Journal* 175, 177.

34 J Dawson and G Szmukler, 'Fusion of Mental Health and Incapacity Legislation' (2006) 188 *The British Journal of Psychiatry* 504; G Szmukler, R Daw and J Dawson, 'A Model Law Fusing Incapacity and Mental Health Legislation' (2010) 11 *Journal of Mental Health Law* 11; S Callaghan and C Ryan, 'Is There a Future for Involuntary Treatment in Rights-Based Mental Health Law?' (2014) 21 *Psychiatry, Psychology and Law* 747.

35 See generally, above n 34.

36 Callaghan and Ryan, above n 34.

37 Ibid.

38 P Bartlett, '"The Necessity Must Be Convincingly Shown to Exist": Standards for Compulsory Treatment for Mental Disorder under the Mental Health Act 1983' (2011) 19 *Medical Law Review* 514, 541; Szmukler, Daw and Dawson, above n 34.

professionals could not secure consent for matters requiring emergency intervention, a series of safeguards would be activated to uphold, as far as possible, the person's will and preferences.

The views stated in the previous paragraph are, of course, deeply controversial.[39] For example, the CRPD Committee has commented that the CRPD 'does not permit perceived or actual deficits in mental capacity to be used as justification for denying legal capacity'.[40] The view that decision-making ability assessments are *intrinsically* discriminatory is one of the most prominent and troubling among a range of criticisms of such tests.

2 *Criticisms of Decision-Making Ability Tests*

The proposals set out in the previous section raise a number of dilemmas. First, the functional approach continues to strip some of the rights of the person deemed incapable.[41] Decision-making power over certain aspects of a person's life and property continue to be restricted. Kristin Booth Glen has argued that '[w]hat remains unquestioned, is that once a person is deemed incapacitated, however defined or established, said person is deprived of the right and power to make – and act on – her own decisions, instead conferring that power on another'.[42] For Glen, 'regardless of the procedural protection she is afforded, the respect given her past views, and the commitment to enhancing or re-establishing capacity, as to her *incapacity*, the person under guardianship is *not, or is no longer, a legal actor*',[43] an argument that could apply equally to mental health law.

Secondly, it is extremely difficult to design capacity tests with the sensitivity to evaluate the autonomy of the individual. Genevra Richardson has written that '[i]f the test of mental capacity is set too high, it will exclude our truly autonomous choices … but if it is set too low it may accord respect to choices that do not reflect our true wishes'.[44] In case law, courts have tended to interpret the definition of mental capacity fairly flexibly in order to achieve

39 Committee on the Rights of Persons with Disabilities, above n 1, 3 [13]; E Flynn 'Mental (In)capacity or Legal Capacity? A Human Rights Analysis of the Proposed Fusion of Mental Health and Mental Capacity in Northern Ireland' (2013) 64(4) *Northern Ireland Legal Quarterly* 485; J Dawson, 'A Realistic Approach to Assessing Mental Health Laws' Compliance with the *UNCRPD*' (2015) 40 *International Journal of Law and Psychiatry* 70.

40 Committee on the Rights of Persons with Disabilities, above n 1, 6 [25] (citation omitted).

41 Dhanda, above n 21.

42 Glen, above n 27.

43 Ibid. 118 (emphasis in original).

44 G Richardson, 'Mental Capacity in the Shadow of Suicide' (2013) 9(1) *International Journal of Law in Context* 87, 90.

the desired outcome.[45] This flexibility can be seen as necessary to avoid too rigid an application of the capacity-incapacity binary. However, the potential for inconsistency remains, and this flexibility does not provide strong grounds for a person to claim rights.[46] Richardson has argued, in the context of courts responding to extreme self-harm and suicide, that '[i]n neither principle nor practice is this entirely satisfactory'.[47] Nevertheless, she proceeds to query whether, at least in theory, the concept of supported decision-making may provide 'equally troubling, if different, outcomes'.[48] I will explore some of these comparable pitfalls and potentially intractable ethical dilemmas facing the CRPD support framework in Chapter 7.

The criticisms set out above do not concern direct discrimination against persons with disabilities – the drawbacks of decision-making ability tests would apply to all. However, *indirect* discrimination looms, and it seems inevitable that decision-making ability testing will disproportionately affect people with intellectual, cognitive and psychosocial disabilities. The criteria of decision-making ability tests relate to cognition, rationality and intellectual ability. Aside from failing capacity tests more often, people with disabilities are more likely to be subject to testing where others are not. Yet Articles 2 and 5 of the CRPD clearly prohibit laws that discriminate against people with disability in their purpose *or effect*.[49] This does not appear to provide strong grounds to accommodate persons with disabilities 'as part of human diversity and humanity'.[50] In Bach and Kerzner's words:

> To make recognition of legal capacity dependent on a particular set of decision-making skills, as most current capacity assessment tools do, is to import ableist assumptions about what the demonstration of decision-making ability entails. This approach to definition reproduces disability 'status' as the basis for restricting legal capacity, a clear violation of the CRPD, and systematically discriminates against people with intellectual, cognitive, psychosocial and communication disabilities; people whose disabilities may entail challenges with managing decision making.[51]

The Canadian Association of Community Living has argued that assessments of decision-making ability *could* determine the type of *support* that a person

45 Ibid.
46 Ibid.
47 Ibid. 91.
48 Ibid. 103. See also L Series, 'Relationships, Autonomy and Legal Capacity: Mental Capacity and Support Paradigms' (2015) 40 *International Journal of Law and Psychiatry* 80.
49 CRPD arts 2 and 4.
50 CRPD art 3(d).
51 Ibid.

needs in order to exercise legal capacity.[52] Yet, as noted previously, the CRPD Committee has rejected this proposition, commenting that 'the provision of support to exercise legal capacity should not hinge on mental capacity assessments; new, non-discriminatory indicators of support needs are required'.[53] I will return to this argument in Chapter 7 and consider if it is possible to provide 'disability-neutral' tests of decision-making ability in order to identify useful support.[54]

a Criticisms of Decision-Making Ability Tests in Mental Health Law

Commentators have raised significant concerns about the proposal to use decision-making ability assessments in the mental health context. Tom Burns, criticising the proposal from a clinical perspective, argues that it ignores the balance between beneficence and restricting autonomy that has 'always lain at the heart of psychiatric practice'.[55] Burns comments that 'only with the most tortuous logic can the compulsory detention of a distraught adolescent intent on suicide because of a broken love-affair be justified in terms of capacity'.[56]

From a rights-based perspective, Peter Bartlett has noted that flexibility in the assessment requirement of understanding and appreciating the nature and consequences of the decision 'has led to allegations that capacity means agreeing with the psychiatrist':

> it is difficult to see that the incapacity can sensibly be separated from the mental disability, given that it is the mental disability that is the direct cause of the incapacity. Insofar as the use of the disability as a criterion is discriminatory, therefore, the use of incapacity as a detention criterion merely moves direct discrimination into indirect discrimination, and this is not really a significant advance.[57]

52 Canadian Association of Community Living, *Submission to the Draft General Comment on Article 12 of the Convention – Equal Recognition before the Law and Draft General Comment on Article 9 of the Convention – Accessibility* (February 2014) <www.ohchr.org>.

53 Committee on the Rights of Persons with Disabilities, above n 1, 7 [29](i).

54 See Chapter 7, Section B(4)–(5).

55 T Burns, 'Mental Illness Is Different and Ignoring Its Differences Profits Nobody' (2010) 20 *Journal of Mental Health Law* 34, 37.

56 Ibid. 36. Cf G Szmukler, R Daw and J Dawson, 'Response to the Commentaries' (2014) 20 *Journal of Mental Health Law* 89.

57 P Bartlett, 'A Mental Disorder of a Kind or Degree Warranting Confinement: Examining Justifications for Psychiatric Detention' (2012) 16(6) *International Journal of Human Rights* 831, 832.

Interestingly, in Burns's reference to a 'distraught adolescent intent on suicide', he continues to note that if a mental capacity assessment *were* required to impose treatment, 'few psychiatrists would hesitate to use it if they "had to"; beneficence so clearly overwhelms autonomy in this situation'.[58] This observation supports Bartlett's contention about the flexibility of the test. It also supports Phil Fennell's criticism that the rights-based rhetoric of mental health law is undermined by the lack of substantive rights protection in practice, where, instead, mental health law codifies clinical discretion to treat and detain.[59]

Recent law reform efforts in Northern Ireland highlight issues that may arise when using decision-making ability assessments in the quest for non-discrimination in the mental health context.[60] Lawmakers sought to design the Draft Mental Capacity Bill 2008 (Northern Ireland) to 'fuse' mental health law and mental capacity law to avoid relying on a diagnosis of mental illness as a criterion for detention and involuntary treatment.[61] The bill appears to expand somewhat the criteria for decision-making inability beyond typical functional assessments. The accompanying policy material states that '[i]t will not be sufficient for a person to have a cognitive understanding of the information relevant to the decision'.[62] Instead, a 'person whose insight is distorted by their illness or a person suffering from delusional thinking as a result of their illness, may not … meet this element of the test'.[63] This may widen the interpretative flexibility of mental capacity assessors by including 'insight' (although there is some evidence that assessors in the United Kingdom are currently using this approach, as I will discuss shortly). This seems a somewhat inevitable step in applying mental capacity assessments to the mental health context.

The use of 'insight' as a criterion in decision-making ability tests may cause significant issues which do not appear to have been addressed in theory or practice. First, 'insight' is a notoriously slippery term that is difficult, if not impossible, to substantiate in relation to a person, because it refers to a 'subjective report of his or her internal state'.[64] Second, it is difficult for

58 Burns, above n 55, 36.
59 See Chapter 3, Section C(4).
60 Draft Mental Capacity Bill 2014 (Northern Ireland).
61 Minister of the Department of Health, Social Services and Public Safety in Northern Ireland, Northern Ireland Department of Justice, 'Draft Mental Capacity Bill (NI) Consultation Document' (Government of Northern Ireland, May 2014) <www.dhsspsni.gov.uk>.
62 Ibid. [2.2].
63 Ibid.
64 R Keefe, 'The Neurobiology of Disturbances of the Self: Autonoetic Agnosia in Schizophrenia,' in XF Amador and AS David (eds), *Insight and Psychosis* (Oxford University Press, 1998) 142, 159.

any external review mechanism to evaluate claims about the *absence* rather than the existence of a characteristic, such as self-harm or violent acts against others. Kate Diesfeld and Stefan Sjöström investigated how the term 'insight' was employed in twenty-five decisions from mental health review proceedings in Victoria, Australia, describing its application as 'problematic'.[65] While, in their view, the term provides 'interpretative flexibility' to usefully resolve complex issues and 'mediate between expert and lay discourse',[66] they concluded that there was little clarity as to how the term was used, a confused logic evident in its application, and 'frequent allusions to an implicit and undefined scale of insight, offering the appearance of objectivity'.[67] Mark Sullivan and Betty Ferrell argue that the application of 'insight' can work as a 'stigmatizing prelude' to continued detention.[68]

There is some evidence suggesting that public authorities in England and Wales are already using 'insight' in mental capacity assessments under the Mental Capacity Act 2005 (England and Wales).[69] Charlotte Emmett and colleagues found that '[w]here assessors did not agree with patients' decisions, they were prone to interpret the decision as lacking insight and, thus, the decision maker as lacking capacity'.[70] Val Williams and colleagues analysed how assessments of mental capacity were taking place under the act and argued that 'there was a dilemma about the difference between someone with capacity who made an "unwise decision" and someone who lacked capacity … The two matters were often confusingly conflated within the notion of "lack of insight" which was a commonly cited reason for assessing a lack of capacity'.[71] Northern Irish law reformers sought to prevent the conflation of decision-making ability with 'unwise decisions'. As criteria for compulsion, they proposed the 'prevention of serious harm conditions' in relation to treatment[72] as well the consideration of resistance by the relevant person to provision of certain treatment[73] and some restrictions on providing 'treatment with serious

65 K Diesfeld and S Sjöström, 'Interpretive Flexibility: Why Doesn't Insight Incite Controversy in Mental Health Law?' (2007) 25 *Behavioral Sciences and the Law* 85.

66 Ibid. 98.

67 Ibid. 85.

68 M Sullivan and B Ferrell, 'Ethical Challenges in the Management of Chronic Nonmalignant Pain: Negotiating through the Cloud of Doubt' (2005) 6 *The Journal of Pain* 2, 5.

69 C Emmett et al., 'Homeward Bound or Bound for a Home? Assessing the Capacity of Dementia Patients to Make Decisions About Hospital Discharge: Comparing Practice with Legal Standards' (2013) 36 *International Journal of Law and Psychiatry* 73.

70 Ibid. 78.

71 V Williams et al., *Making Best Interests Decisions: People and Processes* (Policy Research Programme, Department of Health, United Kingdom, 2011) 159 <www.mentalhealth.org.uk>.

72 Draft Mental Capacity Bill (Northern Ireland) s 19(1).

73 Ibid. s 20.

consequences' (such as side effects, serious pain and distress).[74] However, the issues raised in this section highlight serious concerns from both a human rights and a pragmatic perspective, which appear to remain unaddressed in calls to use decision-making ability as the central grounds for involuntary psychiatric intervention.

3 *CRPD-Based Law Reform Directions*

Some jurisdictions have adopted elements of the CRPD support framework even as they retain decision-making ability assessments and substituted decision-making. In such cases, legislation reserves substituted decision-making for extreme cases and provides for alternative support mechanisms along the way.

Canadian adult guardianship/mental capacity laws include supported decision-making measures which give statutory power to informal supporters of people with complex communication or decision-making support needs.[75] Lawmakers designed the mechanisms for people with intellectual and cognitive disability (and, nominally, those with psychosocial disability).[76] The Representation Agreement Act 1996 in British Columbia is particularly innovative in this respect, with provision for a contractual agreement between two or more adults to formalise a support relationship.[77] The individual can appoint a person ('associate') to help him or her make various decisions regarding personal, health and financial matters.[78] 'Associates' have no authority to make decisions for decision-makers, but they do have statutory powers to gather information and assist them to communicate. Section 8(1) of the act allows an adult to make a representation agreement, even if the adult cannot pass a mental capacity assessment to make a contract 'managing his or her health care, personal care or legal matters' or manage his or her financial affairs.[79] In deciding whether an adult is capable of entering a representation agreement, the following factors are considered:

74 Ibid. s 18.

75 R Gordon, 'The Emergence of Assisted (Supported) Decision-Making in the Canadian Law of Adult Guardianship and Substitute Decision-Making' (2000) 23(1) *International Journal of Law and Psychiatry* 61.

76 There was also an express interest in protecting the rights of elder citizens who were increasingly becoming subject to adult guardianship laws. Reform has taken place in the jurisdictions of Quebec, Ontario, British Columbia, Manitoba, Prince Edward Island and the Northwest Territories, and has been discussed in Nova Scotia and Yukon. Ibid.

77 Representation Agreement Act R.S.B.C. 1996 c 405.

78 Ibid. s 8.

79 Ibid. s 8(1).

(a) whether the adult communicates a desire to have a representative make, help make or stop making decisions;
(b) whether the adult demonstrates choices and preferences and can express feelings of approval or disapproval to others;
(c) whether the adult is aware that making the representation agreement or changing or revoking any of the provisions means that the representative may make, or stop making, decisions or choices that affect him or her;
(d) whether the adult has a relationship with the representative that is characterized by trust.

The legislation promotes an early intervention approach for use prior to problems and conflicts developing – that is, not during emergencies. As soon as a person with an intellectual disability reaches adulthood in British Columbia, he or she is encouraged to enter into a representation agreement.[80] People may also use representative agreements for advance planning in the mental health context.[81] Signing an agreement helps to remind all concerned – parents, family and friends – of their role in supporting the decision of an equal citizen and a peer (rather than a minor) who deserves a full human life.[82] However, the Representation Agreement Act 1996 functions *alongside* guardianship/mental capacity laws that are more typical and maintain substituted decision-making arrangements based on decision-making ability assessments.[83] Typical mental health legislation also remains in British Columbia and can override powers under the Representation Agreement Act 1996.[84]

In the Republic of Ireland, the Assisted Decision-Making (Capacity) Act 2015 was enacted with the explicit aim of supporting people to exercise their legal capacity in accordance with the CRPD, including by discarding the 'best interests' standard.[85] Reformers aimed to introduce a non-discriminatory formulation of legal capacity and decision-making support into

[80] Not only does the agreement afford legal protections to the individual and his or her supporters, it also functions symbolically to affirm the equal legal status of the person. Gordon, above n 75, 61.

[81] S Friday, *Representation Agreements and Supported Decision-Making* (May 2005) Vancouver/Richmond Mental Health Network Society Website <http://francais.ccamhr.ca/communications/repaggreements.html>.

[82] Ibid.

[83] Health Care (Consent) and Care Facility (Admission) Act R.S.B.C. 1996 c 181; Adult Guardianship Act R.S.B.C. 1996 c 6; Public Guardian and Trustee Act R.S.B.C. 1996 c 383.

[84] Representation Agreement Act R.S.B.C. 1996 c 405 s 11(1).

[85] Assisted Decision-Making (Capacity) Act 2015 No 64 (Ireland). See E Flynn, 'Assisted Decision-Making (Capacity) Bill 2013 Finally Published' in *Human Rights in Ireland* (17 July 2013) <www.humanrights.ie>.

law.[86] In her second stage speech during the passage of the act into Irish law, Kathleen Lynch, Minister for Justice, Equality and Defence, commented that '[f]or too long, we have operated in accordance with a paternalist paradigm in which decisions have been made on behalf of people rather than by them and in which decisions have been made in their "best interests" rather than in accordance with the [sic] will and preferences'.[87] The act introduced a number of statutory mechanisms to assist people with making decisions, including 'decision-making assistance agreements', 'co-decision-making agreements' and the appointment of 'decision-making representatives'.[88] Decision-making assistants function in broadly the same way as associates do in British Columbia. A co-decision-making agreement enables a person to enter into an agreement with another person in order to 'co-authorise' joint decisions on specific issues about the person's life. (For example, a person prone to spending sprees may choose to appoint a co-decision-maker to sign off on the making of large transactions.) Both decision-making categories offer a way to operationalise relational understandings of autonomy and to respect different ways citizens make decisions. The decision-making representative role would appear to function in the same way as substituted decision-making under typical adult (in)capacity laws, whether 'deputyship' under the Mental Capacity Act 2005 (England and Wales)[89] or 'guardianship' under the Protection of Personal and Property Rights Act 1988 (New Zealand),[90] although the principles of the Assisted Decision-Making (Capacity) Act would appear to give greater emphasis to the person's will and preferences than pre-CRPD guardianship/mental capacity laws.[91] Further, the act continues to rely on decision-making ability assessments to determine when decision-making representatives can be imposed.[92] Further, the less 'intensive' support mechanisms – decision-making assistance and co-decision-making agreements – do not seem to be available to those who cannot demonstrate sufficient decision-making ability[93] (in contrast to representation agreements in British Columbia, for example).

Since the CRPD came into force, there have been some changes to mental health legislation in the jurisdictions considered by this book. The following

86 Flynn, above n 86.

87 An Roinn Dlí agus Cirt agus Comhionannais/Department of Justice and Equality, 'Speech by Minister for Justice, Equality and Defence at the Assisted Decision – Making (Capacity) Bill 2013: Consultation Symposium' (Dublin Castle, 25 September 2013).

88 Assisted Decision-Making (Capacity) Act 2015 No 64 (Ireland) s 10 pt 4 ch 5.

89 Mental Capacity Act 2005 (c 9) (England and Wales) ss 15–20.

90 Protection of Personal and Property Rights Act 1988 No 4 (NZ) pt 2.

91 Assisted Decision-Making (Capacity) Act 2015 No 64 (Ireland) s 8.

92 Ibid. ss 37–38.

93 Ibid. s 10(1). See also s 24(2)(b).

chapter examines these changes in greater detail. To offer a brief example, consider that seven out of eight jurisdictions in Australia have undertaken mental health law reviews since the coming into force of the CRPD.[94] According to Sascha Callaghan and Christopher Ryan, lawmakers pursued amendments to achieve CRPD compliance and to meet 'the central challenge established in article 12'.[95] Typical changes include advance planning provisions for individuals to set out wishes and preferences in advance of mental health crises[96] and provisions to enable the nominating of representatives to inform decision-making following involuntary psychiatric intervention orders.[97] Some jurisdictions have introduced decision-making ability assessment as a criterion for involuntary psychiatric intervention,[98] while others have introduced the criterion of decision-making inability only in relation to some matters, such as refusing involuntary electroconvulsive treatment.[99] For example, in the Australian Capital Territory, an involuntary order is still permitted for a patient who 'has decision-making capacity ... but refuses to consent', although such an order would need to take account of the set of 'rights' outlined in the 'Principles applying to the Act'.[100]

The CRPD has also influenced regional changes to law and policy. Examples include decisions made by the European Court of Human Rights,[101] as well as the content of the European Disability Strategy 2010–2020,[102] both of which have been influenced by the prerogatives of Article 12 and the broader

94 The exception is the Northern Territory.

95 S Callaghan and C Ryan, 'An Evolving Revolution: Evaluating Australia's Compliance with the Convention on the Rights of Persons with Disabilities in Mental Health Law' (2016) 39(2) *University of New South Wales Law Journal* 596, 597.

96 See, e.g., Mental Health Act 2016 (Qld) s 53; Mental Health Act 2015 (ACT) ss 56(1), 62(5)–(6); and Mental Health Act 2014 (WA) s 7(2). See, generally, P Weller, *New Law and Ethics in Mental Health Advance Directives: The Convention on the Rights of Persons with Disabilities and the Right to Choose* (Routledge, 2013).

97 Mental Health Act 2015 (ACT) ss 15(4), 19–23; Mental Health Act 2016 (Qld) s 25(2); Mental Health Act 2013 (Tas) s 3; Mental Health Act 2007 (NSW) ss 71–2; Mental Health Act 2014 (Vic) ss 23–4; Mental Health Act 2014 (WA) pt 16 div 3.

98 See, e.g., Mental Health Act 2013 (Tas) s 40(e); Mental Health Act 2014 (WA) ss 25(1)(c),(2)(c); Mental Health Act 2016 (Qld) s 12(1)(b). These jurisdictions apply involuntary treatment only to those patients who are unable to consent to treatment themselves.

99 See, e.g., Mental Health Act 2014 (Vic) s 71(1); Mental Health Act 2007 (NSW) ss 12, 14, 15; Mental Health Act 2015 (ACT) ss 6, 58(2)(b)(ii).

100 Mental Health Act 2015 (ACT) ss 6, 58(2)(b)(ii).

101 The European Court of Human Rights has increasingly used Article 12 of the CRPD as an aid to interpretation in cases concerning legal capacity. See, e.g., *Lashin v Russia* (2012) ECHR 63; *MS v Croatia* (2013) ECHR 378; *Sýkora v The Czech Republic*; *DD v Lithuania* (2012) ECHR 10; *Stanev v Bulgaria* (2012) ECHR 46; *Seal v UK* (2010) ECHR 1976.

102 European Commission, *European Disability Strategy 2010–2020: A Renewed Commitment to a Barrier-Free Europe* (2010).

CRPD support framework. The Commissioner for Human Rights in the Council of Europe has noted that the majority of European legal capacity regimes are out of date and in urgent need of reform.[103] Fiona Morrissey has argued that the European Union and the Council of Europe are now moving in a common direction and assisting member states to reform legal capacity law and policy to comply with Article 12.[104] The Organization of American States has taken similar steps.[105]

The reform schema set out in this section retains substituted decision-making based on assessments of decision-making ability (or, in the case of typical mental health legislation, a status-based diagnostic threshold). In relation to this broad reform strategy, Mary Donnelly states that mental capacity 'operates along a continuum ranging from wholly incapable to highly capable', thus providing a more nuanced means of intervening with appropriate support and protection.[106] This trend could conceivably place supported decision-making mechanisms in the first stages of what John Brayley has described as a 'stepped up' spectrum of regulations.[107] The spectrum would range from independent legal decision-making at one end, to supported decision-making as a middle step, to substituted decision-making in extreme cases.[108] In this sense, law reform would be aimed at further de-linking conventional *mental* capacity from *legal* capacity by promoting the notion that people who do not meet decision-making ability tests can still maintain and exercise legal capacity with support.

[103] Council of Europe Commissioner for Human Rights, 'Who Gets to Decide? Right to Legal Capacity for Persons with Intellectual and Psychosocial Disabilities' (Comm DH/Issue Paper, Strasbourg, 20 February 2012).

[104] F Morrissey, 'The United Nations Convention on the Rights of Persons with Disabilities: A New Approach to Decision-Making in Mental Health Law' (2012) 19 *European Journal of Health Law* 423, 439–40.

[105] See Committee for the Elimination of All Forms of Discrimination Against Persons with Disabilities, 'General Observation of the Committee for the Elimination of All Forms of Discrimination against Persons with Disabilities on the need to interpret Article I.2(b) in fine of the Inter-American Convention on the Elimination of All Forms of Discrimination against Persons with Disabilities in the context of Article 12 of the United Nations Convention on the Rights of Persons with Disabilities' (OEA/Ser.L/XXIV.3.1, CEDDIS/doc.12(I-E/11) rev.1, 28 April 2011).

[106] M Donnelly, 'Best Interests, Patient Participation and the Mental Capacity Act 2005' (2009) 17(1) *Medical Law Review* 1, 11.

[107] J Brayley, 'Supported Decision-Making in Australia: Presentation Notes' (Presentation to the Victorian Office of the Public Advocate and Victorian Law Reform Commission, 2009) 6 <www.opa.sa.gov.au>; see also M Bach and L Kerzner, *A New Paradigm for Protecting Autonomy and the Right to Legal Capacity* (Report to the Law Commission of Ontario, 2010) 66–7 <www.lco-cdo.org>.

[108] Gordon, above n 75.

The CRPD Committee has unequivocally stated that such legislative frameworks do not conform to the CRPD. Regardless, some States Parties and commentators have maintained an interpretation of the CRPD that consolidates the functional and status-based approaches but buttresses the concept of 'will and preference'. From this view, supported decision-making *complements* substituted decision-making and provides a more nuanced appreciation of legal capacity, autonomy and personhood.

a Bach and Kerzner's Model

A number of efforts have been made to develop a comprehensive legal and policy framework for guaranteeing universal legal capacity. The Law Commission of Ontario commissioned a report by Michael Bach and Lara Kerzner to conceptualise one such framework, which resulted in one of the most detailed proposals for legislation aimed at guaranteeing legal capacity for all citizens.[109] The proposal is premised on the view that mental health law should be repealed because it is discriminatory and violates the CRPD.[110] However, Bach and Kerzner propose new, seemingly disability-neutral emergency powers that could include involuntary intervention in response to extreme mental health crises.[111]

The alternative scheme draws upon three main categories for legally regulated decision-making: 'legally independent', 'supported' and 'facilitated'. Each category would be accompanied by a proportionate level of legal oversight, ranging from non-intervention to the provision of support mechanisms designed to help develop 'decision-making capabilities'.[112] In keeping with the universal design principle of the CRPD, the authors sought to create a framework that would cover all people requiring support to exercise legal capacity.

A status of 'legal independence' refers to an adult exercising his or her legal capacity to make decisions without any legally recognised decision-making supporters or representatives. Authorities must presume agency to understand

[109] Bach and Kerzner, above n 107.
[110] Ibid. 134–40.
[111] Ibid. 134.
[112] Bach and Kerzner use the term 'decision-making capability' in a very specific way. Rather than referring to individual abilities or capacities, it instead refers to '"capabilities to function" where function refers to the getting of things done or making things happen that are important to individuals or communities'. Further, capabilities for decision-making are 'a combination of … individual decision-making "abilities" and of decision-making "supports" and accommodations'. They use these terms 'as a way to conceptually integrate recognition of the functional diversity of individuals with an understanding of the array of supports and accommodations a person might need to enjoy and exercise his or her legal capacity'. Ibid. 20–2.

information relevant to a decision and to appreciate the reasonably foreseeable consequences of a decision.[113]

'Supported decision-making status' would be similar in nature to an 'associate' under British Columbia's Representation Agreement Act 1996. Trusted individuals or a network of individuals would assist a person to make decisions by, for example, enabling access to interpretation and plain-language support, or to communicate with people.[114] Bach and Kerzner write that 'supported decision making distributes decision-making abilities required for competent decision-making processes across an individual and his/her supporters, as directed by the individual's will and/or intention'.[115]

'Facilitated decision-making' is the most intensive form of 'support' and refers to a legal status in which 'others facilitate the making of needed decisions'.[116] Clearly, this resembles substituted decision-making, although Bach and Kerzner have made efforts to discard the notion of substitution and give priority to a person's will and preference[117]; for example, they promote a 'best interests' standard that is '[b]ased on the facilitator(s)' best understanding of the person's prior wishes, instructions and values' and meets a number of other criteria.[118]

To determine which of their three decision-making categories is appropriate for a particular person, Bach and Kerzner discard any notion of incapacity as it is understood in common-law jurisprudence.[119] They propose a new test, which they claim is non-discriminatory, to assess whether a person has an impaired ability to make decisions and requires support to exercise his or her legal capacity.[120] In addition to the 'understand and appreciate' test for mental capacity assessments, the proposed test should consider, as per the Representation Agreement Act 1996, a person's ability to express desire, to demonstrate the existence of trusting relationships and to express the desire to be helped in making decisions.[121] They suggest this approach to avoid the supported/substituted dichotomy and to provide a more nuanced understanding of decision-making. The test would create a much higher threshold for moving a person into facilitated decision-making status than currently exists

113 Ibid. 148.
114 Ibid. 23.
115 Ibid.
116 Ibid. 91.
117 Ibid. 82–94.
118 Ibid. 93.
119 Richardson, above n 44, 95.
120 Bach and Kerzner, above n 107, 134–40.
121 Ibid. 24, 61, 85.

in law when determining whether the person lacks mental capacity. Attention would shift to the person's identity and 'life story'; if the person can act in such a way that at least one individual whom he or she trusts can attribute a will, intention or preference to the person concerned which fits with that person's 'life story', then supported decision-making will be employed,[122] not facilitated decision-making.

Yet, even within Bach and Kerzner's proposal, there remains some ambiguity about the criteria for applying a facilitated decision-making arrangement. Bach and Kerzner describe a scenario in which a man with intellectual disabilities is acting in an aggressive and paranoid manner and in which his parents – his key supporters – are finding it difficult to cope, so they invite him to see a doctor.[123] Under Bach and Kerzner's scheme, the man's wish not to see a doctor must be respected alongside a requirement that his parents receive intensive planning support, in the event that both the man and his parents are experiencing 'serious adverse effects'.[124] However, Bach and Kerzner subsequently state that '[a]t some point … the parents may perceive the son's condition as deteriorating to the extent that he can no longer express his will and/or intentions *in ways that would direct reasonable consequential action*', at which point the parents could apply to the tribunal for a facilitated decision-making arrangement (which permits some substituted decisions in the form of 'substituted judgments').[125] Bach and Kerzner's phrasing is noteworthy. They do not suggest that the man is no longer able to express his will and preference, simply that he cannot do so in a way '*that would direct reasonable consequential action*'. It is ambiguous as to whether this constitutes a subtle caveat that a person's expression of will must direct *reasonable* consequential action. This caveat would seem to admit that a person's will and intention could be overridden based on their decision-making ability after all.

An alternative reading is that Bach and Kerzner conceptualise 'will' in such a way that, at the point where consequential action deriving from will becomes difficult to understand to key supporters or contradicts the relevant person's 'life story', then that will becomes 'unclear' and requires arbitration by the 'Legal Capacity and Support Office and Administrative Tribunal'.[126] The tribunal would then decide how to mediate the confusion. It is unclear whether this is what Bach and Kerzner meant, but either way, the criteria they use to determine which category of decision-making should apply to a person

[122] Ibid. 47.
[123] Ibid. 144.
[124] Ibid.
[125] Ibid.
[126] Ibid. 141.

risks retaining the negative effects of current law – by placing a burden on people with disabilities to 'prove' the reasonableness of their decision-making ability – which is precisely what the authors sought to avoid in the first place.[127] Other efforts to implement a universal legal capacity approach are facing similar difficulties, as discussed in Chapter 7.[128]

Regardless, there are two distinct advantages to Bach and Kerzner's proposal. First, the proposal recognises that an individual should not have to pass a functional assessment of decision-making ability in order to access supported decision-making. Second, the proposal recognises that a person's ability to make decisions and exercise agency can either reside in the individual or reside interdependently with his or her supporters. Nevertheless, the proposal is still subject to some of the problematic features associated with assessing mental capacity. Under the scheme, an individual could claim to be legally independent, but if he or she does not meet a certain level of understanding as determined by the proposed tribunal, then his or her legal capacity to make a decision could be removed or 'facilitated'. This removal or 'facilitation' would seem to occur on the basis of decision-making ability, thus raising the spectre of disability-based discrimination outlined in Section 2 of this chapter.

b Universal Legal Capacity: The CRPD Challenge

What, then, would it mean for law and policy to guarantee legal capacity as 'a universal human attribute'?[129] While this ambitious reform goal remains somewhat opaque, the CRPD Committee and others have indicated that it can be characterised by a number of features. The CRPD Committee's non-exhaustive description of a 'supported decision-making regime' provides a useful starting point in identifying these features and is worth citing in full:

> While supported decision-making regimes can take many forms, they should all incorporate certain key provisions to ensure compliance with article 12 of the Convention, including the following:
>
> (a) Supported decision-making must be available to all. A person's level of support needs, especially where these are high, should not be a barrier to obtaining support in decision-making;
> (b) All forms of support in the exercise of legal capacity, including more intensive forms of support, must be based on the will and preference of

[127] Richardson, above n 44, 95–6.
[128] See Chapter 7, Section B(4).
[129] Dhanda, above n 21, 457–8.

the person, not on what is perceived as being in his or her objective best interests;

(c) A person's mode of communication must not be a barrier to obtaining support in decision-making, even where this communication is non-conventional, or understood by very few people;

(d) Legal recognition of the support person(s) formally chosen by a person must be available and accessible, and States have an obligation to facilitate the creation of support, particularly for people who are isolated and may not have access to naturally occurring support in the community. This must include a mechanism for third parties to verify the identity of a support person as well as a mechanism for third parties to challenge the action of a support person if they believe that the support person is not acting in accordance with the will and preferences of the person concerned;

(e) In order to comply with the requirement, set out in article 12, paragraph 3, of the Convention, for States parties to take measures to "provide access" to the support required, States parties must ensure that support is available at nominal or no cost to persons with disabilities and that lack of financial resources is not a barrier to accessing support in the exercise of legal capacity;

(f) Support in decision-making must not be used as justification for limiting other fundamental rights of persons with disabilities, especially the right to vote, the right to marry, or establish a civil partnership, and found a family, reproductive rights, parental rights, the right to give consent for intimate relationships and medical treatment, and the right to liberty;

(g) The person must have the right to refuse support and terminate or change the support relationship at any time;

(h) Safeguards must be set up for all processes relating to legal capacity and support in exercising legal capacity. The goal of safeguards is to ensure that the person's will and preferences are respected;

(i) The provision of support to exercise legal capacity should not hinge on mental capacity assessments; new, non-discriminatory indicators of support needs are required in the provision of support to exercise legal capacity.[130]

The General Comment makes it clear that unsoundness of mind 'and other discriminatory labels are not legitimate reasons for the denial of legal capacity', which would include decision-making ability assessments, given that

[130] Committee on the Rights of Persons with Disabilities, above n 1, 6–7 [29].

'perceived or actual deficits in mental capacity must not be used as justification for denying legal capacity'. Such an approach would represent a definitive break between legal capacity and decision-making ability.

This requires rejecting the concept of a 'rebuttable presumption of mental capacity'. Oliver Lewis and Michael Bach have argued that 'a presumption of mental capacity is meaningless' as it does not help to protect the individual's human rights.[131] Similarly, the European Commissioner for Human Rights has argued for a non-derogable '*assumption* of [legal] capacity',[132] for which automatic recognition means an immediate focus on supports.[133] The task would move from assessing whether someone passes a capacity test to providing a suite of supports to help the person exercise legal capacity. Accordingly, the positive obligation on governments to provide 'support to exercise legal capacity' should be generally available, and more intensive forms of support would be activated when a person's will and preference appears to be unclear, tentative and/or absent.[134] At this point, a support process would be initiated to augment decision-making and assist the individual to exercise his or her legal capacity by seeking to give expression to his or her 'will, preference and rights'[135]; however, in rare circumstances, it would still be necessary to draw upon the 'best interpretation of a person's rights, will and preference'.[136]

The OHCHR, the UN Special Rapporteurs on Torture, Disability and Health and other commentators have endorsed this broad reform proposal.[137] A number of efforts have been made to refine this approach,[138] as previously

[131] O Lewis and M Bach, 'How Northern Ireland Can Avoid Making a Big "Mental Capacity Law" Mistake' (23 April 2014) <www.mdac.info>.

[132] Council of Europe Commissioner for Human Rights, above n 103, 19 (emphasis added); Juan E Méndez, Special Rapporteur, Statement on Torture and Other Cruel, Inhuman or Degrading Treatment or Punishment, 22nd sess, Human Rights Council, Agenda Item 3 (4 March 2013) <www.ohchr.org>.

[133] Ibid.

[134] T Minkowitz, 'Legal Capacity as Right, Principle and Paradigm: Submission to the Committee on the Rights of Persons with Disabilities in Response to Its Call for Papers on Theoretical and Practical Implementation of Article 12' (Prepared for the World Network of Users and Survivors of Psychiatry, 17 June 2011) <www.chrusp.org>. CRPD art 12(4).

[135] CRPD art 12(4).

[136] Committee on the Rights of Persons with Disabilities, above n 1, 5 [21].

[137] Office of the High Commissioner for Human Rights, '"Dignity Must Prevail" – An Appeal to Do Away with Non-consensual Psychiatric Treatment World Mental Health Day – Saturday 10 October 2015', Geneva, 8 October 2015 <www.ohchr.org>; JE Méndez, *Report of the Special Rapporteur on Torture and Other Cruel, Inhuman or Degrading Treatment or Punishment*, UN Doc A/HRC/22/53 (1 February 2013) [81].

[138] See, e.g., The Australian Law Reform Commission, *Equality, Capacity and Disability in Commonwealth Laws* (2014); W Martin et al., 'The Essex Autonomy Project Three Jurisdictions Report: Towards Compliance with CRPD Art. 12 in Capacity/Incapacity Legislation across the UK' (University of Essex, 6 June 2016) <www.autonomy.essex.ac.uk>; P Gooding, 'Navigating

discussed. In their analysis of Northern Ireland's proposed 'fusion' law, Lewis and Bach argue that six things can help achieve a guarantee of equal recognition before the law:

> A legal right to supports in decision-making and a corresponding obligation on government to establish these supports;
> A legal prohibition on findings of 'incapacity', the imposition of substitute decision-making measures and detention, with a focus instead on human rights-compliant alternatives;
> A legal obligation to explore alternatives to substituted decision-making;
> A duty on 'third parties' (doctors, banks, coffee shops) to make accommodations (adjustments) to ensure that the person with a disability can exercise their autonomy, and have their decisions made with support as legally valid;
> A right to advocacy in the mental health system, and access to free and quality legal representation;
> A duty on government to engage people with disabilities, their representative organisations and communities in developing and delivering supports.[139]

Based on these (quite broad) proposals, a key function of legislation would be to define legal capacity and recognise the range of ways that persons can exercise it. Another function would be to facilitate support and provide arbitration to resolve any disputes about that support, including disputes about the 'best interpretation of a person's will, preferences and rights'. If these functions remain the primary task of legislation, then neither diagnostic thresholds nor decision-making ability assessments (at least in theory) would be necessary.

c Repealing Substituted Decision-Making under Mental Health Law

It is worth briefly outlining the proposals for ending mental health law in its current form, in pursuit of guaranteeing equal recognition before the law. Two broad options appear.

The first option is that mental health legislation should be dissolved entirely and that certain 'powers' under mental health law, if they are retained at all, should be moved elsewhere in law and made disability-neutral.[140] These

the "Flashing Amber Lights" of the Right to Legal Capacity in the United Nations Convention on the Rights of Persons with Disabilities: Responding to Major Concerns' (2015) 15(1) Human Rights Law Review 45.

139 Lewis and Bach, above n 131.

140 See, e.g., T Minkowitz, 'Abolishing Mental Health Laws to Comply with the Convention on the Rights of Persons with Disabilities' in B McSherry and P Weller (eds), *Rethinking*

powers could include: emergency procedures where a person's will and preference are unclear, adult protection measures seeking to prevent harm perpetrated by others against persons with psychosocial disabilities, or laws of 'civil' detention that allow for 'dangerous persons' to be detained for public protection purposes. The goal of contemporary mental health law to secure resources for those most in need could then be attended by new forms of statutory support, whether related to representative support (as under the Assisted Decision-Making [Capacity] Act 2015), advocacy support (as under Swedish law) and so on.

A second broad option would be to retain the function of mental health law to ensure access to services for people in mental health crises, but discard its powers to detain and treat involuntarily. Amita Dhanda has argued that the CRPD invites lawmakers 'to see the commonalities between persons with and without disabilities'.[141] Thus, for Dhanda, mental health law could potentially provide all citizens with positive rights, such as the right to enjoyment of the highest attainable physical and mental health and the right to an adequate standard of living and social protection.[142] Such legislation, instead of circumscribing involuntary interventions, would be concerned solely with providing positive rights in the form of a wide range of supports that could be used or refused. This would effectively impose 'coercive orders' on the state, which would be obliged to ensure voluntary services for all who needed them.

For both of these ambitious law reform options, the vision for large-scale change requires ending certain functions of mental health law. Many governments considered in this book show no sign of pursuing these reform pathways in the short or even medium term. However, in Germany, as noted previously, two states invalidated mental health legislation, which reportedly caused a sharp drop in involuntary psychiatric interventions.[143] If these reports are

Rights-Based Mental Health Laws (Hart, 2010) 151; D Webb, 'An New Era in Disability Rights; A New Human Rights Charter Plus a New United Nations Convention', Insane Australia <www.thinkingaboutsuicide.org>; Bach and Kerzner, above n 107.

[141] A Dhanda, 'Mental Health Law Reform in the New and Old Paradigm of Legal Capacity' (Presentation, 'Mental Health Law Reform: New Perspectives and Challenges', National University of Ireland, 23 June 2013) <www.archive.amnesty.ie>.

[142] Article 25 of the CRPD requires States Parties to recognise 'the right of everyone to the enjoyment of the highest attainable standard of health without discrimination on the basis of disability'. This includes an expectation that States Parties '[p]rovide those health services needed by persons with disabilities specifically because of their disabilities'. CRPD art 25(b).

[143] As noted previously, some form of involuntary treatment remained permissible in the two jurisdictions concerned, but only in life-threatening emergencies. See Chapter 3, Section D(3). See also M Zinkler, 'Germany without Coercive Treatment in Psychiatry – A 15 Month Real World Experience' (2016) 5(1) *Laws* 15.

verified, German law reform efforts may provide an impetus for governments considered in this book to follow suit.

ABOLISHING INVOLUNTARY OUTPATIENT TREATMENT The strong grounds for repealing involuntary outpatient treatment laws is one area of law reform that seems more straightforward.[144] Extensive evidence points to the ineffectiveness of community treatment orders ('CTOs') and other forms of involuntary outpatient treatment.[145] Sonia Johnson rightly points out that 'the case for urgent review of this legislation, both at government level and within the professions involved in CTO use, is now strong'.[146] The CRPD Committee has specifically called for States Parties to repeal legal provisions for involuntary outpatient treatment on human rights grounds and has argued for the replacement of CTOs with supported decision-making measures.[147] While the repeal of mental health legislation in its entirety appears to be a highly demanding reform process, the repeal of legal provisions for involuntary outpatient treatment seems to be far less challenging. The development of alternative support arrangements, which may be required, could occur with reference to the wide range of practices listed in the next chapter.[148] CTOs have been criticised by Gunvant Patel for potentially 'sabotaging' learning and growth and reifying relapse prevention and risk management.[149] The CRPD offers a countervailing legislative, policy and practice framework by asking what would be required to enhance the agency of individuals, including with respect to gaps in the support available to them.

Many people will ask how governments can take the CRPD Committee seriously when some mental health crises clearly require intervention against a person's expressed wishes. Other questions will follow. What about a person who is self-harming, attempting suicide or seeking to harm others based on profoundly delusional beliefs? How do emergency ward staff 'support the legal capacity' of an aggressive man with acute methamphetamine psychosis who

[144] See Chapter 3, Section C(3).

[145] R Heun, S Dave and P Rowlands, 'Little Evidence for Community Treatment Orders – A Battle Fought with Heavy Weapons' (2016) 40 *BJPsych Bulletin* 115.

[146] S Johnson, 'Can We Reverse the Rising Tide of Compulsory Admissions?' (2013) 381(9878) *The Lancet* 1603.

[147] Committee on the Rights of Persons with Disabilities, *Concluding Observations of the Committee on the Rights of Persons with Disabilities (Australia)* (advance unedited version) 10th sess, UN Doc CRPD/C/AUS/CO/1 (2–3 September 2013) [34].

[148] Forms of independent advocacy may be particularly beneficial, as would assessments seeking to identify (and plug) the gaps in support available to persons. See Chapter 6, Section B.

[149] G Patel, 'Community Treatment Orders in Victoria: A Clinico-Ethical Perspective' (2008) 16(5) *Australasian Psychiatry* 340, 341.

has not slept for weeks on end? Why did the CRPD Committee exclude from its deliberation the 'less extreme' views of mental health professionals and mental health service users who *endorse* involuntary psychiatric intervention? Can it really be said that mental capacity/decision-making ability assessments are *intrinsically* discriminatory? Won't assessments of ability be essential to identify people's support needs, including the safeguards required for those who 'exercise legal capacity' in substantially different ways, such as someone in a state of catatonic depression? Does the CRPD Committee's emphasis on will and preference fetishise 'choice' in a way that goes against the view of autonomy as interdependent and relational in nature as espoused in the CRPD? And even if lawmakers set aside matters of principle, where is the evidence that 'supported decision-making' works? Who is to say that such practices will not cause more problems than they address?

I will directly engage these criticisms in Chapter 7. Before doing so, however, it is useful to further ground the discussion in practical politics, and to consider efforts to implement different elements of the CRPD support approach in practice.

C CONCLUSION

The CRPD support approach shifts the focus from assessing decision-making ability and regulating substituted decision-making to calling for a range of supports and mechanisms to safeguard a person's 'will, preference and rights'. Domestic law reform thus far has tended to retain assessments of decision-making ability and substituted decision-making measures, even as governments can be seen to introduce an expanding array of support mechanisms. This latter reform strategy is in keeping with the explicit interpretative declaration of some governments regarding what they understand the CRPD to mean,[150] even as it varies from the CRPD Committee's call for the prohibition of involuntary mental health treatment.

From a political perspective, the CRPD Committee's 'hard' proposals could be seen to set the bar too high, in which case governments might not 'come to the table' on reforms. The CRPD may then become an ineffective piece of human rights law. This is a possibility, but there is no evidence so far to suggest that an outright rejection of *all* CRPD directives will take place.

[150] Canada signed the CRPD in 2007 and ratified it in 2010 with a declaration and reservation specifying that its understanding of Article 12 permitted substitute as well as supported decision-making. See CRPD: Reservations and Declarations (Canada) (UNHCR, 2008) <treaties.un.org>.

Instead, various States Parties have taken clear steps to integrate the CRPD into law and policy, including in the mental health context. Such steps have been taken even as governments have stopped short of abandoning incapacity determinations and diagnostic thresholds in mental health law and substituted decision-making. As such, it seems unlikely that governments are adamantly opposed to the 'universal legal capacity' model. Instead, it may be that policymakers and other public officials cannot yet conceptualise – or generate enough political will to develop and implement – a system that 'guarantees legal capacity'. Given the entrenched marginalisation of persons with psychosocial disability that appears to persist today, it is perhaps not difficult to see why such political imagination is missing. Government concerns may revolve around the resource implications of providing what appears to be the unlimited support required to guarantee equal standing before the law for all, or the apparent need to amend the numerous laws in which mental incapacity determinations appear. As the European Commissioner of Human Rights has observed, no jurisdiction has met the high standards of Article 12 – doing so is 'path-breaking work'.[151]

Despite these challenges, all jurisdictions considered in this book have taken some steps to overlay the CRPD onto domestic law, policy and practice in the mental health context. Clearly, there remain conceptual ambiguities in the application of the CRPD support framework in this way. However, this ambiguity can be defended – a defence that I have pursued throughout Chapters 4 and 5 – particularly given that ideas about support, agency and equality have an essential ambiguity. Instead of these ambiguities being glossed over or ignored, they should be clearly identified and subjected to public debate. Notwithstanding the CRPD Committee's broad requirements for creating a 'supported decision-making regime', the value attributed to various aspects of the support framework will need to be decided as a matter for democratic discussion. The ambiguities discussed here are not unique to the mental health context, but rarely have the specific issues of mental health law

[151] Council of Europe Commissioner for Human Rights, 'Who Gets to Decide? Right to Legal Capacity for Persons with Intellectual and Psychosocial Disabilities' (Comm DH/Issue Paper, Strasbourg, 20 February 2012) 20. Similarly, the OHCHR handbook on the CRPD for parliamentarians emphasises the difficulty in operationalising supported decision-making within a legislative and policy framework. It states that '[w]hile some good models of support networks exist, there is generally *no clear policy framework*; guardianship laws and practice still dominate' – a view which largely stands today. UN Office of the High Commissioner for Human Rights, 'Chapter Six: From Provisions to Practice: Implementing the Convention, Legal Capacity and Supported Decision-Making', *UN Handbook for Parliamentarians on the Convention on the Rights of Persons with Disabilities* (2007) <www.un.org> (emphasis added).

been subject to rigorous public debate (perhaps due to 'sanism' or stigma). Regardless of uncertainties that remain about the 'hard' reading of the CRPD Committee, the pragmatic and pluralistic approach of the CRPD appears to provide enough 'overlapping consensus' to reimagine how the law addresses the complexities of mental health, disorder, distress and disability.

6

Practical Examples of the CRPD Support Framework in the Mental Health Context

A INTRODUCTION

In Chapters 4 and 5, I highlighted how the support approach of the CRPD[1] emphasises state duties to provide resources to strengthen agency and self-determination. This theoretical shift captures areas of consensus regarding the need for proactive measures of support and expands the purview of justice in the mental health context beyond the vexing question of involuntary treatment. States Parties to the CRPD are obliged to provide resources for persons with psychosocial disability to enjoy substantive rights in many areas of life, including independent living and being included in the community, health, home and family, education and employment. This is not to ignore matters of 'coercive care', but rather to seek ways of resolving difficulties by referencing practical efforts exemplary of the CRPD support framework today. Numerous actors – from persons with psychosocial disability to professionals, government agencies and academics – have proposed, developed and implemented practical measures.[2] Many of these practices appear outside the bounds of mental health legislation in a range of areas of law, policy and programming and in informal arrangements between individuals, their families and communities, as the following non-exhaustive list demonstrates.

1 Convention on the Rights of Persons with Disabilities, opened for signature 30 March 2007, Doc.A/61/611 (entered into force 3 May 2008).

2 See, e.g., P Weller, 'Supported Decision-Making and the Achievement of Non-Discrimination: The Promise and Paradox of the Disabilities Convention' (2008) 26(2) *Law in Context* 85; F Morrissey, 'The United Nations Convention on the Rights of Persons with Disabilities: A New Approach to Decision-Making in Mental Health Law' (2012) 19 *European Journal of Health Law* 423; S Pathare and LS Shields, 'Supported Decision-Making for Persons with Mental Illness: A Review' (2012) 34(2) *Public Health Reviews* 1.

B LEGISLATION

1 *Advance Planning and Representative Support*

Two major measures for promoting the will and preference of persons with psychosocial disability are advance planning and nominated representative schemes.[3] Advance directives (sometimes referred to as 'advance statements' or 'Ulysses agreements') refer to freely made decisions designed to bind oneself or direct others to action in the future. The CRPD Committee has written:

> For many persons with disabilities, the ability to plan in advance is an important form of support, whereby they can state their will and preferences which should be followed at a time when they may not be in a position to communicate their wishes to others. All persons with disabilities have the right to engage in advance planning and should be given the opportunity to do so on an equal basis with others.[4]

Penelope Weller has argued that advance directives are a practical method for formalising supported decision-making in ways that 'take account of varying mental health conditions and the specific institutional contexts in which mental health treatment is provided'.[5] An advance directive can strengthen self-determination by clarifying a person's will and preference before mental health crises occur.[6] These mechanisms exist in laws throughout the common-law world, in mental health legislation and elsewhere. Notwithstanding the incongruence of mental health law (at least in its current form) and the CRPD,[7] it may be possible to draw upon some existing mechanisms within mental health law to build new CRPD-compliant legal frameworks.

In Scotland, under the Mental Health (Care and Treatment) (Scotland) Act 2003 ('MHCT Act'),[8] the treating clinician and the mental health tribunal

3 See, e.g., Department of Health, *Exposure Draft Mental Health Bill 2010, Explanatory Guide* (Victorian Government, 2010); D Sachan, 'Mental Health Bill Set to Revolutionise Care in India' (2013) 382(9889) *The Lancet* 296; Department of Health (Ireland), *Interim Report of the Steering Group on the Review of the Mental Health Act 2001* (2012) 11 <www.dohc.ie>.

4 Committee on the Rights of Persons with Disabilities, *General Comment No 1: Article 12: Equal Recognition Before the Law*, 11th sess, UN Doc CRPD/C/GC/1 (19 May 2014) [17].

5 Weller, above n 2. See also P Weller, *New Law and Ethics in Mental Health Advance Directives: The Convention on the Rights of Persons with Disabilities and the Right to Choose* (Routledge, 2013).

6 LA Campbell and SR Kisely, 'Advance Treatment Directives for People with Severe Mental Illness' (2009) (1) *Cochrane Database of Systematic Reviews*, doi: 10.1002/14651858.CD005963.pub2.

7 See Chapter 2.

8 Mental Health (Care and Treatment) (Scotland) Act 2003 (Scot) asp 13, s 276(3).

must 'have regard to the wishes specified in' a person's advance statement.[9] 'Personal statements' can accompany the advance statement to provide instructions about financial or other personal matters.[10] Representative support is also available under the MHCT Act.[11] The MHCT Act allows for the appointment of a 'named person' from among someone's peers, associates, family members and other informal supporters.[12] Appointments are made either by the person concerned or by a mental health tribunal during periods of crisis.[13] Default nomination of relatives and other supporters can occur, subject to certain rules and regulations.[14] Named persons must be informed and consulted about aspects of the person's care should he or she become subject to civil commitment. Currently, the role contains elements of substituted decision-making – for example, the named person is able to 'make decisions on (the person's) behalf'.[15] Similar statutory recognition of 'named' or 'nominated' representatives appears in mental health legislation throughout the world.[16]

As noted previously, advanced planning and nominated person schemes exist outside mental health law, including within the Representation Agreement Act 1996 in British Columbia, Canada.[17] The Vancouver/Richmond Mental Health Network Society describes the potential benefits of representation agreements in the mental health context as follows:

> Mark had episodes of mood disorder. Each episode created great disruption in his life. Not only did Mark have to struggle to get treatment, but he also suffered unpredictable consequences afterwards. Sometimes his bank account was overdrawn, or he had lost his job or housing. Out of desperation, Mark decided to try a Ulysses Agreement. He asked four members of his extended family to act as his Representatives. He divided their responsibilities into three major areas: health care, financial affairs and employment. He very

9 An advance statement, in law, does not have to be adhered to. However, the Mental Welfare Commission for Scotland has to be informed if advance statements are overridden. Mental Health (Care and Treatment) (Scotland) Act 2003 asp 13, s 276(3).

10 Scottish Executive, *The New Mental Health Act: A Guide to Advance Statements* (2005) 9 <www.scotland.gov.uk>.

11 Mental Health (Care and Treatment) (Scotland) Act 2003 (Scot) asp 13, c 1, ss 250–8.

12 Ibid. s 250.

13 See, generally, Ibid. asp 13 c 1.

14 Ibid. For example, section 253 refers to the power of those subject to the MHCT Act to declare a person ineligible to become a named person.

15 Scottish Executive, above n 10, 7.

16 Mental Health Act 2015 (ACT) ss 15(4), 19–23; Mental Health Act 2009 (SA) s 47; Mental Health Act 2016 (Qld) s 25(2); Mental Health Act 2013 (Tas) s 3; Mental Health Act 2007 (NSW) ss 71–2; Mental Health Act 2014 (Vic) ss 23–4; Mental Health Act 2014 (WA) pt 16 div 3.

17 Representation Agreement Act R.S.B.C. 1996 c 405, ss 2(a), 8.

> clearly described the circumstances that would signal his Representatives to act on his behalf and also said what he wanted them to do. His doctor agreed to help. Mark and his family members executed the agreement. His Representatives have acted on the agreement several times. They've used it to freeze bank accounts and credit cards, to help Mark get treatment and to manage his personal affairs. The banks and professionals who have been called on by the Representatives have honoured the agreement. In retrospect, Mark says that having a Ulysses Agreement 'saved his life'. He no longer has to pick up the pieces and start over after each episode of illness.[18]

This example highlights how statutory advance planning and representative support could meet two key challenges posed by the CRPD: eschewing mental capacity assessments or civil commitment criteria and remaining disability-neutral. The activation of a representative agreement does not rely on a person being made involuntary under the terms of mental health law, or incapacitated under the terms of adult (in)capacity laws; instead, Mark was able to 'very clearly describe … the circumstances that would signal his Representatives to act on his behalf'. Further, the advance planning and representative support enabled by the legislation is accessible to a wide range of people who may require advance planning to exercise legal capacity (for example, older persons, those facing end-of-life decisions, young adults with intellectual disability). Advance planning clearly does not need to operate within mental health law in order to benefit persons with psychosocial disability. Despite these points, British Columbian mental health law does provide powers to override a representation agreement,[19] which would fall short of the 'universal design' standard of the CRPD. According to the Vancouver/Richmond Mental Health Network Society, the inability of representatives 'to refuse consent' to any treatment decisions under mental health legislation 'denies to people who have been detained under the Mental Health Act of BC the right to have a representative ensure that their wishes are respected with regard to their mental health care – a right that every other citizen concerned with any other aspect of their health is guaranteed by the Representation Agreement Act'.[20]

A key challenge for reformers seeking to develop CRPD-compliant advance planning and representative functions will be to ensure that people with

[18] Vancouver/Richmond Mental Health Network Society, *Representation Agreements and Supported Decision-Making* (May 2005) <http://francais.ccamhr.ca/communications/repaggreements.html>.

[19] Representation Agreement Act R.S.B.C. 1996 c 405, s 11(1).

[20] Vancouver/Richmond Mental Health Network Society, above n 18.

disabilities have the right to engage in advance planning on an equal basis with others. The CRPD Committee has noted that:

> States parties can provide various forms of advance planning mechanisms to accommodate various preferences, but *all the options should be non-discriminatory*. Support should be provided to a person, where desired, to complete an advance planning process. The point at which an advance directive enters into force (and ceases to have effect) should be decided by the person and included in the text of the directive; it should not be based on an assessment that the person lacks mental capacity.[21]

Achieving consistency in the application of advanced planning mechanisms where individuals or supporters set the terms by which they are activated, will be challenging. However, this style of advance planning and representational support is not without precedent, as demonstrated in the account of the Vancouver/Richmond Mental Health Network Society noted previously. The non-discrimination prerogative will also raise tensions with the exceptional status given to people with psychiatric diagnoses in most jurisdictions. After all, advance planning in general health settings encompasses refusal of life-saving treatment. Yet, in mental health settings, even a person with mental capacity would be unable to have an advance directive refusing treatment under the vast majority of mental health laws considered in this book.[22]

2 *Assessing Support (Not Individual Deficits) and Mandating Services: Argentina's National Mental Health Law*

Other mechanisms within mental health legislation are worth considering for their potential to inform a broader scheme of CRPD-based support in the mental health context. Argentina's National Mental Health Law 2010 ('NMHL')[23] contains an innovative mechanism to strengthen the self-determination of service users and take into account the harmful effects of involuntary treatment.[24]

[21] Committee on the Rights of Persons with Disabilities, above n 4, [17].

[22] An exception to this generalisation is likely to be the mental health law of Ontario, Canada, under which a person can be detained due to an apparent or diagnosed mental disorder, although treatment cannot be imposed involuntarily, even when it may 'alleviate the disorder'. Ontario Mental Health Act R.S.O. 1990 ch M.7. See JE Gray and RL O'Reilly, 'Supreme Court of Canada's "Beautiful Mind" Case' (2009) 32(5) *International Journal of Law and Psychiatry* 315.

[23] Law No 26657, 3 December 2010 [32041] BO 1; 'Mental Health Regime', House of Representatives Res D-276/07 (7 March 2007) art 1.

[24] FJ Bariffi and MS Smith, 'Same Old Game but with Some New Players: Assessing Argentina's National Mental Health Law in Light of the Rights to Liberty and Legal Capacity under the

Article 42 of the NMHL requires all restrictions to be based on interdisciplinary evaluations that seek to assess not just the person but the availability of support in his or her life, in relation to which voluntary supports could be court-ordered.[25] Francisco Bariffi and Matthew Smith argue that 'the evolving practice arising from the "interdisciplinary evaluation" requirement suggests that interdisciplinary teams aware of the CRPD may prove effective in promoting the replacement of restrictions with supported decision-making arrangements'.[26] The existing teams – consisting of psychiatrists, psychologists, lawyers and social workers – reportedly exceed the minimal requirements of Article 42 in practice.[27] Each evaluation, which includes interviews, an assessment of available support and consideration of daily routines, results in a recommendation for the establishment of a supported decision-making plan around that person.[28] The evaluation team reportedly uses the CRPD as a guide when communicating and reporting to judges, including highlighting a person's communication needs, the extent to which past experiences of involuntary treatment from the person's view have compromised his or her autonomy and personal development, and the extent of the person's existing informal and formal supports, including possible gaps that could be remedied with services.[29] Bariffi and Smith argue that such measures 'contribute to increasing judges' alternatives regarding incapacitations that promote the supported exercise of legal capacity'.[30] Further, it 'prompts judges to address issues related to supported decision-making'.[31]

By promoting a range of available supports, the support framework of the CRPD invites interdisciplinary responses to mental health support. John Brayley notes that '[t]he practise of facilitating supported decision-making arrangements does not belong to any one particular profession'.[32] Relevant disciplines may include social work, law, psychiatry, psychology, nursing and the emerging field of peer-support workers, but may also include community-based

United Nations Convention on the Rights of the Persons with Disabilities' (2013) 31(3) *Nordic Journal of Human Rights* 325.

25 Law No 26657, 3 December 2010 [32041] BO 1; 'Mental Health Regime', House of Representatives Res D-276/07 (7 March 2007) art 42.

26 Bariffi and Smith, above n 24, 339.

27 Ibid. 339.

28 Ibid.

29 Ibid, 339–40.

30 Ibid.

31 Ibid.

32 South Australia Office of the Public Advocate, 'Developing a Model of Practice for Supported Decision-Making: Background Information to Assist the Facilitation of Agreements' (2011) Office of the Public Advocate and Julia Farr MS McLeod Benevolent Fund, 32, s 4.3.2. <www.opa.sa.gov.au>

workers trained to facilitate support from within a person's social context. (I will discuss family-based support shortly.)

The use of interdisciplinary teams in providing support could begin to disperse the concentration of power that may reside with authorised persons under current mental health laws (typically clinicians). A team of multidisciplinary actors might also help to clarify the constituent motives for decision-making under current laws, which can be exceedingly complex.[33] Presently, such motivations include providing therapeutic support, undertaking risk assessment for both the person and the public, and taking into account the available resources. Brayley argues that individualised funding packages, in combination with supported decision-making and person-centred planning, can help to separate the constituent motives for decisions about service delivery.[34] 'Person-centred care' in the health context is described by the Institute of Medicine as care that is 'respectful of and responsive to *individual* patient preference, needs, and values and ensur[es] that patient values guide all clinical decisions' – a concept that at first glance seems to reflect the emphasis placed on will and preference under the CRPD support framework.[35] Under the Argentinian NMHL, interventions are based on interdisciplinary evaluations, which suggests that interdisciplinary teams aware of the CRPD could effectively promote the replacement of 'best interests' restrictions with CRPD-based support arrangements – at least as far as assessing the supports available and mandating the provision of resources to plug gaps.[36] The use of supported decision-making to clarify the decision-making process can assist a person, and his or her supporters, to determine the most useful and appropriate avenues of support.

The NMHL, once again, clearly does not accord with the high standards of the CRPD; it does not question the legitimacy of involuntary treatment and engenders a rebuttable presumption of a person's mental capacity. Nonetheless, Bariffi and Smith rightly advance this 'rights-based approach' to civil commitment as a means by which government agencies, which play a crucial role in implementing law reform, can promote obligations under the CRPD in the operation of existing law.[37]

33 See Chapter 3, Section E(4).

34 J Brayley, 'Supported Decision-Making in Australia: Presentation Notes' (2009) Presented to Victorian Office of the Public Advocate and Victorian Law Reform Commission, 7–9 <www.opa.sa.gov.au>.

35 Institute of Medicine, *Crossing the Quality Chasm: A New Health System for the 21st Century* (National Academy Press, 2001).

36 Bariffi and Smith, above n 24, 339.

37 Ibid.

3 *Independent Advocacy: Sweden's 'PO Skåne'*

One of the most commonly cited statutory mechanisms to support people with psychosocial disabilities to exercise legal capacity is from Sweden. It arranges for the judicial appointment of a legal mentor or personal ombudsman (often referred to as an 'assistant' or 'advocate') to assist a person to make legal decisions in a facilitative rather than coercive fashion.[38] In its *Handbook for Parliamentarians on the CRPD*, the OHCHR recommend the 'PO Skåne' program as an appropriate supported decision-making statutory mechanism for persons with psychosocial disability.[39] Elsewhere, Stanley Herr describes Sweden as 'one of the most advanced countries in developing legal techniques to reinforce rather than disregard a person's capacity for making choices'.[40]

According to the PO Skåne website, support workers start by making contact with people experiencing mental health crises or extreme mental states, including individuals who may live entirely in their own 'symbolic world'.[41] Individuals are then invited to share their goals in order to guide the work of their assistants.[42] According to Maths Jesperson, the model follows the social model of disability by 'rejecting the notion that the problem is within the individual' – instead, 'it is the society which does not meet the person in such a way that he or she can function':

> If some people have difficulties communicating and expressing their wishes, the solution is to develop a relationship with the person and find ways to make it possible for the person to express and communicate what he or she wants. A Personal Ombudsperson (PO) ... has the skills required to advocate effectively for a client's rights in front of various authorities or in a court of law. All the PO's of PO-Skåne have academic degrees or similar education. Most of them are social workers, some are lawyers. They come from various ethnic backgrounds. The PO is not in alliance with psychiatry or social services or any other authority and not with the client's relatives or any other

[38] L Salzman, 'Guardianship for Persons with Mental Illness – A Legal and Appropriate Alternative?' (2011) 4 *St. Louis University Journal of Health Law and Policy* 279.

[39] UN Office of the High Commissioner for Human Rights, 'Chapter Six: From provisions to practice: implementing the Convention, Legal Capacity and Supported Decision-Making', *United Nations Handbook for Parliamentarians on the Convention on the Rights of Persons with Disabilities* (Geneva, 2007) 89 <www.un.org>.

[40] S Herr, 'Self-determination, Autonomy, and Alternatives to Guardianship', in S Herr, LO Gostin and H Hong-Ju Koh (eds), *The Human Rights of Persons with Intellectual Disabilities* (Oxford University Press, 2003) 432.

[41] PO Skåne website (English) 'Swedish User-Run Service with Personal Ombud (PO) for Psychiatric Patients' <www.po-Skåne.org>.

[42] Ibid.

> person in the client's surroundings. The PO works only with the consent of his or her client. The PO does only what the client wants him or her to do. It can take a long time, sometimes several months, before the client knows and dares to tell the PO what kind of help he or she wants. The PO has to wait, even though a lot of things in the client's life may be in chaos. It usually takes the PO several years to develop a long-term relationship and build enough trust to be able to address essential matters. In other models, it is usually the clients who have to adjust to the bureaucratic system, but the PO-Skåne service works the other way. The PO's have to be very flexible and creative and unconventional in finding ways to work with their clients. Many clients are very suspicious or hostile or hard to reach for other reasons. The PO has to go out and meet them where they are. Making contact sometimes takes several months. It could involve going out to the park to start talking to a homeless person or talking through the mail drop with someone who lives barricaded in their apartment.[43]

A report by the Swedish National Board of Health and Welfare indicates that being a 'care demander' is an important function of the PO.[44] He or she 'make[s] demands on the public authorities that are responsible for people with serious psychiatric disabilities, to ensure that they are receiving the help and service to which they are entitled'.[45] According to the report, this function reduces the number of mental health crises that a person experiences and leads to savings of up to seventeen times the cost of the service itself; the PO's facilitative role in coordinating between services can help address weaknesses in service provision.[46] The status of the PO as a statutorily recognised advocate may be crucial in holding services accountable in this way.

To gain a brief sense of how the PO scheme might operationalise elements of the CRPD support framework, consider the following case, described by the Swedish National Board of Health and Welfare:

> After a stay in hospital, a client wanted to live in a flat of his own. Since this was the client's wish, he was supported by the PO, while many other professionals involved with the client advised against it, saying that it would not

43 M Jesperson, 'How Can We Accomplish What Needs to Be Done? 1. Positive Measures Relating to Key Articles of the Convention, Article 12: Models for Supported Decision-Making and Totally Voluntary Services (1. Supporting Decision-Making)' in T Minkowitz (ed), *Implementation Manual for the United Nations Convention on the Rights of Persons with Disabilities* (World Network of Users and Survivors of Psychiatry, February 2008) 29–30 <www.psychrights.org>.

44 Swedish National Board of Health and Welfare, 'A New Profession is Born – Personligt ombud, PO' (Västra Aros, Västerås, November 2008) 10 <www.personligtombud.se>.

45 Ibid.

46 Ibid.

> work out. This in fact turned out to be the case: the client eventually moved into housing with special support and was very happy there. Professionals in the social services and psychiatric services thought that this was an unnecessary failure, while the PO's view was that the reason why the client was so happy in the special housing was that he had been given the chance to live in his own flat.[47]

The emphasis of the PO on respecting the will and preference of the client in this case, rather than prioritising risk-aversion or 'best interests' recommendations by experts, demonstrates how supported decision-making can be provided in practice. It is noteworthy that there is little in the way of robust research on the operation of the scheme (at least for English-language readers), including its operation in Anglo-Celtic jurisdictions. Nevertheless, the PO scheme seems particularly compelling as an alternative to involuntary outpatient treatment and offers a practice that appears to capture the *ethos* of CRPD-oriented support. Providing support for clients to exercise a range of rights outside of hospital (including those related to autonomy, independent living, health) could disrupt the existing emphasis in involuntary treatment in general, and involuntary outpatient treatment in particular, on relapse prevention, coercion and risk management.[48]

C POLICY AND PROGRAMMING

Policies and programs clearly overlap with legislative mechanisms, including those outlined in the previous section. For example, there are a number of non-statutory schemes for advance planning and for the type of individual advocacy of the PO scheme (though the extent to which the statutory standing of the PO affects the role compared to non-statutory advocacy may be important). Tina Minkowitz has suggested that development of a CRPD-based support framework in the mental health context 'will require innovation and should draw on existing programs that may not have been understood as support in the exercise of legal capacity'.[49] This could include '[p]eer support, recovery-based services, community support networks, and personal assistance, [which] may all help people with psychosocial disabilities in ways related to decision-making or the exercise of legal capacity'.[50] The following

47 Ibid.

48 Ibid.

49 T Minkowitz, 'The United Nations Convention on the Rights of Persons with Disabilities and the Right to Be Free from Non-Consensual Psychiatric Interventions' (2007) 34(2) *Syracuse Journal of International Law and Commerce* 405, 409.

50 Ibid.

practices in policy and programming appear to capture different aspects of the support framework outlined in Chapters 4 and 5.

1 *The South Australian Supported Decision-Making Model*

The South Australian Office of the Public Advocate ('OPA') trialled a non-statutory supported decision-making program in 2010.[51] OPA described the process as 'setting up supported decision-making agreements, and supporting the participants with those agreements'.[52] Following the initial trial, the model was further developed by the South Australian Health Services Complaints Commission ('HSCC').[53] The HSCC described the program thus:

> The model is centred on a person with a disability ('the decision-maker') and one or more supporters. Supporters are drawn from the immediate family or social networks of the decision-maker and commit to assist the decision-maker to make decisions in areas of their own choosing.
>
> Facilitators are workers in disability agencies. They:
>
> - conduct particular processes to recruit decision-makers;
> - support decision-makers to choose their supporters;
> - assist with recruitment of supporters if required, and provide ongoing support to those supporters (some of whom must make significant shifts in previous beliefs and behaviours to be able to operate as a supporter);
> - facilitate meetings involving the decision-maker and their supporters in which the decision-maker selects the decisions they wish to make, and is supported to make them;
> - facilitate meetings between the decision-maker, their supporters and other 'team members' who can assist with the implementation of decisions;
> - provide follow-up between meetings to keep the process moving forward.
>
> The model is intended to work by ensuring 'expressed wish' decision-making (that is, decisions made by and reflecting the expressed wishes of the participant) rather than 'best interests' decision-making … In doing so,

[51] South Australia Office of the Public Advocate, Developing a Model of Practice for Supported Decision-Making: Background Information to Assist the Facilitation of Agreements (2011) <www.opa.sa.gov.au>.

[52] Ibid. 5.

[53] Community Matters, *HCSCC Supported Decision Making Program 2014–15: Evaluation Report* (Health and Community Services Complaints Commissioner's Office, 2015) <www.hcscc.sa.gov.au>.

> it expected to build the capacity of the decision-maker by enabling them to identify and access support for decision making, helping them understand the options and consequences of each decision, building awareness and understanding of their rights, and building skills in decision-making and negotiation. The project also expected to build capacity in the family and friends who act as supporters, who learn to support decision making rather than to make the decisions for the person with a disability. Facilitators act as coaches for supporters, ensuring that they develop the knowledge, skills and attitudes necessary to support the individual in making their own decisions ...
>
> Finally, the project was expected to build the capacity of workers to act as facilitators of the SDM process and to influence the capacity of organisations to implement expressed wish decision-making.[54]

Supports centre on a range of areas of life, including finances, healthcare, accommodation and lifestyle.[55] Both the OPA trial and the HSCC program were small-scale, with twenty-six decision-makers in the former[56] and twenty-one in the latter[57]; however, both encompassed interactions beyond simply the decision-makers themselves, also including their informal supporters, service providers and others, whose combined number would have been dozens, perhaps hundreds.

Evaluations of the programs were positive, with minor exceptions. For the OPA iteration of the model, the researchers hypothesised that support could offer an alternative to people at risk of being placed under guardianship, and as an early intervention strategy for people to prevent problems occurring in the future; the aim was to 'facilitate age appropriate responses and skills in self-determination',[58] and to identify 'the wider possible benefits of supported decision-making'.[59] According to an independent evaluation, the programme achieved these aims:

> [T]here were specific benefits to most of the participants. These were seen in their increased confidence in themselves and in their decision making. There was evidence of improvement in decision making skills. Participants described the growth in their support networks. Many reported that [they] felt more in control of their lives. Participants gave evidence that they had

54 Ibid. 10.

55 Ibid.

56 M Wallace, Evaluation of the Supported Decision Making Project Office of the Public Advocate (Muirgen Nominees, 2012) 4 <www.opa.sa.gov.au>.

57 Community Matters, above n 53, 14 [1.5].

58 D Chartres and J Brayley, *Submission to the Productivity Commission: Inquiry into Disability Care and Support* (Office of the Public Advocate, South Australia, August 2010) 12 [42].

59 Ibid. 12 [43].

> increased their engagement with the community, either through expanding their options or through making decisions that changed their circumstances.
>
> Supporters reported positive changes. They reported on increases in supported decision making in the lives of the participants, changes to the way they considered decision making with the participants, and positive improvements in the nature and quality of their interpersonal relationships. The evaluation gives evidence that Supported Decision Making was both a companion process and viable alternative to substitute decision making for participants who were initially on Guardianship Orders.[60]

Since the trial, the authors have continued to promote supported decision-making in policy, including a 'population-based' policy model.[61]

For the HSCC iteration of the project, the evaluation included identifying where the supported decision-making programme '[wa]s and [wa]s not effective'[62] and listing the outcomes of the project 'for decision-makers, support people, facilitators and organisations'.[63] The evaluators summarised the overall outcomes thus:

> Positive outcomes included goal-setting, increased confidence, greater assertiveness, reduced frustration and anger with consequent impacts on service personnel and costs, increased autonomy in daily living, greater variety in activities, higher levels of engagement in community activities and organisations, increased literacy and numeracy, work related skills, changed employment and in one case, a decision to get married. For at least two, probably three and perhaps more of these decision-makers, outcomes are likely to reduce costs the participating organisations. (Greater clarity about the extent to which costs may be saved will require a proper economic evaluation). Other than the direct costs of running the program, no increases in costs were reported. Outcomes for trainee facilitators included increased skills and knowledge, and changed ways of working, not just with decision-makers but also with other clients. Some supporters reported positive outcomes for themselves, including increased satisfaction, greater awareness of the capacities of the decision-maker, and in one case, a significant change in life direction. One supporter reported increased tension in their relationship with the decisionmaker. Outcomes for organisations included changed practice by participating staff and some knowledge and skills diffusion to other staff, and some minor changes to management thinking. No significant policy or

60 Wallace, above n 56, 4–5.

61 South Australia Office of the Public Advocate, *Annual Report 2012–2013 | Promoting Rights and Interests* (2013) 52 <www.opa.sa.gov.au>.

62 Community Matters, above n 53, 5.

63 Ibid. 6.

service changes were identified. Some managers reported that the program was more expensive to implement than had been anticipated.[64]

There were a few exceptions to the generally positive reports of individuals, families, workers and agency representatives. One of the eight services that engaged with the project 'did not report positive outcomes ... [following] significant tensions in relationships between families and the organisation'.[65] Overall, the evaluators of the HSCC-supported decision-making program recommended that it 'should be continued and expanded' and called for further research to refine and expand the practice.[66]

2 *Family-Based and Collaborative Practices*

Given the high priority that the CRPD places on relationships,[67] a person's social context becomes a natural site to direct support. Most people with a disability, including in the mental health context, have strong and mutually supportive relationships with their families and supporters, relationships that are frequently the most enduring in their lives. Family members, in the broad sense of the term, assist in ways directly relevant to strengthening self-determination, including providing financial and decision-making support, emotional support and encouragement, and advocacy, as well as promoting learning and development. Families and close supporters store a person's life history, interpret individuality and communication, share social activities and introduce new opportunities. They can also act as vehicles for accessing services, raising complaints and passing on compliments, monitoring service quality, coordinating support and helping to manage individual funding. They provide expertise on identifying a person's needs, will and preferences, and can assist the person and services with communication and planning.[68]

There are certainly exceptions to this trend which must be taken seriously. John McCarthy has written that '[t]he value of a good relative cannot be overestimated or overstated', and yet '[t]he damage caused by a bad relative

64 Ibid.

65 Community Matters, above n 53, 8.

66 Ibid 7.

67 See Chapter 4, Section C(6).

68 In 2008, for example, 97.5 per cent of people with severe and profound impairments in Australia who were under the age of sixty-five lived in the community. Of these, 84 *per cent of people with 'severe and profound limitations' lived with family*, according to the Australian Institute of Health and Welfare, while 10 per cent lived alone and 3.2 per cent lived with unrelated individuals. Australian Institute of Health and Welfare, *Bulletin* 61 (2008).

cannot be understated or underestimated'.[69] To prioritise the constitutive relationships in which a person exercises self-determination would conceivably require measures to help *prevent* and *resolve* conflicts between supporter and supported person (or address abuse against the person). After all, mental health crises may place considerable stress on personal relationships and may even *emerge* as a result of violent or otherwise troubled relationships, in which case avenues to exit such relationships might also form part of the support measures being offered to persons with disabilities.

In less extreme scenarios, support that accords with the CRPD might also generate practical measures to address issues related to family and supporters who act (inadvertently or otherwise) in ways that undermine a person's agency. The South Australian supported decision-making program operationalised precisely this function: a key part of the supporter role involved providing 'ongoing support to those supporters (some of whom must make significant shifts in previous beliefs and behaviours to be able to operate as a supporter)'.[70] Supported decision-making measures ideally affirm to all parties that the person making decisions is a peer and an equal citizen, with rights and entitlements, rather than a passive patient whose preferences can be overlooked or dismissed. As noted previously, Robert Gordon refers to this symbolic function as a central component of supported decision-making legislation in Canada,[71] a function buttressed by practical tools for families and supporters.[72]

Numerous existing practices in this area are likely to serve this facilitative function. A number of clinical studies have highlighted the benefits of involving family in mental health service provision, including what is sometimes referred to as 'family psycho-education' and 'home based behavioural interventions'.[73] Existing initiatives, which can be found in mental health policy worldwide, are informative. For example, the Medical Council of New Zealand adopted 'Māori-based strategies' which strongly promote engagement

69 J McCarthy, 'Do Doctors Have the Capacity to Decide? In the Equality Debate, Nurses Must Step Up to the Plate!' (Presentation to the Irish Institute of Mental Health Nursing, 2nd Annual Symposium, 2 June 2011).

70 Community Matters, above n 53, 5 (bracketed text in original).

71 R Gordon, 'The Emergence of Assisted (Supported) Decision-Making in the Canadian Law of Adult Guardianship and Substitute Decision-Making' (2000) 23(1) *International Journal of Law and Psychiatry* 61.

72 Ibid.

73 See, e.g., AN Cohen et al., 'The Family Forum: Directions for the Implementation of Family Psychoeducation for Severe Mental Illness' (2008) 59 *Psychiatric Services* 40; G Pitschel-Walz et al., 'The Effect of Family Interventions on Relapse and Rehospitalization in Schizophrenia: A Meta-Analysis' (2004) 2(1) *FOCUS* 78; F Pharoah et al., 'Family Intervention for Schizophrenia' [2010] (12) *Cochrane Database of Systematic Reviews*, doi:10.1002/14651858.CD000088.pub3.

with a person's *whānau* (which roughly translates as 'family' but includes broader community ties).[74] These practices have even been incorporated into New Zealand's mental health law,[75] although the extent to which they have been operationalised remains unclear and no standard practice guidelines exist.[76] Within existing mental health law, Terry Carney has argued that mental health tribunals could do more to appreciate the significance of the social networks of people who stand before them.[77] By creating 'relational space' for tribunal adjudications, he argues, greater consideration could be given to the views of family members, friends and other informal support people.[78]

The Open Dialogue approach to acute psychosis is a practice developed in Finland in which care decisions are made in the presence of the individual and his or her wider networks.[79] Minkowitz suggests that the practice appears to accord with the emphasis in the CRPD on involving 'social networks in finding solutions'.[80] Russell Razzaque and Lisa Wood describe it as follows:

> [Open Dialogue] involves a psychologically consistent family and social network approach to mental health care – especially in crisis – where all psychotherapeutic treatment is done in the presence of the patient's support system. The aim is to develop a dialogical communication between the patient and their support system as a therapeutic intervention. The primary focus of service provision is around regular 'network meetings' between the patient and his/her immediate network of friends, carers and family, and several consistently attending members of the clinical team. The aim is to empower the family and social network via a process of dialogical communication, which involves the equal hearing of all voices and perspectives as both a means and an objective of treatment in itself.

74 Medical Council of New Zealand, Statement on Best Practices When Providing Care to Māori Patients and Their Whānau (2006) 2 <www.mcnz.org.nz>. See also Ministry of Health New Zealand, Involving Families: Guidance for Involving Families and Whanau of Mental Health Consumers/tangata whai ora in Care, Assessment and Treatment Processes (2000) <www.health.govt.nz>.

75 Mental Health (Compulsory Assessment and Treatment) Act 1992 (NZ) ss 5 and 65.

76 H Elder and R Tapsell, 'Maori and the Mental Health Act' in J Dawson and K Gledhill (ed), *New Zealand's Mental Health Act in Practice* (Victoria University Press, 2013) 249. See also A Douglass, *Mental Capacity: Updating New Zealand's Law and Practice* (Report for the New Zealand Law Foundation, Dunedin, July 2016) 61 [2.66] <www.aspenltd.co.nz/mc/assets/Full_Report.pdf>.

77 T Carney 'Australian Mental Health Tribunals – "Space" for Rights, Protection, Treatment and Governance?' (2012) 35 *International Journal of Law and Psychiatry* 1.

78 Ibid.

79 J Seikkula and M Olsen 'The Open Dialogue Approach to Acute Psychosis: Its Poetics and Micropolitics' (2003) 42 *Family Processes* 403.

80 T Minkowitz, 'Abolishing Mental Health Laws to Comply with the Convention on the Rights of Persons with Disabilities' in B McSherry and P Weller (eds), *Rethinking Rights-Based Mental Health Laws* (Hart, 2010) 151, 175.

Currently, research on this practice consists of small-scale studies based in Western Lapland, Finland, which focus on people with first-episode psychosis.[81] For example, preliminary results of a two-year follow-up found that a group of people with a first-instance diagnosis of schizophrenia who used the approach 'were hospitalized for fewer days, family meetings were organised more often and neuroleptic medication was used in fewer cases'.[82] Jaako Seikkula and colleagues reported that participants experienced 'fewer relapses and less residual psychotic symptoms and their employment status was better than in the (non-participating) comparison group'.[83] There has been some consideration of how the practice could be translated to broader mental health policy – again in Western Lapland – with reportedly promising results.[84] Russell Razzaque and Tom Stockman describe 'peer-supported open dialogue' as a variant of the Finnish practice, which is being trialled in six National Health Service trusts in the United Kingdom commencing in 2016.[85] They describe how a 'core principle of the approach is the provision of care at the social network level, by staff who have been trained in family, systems and related approaches'.[86] However, rigorous empirical analysis of Open Dialogues is yet to occur, and its application in the Anglosphere remains largely untested, although studies are beginning to emerge.[87]

Similarly, Intentional Peer Support has been advanced by the Centre for the Human Rights of Users and Survivors of Psychiatry as a form of supported decision-making.[88] Intentional Peer Support is designed to be applied both prior to emergency mental health crises, but also during them if need be.[89]

81 See, e.g., Seikkula and Olsen, above n 79; J Seikkula et al., 'Open Dialogue Approach: Treatment Principles and Preliminary Results of a Two-year Follow-up on First Episode Schizophrenia' (2003) 5(3) *Ethics and Human Sciences and Services* 163; J Aaltonena, J Seikkulaa and K Lehtinen, 'The Comprehensive Open-Dialogue Approach in Western Lapland: I. The Incidence of Non-Affective Psychosis and Prodromal States' (2011) 3(3) *Psychosis* 179.

82 Seikkula et al., above n 81.

83 Ibid.

84 Aaltonena, Seikkulaa and Lehtinen, above n 81.

85 R Razzaque and T Stockmann, 'An Introduction to Peer-Supported Open Dialogue in Mental Healthcare' (2016) 22 *BJPsych Advances* 348.

86 Ibid. For a detailed overview of Open Dialogue and its applicability in policy and practice, see J Seikkula and B Alakare, 'Open Dialogues Mobilise the Resources of the Family and the Patient' in S McNab and K Partridge, *Creative Positions in Adult Mental Health: Outside In-Inside Out* (Karnac Books, 2014) 131–49.

87 See, e.g., M Olson, J Seikkula and D Ziedonis, *The Key Elements of Dialogic Practice in Open Dialogue* (University of Massachusetts Press, 2014); R Razzaque and T Stockmann, 'An Introduction to Peer-Supported Open Dialogue in Mental Healthcare' (2016) 22 *BJPsych Advances* 348.

88 See Center for the Human Rights of Users and Survivors of Psychiatry, 'Good Practices', n.d. <www.chrusp.org>.

89 See, generally, <www.intentionalpeersupport.org>.

Intentional Peer Support focuses on the social *relations* between people experiencing profound distress, and is aimed at addressing the patterns of power and authority that impact on the exercise of individual agency.[90] There is currently no peer-reviewed research on Intentional Peer Support; however, this practice may be useful in operationalising elements of the CRPD support framework.[91] Julie Repper and Tim Carter undertook a meta-analysis of studies on peer support workers more generally, and reported that the presence of peer support workers in services 'can lead to a reduction in admissions among those with whom they work', and that 'associated improvements have been reported on numerous issues that can impact on the lives of people with mental health problems'.[92] With sufficient training, supervision and management, they argue, this cohort has the 'potential to drive through recovery-focused changes in services'[93] (I will discuss 'recovery-oriented services' shortly).

These initial, and quite brief, observations about collaborative and family-based support are meant to offer a glimpse into what might be required to apply the relational focus of the CRPD in practice. Any practical law and policy reform towards supported decision-making will face a number of important questions related to family and other supporters. For example, how will legislation stipulate the need for service providers to understand a person's social context? How will family and supporter representative groups respond to the proposition of expanding the scope for risk-taking? How will these concerns be addressed without reverting to protective measures that curtail the rights of people with disabilities on an unequal basis with others? What are the consequences of potentially formalising previously informal relationships? Careful consultation involving persons with disabilities and their families, friends and other informal supporters is likely to be required in any attempt to address these questions in legal or political terms.

3 *Advance Planning*

Advance planning can take non-statutory forms. One example is a 'joint crisis plan', a form of advance agreement from the United Kingdom which is written

90 Ibid.

91 For a theoretical perspective on the benefits of peer support, see S Mead, D Hilton and L Curtis, 'Peer Support: A Theoretical Perspective' (2001) 25(2) *Psychiatric Rehabilitation Journal* 134.

92 J Repper and T Carter, 'A Review of the Literature on Peer Support in Mental Health Services' (2011) 20(4) *Journal of Mental Health* 392.

93 Ibid.

by an individual in collaboration with his or her clinicians.[94] Joint crisis plans were trialled in England and developed in consultation with national service-user groups, including 'detailed development work with service users in south London'.[95] Claire Henderson and colleagues conducted a study that looked at engaging patients and professionals in active joint planning for future crises as a means of reducing compulsory admissions.[96] Their trial found that the 'use of joint crisis plans reduced compulsory admissions and treatment in patients with severe mental illness'.[97] However, the 2013 follow-up trial was unable to replicate the previous results, although the authors argued 'that patchy implementation and lack of real commitment are more likely culprits', and that 'one meeting between patients and professionals is unlikely to be sufficient to counteract a culture of professional dominance in decision making where this prevails'.[98] While joint crisis plans are not a panacea for rising rates of compulsion – as Thomas and Cahill write, 'the idea that we can soothe the pain of greater compulsion with the balm of advance statements is simplistic'[99] – the practice offers a workable measure to avoid non-consensual interventions under current conditions.

4 *Reducing and Eliminating Seclusion and Restraint in Mental Health Settings*

Eliminating seclusion and restraint clearly helps to advance human rights in the mental health system. Seclusion and restraint in mental health settings restrict autonomy and liberty, and perhaps the right to respect for physical and mental integrity and the right to be free from torture, or cruel, inhuman or degrading treatment.[100] Seclusion and restraint, including physical, mechanical and chemical restraint, are generally understood to be traumatising, even when some view them as necessary.[101] A number of initiatives around

94 C Henderson, et al., 'Effect of Joint Crisis Plans on Use of Compulsory Treatment in Psychiatry: Single Blind Randomised Controlled Trial' (2004) 329 *British Medical Journal* 136.

95 Ibid.

96 Ibid.

97 Ibid.

98 G Thornicroft et al., 'Clinical Outcomes of Joint Crisis Plans to Reduce Compulsory Treatment for People with Psychosis: A Randomised Controlled Trial' (2013) 381(9878) *Lancet* 1634.

99 See P Thomas and A Cahill, 'Compulsion and Psychiatry – The Role of Advance Statements: Liberation Cannot Be Handed to the Oppressed by the Oppressor' (2004) 329 *British Medical Journal* 123.

100 S Kumble and B McSherry 'Seclusion and Restraint: Rethinking Regulation from a Human Rights Perspective' (2010) 17(3) *Psychiatry, Psychology and Law* 551, 554–55.

101 Ibid. 551.

the world suggest that reducing and eliminating seclusion and restraint in mental health settings is a key priority for governments, disability organisations and others.[102] Variable rates of seclusion and restraint in mental health services indicate that they can be significantly reduced and, in some cases, eliminated.[103] Factors contributing to a decline in instances of seclusion and restraint include increased availability of 'low-intensity rooms' and gender-specific areas, hospital-driven attention to seclusion practices, improved data collection, workforce development, consumer roles in inpatient settings and debriefing tools.[104]

D THE HUMAN RIGHTS MODEL OF DISABILITY IN MENTAL HEALTH

As discussed in Chapter 2, the human rights model of disability conceptualises disability as arising from the interaction between a person's impairment and the external physical and social barriers to his or her full and effective participation in society on an equal basis with others.[105] From this perspective, by intervening strategically in the physical and social world, disability can be effectively dismantled, even as 'impairment' remains.[106]

The human rights model is likely to raise conceptual and practical tensions with disabilities more commonly linked to 'illness', such as AIDS, diabetes or, indeed, mental illness. For mental health law and policy, a human rights–oriented system appears to invite an adjustment of the dominant explanatory framework. Long-standing debates on the social model of disability provide

102 See, e.g., Mental Health Commission (Australia), *National Seclusion and Restraint Project* (2013) <www.mentalhealthcommission.gov.au>; M O'Hagan, M Divis and J Long, Best Practice in the Reduction and Elimination of Seclusion and Restraint; Seclusion: Time for Change (Te Pou Te Whakaaro Nui: The National Centre of Mental Health Research, Information and Workforce Development, 2008).

103 See, e.g., DC Donat, 'An Analysis of Successful Efforts to Reduce the Use of Seclusion and Restraint at a Public Psychiatric Hospital' (2003) 54(8) *Psychiatric Services* 1119; GM Smith et al., 'Special Section on Seclusion and Restraint: Pennsylvania State Hospital System's Seclusion and Restraint Reduction Program' (2005) 56(9) *Psychiatric Services* 1115; K Huckshorn, 'Re-Designing State Mental Health Policy to Prevent the Use of Seclusion and Restraint' (2005) 33(4) *Administration and Policy in Mental Health and Mental Health Services Research* 482.

104 For a range of strategies for reducing and eliminating seclusion and restraint practices, see above n 103. See also KA Huckshorn, et al., 'Reducing Seclusion and Restraint Use in Mental Health Settings: Core Strategies for Prevention' (2004) 42(9) *Journal of Psychosocial Nursing and Mental Health Services* 22.

105 See Chapter 2, Section B(1).

106 See, generally, C Thomas, 'How Is Disability Understood? An Examination of Sociological Approaches' (2004) 19(6) *Disability and Society* 569. For a critique of the social model, see T Shakespeare, *Disability Rights and Wrongs* (Routledge, 2006).

some sense of what this adjustment might require. A prominent theorist on the social model of disability, Mike Oliver, has argued: 'To put the matter unequivocally, the medicalisation of disability ha[s] given doctors power and left disabled people powerless. The social model is not an attempt to take power away from doctors and give it to disabled people, but a prescription for sharing power'.[107] There are potential downsides to such an adjustment. A prominent critic of the social model of disability, Tom Shakespeare, warns against overstating its constructivist element.[108] Disability, he argues, should not be 'defined entirely in terms of social oppression, social relations and barriers'.[109] To do so, he argues, can belittle the bodily experience of pain, physiological trauma and, in the context of mental health, psychological pain, mental illness and extreme distress.[110] Hence, denying impairment might be just as damaging as doing the opposite.

It is generally agreed among legislators, professionals, persons with psychosocial disability, family members and other supporters that whether a particular experience is defined as mental illness, disorder or disability, *some* kind of distress or an extreme emotional state exists and is located in the body. This broad agreement puts to rest any suggestion that such experiences are entirely socially constructed. At the same time, there is broad agreement about the existence of mental health–based discrimination and prejudice that causes profound material and psychic damage to individuals and those around them. In accepting both propositions – and avoiding a reductive characterisation of either – the task remains to balance diverse views on mental distress and disability in law, policy and practice.

Mediating 'social' and 'medical' considerations in this way is not novel. Throughout modern history, the mental health field has been driven, in part, by tensions between social and medical views on distress, madness and impairment. According to Stefan Priebe and colleagues, '[a] tension between a neurobiological and a social model has characterised psychiatry since the establishment of academic psychiatry in the mid-nineteenth century'.[111] They consider that 'this tension has been productive', although they ultimately argue for a 'social model of psychiatry', which is likely to 'generate real progress and, simultaneously, make the profession more attractive'.[112]

[107] M Oliver, *The Politics of Disablement* (MacMillan, 1990) 6.
[108] See, generally, Shakespeare, above n 106.
[109] Ibid. 31.
[110] Ibid.
[111] S Priebe, T Burns and T Craig, 'The Future of Academic Psychiatry May Be Social' (2013) 202(5) *The British Journal of Psychiatry* 319.
[112] Ibid.

In the past, some rights-based strategies for mental health law reform have focused on critiquing the scientific basis of psychiatry.[113] Critics have referred to the practice of clinicians in medical fields other than psychiatry who weigh observable facts alongside the subjective reports of patients.[114] For psychiatrists, by contrast, the 'objective' indicators of mental disorder – such as abnormal brain activity, physical lesions or biochemical 'imbalance' – remain elusive, despite a decades-long scientific search.[115] However, such criticisms may not provide a good basis for law and policy reform. Nikolas Rose points out that there is a low correlation of non-psychiatric diagnoses and such indicators, including a lack of biological indicators for certain *physical* illnesses, such as migraines, and many other debilitating conditions.[116] Further, medicine has long been practised beyond disease eradication in areas such as grief, childbirth and infertility.[117] Rose has argued that law and policy reformers are better off focusing direct 'attention and resources … [on] analysing the specific problems of diagnostic processes and classificatory systems'.[118] This recommendation – to focus on the destructive aspects that can result from 'diagnostic processes and classificatory systems' rather than their scientific *validity* – appears prudent given that commentators have debated the reliability of psychiatric diagnosis for many decades, and appear likely to do so for decades to come.[119]

[113] For example, some proponents of the 'new legalism' that motivated 1980s mental health law reform called for increased legal regulation of clinical discretion by claiming that psychiatry is fundamentally different from other medical fields. Gostin, for example, submitted that 'clinical' judgments would come under greater scrutiny by legal professionals who have no special interest in maintaining spurious scientific claims or the mystique of psychiatry. See L Gostin, 'The Ideology of Entitlement: The Application of Contemporary Legal Approaches to Psychiatry' in P Bean (ed), *Mental Illness: Changes and Trends* (Wiley, 1983) 50.

[114] M Slade, *Personal Recovery and Mental Illness: A Guide for Mental Health Professionals* (Cambridge University Press, 2009) 8.

[115] Ibid.

[116] N Rose, 'Unreasonable Rights: Mental Illness and the Limits of the Law' (1985) 12(2) *Journal of Law and Society* 204.

[117] Ibid. 481.

[118] Ibid. 205.

[119] For criticism of dominant psychopharmacological approaches to mental illness, see J Moncrieff, *The Myth of the Chemical Cure: A Critique of Psychiatric Drug Treatment* (Palgrave Macmillan, 2009); Slade, above n 114; British Psychological Society, Division of Clinical Psychology, 'DCP Position Statement on Classification' <dcp.bps.org.uk>. Cf. P Kramer, 'In Defense of Antidepressants', *The New York Times*, 9 July 2011; JA Lieberman, 'DSM-5: Caught between Mental Illness Stigma and Anti-Psychiatry Prejudice' on *Scientific American* (20 May 2013) <blogs.scientificamerican.com/>; T Burns, *Our Necessary Shadow: The Nature and Meaning of Psychiatry* (Penguin, 2014).

What, then, are the problems associated with 'diagnostic processes and classificatory systems', and what can the CRPD offer to address them? For some commentators, the 'supported decision-making model', in Kohn, Blumenthal and Campbell's terms, 'seeks to avoid the use of disabling labels such as "incompetent"',[120] which might well apply to disease vocabularies in the mental health context.[121] Interestingly, the British Psychological Society, Division of Clinical Psychology ('DCP') has called for the abandonment of psychiatric diagnostic systems.[122] In a document accompanying the *DCP Position Statement on the Classification of Behaviour and Experience in Relation to Functional Psychiatric Diagnoses*, the current DCP chair stated: 'This is the latest in a series of documents arguing for psychological and interdisciplinary understanding of experiences such as hearing voices, despair and mood swings. Our statement calls for a paradigm shift away from an outdated disease models [sic], towards one which gives much more weight to service user experience and psychosocial approaches'.[123] It is worth remaining cautious regarding the restorative value of recasting terminology. In another context, Henry Louis Gates claimed that efforts to curb 'offensive speech' can detract from civil rights advocacy, and specifically efforts to address underlying economic disadvantage.[124] The analogy is imperfect, as solely focusing on civil rights and economic disadvantage in the mental health context would seem overly 'constructivist', to use Shakespeare's term. Yet Gates's critique usefully turns the spotlight from speech acts to the locus of power imbalance, which includes the material conditions available to a person (for example, safe housing, accessible health services and so on). In a similar vein, Barbara Taylor writes critically about so-called empowering language in current mental health policy, and highlights the inadequacy of focusing too heavily on finding the right terminology: 'a closer look at the language of mental health policy is revealing, taking us into a Humpty Dumpty land of key-words – "recovery", "wellness", "choice" – whose meanings, as in the case of Lewis Carroll's prolix egg, depend on the power of those employing them: a topsy-turvy world where it is easy to lose track of

[120] NA Kohn, JA Blumenthal and AT Campbell, 'Supported Decision-Making: A Viable Alternative to Guardianship?' (2013) 117(4) *Pennsylvania State Law Review* 1111, 1114–5.

[121] See Chapter 3, Section D(5).

[122] See British Psychological Society, Division of Clinical Psychology, 'DCP Position Statement on Classification' <dcp.bps.org.uk>.

[123] Ibid.

[124] HL Gates, 'Let Them Talk: Why Civil Liberties Pose No Threat to Civil Rights' (1993) 37 *New Republic* 27.

the distinction between sense and nonsense, crazy and sane'.[125] Reorienting mental health law and policy towards a social model of disability and beyond a mere vocabulary change demands political imagination, and attention should turn to the foundations of destructive power relations that contribute to disadvantage.

Presenting the 'medical model' and 'human rights model' as diametrically opposed would be misleading (and potentially counterproductive). As early as the 1980s, Peter Sedgwick resisted the characterisation of physical diseases as the realm of scientific fact, while also critiquing the notion of mental health diagnosis as subjective deviancy labelling.[126] Sedgwick called for a unitary concept of health that could avoid the physical-mental divide, which he referred to as 'psycho-medical dualism', and instead promote a broader understanding *and politicisation* of illness and health.[127] This proposal for socialised medicine included, for example, the 'insertion of windows into working-class houses'[128] and the 'provision of a pure water supply and an efficient sewage disposal'.[129] Sedgwick sees this shift in understanding 'illness' as useful because it 'politic[ises] medical goals'.[130] He argues explicitly that 'without the concept of illness – including that of mental illness … we shall be unable to *make demands* upon the health service facilities of the society in which we live'.[131] Sedgwick criticised the insistent demands for 'negative rights' among service user and ex-patient groups, which he argued constituted nothing more than 'the ritualistic evasion of the serious questions of long-term psychiatric care'.[132] Although he called for grass-roots initiatives, which insist upon the 'countervailing power of voluntary social initiative, outside the bureaucratic compass of the state',[133] he ultimately believed that this would be delivered through a unitary illness model. 'The future', he predicted in 1982, 'belongs to illness'.[134]

Cresswell and Spandler argue that Sedgwick was off the mark, even as his analysis remains relevant today.[135] In a passage worth citing in full, they

[125] B Taylor, *The Last Asylum: Memoir of Madness in Our Times* (Penguin Random House, 2014) 251.
[126] P Sedgwick, *Psychopolitics* (Pluto Press, 1982).
[127] Ibid. 43–65.
[128] Ibid. 39.
[129] Ibid.
[130] Ibid. 40.
[131] Ibid.
[132] Ibid. 241.
[133] Ibid. 252.
[134] Ibid. 39.
[135] M Cresswell and H Spandler, 'Psychopolitics: Peter Sedgwick's Legacy for the Politics of Mental Health' (2009) 7(2) *Social Theory and Health* 129.

critique his assumption that service user groups would necessarily adopt a 'negative rights'–based agenda, which is always against psychiatric 'abuses' but never for psychiatric 'uses':

> On the contrary, whilst such movements have been highly autonomous, they have been simultaneously the product of alliances between workers, service users and political activists (notably feminists). Moreover, these have led to the 'development of new programmes, demands and services' from service users and workers alike … For example, the politicisation of issues such as 'self-harm' and 'hearing voices' – which psychiatry traditionally subsumes beneath 'illness' categories – has resulted in a number of self-help strategies and practices such as 'harm minimisation' and 'coping with voices' pursued via non-medical, consensual means. Such developments have also challenged Sedgwick's insistence that the 'unitary conception of illness' is the necessary precursor to politicisation of the mental health field. In fact, the organisations [that pursued the previously noted reform] have explicitly rejected the notion of 'illness'; and have sought instead to locate the specificity of experience, such as 'hearing voices' or 'self harm', deploying alternative concepts and frameworks such as 'mental distress' or even 'madness'. The mobilisation of such groups has revolved around the discursive ensemble 'trauma/abuse/distress' rather than the 'Sedgwickian' ensemble 'illness/disease'. Such frameworks attest to the importance of personal histories of trauma and abuse, as well as iatrogenic degradations experienced within the mental health system itself.[136]

Cresswell and Spandler suggest that the voices of service users and others with psychosocial disability can play a crucial role in unpacking the relationships between bodily pain and distress and structural, disabling barriers to a fulfilling life.[137] Recent literature in this area provides fertile ground for the 'co-production' or 'co-design' of laws, policy and practice in the mental health context. The notion of co-design is one of the core requirements of a CRPD support framework (and a key recommendation of this book).[138] This is not to suggest that other voices should be excluded from public deliberation. It would be odd to suggest that only people who have attracted a mental health diagnosis ought solely to determine political and legal responses to impairment and disability in the mental health context. Broad alliances – including groups connected to health, justice, employment, housing and economics – seem

[136] Ibid. 137–8.

[137] See, particularly, H Spandler, J Anderson and B Sapey (eds), *Madness, Distress and the Politics of Disablement* (Policy Press, 2015).

[138] See Conclusion, Section B(2).

necessary to address the myriad issues flowing from severe mental health issues and psychosocial disability.

Infusing mental health policy with the insights gained from the complex debates around the 'social' and 'human rights' models of disability will be politically and technically challenging. Public health scientists may be well placed to bridge the conceptual divide between Sedgwick's 'illness/disease' model and Cresswell and Spandler's 'trauma/abuse/distress' model, including those concerned with social epidemiology and the social determinants of disability and impairment. The 'systems view' promoted by the CRPD gives prominence to the experience of persons with psychosocial disabilities with their family and other intimate relations, or with employers and neighbours more distantly, and in relation to social structures, such as gender, race, economics and forms of government power.[139] Engaging with this social context beyond the abstract might seem a daunting task for those who deal with the day-to-day dilemmas of mental health crises – and for policymakers who seek to address macro-level law making and resource distribution. However, there are a number of approaches in law, policy and practice that have already pursued this task. For the purposes of this section, I will discuss some of these approaches below, namely 'recovery-oriented practice', 'trauma-informed services', informal safeguarding and community development, and anti-discrimination law.

1 *Recovery-Oriented Practice*

'Recovery'-oriented mental health policy and practice aims to enhance the agency of people and to avoid what Pamela Fisher describes as interventions 'being done to' people.[140] This approach places a high priority on respect for self-determination and supporting the capabilities of each individual. Tina Minkowitz has argued that 'recovery-oriented practices' can help us understand supported decision-making in the mental health context:

> Supported decision-making can be understood, from a user/survivor point of view, as an application of the recovery perspective to the situation of decision-making. The recovery perspective is centred on individual strength and capability and the belief that madness is a temporary state of distress and disruption. It emphasizes hope and cultivation of the person's own abilities

[139] J Nedelsky, *Law's Relations: A Relational Theory of Self, Autonomy, and Law* (Oxford University Press, 2011) 4.

[140] P Fisher, 'Questioning the Ethics of Vulnerability and Informed Consent in Qualitative Studies from a Citizenship and Human Rights Perspective' (2012) 6 *Ethics and Social Welfare* 2, 12.

> of self-reflection and development of skills particularly with experiences that might otherwise gain power over the individual.[141]

Some proponents of the recovery model of mental health service provision have emphasised features of the model that have parallels with the 'universalism' of the CRPD. Pat Deegan writes: 'The goal of the recovery process is not to become normal. The goal is to embrace our human vocation of becoming more deeply, more fully human'.[142] On the specific issue of diagnosis, Michael Slade has argued that the recovery approach values varied ways of explaining mental distress.[143] He discusses the potentially disabling role of diagnosis, and considers ways in which clinicians might respond to this paradox:

> If diagnosis is one of the many ways of understanding, what does this mean for clinicians? A truly evidence-based clinician (i.e. one who recognises the limitations of their worldview) would offer their expertise as a resource, which may or may not be helpful to or utilised by the patient. This clearly will involve a role transition. It may be reasonable to state to a patient, '*You have meningitis*', if this is the best available explanation. The statement '*You have depression*' is a different animal – it should more precisely be stated as '*Your experience can be understood as depression*'. This then becomes an informed suggestion about how it might be helpful to understand the experience, rather than an authoritative pronouncement about what is really going on.[144]

The recovery approach, like the human rights model of disability, seems to encompass a range of ways to explain impairment and disablement, thus creating a broad and permissive framework of discussable ideas. However, 'recovery' is understood in varied and sometimes contradictory ways.[145] 'Recovery principles' have been incorporated into some mental health laws. For example, the Victorian Mental Health Act 2014 includes 'promot[ing] the recovery of persons who have mental illness' as a key objective,[146] a point that is reiterated a number of times throughout the act.[147] Others have argued that recovery is

[141] T Minkowitz, *No-Force Advocacy by Users and Survivors of Psychiatry* (Mental Health Commission New Zealand, 2005) 19 <www.mhc.govt.nz>.

[142] P Deegan, 'Recovery as a Journey of the Heart' (1996) 19(91) *Psychosocial Rehabilitation Journal* 91.

[143] Slade, above n 114, 17–8.

[144] Ibid. (emphasis in original).

[145] David Pilgrim and Ann McCranie distinguish between four main meanings attributed to the term: recovery as a 'personal journey', recovery as 'therapeutic optimism', recovery as a 'critique of services' and recovery as a 'model of social disability'. D Pilgrim and A McCranie, *Recovery and Mental Health: A Critical Sociological Account* (Palgrave MacMillan, 2013).

[146] Mental Health Act 2014 (Vic) s 10(f).

[147] See, e.g., Ibid. ss 10(d)(i), 10(d)(h), 55(2)(a),

inimical to involuntary treatment.[148] Mary O'Hagan notes that 'legal coercion erodes all the cornerstones of the recovery philosophy, yet it remains a core response in our mental health systems'.[149] It is outside the scope of this paper to elaborate, in detail, on the diverse understandings of 'recovery' and its links to 'human rights–based' support, although this relationship would benefit from further exploration.

2 *Trauma-Informed Approaches*

A 'trauma-informed' approach to service provision appears to overlap with the human rights model of disability by drawing attention to external disabling barriers to the enjoyment of rights. Denise Elliott and colleagues describe trauma-informed services as:

> those in which service delivery is influenced by an understanding of the impact of interpersonal violence and victimization on an individual's life and development. To provide trauma-informed services, all staff of an organization … must understand how violence impacts the lives of the people being served, so that every interaction is consistent with the recovery process and reduces the possibility of retraumatization.[150]

Maxine Harris and Roger Fallot have argued that, in light of significant evidence to suggest that the majority of mental health and welfare recipients have survived physical or sexual violence, '[s]ystems *serve* survivors of childhood trauma without *treating* them for the consequences of that trauma; more significant, systems serve individuals without even being aware of the trauma that occurred'.[151] A number of personal accounts of mental health services support this view. Tony Cain has written:

> During every incarceration, every institutionalization, every court-ordered drug treatment program, it was always the same: I was always treated like a

[148] See C Maylea, 'A Rejection of Involuntary Treatment in Mental Health Social Work' (2016) *Ethics and Social Welfare*, doi:10.1080/17496535.2016.1246585; M O'Hagan, 'Force in Mental Health Services: International User/Survivor Perspectives' in *World Federation for Mental Health Biennial Congress* (Melbourne, Australia, 2003); M O'Hagan, 'Legal Coercion: The Elephant in the Recovery Room' (Scottish Recovery Network, 17 January 2012) <www.scottishrecovery.net>.

[149] O'Hagan, above n 148.

[150] DE Elliott et al., 'Trauma-Informed or Trauma-Denied: Principles and Implementation of Trauma-Informed Services for Women' (2005) 33(4) *Journal of Community Psychology* 461, 462.

[151] M Harris and RD Fallot, 'Envisioning a Trauma-Informed Service System: A Vital Paradigm Shift' (2001) 89 *New Directions for Mental Health Services* 3.

hopeless case. It wasn't until I finally entered a recovery-oriented, trauma-informed treatment program a little more than four years ago, where I felt safe and respected, that I could begin to heal … Someone finally asked me "What happened to you?" instead of "What's wrong with you?"[152]

Indigo Daya has also written about her own early trauma and its impact on her experience with mental health services:

During hundreds, perhaps thousands, of contact hours with mental health professionals, not one single doctor, nurse, therapist or community worker ever once asked me about past trauma. No-one knew about my childhood experiences of violence at home, bullying at school, a terrifying two-week long abduction and rape at the age of thirteen, or how they might be linked to my madness. I certainly wasn't going to bring it up. I didn't know how, and even if I did, I felt far too ashamed and confused. I was told that I had a chemical imbalance in my brain, and I gave over to being medicated, hospitalised, given shock treatment and put on the pension.

Daya goes on to describe her efforts to explore the impact of her traumatic past:

[W]ith indescribable trepidation, but inspired by my peers, I began to explore 'that thing that had happened when I was thirteen'. I talked to a therapist, but then I went completely mad again. This, of course, is exactly why many people say we shouldn't talk about trauma. But they're wrong. I did end up psychotic, suicidal, back in hospital, back on medication, and being told by a psychiatrist that I had come too far to risk it all now. My trauma was in the past and it would only keep me sick to talk about it. I must get back on medication and forget the past. I fought and fought. I knew that I was right. And then I remembered how the system really works, so I lied. I told the doctors they were right. I drew up a 'sensible' recovery plan for myself, and got discharged. Then I went straight to [the Centre against Sexual Assault] and got myself an amazing counsellor … And while it was painful, I began to find a way to really heal.[153]

Daya's and Cain's accounts, albeit only two individual perspectives, highlight how service providers may ignore relevant social determinants of distress. To do so risks imposing interventions that are controlling and coercive, which may be experienced as shaming and even retraumatising. Writing from a psychoanalytical perspective, Robert Stolorow argues that '[t]o attribute the

[152] Cited in L Rosenberg, 'We Must Do More' [2011] (2) *National Council Magazine* 6 <www.thenationalcouncil.org>.

[153] I Daya, 'The Blog that Shouldn't Be Written. And Why I'm Writing It' on I Daya, *The Blog that Shouldn't Be Written* (10 May 2015) <www.indigodaya.com/the-blog-that-shouldnt-be-written-and-why-im-writing-it/>.

affective chaos or schizoid withdrawal of patients who were abused as children to "fantasy" or to "borderline personality organization" is tantamount to blaming the victim and, in doing so, reproduces features of the original trauma'.[154] A less intrusive and more socially contextual response is to make a range of supports available to people, amongst which trauma-informed support appears to be a logical addition.

Clearly, not all people will benefit from trauma-informed support services. Many trauma survivors do not develop mental health issues, just as many people who attract diagnoses have *not* experienced trauma in the commonsense understanding of the term. For the purposes of this chapter, the trauma-informed approach highlights how the human rights model of disability can direct focus to preparing *others* by helping create a more inclusive (and, hence, less disabling) society. While trauma-informed services draw attention to the impact of violence, including the sheer pervasiveness of physical and sexual assault and its consequences for survivors, there are other mental health–related initiatives aimed at improving equity. In this respect, Anne Plumb asks how we can create 'societies in which people may thrive emotionally and mentally' and suggests that '[w]e need to name sexual abuse, marital violence, bullying, exploitation, deprivation and so on'.[155] For those who share Plumb's view, it is perhaps reassuring that numerous mental health professionals and other mental health advocates have worked together to confront such issues, including those concerning the human rights of lesbian, gay, bisexual and transsexual people,[156] as well as refugees and asylum seekers.[157]

3 *Informal Safeguards, Community Development and Social Inclusion*

As discussed in Chapter 4, informal safeguards are relevant to discussions about mental health and human rights.[158] The Western Australian Mental

[154] R Stolorow, *Trauma and Human Existence* (Routledge, 2007) 11.

[155] A Plumb, 'UN Convention on the Rights of Persons with Disabilities: out of the frying pan and into the fire? Mental health service users and survivors aligning with the disability movement' in Spandler, Anderson and Sapey, above n 137, 185–6.

[156] Royal College of Psychiatrists, 'Royal College of Psychiatrists' Statement on Sexual Orientation' (Position Statement, PS02/2014, April 2014).

[157] See, e.g., Royal Australian and New Zealand College of Psychiatrists, *Australian Human Rights Commission National Inquiry into Children in Immigration Detention 2014: RANZCP Response – May 2014* (2014) <www.ranzcp.org>; M Hopwood, Royal Australian and New Zealand College of Psychiatrists, Submission to the Senate Inquiry into the Conditions and Treatment of Asylum Seekers and Refugees at the Regional Processing Centres in the Republic of Nauru and Papua New Guinea, 8 April 2016 <www.ranzcp.org>.

[158] For an earlier discussion of informal safeguards, see Chapter 4, Section C(8).

Health Commission ('WAMHC') has undertaken systemic reform efforts to implement a 'self-directed approach' to mental health service provision, which includes efforts to foster 'informal or natural, intentional safeguard arrangements'.[159] These efforts demonstrate how informal safeguards can be applied to the mental health context in practice. According to the WAMHC, self-directed mental health service provision aims to 'empower … people with mental illness and/or mental health problems, along with their families and carers, to be in charge of planning how they are supported and to have choice and flexibility in what supports and services they receive and how these are delivered'.[160] The WAMHC's report provides an example:

> Mick has spent the last two years in hospital away from his local community. During his last few months in hospital, Mick was introduced to Janine and Bob, an Aboriginal couple who will be supporting Mick when he moves back into the community. For several months while Mick was in hospital, Janine and Bob spent a lot of time getting to know Mick, and now that a new home in the community has been found for him, they will become a bigger part of his life. Mick is very happy for Janine and Bob to share his new home with him and in exchange, they will help Mick to re-establish existing, and develop new relationships within his community. Sharing household tasks will also help to increase Mick's independence. This living and sharing arrangement will minimise the risk of exploitation by others, something that has happened to Mick in the past. Janine and Bob will also help Mick to rebuild connections to his country and people. They also plan to enjoy shared interests such as fishing, and help Mick to test out new things he might enjoy. As Janine and Bob come to know Mick more, they will be very aware of the early warning signs of any deterioration in Mick's mental health and assist him to seek the necessary support when it is needed.[161]

From the perspective of the WAMHC, the natural, informal or intentional support approaches to mental health service provision are not intended to replace formal safeguards (for example, legal avenues to address exploitation by others or the provision of professional independent living services).[162] Instead, the expansion of safeguarding to include social inclusion is designed to complement existing formal avenues provided by legislation and other areas of law. The WAMHC has developed guidelines on the two safeguarding systems:

[159] Government of Western Australia, Mental Health Commission, *Draft Safeguards Framework for Individualised Support and Funding* (May 2013) 2 <www.mentalhealth.wa.gov.au>.

[160] Ibid.

[161] Ibid.

[162] Ibid.

- Formal safeguard systems should not interfere with the flexibility and creativity of informal safeguards.
- Formal safeguards should be able to respond to concerns raised by people in informal safeguarding roles.
- The people involved in formal and informal safeguards should understand and respect each other's roles.
- Everyone involved in safeguarding should be open to evaluating how safeguards are working and changing things that are not going well.[163]

The report acknowledges that the personalised nature of such informal safeguards makes it 'difficult to prescribe a standard package of safeguards to apply to everyone'.[164] In this instance, personalisation makes standardisation difficult, which may pose operational difficulties; however, they do not seem insurmountable. Indeed, there is some evidence to suggest that placing less emphasis and reliance on 'models' in care and service delivery might produce better outcomes, particularly when promoting individualised and local area solutions.[165]

Informal safeguards can relate to efforts to improve independent living and social inclusion. As noted previously, Article 19 of the CRPD requires that persons with disabilities are provided with the 'personal assistance necessary to support living and inclusion in the community, and to prevent isolation or segregation from the community'.[166] Quinn has argued that Article 12 is meant to operate in conjunction with Article 19, which can help create the 'building blocks' for a person to enjoy equality before the law; practical examples include having a safe home, a valued social role, a connection to community and so on.[167] This vision for community development can be incorporated into efforts to reduce formal safeguards.

One example of such a service, the Local Area Coordination Network, has been used in different parts of the United Kingdom, Australia and New Zealand to support people with a range of different needs, including mental health needs, to avoid relying solely on health and social care services

[163] Ibid. 5.
[164] Ibid.
[165] See, e.g., M Bleasdale, 'Supporting the housing of people with complex needs', Australian Housing and Urban Research Institute (2007).
[166] CRPD art 19(b).
[167] G Quinn, 'Rethinking Personhood: New Directions in Legal Capacity Law and Policy' (Paper, New Foundations for Personhood and Legal Capacity in the 21st Century Conference, University of British Columbia, 29 April 2011) 17 <www.nuigalway.ie>.

for social contact.[168] This practice involves community workers based in particular neighbourhoods, whose role is to build relationships, identify problems and help connect people to community associations.[169] Local Area Coordination, informal safeguards and other social services that facilitate community engagement aim to personalise support by asking people what their preferences and life goals are, while also grounding people in their local social sphere and working to connect them with existing services, businesses and community organisations (rather than congregated, disability-specific services).[170]

Sharing Voices, based in Bradford, United Kingdom, is one example of an innovative support program for at-risk people with severe mental health issues, who often face social exclusion, isolation and discrimination. According to Robyn Edwards and colleagues, Sharing Voices:

> is a community development mental health project focusing on developing and raising awareness of mental health wellbeing amongst marginalised black and migrant communities and people. Sharing Voices develops services that are culturally appropriate to the needs of these communities and that contribute to improved health outcomes … A community based approach is utilised; engaging communities in dialogue to articulate their own understanding of mental health and illness and to design solutions appropriate for black and minority ethnic communities … The groups emphasise the concept of mutual aid and self-help; the role of the community worker is to respond to the needs identified by local participants. To complement the centre-based gatherings, social exclusion outreach teams work with people in their homes to assist them access mainstream services and activities. The project promotes independent living and engagement in community activities, by developing capacity within communities and supporting the development of self-help initiatives and community networks.[171]

[168] See, e.g., R Broad, *People, Place, Possibilities* (Centre for Welfare Reform, 2015); Ministry of Health (NZ), 'Local Area Coordination: Walking Alongside Disabled People and their Families/Whānau to Assist Them to Live Good, Everyday Lives Within Welcoming Communities, Hapū and Iwi', n.d. <www.health.govt.nz>.

[169] Ibid.

[170] See, generally, A Power, J Lord and A deFranco, *Active Citizenship and Disability: Implementing the Personalisation of Support* (Cambridge University Press, 2013); see also G Quinn and MA Stein, 'Challenges in Realising the Right to Live in the Community' in *ECCL European Coalition for Community Living Focus on Article 19 of the United Nations Convention on the Rights of Persons with Disabilities* (ECCL, 2009).

[171] R Edwards et al., 'Housing and Associated Support for People with Mental Illness or Psychiatric Disability' (SPRC Report 4/09, University of New South Wales, Social Policy Research Centre and Griffith University, Disability Studies and Research Centre, May 2009) 51 [7.4].

According to the Sharing Voices Bradford website, the service was established on the basis that 'an individual's mental health experiences often arise from issues around: poverty, racism, unemployment, loneliness, family conflicts, relationship difficulties and cannot be merely understood through biological terms alone. So listening to peoples own explanation and helping them find their solutions to problems is a key part of our work'.[172] This book has not engaged in detail with mental health and human rights issues for specific minority communities, including people who are LGBTI and/or culturally and linguistically diverse. However, a logical step in the expanded scope of the human rights model of disability is to take into account the social and economic determinants of impairment, distress and disablement, in relation to which racism and homophobia are undoubtedly contributing factors for many people. Practices of 'informal safeguarding', community development and other efforts to foster social inclusion highlight ways of creating less intrusive and more socially contextual responses to mental health crises and psychosocial disability that are in step with the human rights model of disability promoted in the CRPD.

4 *Repealing Discriminatory Law*

While the focus of this book has been on mental health legislation, there remain a range of other laws that explicitly discriminate against persons with psychosocial disabilities. Setting aside mental health legislation, almost all modern democracies include prejudicial restrictions on equal standing before the law for persons with psychosocial disability. Under the Electoral Act 1918 (Australia), for example, persons of 'unsound mind' are not entitled to have their names on the electoral roll or to vote in elections, and may be removed from the electoral roll following objection and with the endorsement of a health professional.[173] Similar laws exist throughout the United States.[174] Efforts to instil a human rights model of disability in law and policy would be incomplete without addressing these forms of institutional 'sanism'.[175] By abolishing discriminatory, disability-based exceptions

[172] Sharing Voices Bradford <www.sharingvoices.net>.

[173] Electoral Act 1918 (Cth) (Australia) s 93(8)(a).

[174] See, generally, Judge David L. Bazelon Center for Mental Health Law, 'State Laws Affecting the Voting Rights of People with Mental Disabilities' (updated 2012).

[175] See ML Perlin, 'Things Have Changed: Looking at Non-Institutional Mental Disability Law Through the Sanism Filter' (2002–2003) 46 *New York Law School Review* 535, 539; see also M

in law, governments can take an important step towards implementing the CRPD anti-discrimination directives. One example of how this might occur is found in the Mental Health (Discrimination) Act 2013 in England and Wales.[176] This act was designed explicitly to remove major forms of discrimination from the law, and to repeal laws that prevented people with mental health issues from serving on a jury, being a director of a company or serving as an MP.[177]

Incorporating a 'human rights model' of disability will pose many challenges and will give rise to issues too numerous for this book to consider. Instead, this brief discussion considers where the human rights model of disability can build upon existing strategies – through recovery-oriented practice, trauma-informed services and anti-discrimination measures – to reorient law, policy and practice to take into account the 'attitudinal and environmental barriers that hinder [persons with disabilities'] full and effective participation in society on an equal basis with others'.[178]

E CONCLUSION

Some commentators claim that to 'abolish policies and legislative provisions that allow or perpetrate forced treatment'[179] would do more harm than good.[180] Yet it is generally agreed, including among those who maintain the need for coercive powers, that current systems can inhibit self-determination, dignity and respectfulness, and that more could be done to strengthen the agency of persons with psychosocial disability. This consensus provides fertile ground to develop law, policy and practice that seeks to improve the effectiveness of support for persons with psychosocial disability and strengthen their self-determination. Numerous other examples could have been listed in this chapter,

Perlin and DA Dorfman, 'Sanism, Social Science, and the Development of Mental Disability Jurisprudence' (1993) 11(1) *Behavioral Sciences and the Law* 47.

176 Mental Health (Discrimination) Act 2013 ch 8.

177 Ibid. ss 1, 2, 3.

178 CRPD, preamble (e).

179 Committee on the Rights of Persons with Disabilities, above n 4, [42].

180 See, e.g., J Dawson, 'A Realistic Approach to Assessing Mental Health Laws' Compliance with the UNCRPD' (2015) 40 *Mental Capacities and Legal Responsibilities* 70; M Freeman et al., 'Reversing Hard Won Victories in the Name of Human Rights: A Critique of the General Comment on Article 12 of the UN Convention on the Rights of Persons with Disabilities' (2015) 2 *Lancet Psychiatry* 844; J Dute, 'Should Substituted Decision-Making Be Abolished?' (2015) 22 *European Journal of Health Law* 315.

including initiatives related to housing,[181] employment[182] and community-based services.[183]

Alongside rights in the CRPD to ensure freedom from coercive interventions by governments on an unequal basis, the States Parties are obliged to provide the resources necessary for persons with disabilities to exercise rights. In the mental health context, Peter Bartlett summarises a broad argument for improving the range of services available when he observes:

> If appropriate services and supports are provided, the argument goes, compulsion will be no more necessary for people with mental disabilities than for anyone else. There is much to recommend this view in many circumstances, including those related to psychiatric and related detention. Thus, in much of Europe, provision of proper community housing and community support would provide an option likely to be preferred by many people with mental disabilities. If services are provided that people want, it will not be necessary to force them to use them. For a large number of people in psychiatric and related institutions this is almost certainly a convincing argument. And, if the state refuses to offer services that people do want to use, it is ethically dubious to force them to use services they do not want to use.[184]

The examples listed in this chapter identify practical measures that operate more squarely within a human rights framework and can help to create indicators and benchmarks, undertake impact assessments and budgetary analyses, and so on. They can assist individuals, families and service providers to avoid practices that encourage compliant and passive behaviour, or that

[181] A significant body of evidence indicates that safe, affordable housing can be effective in improving health and self-determination in other areas of life. See, e.g., L Wood et al., *What Are the Health, Social and Economic Benefits of Providing Public Housing and Support to Formerly Homeless People?* (AHURI Final Report No 265, Australian Housing and Urban Research Institute, Melbourne, 2016) <www.ahuri.edu.au>; D Fitzpatrick-Lewis, 'Effectiveness of Interventions to Improve the Health and Housing Status of Homeless People: A Rapid Systematic Review' (2011) 11 *BMC Public Health* 638.

[182] Individual Placement and Support, for example, is an employment practice in the United Kingdom for which the 'overriding philosophy', according to Miles Rinaldi and colleagues, 'is that anyone is capable of working competitively in the community if the right kind of job and work environment can be found and the right kind of support provided. Thus, the primary goal is not to change the individual, but to find a natural match between the individual's strengths and experiences and a job in the community'. M Rinaldi et al., 'Individual Placement and Support: From Research to Practice' (2008) 14(1) *Advances in Psychiatric Treatment* 50.

[183] For more examples, see the Zero Project <www.zeroproject.org>.

[184] P Bartlett, 'A Mental Disorder of a Kind or Degree Warranting Confinement: Examining Justifications for Psychiatric Detention' (2012) 16(6) *International Journal of Human Rights* 831, 834.

persecute anger or dissent. The examples also demonstrate the wide range of practices – information supports, communication and interpretative supports, life-planning tools, advocacy, formal and administrative representational supports, and relationship-building supports[185] – which promote the different rights set out in the CRPD. In this sense, Carney rightly argues that 'uniformity of approach may appeal to purists or academic commentators, [but] overlooks the need to accommodate local values, institutions and patterns of administration'.[186]

However, within the pragmatic and pluralistic approach of the CRPD, a number of concrete requirements seem inevitable. For example, it seems necessary to create legislation that offers different statutory mechanisms for support to exercise legal capacity; for example, through 'representative agreements', 'assisted decision-making agreements', advance planning mechanisms, independent advocates and so on. Creating an 'assisted legal capacity' statute or integrating statutorily recognised support measures into other areas of law, such as those related to powers of attorney, may be the necessary first step for governments to develop effective safeguards from which to 'take the leap of faith' and repeal or fundamentally alter mental health law. Looking beyond law, as this chapter has demonstrated, some policy and programming can incorporate – and has incorporated – CRPD directives in practice. These measures demonstrate that various short- and medium-term changes can be pursued under current social conditions.

185 G Davidson et al., 'Good Practice in Supported Decisionmaking under Modern Mental Capacity Legislation: A National Disability Authority Working Paper' (National Disability Authority, 2012) 5.

186 T Carney, 'Guardianship, Citizenship, and Theorizing Substitute-Decision-Making Law', Legal Studies Research Paper, Sydney Law School, No 12/25.

7

Navigating the 'Flashing Amber Lights' of the CRPD Support Framework: Addressing Major Concerns

A INTRODUCTION

In this chapter I will examine major concerns raised about the support framework of the CRPD and its challenging implications for mental health law and policy.[1] I will set out a list of questions raised by scholars and other commentators regarding the CRPD in the mental health context, pinpointing controversies and highlighting ongoing practical and conceptual issues. In particular, I will consider General Comment No 1 of the CRPD Committee, which was adopted in 2014 and provides specific interpretative guidance on Article 12 of the CRPD.[2]

As outlined in Chapters 4 and 5, CRPD directives for realising universal 'legal capacity' are purported to produce a number of benefits, including: promoting people's self-determination, authority and control over their own lives;[3] using a more realistic account of autonomy and decision-making that takes into account people's *inter*dependence with others;[4] providing a more transparent process for pinpointing moral dilemmas in relation to those whose will and preference is unclear or unknown or may fundamentally compromise

[1] Convention on the Rights of Persons with Disabilities, opened for signature 30 March 2007, Doc.A/61/611 (entered into force 3 May 2008).

[2] Committee on the Rights of Persons with Disabilities, *General Comment No 1: Article 12: Equal Recognition Before the Law*, 11th sess, UN Doc CRPD/C/GC/1 (19 May 2014).

[3] T Minkowitz, 'The United Nations Convention on the Rights of Persons with Disabilities and the Right to Be Free from Non-consensual Psychiatric Interventions' (2007) 34(2) *Syracuse Journal of International Law and Commerce* 405.

[4] R Gordon, 'The Emergence of Assisted (Supported) Decision-Making in the Canadian Law of Adult Guardianship and Substitute Decision-Making' (2000) 23(1) *International Journal of Law and Psychiatry* 61; P Gooding, 'Supported Decision-Making: A Rights-Based Disability Concept and Its Implications for Mental Health Law' (2013) 20(3) *Psychiatry, Psychology and Law* 431, 436.

other rights;[5] and even realising a 'frontier of justice' by extending core civil rights to persons with disabilities.[6]

Yet despite these apparent benefits, the terms of Article 12 and the CRPD Committee's comments have been criticised by a number of commentators.[7] The list presented in this chapter is not exhaustive.[8] I have listed concerns that have been raised repeatedly by academics, law reformers, governments, service users, families and others, or where issues identified throughout this book present significant risks or ambiguities. The intention here is to raise a range of critical issues and present possible counterarguments, in order to better examine which issues the various interpretations and implementation strategies may or may not address.

In evaluating the benefits and drawbacks of the CRPD, the use of mental capacity assessments or the universal legal capacity approach, it is important to ask whether the law is appropriate for solving personal and social difficulties. One possibility is that any benefits from using the law for social justice in this way are overwhelmed by other powerful forces in society, such as resource allocation, accessible housing and wealth disparity.[9] Consider, for example, the mounting evidence that people who are socially and economically disadvantaged experience higher levels of stress than others, increasing the likelihood of physical and mental health issues, and hence rights restrictions under

5 M Bach and L Kerzner, *A New Paradigm for Protecting Autonomy and the Right to Legal Capacity* (Report to the Law Commission of Ontario, 2010) <www.lco-cdo.org>.

6 A Dhanda, 'Legal Capacity in the Disability Rights Convention: Stranglehold of the Past or Lodestar for the Future?' (2007) 34 *Syracuse Journal of International Law and Commerce* 429, 433.

7 See, e.g., P Fennell and U Khaliq, 'Conflicting or Complementary Obligations? The UN Disability Rights Convention, the European Convention on Human Rights and English Law' (2011) 6 *European Human Rights Law Review* 662; A Ward, 'Adults with Incapacity: Freedom and Liberty, Rights and Status: Part 1' (2011) 5 *Scots Law Times* 21; T Carney and F Beaupert, 'Public and Private Bricolage – Challenges Balancing Law, Services and Civil Society in Advancing CRPD Supported Decision-Making' 2013 36(1) *UNSW Law Journal* 175.

8 For a fuller range of concerns raised about Article 12 of the CRPD, see the 73 submissions to the CRPD Committee in response to its draft General Comment. Committee on the Rights of Persons with Disabilities, 'Submissions to the Draft General Comment on Article 12 of the Convention – Equal Recognition before the Law and Draft General Comment on Article 9 of the Convention – Accessibility', UN Office for the High Commission for Human Rights <www.ohchr.org>.

9 See, e.g., M Jones and LA Basser-Marks, 'The Limitations on the Use of Law to Promote Rights: An Assessment of the Disability Discrimination Act 1992' in M Haurit, C Sampford and S Blencowe (eds), *Justice for People with Disabilities – Legal and Institutional Issues* (Federation Press, 1998); M Maroto and D Pettinicchio, 'The Limitations of Disability Antidiscrimination Legislation: Policymaking and the Economic Well-being of People with Disabilities' (2014) 36(4) *Law and Policy* 370.

mental health legislation.[10] Nevertheless, as Clive Unsworth has argued, the law authoritatively creates the power structures, institutions and incentives of disability service 'systems', which directly shape the lives of people with disabilities and their families.[11] The issues listed in this chapter are relevant to all those who are implicated in the disconnect between the CRPD and current law and policy, including mental health professionals, lawyers, judges and social service providers, all of whom may influence developments in the near future. The core significance of these issues to persons with psychosocial disability rests on their being among the last groups to hold and exercise decision-making rights on an equal basis with others.[12]

B MAJOR ISSUES WITH 'UNIVERSAL SUPPORT' AND THE PROHIBITION OF COERCION UNDER THE CRPD

1 *What about Someone in a Profound Psychosis or Someone in a Coma? Surely There Are Limits to Non-Coercion?*

Perhaps the most common critique of calls to replace substituted decision-making with supported decision-making is captured by the following questions: What about a person who is unconscious, or what about a person in a state of profound psychosis? How can Article 12 apply when a person is incapable of expressing any will or preference in the strict sense, or cannot consistently express a sense of yes and no? This may also include someone who has been institutionalised for decades, someone who is socially isolated and has no connection to others from whom to gain support, or someone who is profoundly depressed and is not expressing any wish or preference and/or is uncommunicative and unmoving.

In part, proponents who reject the view that some form of substituted decision-making should be retained have argued against acknowledging decision-making 'incapacity' or 'incompetency'. Doing so risks fixing such a status without any countervailing incentive to accommodate residual expressions of a person's will and preference.[13] This risk is particularly relevant to

[10] Maroto and Pettinicchio, above n 9; P Persson and M Rossin-Slater, 'Family Ruptures, Stress, and the Mental Health of the Next Generation' (Working Paper, 2015); S Kunz-Ebrecht, C Kirschbaum and A Steptoe, 'Work Stress, Socioeconomic Status and Neuroendocrine Activation over the Working Day' (2004) 58 *Social Science and Medicine* 1523.

[11] C Unsworth, *The Politics of Mental Health Legislation* (Oxford University Press, 1987).

[12] E Saks, 'Mental Health Law and the Americans with Disabilities Act: One Consumer's Journey' (2016) 4(1) *Inclusion* 39, 43.

[13] Dhanda, above n 6.

people with disabilities, given the long history of such people being considered to have limitations that are 'natural' and fateful but are in fact socially engineered, born from low expectations or a lack of accommodations due to underdeveloped or unavailable assistive technology.[14] In a recent iteration of this pattern, Lorina Naci and Adrian Owen have produced evidence suggesting that it is possible to open up communication with a small but significant proportion of people in a so-called persistent vegetative state.[15] Naci and Owen used functional magnetic resonance imaging data to establish a form of brain communication with comatose persons: 'despite the apparent absence of external signs of consciousness', they reported that 'a significant small proportion of patients with disorders of consciousness can respond to commands by wilfully modulating their brain activity, even respond to yes or no questions, by performing mental imagery tasks'.[16] Such studies add a pragmatic dimension in response to queries about whether there is any justification for 'locking in' a categorical notion of incapacity.

Nevertheless, there will remain individuals for whom no relationships of trust exist and not enough intention is expressed to guide decision-making. There are clear risks to stretching the meaning of the term 'supported decision-making' to cover situations where decisions are being made *for* rather than *by* a person. In this vein, Gerard Quinn has asked the question:

> what's worse: stretching a fiction (100% support) to the point that it is visibly at odds with reality – a factor that is only likely to be seized on by States acting out of abundant caution and enter declarations or reservations ring-fencing substitute decision-making – or, admitting the obvious and then using our talents to lock in the exception and transform how decisions are 'made for' people?[17]

More decisively, he concludes, '[w]e cannot trade-off the reality that decisions will be "made for" some people under the carpet in the hope of cementing into place the paradigm shift only for the majority'.[18] Acknowledging that decisions will be 'made for' some people, particularly in times of emergency,

[14] S Wong, 'Justice and Cognitive Disabilities: Specifying the Problem' (2008) 9(1) *Essays in Philosophy* 1, 12.

[15] L Naci and A Owen, 'Making Every Word Count for Nonresponsive Patients' (2013) *JAMA Neurology* 3686.

[16] Ibid.

[17] G Quinn, 'Personhood and Legal Capacity: Perspectives on the Paradigm Shift of Article 12 CRPD' (Paper presented at the Conference on Disability and Legal Capacity under the CRPD, Harvard Law School, 20 February 2010) 16 <www.nuigalway.ie>.

[18] Ibid. 18.

raises immediate difficulties. Some types of psychosis and extreme self-harm, for example, raise particularly challenging issues. (I will discuss these issues shortly).

The CRPD Committee offers some interpretative guidance on this point. It indicates that Article 12 requires discarding the term 'substituted decision-making', even as *some* of the practices currently seen to operate under the term may be retained. The CRPD Committee refers to use of an interpretation by a third party, based on the perceived wishes of the person, as a way out of many of the difficulties described in the coma scenario and like situations. For the comatose patient, use of the 'best interpretation' by friends or family, or even by public officials who seek to identify the wishes and preferences of the individual based on his or her life story, values and beliefs, would conform with the concept of support advanced in Article 12 of the CRPD. From the perspective of the CRPD Committee:

> Where, after significant efforts have been made, it is not practicable to determine the will and preference of an individual, 'best interpretation of will and preference' must replace 'best interests' determinations. This respects the rights, will and preferences of the individual, in accordance with article 12, paragraph 4. The 'best interests' principle is not a safeguard which complies with article 12 in relation to adults. The 'will and preferences' paradigm must replace the 'best interests' paradigm to ensure that persons with disabilities enjoy the right to legal capacity on an equal basis with others.[19]

States wishing to realise this interpretation will be confronted with the challenge of situations in which the 'best interpretation' approach would not appear to quite fit. This could include a person who is non-verbal, requires intensive support and has no financial experience or apparent preference regarding her personal finances. On what basis should a supporter make investment choices with her money? The Victorian Law Reform Commission ('VLRC') has suggested that the guiding principle in these exceptional instances should be an overarching goal of 'promoting the personal and social wellbeing' of the supported person, with other principles applied in certain circumstances, such as the 'prudent person principle', when administering a person's finances.[20] A difficulty arises in applying 'support to exercise legal capacity' in accordance

[19] Committee on the Rights of Persons with Disabilities, above n 2, [21] 5.

[20] For example, when making financial decisions, the VLRC proposed that 'financial decision makers should be required to apply the prudent person principle in managing a person's finances *to the extent this promotes their personal and social wellbeing*'. Victorian Law Reform Commission, *Guardianship: Final Report* 24 (2012) 398, s 17.139 (emphasis in original).

with the CRPD when at first glance this approach seems indistinguishable from the 'best interests' standard.

But while it might be impossible to stretch the fiction that the person is being supported to 'make' a decision in these exceptional scenarios, it is not inconceivable to suggest that the 'best interpretation' of the person's will and preferences by supporters could be the main driver in a decision, even as other guiding principles apply, such as the various rights of the person relevant to the decision. For example, supporters wishing to make a decision for a person who is non-communicative and unmoving in a state of catatonic depression could reasonably presume that the person wishes to be free from harm and to be removed to a place of safety. Separate questions arise as to the role of the law in the removal of such a person to a place of safety, what such a place looks like and the mechanisms required for addressing exploitation, neglect and abuse, including arbitration procedures to resolve possible disputes about the 'best' interpretation of the person's will and preference. These do not seem like insurmountable barriers to applying the CRPD support framework to the 'hard cases' often advanced in debates about disability, mental health and legal capacity.

The CRPD Committee included 'rights' as a third element of the 'best interpretation of will and preference' determination, stating that any such determination must respect 'the *rights*, will and preferences of the individual', which conforms with the text of Article 12(4).[21] Although the rights element is not specifically emphasised or elaborated upon by the CRPD Committee, it is likely to receive attention by states wishing to address ambiguities in 'best interpretation' determinations. In recent law reform activity in Australia, for example, the Australian Law Reform Commission recommended that 'if it is not possible to determine what the person would likely want, the representative must act to promote and uphold the person's human rights and act in the way least restrictive of those rights'.[22] An important issue to resolve under such a scheme is to ascertain the point at which it is 'not possible to determine what the person would likely want'. Identifying this point will pose challenges, including questions as to who decides, how they decide and the extent of support that must be provided before such a decision is made. Another challenge will arise in instances where a person's 'rights' are seen to conflict with a representative's 'best interpretation of the person's will and preference' (or indeed the person's own expressed wishes, as discussed later in the chapter). States

[21] Committee on the Rights of Persons with Disabilities, above n 2, 5 [21] (emphasis added).

[22] Australian Law Reform Commission, *Equality, Capacity and Disability in Commonwealth Laws* (2014) rec 3–3(2)(d).

wishing to heed the General Comment will be required to set boundaries as to how far the best interpretation of will and preferences might stretch, whilst giving due consideration to 'rights, will and preference' in establishing such boundaries.

2 *Manipulation and Undue Influence by Supporters*

The scenarios discussed in the previous section raise another common critique of proposals for implementing Article 12 – that is, supported decision-making and other CRPD-based support opens up the possibility of manipulation and unchecked abuse against people with disabilities. Adrian Ward argued that Article 12 was the result of 'inept drafting', where the definition of capacity is confused and confusing, which will lead to the unbridled manipulation of people by so-called supporters.[23] He argued that a 'lack of clarity on this issue means that any reference to supported decision-making should be viewed as a flashing amber light requiring vigilance to distinguish between the adult's own competent decision, made without undue influence, on the one hand, and on the other a decision more truly reflective of the views and values of the supporter, masquerading as the supported decision of the adult, but in fact straying into the area of *de facto* substituted decision-making'.[24] Certainly, evidence is required to measure the incidence of undue influence, coercion or abuse in supported decision-making arrangements, including the identification of factors that may encourage or discourage subtle coercion and substituted decision-making.

As a starting point, it is important to note that all adults are subject to influence, pressure, manipulation and subtle coercion by those close to them. Hannah Arendt highlights this point with reference to the interdependence of human beings, arguing that 'the human capacity for freedom … by producing the web of relationships, seems to entangle its producer to such an extent that he appears more the victim and the sufferer than the author and doer of what he has done'.[25] This does not leave humans without agency; instead, Arendt argues, agency is expressed within an inevitable human plurality.[26] This point remains important so as to avoid lowering standards for state intrusion into the lives of people with disabilities (and their decision-making) compared to the general population. Avoiding disability-specific exceptions

23 A Ward, 'Adults with Incapacity: Freedom and Liberty, Rights and Status: Part 1' (2011) 5 *Scots Law Times* 21.
24 Ibid.
25 H Arendt, *The Human Condition* (University of Chicago Press, 1958) 234.
26 Ibid.

to the right to be free from government interference is important, given that states have historically used the alleged incapacity and dependence of persons with disabilities to justify exceptions to normative rights (leading, for example, to the institutionalisation of people with disabilities writ large).[27] Further, the idea that autonomy is an interdependent phenomenon problematises the very distinction between the 'competent decision, made without undue influence, on the one hand', and 'a decision more truly reflective of the views and values of the supporter', on the other. Resolving this line of enquiry requires a clearer definition of 'undue influence'.

According to the CRPD Committee, undue influence is evident 'where the quality of the interaction between the support person and the person being supported includes signs of fear, aggression, threat, deception or manipulation'.[28] Clarifying such definitions at a domestic level will help develop adequate safeguards, including designing appropriate responses, such as placing duties on supporters to refrain from undue influence. Thresholds for undue influence in contract and probate law, which are broader than mental capacity determinations, may provide guidance on this point, including consideration of whether a relationship is characterised by trust and confidence, a power imbalance and so on. Further research is required to identify how these kinds of abuses can be identified and addressed and how to prevent people with disabilities from having their relationships scrutinised to a degree that is detrimental to the point of being unequal to others.

Another concern raised by Nina Kohn, Jeremy Blumenthal and Amy Campbell is that manipulation may arise, not just in the form of deliberate coercion or unconscious influence by supporters, but also in terms of the undue influence arising from 'deliberate deference by the principal decision-maker'.[29] This may include elderly people in mental health services who prefer a decision-making proxy rather than making such decisions themselves, as some research indicates is the case in general health services.[30] Such deference can subvert the goals of supported decision-making, although there is little evidence to support how or when this happens.[31]

Yet, although deference to others is a serious issue requiring concerted efforts to strengthen self-determination, this is an issue that *all* adults must grapple with at an interpersonal level. Most (if not all) people are likely to

27 See, generally, Dhanda, above n 6, 10.

28 Committee on the Rights of Persons with Disabilities, above n 2, 5 [22].

29 NA Kohn, JA Blumenthal and AT Campbell, 'Supported Decision-Making: A Viable Alternative to Guardianship?' (2013) 117(4) *Pennsylvania State Law Review* 1111, 1123.

30 Ibid. n 108.

31 Ibid. 1123.

defer some decisions about themselves to those they trust. This may be magnified if expert advice is given. Indeed, there is some evidence in neuroscience showing that expert advice may, for those receiving it, shut down areas of the brain seemingly active during decision-making processes, particularly when individuals are trying to evaluate a situation involving risk.[32] Nonetheless, manipulation by 'supporters' remains a concern, particularly given the long history of people with psychosocial disabilities having their abilities devalued and suffering abuse in the private sphere.

Finally, it is important to acknowledge the ongoing difficulty of safeguarding against abuse under current substituted decision-making models, particularly at the interpersonal level. Preventing abuse and applying adequate safeguards that balance freedom and protection remains an issue of enormous difficulty under current adult (in)capacity[33] and mental health legislation.[34]

3 *A Widening Gulf between Mental Health Practitioners and the CRPD Committee*

Unsurprisingly, the CRPD Committee's comment on the need to abolish 'legislative provisions that allow or perpetrate forced treatment'[35] has been strongly criticised. Melvyn Freeman and colleagues have argued the following:

> The [CRPD] is a major milestone in safeguarding the rights of persons with disabilities. However, the General Comment on Article 12 … threatens to undermine critical rights for persons with mental disabilities, including the enjoyment of the highest attainable standard of health, access to justice, the right to liberty, and the right to life. Stigma and discrimination might also increase. Much hinges on the Committee on the Rights of Persons with Disabilities' view that all persons have legal capacity at all times irrespective of mental status, and hence involuntary admission and treatment, substitute decision-making, and diversion from the criminal justice system are deemed

32 JB Engelmann et al., 'Expert Financial Advice Neurobiologically "Offloads" Financial Decision-Making under Risk' (2009) 4(3) *PLoS ONE* e4957.

33 The recent House of Lords Select Committee on the Mental Capacity Act 2015 (England and Wales), for example, raised major concerns about whether the safeguards contained within the act are adequate. Select Committee on the Mental Capacity Act 2005, *Mental Capacity Act 2005: Post-Legislative Scrutiny* (House of Lords, Report of Session 2013–14, HL Paper 139, 2014) 91–102 [253–300]. See also Joint Committee on the Draft Mental Incapacity Bill (2002–3) *First Report: Volume II: Oral and Written Evidence* (House of Lords, HL Paper 189–II; House of Commons, HC 1083–II, 2003) [124], [133].

34 See, e.g., P Bartlett and R Sandland, *Mental Health Law: Policy and Practice* (Oxford University Press, 2nd ed, 2007) 169.

35 Committee on the Rights of Persons with Disabilities, above n 2, 11. [42].

indefensible. The General Comment requires urgent consideration with the full participation of practitioners and a broad range of user and family groups.[36]

Freeman and colleagues' concerns, particularly regarding the CRPD Committee's directive to prohibit involuntary psychiatric treatment, have been reiterated elsewhere.[37] Before engaging these concerns, it is worth noting that certain arguments they pursued are based on clear misunderstandings. First, the CRPD Committee has never argued that 'diversion from the criminal justice system [is] indefensible'. It is true that the committee has advanced a consistent position on the need to abolish declarations of incompetency as a means to limit legal capacity or justify a deprivation of liberty (including through declarations of unfitness to stand trial[38] and, possibly, the insanity defence[39]). However, the CRPD Committee has also maintained the consistent view that 'necessary and appropriate modification and adjustments'[40] are needed in order to make the mainstream substance and procedures of law *accessible* to persons with disabilities.[41] There is nothing to suggest that such accessibility measures could not include diversionary programs or an expanded range of sentencing options in responding to offenders with disabilities, as long as those people are not diverted to 'adapted and specialized'[42] processes that do not ensure 'general guarantees of criminal law

[36] M Freeman et al., 'Reversing Hard Won Victories in the Name of Human Rights: A Critique of the General Comment on Article 12 of the UN Convention on the Rights of Persons with Disabilities' (2015) 2 *Lancet Psychiatry* 844.

[37] See, e.g., J Dawson, 'A Realistic Approach to Assessing Mental Health Laws' Compliance with the UNCRPD' (2015) 40 *International Journal of Law and Psychiatry* 70; see, generally, above n 7.

[38] Committee on the Rights of Persons with Disabilities, *Statement on Article 14 of the Convention on the Rights of Persons with Disabilities* (September 2014) <www.ohchr.org> (emphasis added).

[39] See P Gooding and T Bennett, 'The Abolition of the Insanity Defense in Sweden and the United Nations Convention on the Rights of Persons with Disabilities: Human Rights Brinksmanship or Evidence It Does Not Work?' (2017) *New Criminal Law Review* (forthcoming).

[40] CRPD art 2.

[41] See, e.g., Committee on the Rights of Persons with Disabilities, *Concluding Observations of the Committee on the Rights of Persons with Disabilities (Belgium)*, 12th sess, UN Doc CRPD/C/BEL/CO/1 (28 October 2014) [28–9]; Committee on the Rights of Persons with Disabilities, *Concluding Observations of the Committee on the Rights of Persons with Disabilities (Australia)*, 10th sess, UN Doc CRPD/C/AUS/CO/1 (2–3 September 2013) [30]; Committee on the Rights of Persons with Disabilities, *Concluding Observations of the Committee on the Rights of Persons with Disabilities (Mongolia)*, 13th sess, UN Doc CRPD/C/MNG/CO/1 (13 May 2015) [25]; Committee on the Rights of Persons with Disabilities, *Concluding Observations of the Committee on the Rights of Persons with Disabilities (New Zealand)*, 12th sess, UN Doc CRPD/C/NZL/CO/1 (31 October 2014) [34].

[42] CRPD art 2.

and procedure'.[43] Negotiating the line between 'necessary modifications or adjustments' and 'adapted and specialized' processes will be an ongoing challenge. However, this challenge is not intrinsically different to existing tensions negotiated in domestic laws, for example between upholding religious freedoms and ensuring reasonable adjustments,[44] or even those that already exist in disability discrimination law.[45]

Another immediate misunderstanding relates to Freeman and colleagues' insistence that the General Comment 'conflates the notions of disability, a long-term state, and mental capacity, which is based on a time-limited assessment', and that involuntary psychiatric intervention is justified when based upon 'a time-limited assessment of a person's mental state, safety, and decision-making capacity'.[46] As George Szmukler points out, the authors 'overlook the fact that in almost all countries, detention – and in the vast majority of cases involuntary psychiatric treatment – is not based on impaired decision-making capacity at all, but on the status of being diagnosed with a mental disorder coupled with the risk of harm to self or to others'.[47] The use of a diagnostic threshold in this sense does not comply with the CRPD (as I argued in Chapters 2 and 3), which seems to remain a point of general agreement irrespective of the General Comment.[48]

Such misunderstandings suggest a need for awareness-raising regarding the CRPD's implications in the mental health context. Freeman and colleagues reasonably call for action and advocacy on the part of 'clinicians, practitioners, professional organisations, and a wide range of service user groups … to ensure that implementation of the CRPD generates laws and practices that indeed safeguard the rights of persons with mental disabilities'.[49] Any such advocacy should be based on clear information about CRPD content. On this point, States Parties to the CRPD are obliged, under Article 4(1)(i), 'To promote the training of professionals and staff working with persons with disabilities in the rights recognized in this Convention so as to better provide the assistance and services guaranteed by those rights'. Implementing this requirement in the mental health context would help to build upon, and in some

43 Committee on the Rights of Persons with Disabilities, *Concluding Observations on the Initial Report of Ecuador*, 12th sess, UN Doc CRPD/C/ECU/CO/1 (27 October 2014) [29(b)].

44 See, e.g., L Vickers, *Religious Freedom, Religious Discrimination and the Workplace* (Hart, 2008).

45 A Lawson, *Disability and Equality Law in Britain: The Role of Reasonable Adjustment* (Bloomsbury Publishing, 2008).

46 Freeman et al., above n 36.

47 G Szmukler, 'UN CRPD: Equal Recognition Before the Law' (2015) 2(11) *Lancet Psychiatry* e29.

48 Ibid. See also Chapter 3, Section B.

49 Freeman et al., above n 36.

cases resolve, the debates that have been discussed in this book. Much would be gained by clarifying concepts such as accessibility, reasonable accommodation, the human rights model of disability and disability-based discrimination. State-led awareness-raising campaigns among professionals alone are unlikely to bridge the apparent gap emerging between the views of human rights agencies, on the one hand, and some mental health practitioners and their representative organisations, on the other. However, awareness-raising measures would help to dispense with misunderstandings and hone down the focus to important issues; this would increase the likelihood that points of agreement would be pursued in law, policy and practice, and that points of disagreement could be resolved (or at the very least subjected to serious public debate). It is noteworthy that there has been a general absence of detailed information and commentary about the CRPD disseminated by the representative bodies for mental health professionals.[50] This disengagement is striking, given the role of professional bodies in education and training, and in setting and raising professional standards.

Returning to Freeman and colleagues' concerns, the most pressing issue raised is undoubtedly that the CRPD Committee appears to see no role for involuntary psychiatric treatment. As I discussed in Chapter 5, it is not explicitly clear whether the CRPD Committee promotes the outright prohibition of all involuntary psychiatric treatment in all circumstances. Its directive that states 'abolish policies and legislative provisions that allow or perpetrate forced treatment' because 'forced treatment by psychiatric and other health and medical professionals is a violation' of a range of human rights would suggest as much.[51] However, the committee does not seem to have explicitly ruled out possible 'involuntary' treatment under emergency powers, where such powers are 'non-discriminatory in purpose or

[50] At the time of writing, psychiatric and psychological professional bodies, with few exceptions, have tended not to publish specific materials on the CRPD, except indirectly and briefly in materials such as policy submissions and reports by other organisations or speakers. This general omission appears to be the case with the Canadian Psychiatric Association (www.cpa-apc.org), the Canadian Psychological Association, (www.cpa.ca), the Australian and New Zealand Royal College of Psychiatrists (www.ranzcp.org), the Australian Society of Psychology (www.psychology.org.au), the New Zealand Psychological Society (www.psychology.org.nz), the Irish College of Psychiatrists (www.irishpsychiatry.ie) and the Psychological Society of Ireland (www.psihq.ie). The Royal College of Psychiatrists is exceptional in having produced a specific, albeit brief, three-page document on the implications of the CRPD to psychiatrists and mental health law, whilst also including a considerable number of materials on its website. See Royal College of Psychiatrists, 'The Convention on the Rights of Persons with Disabilities (CRPD): Implications for psychiatrists and mental health law' (n.d.) <www.rcpsych.ac.uk>.

[51] Committee on the Rights of Persons with Disabilities, above n 2, 11 [42] (emphasis added).

effect'. What forms of emergency treatment would be acceptable under such a scheme? Is it simply psychiatric treatment that is prohibited? If so, what constitutes psychiatric treatment? Could psychiatric medication be administered to a person in a state of catatonic depression who has not expressed any will or preference on the matter? What if the person's supporters decided, based on 'best interpretation of will and preference', that administering some psychoactive medication was appropriate? Such treatment would remain involuntary even if it did not (necessarily) go against the person's expressed will and preference. The ambiguity of the CRPD Committee on this point raises important questions. One possibility is that the committee views current legal and political norms as being so thoroughly discriminatory against persons with psychosocial disability that to even imagine a detailed legislative alternative for intervention according to a 'best interpretation' approach is impossible. For those responding to the day-to-day dilemmas raised by mental health crises under current social conditions, such a view may seem inadequate. John Dawson has strongly criticised the General Comment, stating that

> the Committee pays no adequate attention ... to the potentially adverse consequences of the positions it takes. It makes no mention of the prospect, for instance, that, if a person cannot be subject to compulsory treatment or institutionalisation under the civil law, they may be subject to imprisonment or preventive detention instead, with no advance in human rights terms. In this fashion, the Committee's approach reveals a famous weakness of rights discourse – its non-consequential character.[52]

Dawson criticises the CRPD Committee, in particular, for dismissing mental capacity assessments as inherently discriminatory, and argues instead for a 'more conservative interpretation' of the CRPD in which 'functional tests of mental capacity *should* be used in mental health law'.[53] Such a view, he argues, would help achieve 'a more balanced interpretation of the Convention as a whole'.[54] I have discussed some of these concerns in detail in Chapter 5, but will elaborate on a key point in the following subsection regarding the manifest need for a threshold to activate processes to make decisions 'for' people in emergency crises or for the purposes of providing ongoing support.

[52] Dawson, above n 37, 73 (citations removed).
[53] Ibid. 71.
[54] Ibid.

4 *The Need for Boundaries between Different Support Arrangements*

Establishing comprehensive support to 'exercise legal capacity' in law and policy would still require 'dividing lines' between different categories of support and safeguarding. This includes separating categories of support and intervention in which a legislative mechanism is required in order to make a decision for or about an individual, such as where his or her wishes and preferences are unclear or unknown (or are discernible only to a small number of people, as may be the case for those with certain communication disabilities).

As discussed in Chapter 5, various categories of support for exercising legal capacity in these situations have been advanced.[55] As noted, Michael Bach and Lara Kerzner have suggested three categories for legal models of support in line with Article 12 of the CRPD: (1) autonomous (or 'legally independent') decision-making, (2) supported decision-making and (3) facilitated decision-making.[56] Accompanying each status is a corresponding level of legal oversight. This would range from non-intervention to the provision of support mechanisms designed to help the person develop 'decision-making capabilities' to facilitation whereby a supporter is appointed to make decisions *for* the person using (in general) the 'best interpretation of his or her will and preference'.[57] Ireland's Assisted Decision-Making (Capacity) Act 2015 introduced similar categories of support.[58]

The challenge arises in setting out criteria for the application of these types of categories in ways that do not discriminate against persons with disabilities – including practices that do not discriminate in effect.[59] As Genevra Richardson has observed, supported decision-making seemingly requires the creation of new boundaries which 'determine when support is to be offered and/or imposed and to provide for cases where decision-making powers are severely

55 See, e.g., S Then, 'Evolution and Innovation in Guardianship Laws: Assisted Decision-Making' (2013) 35 *Sydney Law Review* 133.

56 Bach and Kerzner, above n 5.

57 Bach and Kerzner use the term 'decision-making capability' in a very specific way to refer not to individual abilities or capacities, but instead to '"capabilities to function" where function refers to the getting of things done or making things happen that are important to individuals or communities'. Further, capabilities for decision-making are 'a combination of … individual decision-making "abilities" and of decision-making "supports" and accommodations'. They use these terms 'as a way to conceptually integrate recognition of the functional diversity of individuals with an understanding of the array of supports and accommodations a person might need to enjoy and exercise his or her legal capacity'. Ibid. 20–2.

58 These support categories are: decision-making assistance, co-decision-making and representative decision-making. Assisted Decision-Making (Capacity) Act 2015 No 64 (Ireland) pt 4 ch 5, s 10.

59 Committee on the Rights of Persons with Disabilities, above n 2, 6 [25]; CRPD arts 2, 5.

impaired and, despite all support, a decision with drastic consequences is maintained'.[60] Richardson notes that creating such boundaries would conceivably require some form of functional mental capacity testing and would therefore run counter to the spirit of the CRPD[61] and, more recently, to the explicit interpretation of the CRPD Committee.[62] Indeed, Bach and Kerzner deemed it necessary to include assessments of 'decision-making ability' (albeit differently formulated)[63] to determine boundaries between different support categories,[64] as did the drafters of Ireland's Assisted Decision-Making (Capacity) Act 2015.[65]

The Canadian Association of Community Living ('CACL') echoes Bach and Kerzner and argues that functional assessments of mental capacity can help to identify those who exercise their legal capacity in 'substantially different' ways.[66] In particular, the CACL highlights that some people with more profound disabilities will require supporters to: interpret their unique forms of communication, assist them with developing their will and preference, and translate those wishes into 'particular actions and decisions which enable the person to exercise legal capacity'.[67] For the CACL, functional assessments of mental capacity help determine who requires such arrangements, and can therefore be made non-discriminatory: 'To recognize that people have different decisional abilities is not in itself discriminatory; just as it is not discriminatory to recognize that people have different mobility abilities. The issue is how those different abilities are recognized and supported, and how to ensure equal access and outcomes are not dependent on those differences'.[68] The CACL criticises the CRPD Committee's rejection of assessments of decision-making ability and warns that a 'principle of proportional support is not the answer to these challenges, except at the highest and most abstract level of principle'.[69] Similar arguments have been advanced elsewhere,[70] and

60 G Richardson, 'Mental Capacity in the Shadow of Suicide' (2013) 9(1) *International Journal of Law in Context* 87, 103.

61 Ibid.

62 Committee on the Rights of Persons with Disabilities, above n 2.

63 See Chapter 5, Section C(1).

64 Bach and Kerzner, above n 5.

65 See Chapter 5, Section C.

66 Canadian Association of Community Living, 'Submission to the Draft General Comment on Article 12 of the Convention – Equal Recognition before the Law and Draft General Comment on Article 9 of the Convention – Accessibility', UN Office of the High Commissioner for Human Rights <www.ohchr.org>.

67 Ibid.

68 Ibid.

69 Ibid.

70 See, e.g., W Martin et al., 'Achieving *CRPD* Compliance: Is the Mental Capacity Act of England and Wales Compatible with the UN Convention on the Rights of Persons with

lawmakers are struggling to find alternative, non-discriminatory mechanisms of support, with accompanying safeguards.

The final draft of the General Comment did not heed the CACL's suggestion to endorse ability tests in defined circumstances. Indeed, the CRPD Committee expanded its view that mental capacity tests were prohibited by the CRPD, and stated explicitly that 'the provision of support to exercise legal capacity should not hinge on mental capacity assessments; new, non-discriminatory indicators of support needs are required'.[71] The CRPD Committee also abstained from specifying categories of support, which were conceivably viewed as being too complex and specific, and hence the domain of States Parties. However, the committee did add the 'best interpretation of will and preference' standard to the final draft, which the CACL recommended as a tool for navigating between the more challenging categories of support to exercise legal capacity.[72]

Those wishing to pursue the CRPD Committee's call to discard decision-making ability tests will need to investigate alternative indicators for activating support – or for indicating the *limits* of such support. Only a very small number of commentators have explored this possibility beyond the abstract.[73] For example, a coalition of Australian non-governmental organisations has advanced a national framework to discard 'ability tests'.[74] The coalition describes such functional assessments of mental capacity as providing an 'overarching exception to the right to equal capacity before the law, embedding discrimination against people with disability'.[75] Instead, a determination as to whether a person's will, preference or decision is recognised by the law should focus on 'the integrity of the support process' used to express that decision.[76] This, in turn, requires the testing of *supports* based on the 'functional ability [of those supports] to meet the requirements of a person to make and/or communicate a decision to a third party'.[77] In practice, this would mean that

Disabilities? If Not, What Next? (Essex Autonomy Project Position Paper, Report Submitted to the United Kingdom Ministry of Justice, 22 September 2014) 16–30; Australian Law Reform Commission, above n 22, rec 3–3(2)(d).

[71] Committee on the Rights of Persons with Disabilities, above n 2, 7 [29](i).

[72] Canadian Association of Community Living, above n 66.

[73] See, e.g., People with Disabilities Australia, the Australian Centre for Disability Law and the Australian Human Rights Centre, 'Submission to the Australian Law Reform Commission (ALRC): Equality, Capacity and Disability in Commonwealth Laws, Discussion Paper May 2014 <www.alrc.gov.au>.

[74] Ibid.

[75] Ibid. para 5.

[76] Ibid. para 7.

[77] Ibid.

'[a]ny test of a person's ability to exercise their legal agency is actually a test of whether the supports provided to the person are adequate and appropriate to the task in hand. If not they should be altered until will and preference can be expressed, or it becomes apparent that this is not possible'.[78] Such proposals are in the early stages of conceptual development and their implementation in legislation would constitute a profound shift from centuries of capacity jurisprudence. At a minimum, amendments would be required across a wide range of laws that use mental capacity assessments, and states would need to provide universally accessible support. Perhaps unsurprisingly, then, no state has expressed a willingness to remove entirely functional assessments of mental capacity in light of the CRPD. Yet conceptual alternatives have developed considerably in recent years, and the search for 'dividing lines' between categories of support in line with Article 12, while challenging, appears to promote more explicit consideration of the moral dilemmas at stake in fraught decision-making scenarios in a way that the binary division of mental capacity/incapacity cannot.[79]

5 *Risk Where the Person Is Unaware of Harm Caused*

Despite supported decision-making and broader support under the CRPD challenging the high priority given to risk aversion, a distinct challenge remains where individuals are not aware of the consequences of certain decisions that carry grave danger. This point is illustrated in Elizabeth Farr's account of her own experience of psychosis.[80] After many years of visual and aural hallucinations, Farr felt that she had to perform a dangerous act:

> I thought I was approaching some kind of horrible Enlightenment about which I felt quite ambivalent … The voices told me that in order to reach this Enlightened state I would have, at the appropriate moment, to jump from the seventh floor of a building and land on my head in a certain way. This would put me in a cosmic junction whereupon … I would be able to enlighten all mankind to all the full scope of reality that lay beyond.[81]

Farr's account brings into sharp relief a troubling moral dilemma for which the CRPD offers no easy answers. Bach and Kerzner's proposed law and policy framework leaves some ambiguity on this point. From their view, 'facilitated

78 Ibid. para 11.
79 Richardson, above n 60, 95, 103.
80 E Farr, 'A Personal Account of Schizophrenia', in M Tsuang (ed), *Schizophrenia: The Facts* (Oxford University Press, 1982).
81 Ibid. 4.

decision-making' would be permitted when a person was not able to express intention in 'ways that would direct reasonable consequential action', thus retaining a 'reasonableness' criteria from the functional assessment of decision-making ability/mental capacity.[82]

Bach and Kerzner use the concept of 'serious adverse effects' to provide a threshold for activating emergency safeguarding schemes aimed at maximising autonomy, yet simultaneously limiting legal *agency* in order to address issues of self-harm and the 'unacceptably high rates of abuse and neglect of older adults and people with disabilities'.[83] As a result of his or her actions or those of others, an adult's situation reaches the 'serious adverse effects' threshold if he or she:

> Experiences loss of a significant part of [his or her] property, or [fails] to provide necessities of life for himself or herself or for dependents; or
>
> Experiences serious illness or injury, and deprivation of liberty or personal security; or
>
> Has threatened or attempted or is threatening or attempting to cause physical and/or psychological harm to himself or herself; or
>
> Has behaved or is behaving violently towards another person or has caused or is causing another person to fear physical and/or psychological harm from him or her.[84]

I have argued elsewhere, along with Eilionóir Flynn, that this definition swings the pendulum too far towards paternalistic intervention, and skews the balance between the individual's dignity and the legitimate state impulse to protect its citizens from harm.[85] For example, the risk of loss of property may be significant, but this seems quite a low threshold to warrant *preemptive* action on the part of the state or others who might wish to restrict a person's self-determination.

Early on in debates about the CRPD and mental health law, David Webb (somewhat tentatively) suggested that states insisting on the need for emergency powers to intervene when someone poses a grave risk of suicide may be able to create generic, disability-neutral suicide-prevention legislation.[86]

[82] Bach and Kerzner, above n 5, 144.

[83] Canadian Association of Community Living, above n 66, pt 2, s VI.

[84] Bach and Kerzner, above n 5, 47.

[85] P Gooding and E Flynn, 'Querying the Call to Introduce Mental Capacity Testing to Mental Health Law: Does the Doctrine of Necessity Provide an Alternative?' (2015) 4(2) *Laws* 245.

[86] D Webb, 'Is Involuntary Psychiatric Treatment – Reasonable, Necessary, Justified and Proportionate?' (Paper, Victorian Mental Health Legal Centre Forum: 'Victorian Charter of Human Rights and Responsibilities and Mental Health Rights', 20 May 2008) <www.thinkingaboutsuicide.org>. Sascha Callaghan and colleagues have argued that the risk of suicide should *not* provide grounds for coercive psychiatric treatment given the inaccuracy of

An example would be preserving the right to intervene where a person's life, health or safety is at imminent and grave risk, and failure to intervene would constitute criminal or civil negligence. Notwithstanding the considerable evidence reflecting the inability of experts to predict when someone is going to attempt suicide, this threshold for intervention could conceivably remain 'disability-neutral'. In her meta-analyses of suicide research, Susan Stefan concluded that 'at least half of all suicide attempts and suicides are not caused by serious mental illnesses such as major depression, bipolar disorder, and schizophrenia'.[87]

In a similar vein, Flynn and I have proposed an alternative, restrictive definition of serious adverse effects: 'A situation of serious adverse effects occurs when a person's life, health or safety is at imminent and grave risk, and failure to intervene would constitute criminal or civil negligence'.[88] We argue that this provision could be equally applied to those with and without disabilities, and that determination of an individual's mental capacity would not need to form part of the basis for intervention. This preliminary suggestion was offered in the spirit of advancing debate in the field. Refining such a definition, and comprehensively thinking through its legal and political implications, is beyond the scope of this book (and would likely require a treatise on its own). A small number of initiatives are under way to build upon this definition and refine non-discriminatory thresholds for emergency interventions, and also to work through the theoretical, political and operational issues of adopting them.[89]

Returning to the challenging issue of self-harm, Richardson and others have pointed to another type of exceptional scenario that poses immediate difficulties for the CRPD support framework in the mental health context; that is, where a person's will and preference conflict on a matter of grave concern following efforts to clarify and reconcile his or her will and preference.[90] Anorexia provides a commonly used example of such a bind, where persons with anorexia often express a wish not to eat, but a 'will' to live.[91]

risk assessment tools. See S Callaghan, C Ryan and I Kerridge, 'Risk of Suicide Is Insufficient Warrant for Coercive Treatment for Mental Illness' (2013) 36(5–6) *International Journal of Law and Psychiatry* 374.

87 S Stefan, *Rational Suicide, Irrational Laws: Examining Current Approaches to Suicide in Policy and Law* (Oxford University Press, 2016) 272.

88 Gooding and Flynn, above n 85.

89 See E Flynn and A Arstein-Kerslake, 'DRAFT: State Intervention in the Lives of People with Disabilities – The Case for a Disability Neutral Framework' (Voices of Individuals: Collectively Exploring Self-Determination, National University of Ireland Galway, 2016) <www.ercvoices.com>.

90 Richardson, above n 60.

91 See, e.g., *Re E* (Medical treatment: Anorexia) (Rev 1) [2012] EWCOP 1639 (15 June 2012) (United Kingdom).

Again, a 'best interpretation of will and preference' could be used to guide a decision, but adjudicating its application would be fraught indeed (as it is, I would hasten to add, under current substituted decision-making and 'best interests' approaches). The issue of conflicting will and preference is perhaps one of the most difficult situations in which to apply support within the framework of the CRPD.

It is beyond the scope of this chapter to consider the specific concern of conflicted wishes, will and preference in detail, or to discuss the relative merits and drawbacks of generic suicide-prevention legislation. The more important point here is the apparent need to explicitly define the emergency instances in which legal *agency* can be overridden and in which coercion can occur in ways that do not discriminate on the basis of disability (if this is indeed possible in substantive terms).[92] In international human rights law, 'public order' ('*ordre public*') may be invoked under the terms of the International Covenant on Civil and Political Rights to impose restrictions on the exercise of certain human rights,[93] including freedom of movement, which may help set the boundary between the individual right to legal capacity and countervailing collective interests to restrict that right. However, the General Comment directs that the right to legal capacity (on an equal basis) is non-derogable, even in emergencies.[94] It will be useful to seek guidance in international human rights law on this point. Discovering more suitable alternatives that comply with human rights standards yet provide suitable means for emergency intervention remains an ongoing endeavour for governments and others wishing to comply with the CRPD.

6 *Fetishising 'Choice': When Expressed Wishes Won't Do*

The spectre of people with disability being unaware of the risk that their actions carry raises concerns about an excessive adherence to individual 'choice'. By promoting the 'will and preferences paradigm',[95] does the CRPD – despite its apparent emphasis on interdependence and relational autonomy – risk promoting the false and idealised view of a free and liberal subject? A blind focus

92 See Chapter 4, Section C(7).

93 International Covenant on Civil and Political Rights, opened for signature 19 December 1966, 999 UNTS 171, 1057 UNTS 407 (entered into force 23 March 1976), ratified by Australia on 13 November 1980, art 12. See N Jayawickrama, *The Judicial Application of Human Rights Law: National, Regional and International Jurisprudence* (Cambridge University Press, 2002) 195–7.

94 Committee on the Rights of Persons with Disabilities, above n 2, 2 [5].

95 Ibid. 5 [21].

on expressed wishes ignores the reality that individual expressions of will and preference may be unclear, conflicted or apparently absent. Sascha Callaghan and Chris Ryan describe this concern in the following way:

> The crux of the problem appears to be that while autonomy theory in general is concerned with the concept of 'agency', theories of universal capacity do not yet agree on the extent to which expressions of 'will' and 'preference' must also involve this characteristic and how it could be discerned. Without further attention being given to the requirement of 'agency' in the expression of will and preference, it is not clear that 'respecting my will and preference' can mean anything more that 'do what I say I want right now'. Such an impoverished account of autonomy is presumably not what is intended by those advocates of universal capacity, but without at least some qualifiers, the notion of universal capacity gives us very little to work with to nuance this rather blunt result. This is particularly troublesome in the context of some forms of mental disorder. Compulsions, phobias and addiction have known volitional effects (literally, affects on the will), while others such as anorexia and depression affect values and 'choices', and still others, including psychotic illness, impact the understanding and processing of information upon which a 'will' is formed. Whether all statements about 'what I want' are meaningful acts of 'will' is a difficult question in this context, and too strong an interpretation may yield a rather hollow rendering of the principle of 'respect for autonomy'.[96]

The authors rightly point out that remarkably little attention has been paid to the meanings of 'will' and 'preference', or what it means exactly to respect them according to the terms of the CRPD.

Such ambiguities could have adverse effects where service users are portrayed as isolated, self-interested individuals for whom choice maximisation is seen as an end in itself. Barbara Taylor illustrates one such adverse effect:

> I met with a man who runs a rehab service in London. He complained to me furiously about some support workers who had been using 'choice' as an excuse not to visit people who failed to turn up for things. 'They tell me it's the person's choice – why should they interfere? Someone might be really frightened or depressed, but they don't bother to sit down with them to try and find out why; they just say, "Oh, it's his choice!" and ignore them'. Is choice really more important than care? 'We want people to learn to manage their own situations, not to always rely on somebody else,' I was told by one mental health manager. 'We want people to learn to make their own choices,

96 SM Callaghan and C Ryan, 'Is There a Future for Involuntary Treatment in Rights-Based Mental Health Law?' (2014) 21(5) *Psychiatry, Psychology and Law* 747, 755 (citations omitted).

> instead of looking to someone else for the answers'. This sounded all right until I began to think back to my own attempts to 'manage my situation' when I was very unwell, and some of the deadly choices I made at that time. What I needed then, and what I was fortunate enough to get was effective care.[97]

Taylor's recollection highlights how a service provider might respect a person's expressed wish in the strict sense, but in a way that is effectively neglectful. Respecting 'choice' in such a cynical way would appear to violate positive duties under the CRPD. In addition, persons with psychosocial disabilities may express 'adaptive preferences', a term used by Amartya Sen to describe the way deprived citizens often adapt personal preferences according to their second-class status.[98] Conceptually, the CRPD offers a remedy by setting out fundamental entitlements that must be available to people in meaningful ways, but more work is needed to establish what this guarantee looks like in practice.

Ann Plumb offers some potential solutions with reference to her personal experience. She problematises the CRPD-based emphasis on adhering to a person's will and preference, yet critiques existing substituted decision-making under mental health legislation:

> My first crisis highlights the difficulties for me around legal capacity, freedom, and informed consent (CRPD 12, 14). Unmoving and uncommunicative (believing myself to be accountable to a higher authority than the State, but unsure of what is required of me) what should be done about me? Should I be left alone, respecting my will to stay where I am for as long as I like? Or be forcefully taken for a psychiatric assessment, detained in hospital, and given strong neuroleptics, as happened. Or should there be another option – someone available to engage meaningfully with me, some temporary sanctuary provided while the next step is considered.[99]

Plumb's suggestion – 'someone [being] available to engage meaningfully with me, [the availability of] some temporary sanctuary' – provides a useful frame in which to explore support strategies during mental health crises.[100] She offers

97 B Taylor, *The Last Asylum: Memoir of Madness in Our Times* (Penguin Random House, 2014) 253.

98 See A Sen, Foreword in S Fukuda-Parr and AK Shiva Kumar (eds), *Oxford Handbook of Human Development* (Oxford University Press, 2009).

99 A Plumb, 'Incorporation, or Not, of MH Survivors into the Disability Movement' in JC Anderson and H Spandler (eds), *Distress or Disability: Proceedings of a Symposium Held at Lancaster University* (Technical Report, January 2012) 18, 22–3 <www.researchgate.net>.

100 Ibid. 23.

two possible responses: (1) 'places to go with support away from home', including women-only spaces and other types of 'refuge'; and (2) 'support for people who wish to stay at home in crisis', which might include 'practical support' and 'befriending services',[101] to which might be added many of the practices set out in Chapter 6. These methods will not provide a fail-safe means of respecting someone's 'truly' autonomous wishes, but they offer pathways to avoid a binary between coercion, under current frameworks, and blind adherence to expressed wishes that leads to neglect.

It is also worth noting that the challenge of defining terms like 'will and preference' is not unique to mental health or broader disability law and policy. Thinkers have debated the nature of decision-making since the very beginnings of disciplines such as philosophy, economics and psychology, and their debates continue to shape public policy. A World Bank Group report in 2015, for example, explored major differences in understandings of 'choice' between Milton Friedman's market-constructed 'freedom to choose' and Amartya Sen's understanding of 'development as freedom'.[102] The authors, who erred on the side of Sen's theory, point to ample evidence from behavioural economics and psychology to reveal the irrationality that drives human beings, commenting that '"Economic man" is a fiction, not a reality. Policies that assume that rational decision making will always prevail can go astray in many contexts … Updating the standard assumptions about human decision making is essential to pushing forward the frontier of development policy making'.[103] The mental health context appears to require a similar 'updating of standard assumptions'. Unpacking concepts such as the 'will and preference' paradigm in the mental health context, in particular, could include building upon ideas such as 'temporary sanctuary' or applying social and economic policy lessons about 'choice' to the mental health context. Applying Amartya Sen's notions of 'development as freedom' would also aid in this process.

7 *The Limits of Legislative Mechanisms in Garnering Resources*

Human agency is enhanced by the social, economic and political material requirements that people have for fulfilling their rights. Carney has argued that the success of supported decision-making can be measured by its ability

[101] Ibid.
[102] World Bank, 'World Development Report: Mind, Society and Behaviour' (World Bank Group, 2015) 25.
[103] Ibid.

to draw in resources.[104] The same standard could be applied more generally to the CRPD support framework in the mental health context. I have already emphasised the limited role for legal mechanisms in addressing issues in service provision.[105] Carney argues that legislative mechanisms for supported decision-making can 'only be judged by how well [they] mobilise … public or private resources (such as informal supports of civil society) in accordance with people's individual set of values and preference (in this and other respects); but the point here is that agency is realised only to the extent that resources exist in the external environment'.[106] At the conclusion of its supported decision-making trial, the South Australian Office of the Public Advocate reported that Carney's warning 'turned out to be very much the case in our trial, particularly when people made accommodation or support decisions … that then had to be resourced'.[107]

Importantly, this argument is not directly concerned with cost-effectiveness, but rather focuses on the acknowledgement that achieving human rights is dependent on material conditions. It is worth noting briefly that if an analysis of cost-effectiveness were to be undertaken, it would be important to consider the comparative costs of the existing systems of substituted decision-making.

From a legal perspective, it could be argued that equality before the law is a civil and political right, for which there is arguably no limit to the level of support that must be provided to achieve compliance.[108] Such a pure human rights argument seems unlikely to convince policymakers, and perhaps belies the reality of finite resources. In fiscal terms, attracting sufficient resources for people who require support to exercise legal capacity will continue to present a challenge. A number of governments around the world are transitioning to funding schemes for disability services that are 'self-directed' by those receiving support, or are directed towards assisting people with disabilities to have opportunities and pathways typical of other citizens in the community – lives that are fulfilling and unique. These schemes clearly dovetail with the emphasis on 'choice' in the CRPD support framework and may address certain deficits that currently limit the reasonable expectations of people with

[104] South Australian Office of the Public Advocate, *Annual Report 2012* (2013) 54 <www.opa.sa.gov.au>.

[105] See Chapter 3, Section E.

[106] Ibid. 17.

[107] Ibid.

[108] See, e.g., E Flynn and A Arstein-Kerslake, 'Legislating Personhood: Realising the Right to Support in Exercising Legal Capacity' (2014) 10 *International Journal of Law in Context* 81, 85.

disabilities in making decisions about their lives.[109] But the evidence varies on self-directed funding schemes,[110] and inevitably the issue of the most effective use of government spending to best create support 'ramps' for strengthening agency will need to be carefully considered by reformers and others interested in implementation.

Interestingly, the PO Skåne model, a Swedish personal advocacy service for people with psychosocial disabilities, which was described by the European Commissioner for Human Rights as 'decision-making support in line with Article 12',[111] has a specific function for 'demanding' resources. A report by the Swedish National Board of Health and Welfare indicates that a key role of the personal advocate is as a 'care demander'[112]; the advocate 'make[s] demands on the public authorities that are responsible for people with serious psychiatric disabilities, to ensure that they are receiving the help and service to which they are entitled'.[113] Policymakers facing fiscal restraint may be deterred by such a function. Yet the same report claims that the scheme produces savings of up to seventeen times the cost of the service itself.[114] The saving is explained in the report by a reduction in the number of mental health crises and by the PO's facilitative role in coordinating services and highlighting weaknesses in service provision.[115]

'Informal resources', or 'natural supports', will be just as important in measuring the application of a supported decision-making regime in practice. It is worth reiterating that concepts such as supported decision-making were developed from relationships between people with disabilities and their largely informal support networks.[116] Such ideas were progressed within peer groups, families and advocacy groups, often alongside the development of

[109] See, e.g., National Disability Insurance Scheme Act (No 20) 2013 (Cth), pt 2. See, generally, National Disability Insurance Scheme website <www.ndis.gov.au>; C Ungerson and S Yeandle (eds), *Cash for Care in Developed Welfare States* (Palgrave Macmillan, 2006).

[110] See, e.g., J Glasby and R Littlechild, *Direct Payments and Personal Budgets: Putting Personalisation Into Practice* (Policy Press, 2nd ed, 2009). For positive findings on mental health–based individualised funding, see C Glendinning et al., *Evaluation of the Individual Budgets Pilot Programme: Final Report* (University of York, 2008).

[111] Council of Europe Commissioner for Human Rights, 'Who Gets to Decide? Right to Legal Capacity for Persons with Intellectual and Psychosocial Disabilities' (Comm DH/Issue Paper, Strasbourg, 20 February 2012) 20 [5.2].

[112] Swedish National Board of Health and Welfare, *A New Profession Is Born – Personligt ombud, PO* (Västra Aros, Västerås, November 2008) 10 <www.personligtombud.se>.

[113] Ibid.

[114] Ibid. 23–4.

[115] Ibid.

[116] See Gordon, above n 4, 64.

theory, and applied only later to law and policy.[117] This community-driven feature of the support framework would seem important to retain, and the spirit of the CRPD would surely be missed if support practices were appropriated and taken over by specialised areas of service provision, law, academia or any other area of expertise. On the other hand, it is important that informal efforts by people with disabilities, their families and other supporters do not *replace* government resourcing. (Notably, the potential risks for informal supporters in this equation include a gendered dimension, where informal support is typically provided by mothers, and women more generally.)[118] An innovative attempt to strike this balance in policy terms is illustrated by the supported decision-making trial taking place in Victoria, Australia, coordinated by the Office of the Public Advocate.[119] The OVAL Project aims to mobilise citizen volunteers, using a paid facilitator, to develop freely given relationships around socially isolated persons who may benefit from decision-making support.[120] The OVAL Project aims to recruit, train and match volunteer supporters with 'socially isolated people with decision-making disabilities who wish to receive support with decision-making' about their disability support services.[121]

Resource mobilisation remains a major issue for achieving human rights in the mental health context. This seems unlikely to change under any CRPD support proposals, particularly where current austerity measures in countries such as the United Kingdom and the Republic of Ireland seem to have made the enjoyment of human rights more difficult for persons with disabilities generally, and with psychosocial disability in particular.

8 *'Responsibilisation'* – *Governments Placing Risks on Citizens*

One concern arising from the push to draw on informal supports noted in the previous section is that governments may abrogate their duty to provide support to citizens by conferring various risks and duties on individuals.[122] In

[117] Ibid. Gordon argues that the theory underpinning the concept of supported decision-making includes that of Wolf Wolfensberger. See W Wolfensberger, *A Brief Introduction to Social Role Valorization: A High-Order Concept for Addressing the Plight of Societally Devalued People, and for Structuring Human Services* (Syracuse University Press, 3rd ed, 1998).

[118] R Traustadottir, 'Mothers Who Care: Gender, Disability, and Family Life' (1991) 12(2) *Journal of Family Issues* 211.

[119] Victorian Office of the Public Advocate, 'Supported Decision-Making' (website) (n.d.) <www.publicadvocate.vic.gov.au/advocacy-research/supported-decision-making>.

[120] Ibid.

[121] Ibid.

[122] B Carter and J Chesterman, 'Supported Decision-Making: Background and Discussion Paper' (Office of the Public Advocate Victoria, 2009) 19 <www.publicadvocate.vic.gov.au>.

a more general critique, Michel Foucault argued that the government may discard its duties under the guise of increasing the rights and responsibilities of citizens.[123] According to Foucault, this leads to 'responsibilisation', in which citizens view social risks – such as illness, unemployment and poverty – as existing in the domain of individual responsibility and 'self-care', rather than as matters falling within the state's remit to provide resources.[124]

A key function of mental health legislation and adult (in)capacity law has been the statutory recognition that people cannot be held responsible for decisions in relation to which they are experiencing mental impairment or lack mental capacity. Another key function is that people in mental health crisis may need carefully regulated protective intervention, which may restrict their immediately expressed wishes. Barbara Carter and John Chesterman have argued that '[o]ne of the most positive features' of current substituted decision-making regimes 'is the acceptance of responsibility by the guardian and/or the administrator for the decisions s/he makes at a time in history when many professionals are increasingly reluctant to accept such responsibility'.[125] Concerns may be raised that policies of 'supported decision-making' will draw credibility from the ideas and language of individual human rights, but may result in the unreasonable transfer of risk and uncertainty by the state to persons with disabilities.

These are legitimate concerns, particularly in light of the experience of neglect and underresourced community mental health services, which many people with disabilities faced after deinstitutionalisation. Nevertheless, a number of possible counterarguments can be raised. First, it is questionable whether more 'protectionist' policy frameworks do in fact mitigate risk and uncertainty.[126] Nor is it clear whether 'protectionist' schemes (such as in the post-war era of large-scale psychiatric hospitals) were better able to secure resources to support those in need compared to more 'libertarian' schemes (such as community-based support and rights-based mental health law).

[123] Ibid. Foucault coined the term 'governmentality' to describe a mentality, adopted by citizens, which is most accommodating to systems of power. He was particularly interested in the influence of the prevailing economic ideology. Thus, with 'neoliberal governmentality', citizens who call for less and less intervention by the state could be seen to reflect the neoliberal aim of reducing the scope of government, and particularly the provision of welfare. Overall, Foucault viewed governmentality as a technique for controlling citizens without the state taking responsibility for them. M Foucault, 'Security, Territory, and Population' in P Rabinow (ed), *Ethics: Subjectivity and Truth* (The New Press, 1997) 67.

[124] T Lemke, '"The Birth of Bio-Politics" – Michel Foucault's Lecture at the Collège de France on Neo-Liberal Governmentality' (2001) 30(2) *Economy and Society* 190, 201.

[125] Ibid.

[126] See Chapter 3.

Second, the CRPD framework for realising legal capacity on an equal basis explicitly aims to counterbalance the possibility of 'responsibilisation', at least in theory, by redirecting state duties and resources in strategic ways. An example would be shifting the focus from individual treatment to improving accessibility and reasonable accommodation.[127] Another would be efforts in law and policy to prevent violence against persons with disabilities by decoupling substituted decision-making from protection against abuse, exploitation and neglect by others.[128]

Third, the CRPD explicitly requires disabled people's organisations to be actively involved in the policies that concern them.[129] This involvement could serve as a countervailing force against 'responsibilisation' by building in deliberative processes to ensure that governments are responsive to human rights requirements, including providing the resources needed to enjoy human rights. Disabled people's organisations are also well placed to negotiate the extent of acceptable risks involved in moving away from protectionism and expert-based paternalism.

Nevertheless, the reorientation of state responsibilities in this way may be sound in theory, but would require careful evaluation, monitoring and the deliberative input of service users, persons with disabilities and their supporters to ensure its realisation in practice.

9 *'Net Widening'*

Most commentators on supported decision-making see its potential for introducing a spectrum to what has previously been a crude binary division between those considered capable and those considered incapable of decision-making. A more nuanced spectrum of legislative intervention would help people avoid this binary system. However, Carney has raised the concern that such a spectrum may not help keep people out of substituted decision-making arrangements, but will potentially 'widen the net' and draw *more* people into prescriptive decision-making structures:

> One possible unintended consequence of any additional legal avenue is that of 'net widening' – where supported decision-making orders extend to an additional population rather than apply to those otherwise liable to a guardianship order; a phenomenon that may variously be both a risk (via unnecessary incursions on autonomy and privacy) or a benefit (in facilitating the

[127] CRPD arts 2, 5.
[128] Ibid. art 16.
[129] Ibid. art 33(3).

provision of necessary support and the recognition of such support by third parties).[130]

'Net widening' may be especially likely to emerge from efforts to remove specific mention of disability from mental capacity tests.[131] Lucy Series reiterated this point with reference to English case authority, which 'held that unless mental capacity assessors can show that a person failed the "functional test" *because of* a "disturbance in the functioning of the mind or brain" [as set out in the Mental Capacity Act 2005] then they should be treated as having legal capacity'.[132] In other words, without a causative correlation between the decision and the 'diagnostic criterion', the person cannot be found to lack mental capacity. Removing the criterion, paradoxically, would result in its application to more people generally (and probably more people with disabilities, who are more likely to have their mental capacity called into question).

Similarly, mental capacity law reform efforts in Northern Ireland have included expanded criteria for assessing mental capacity in an effort to remain non-discriminatory against persons with disability.[133] The Draft Mental Capacity Bill 2014 was designed to 'fuse' mental health law and mental capacity law so as to avoid relying on a diagnosis of mental illness as a criterion for detention and involuntary treatment under current mental health legislation.[134] The bill would see an additional criterion in assessment of mental capacity which goes further than the typical functional assessment of mental capacity (the so-called understand-and-appreciate test). The accompanying policy material states, '[i]t will not be sufficient for a person to have a cognitive understanding of the information relevant to the decision'.[135] Instead, a 'person whose insight is distorted by their illness or a person suffering from delusional thinking as a result of their illness, may not … meet this element of the test'.[136] This measure explicitly widens the interpretative flexibility of mental capacity

130 Carney and Beaupert, above n 7, 195.

131 Ibid.

132 L Series, 'Submission to the UN CRPD: Comments on Draft General Comment on Article 12: The Right to Equal Recognition before the Law', Submission 25 to the UN CRPD, 21 February 2014, at 3 <www.ohchr.org> For relevant case law, see *PC and Anor v City of York Council* [2013] EWCA Civ 478.

133 Draft Mental Capacity Bill (Northern Ireland) s 3(1)(c)).

134 Minister of the Department of Health, Social Services and Public Safety in Northern Ireland, Northern Ireland Department of Justice, 'Draft Mental Capacity Bill (NI) Consultation Document', Government of Northern Ireland, May 2014.

135 Ibid. s 2.22.

136 Ibid.

assessors and may indeed result in 'net-widening'.[137] In the mental health context, John Dawson has rejected the claim that the use of mental capacity assessments rather than the diagnostic threshold of mental health legislation will result in 'net-widening', instead arguing that 'in fact [the mental capacity] test seems no more malleable than the vague concepts of mental disorder used in many Mental Health Acts'.[138]

The General Comment does not explicitly respond to concerns raised about 'net-widening'. This is unsurprising, given its mandate to monitor human rights violations against persons with disabilities specifically (and not all vulnerable individuals who may be affected by 'net-widening'). It is highly doubtful that proponents of human rights–based support would welcome any net-widening that occurred as a result of efforts to reduce disability-based discrimination. However, such a development would not raise concerns about disability rights per se (unless, of course, it was disproportionately affecting persons with disabilities). Instead, the focus would turn to basic – and intractable – political questions about the legitimate reach of the law into the autonomy of all citizens and not just the civil rights of a marginalised minority, which seems to be precisely the shift that the CRPD is meant to achieve. Further, the General Comment repeatedly emphasises the need for non-discriminatory measures of support in both form *and effect* and rejects the use of 'mental capacity' assessments altogether, citing them as a barrier to equal recognition before the law. Hence, the concern raised about net-widening rests not on a criticism of the model itself, but rather on its implementation. Given that the support framework of the CRPD is only beginning to be applied, the issue of 'net-widening' demands ongoing attention by reformers.

10 *Gaps in Evidence on the 'Success' of Support to Exercise Legal Capacity*

There is a significant lack of empirical research on implementing a supported decision-making regime. Kohn, Blumenthal and Campbell describe this gap regarding supported decision-making:

> Supported decision-making holds promise both as an alternative to guardianship and as an element of the guardian-ward relationship. If it empowers persons with cognitive and intellectual disabilities to make decisions

[137] As discussed in Chapter 4, it is important to note that the use of 'insight' as a criterion for mental capacity is likely to be implicit in other mental capacity schemes. See Chapter 4, Section E(4).

[138] Dawson, above n 37.

> for themselves, as advocates of supported decision-making claim, it has the potential to advance the interests and human rights of persons with disabilities. However, without more evidence as to how supported decision-making functions in practice, it is too early to rule out the possibility that it may have the opposite effect.[139]

Indeed, there have been extensive discussions of the benefits and possible drawbacks of supported decision-making, most of which 'provide little or no empirical support for their claims'[140]; this is as true of the mental health field as it is of guardianship law. Carney and Beaupert have argued that current proposals are confused and the 'very design and connection [of supported decision-making] to other social supports, remains very much a work in progress', which, if mismanaged, could harm persons with disabilities.[141] Anthony Mason goes a step further and argues that 'proposals for supported decision-making (in legislation) must be based on empirical evidence-based research and pilot programmes which are presently lacking'.[142] Mason concludes that '[a]s things currently stand, the proposals seem to reflect little more than ideals that have not been carefully thought through, with the risk that they will result in experimental law-making'.[143] Certainly, the gap in the empirical evidence on how to effectively realise a broader support framework in line with the CRPD does little to assuage concerns about the concept raised by policymakers, persons with disabilities, professionals, families and others.

However, the paucity of empirical literature is not unique to supported decision-making.[144] As Kohn, Blumenthal and Campbell acknowledge, 'there is also surprisingly little evaluative empirical literature on guardianship',[145] a concern that can be applied to many issues in the mental health context. For example, Mary Donnelly has raised similar concerns about the 'best interests' approach, observing of the literature that, despite its widespread use, 'the conceptual basis for the ["best interests"] standard has remained, for the most

139 Kohn, Blumenthal and Campbell, above n 29, 1157.

140 Ibid. 1129. Important exceptions include the findings of the Law Commission of Ontario, Canada, which commissioned a series of papers as part of the Legal Capacity, Decision-making and Guardianship Project. See Law Commission of Ontario, 'Funded Research Papers: Legal Capacity, Decision-making and Guardianship' <www.lco-cdo.org>. Independently evaluated findings also exist from the South Australian Office of the Public Advocate Supported Decision-making Trial. See Chapter 6, Section C(1).

141 Carney and Beaupert, above n 7, 179.

142 A Mason, Foreword (2013) 36(1) *UNSW Law Journal* 170, 172–3.

143 Ibid.

144 Kohn, Blumenthal and Campbell, above n 29.

145 Ibid. 1111.

part, unexplored'.[146] The lack of evidence to support the efficacy of involuntary outpatient treatment under mental health law, such as 'community treatment orders' and 'assisted outpatient treatment', provides another example of substituted decision-making mechanisms in law that lack a strong evidence base to indicate their success.[147] Arguably, there is also a lack of robust evidence to demonstrate the effectiveness of involuntary treatment and detention more generally, including remarkably few studies on the rationale, frequency and effects of coercive treatment.

It is noteworthy that governments are willing to implement such under-researched coercive measures, the success of which remains largely unproven. One can only speculate upon the reason for retaining 'experimental law-making' in these cases. It is reasonable to hypothesise that risk aversion is a key driver in government priorities regarding many substituted decision-making measures. Service providers and professionals may also strongly support substituted decision-making approaches. Edwina Light and colleagues produced evidence indicating that many service providers are convinced about the effectiveness of community treatment orders,[148] despite large-scale randomised controlled trials failing to support such a view. Such convictions may in turn drive policy and service delivery culture, which adapts to using and relying upon coercive intervention.[149]

It also worth remaining cautious about 'evidence-based law' more generally. Undoubtedly, empirical research is useful to debunk myths that are advanced in legal debates. However, 'evidence-based law' is a relatively new field of enquiry compared to empirical testing in other disciplines, such as medicine and engineering, to which it is seemingly better suited.[150] Jeffrey Rachlinski has argued that empirical testing for medicine, with its uniform mission to treat patients, is more straightforward than for law, where 'law is often politics by other means'.[151] A useful legal and public policy issue to illustrate this point is the death penalty. Abandoning the death penalty, in most jurisdictions to have done so, cannot be explained by the accumulation of empirical evidence highlighting its ineffectiveness in preventing crime; instead, change was driven by evolving ideas as to what is moral and unjust.[152] Rachlinski argues

[146] M Donnelly, 'Best Interests, Patient Participation and the Mental Capacity Act 2005' (2009) 17(1) *Medical Law Review* 1.
[147] See Chapter 3, Section C(3).
[148] E Light et al., 'Out of Sight, Out of Mind: Making Involuntary Community Treatment Visible in the Mental Health System' (2012) 196(9) *Medical Journal of Australia* 591.
[149] Ibid.
[150] J Rachlinski, 'Evidence-Based Law' (2011) 96(4) *Cornell Law Review* 901.
[151] Ibid.
[152] Ibid. 905.

that law often 'sorts winners and losers, rather than right and wrong', and the imposition of empirical legal testing can cloud normative claims.[153]

The call for 'evidence' regarding support to exercise legal capacity must be weighed against the qualitative criteria for justifying the reform of substituted decision-making law and policy. Arstein-Kerslake argues that 'as a moral imperative … equality of people with cognitive disabilities is "right," and is the proper aim of law reform processes'.[154] She further argues that 'the *prima facie* inequality enshrined in legislation is sufficient evidence to demonstrate a need for reform to reach equality and compliance with human rights law'.[155] On this view, one might ask why advocates for supported decision-making regimes are being asked to 'prove' whether such a model works.

Even if human rights are set aside in favour of pragmatic concerns, there are well-documented problems converting empirical studies into evidence-based law.[156] Again, the death penalty is illustrative. John Donohue and Justin Wolfers conducted a meta-analysis of research examining whether the death penalty deterred crime in the United States.[157] They concluded that, despite decades of concerted social scientific inquiry, there has been a consistent failure to demonstrate that the death penalty is more effective than long prison sentences – and yet neither have studies proven that the death penalty is *less* effective for deterring crime than long-term prison sentences.[158] The analogy is, of course, imperfect. However, the methodological complexity of drawing a direct causative link between the death penalty and preventing crime seems comparable to the challenge of measuring the 'success' of replacing substituted decision-making with supported decision-making in law and policy. What measurements could be used for such a comparison? The 'well-being' of subjects is one option; another might be the rate of reported abuse before and after legal change. Yet, in both cases, it would be extremely difficult to indicate direct causality between the conceptual basis for legal change and subsequent events. Again, even if human rights concerns are set aside, it is problematic to base the foundation for implementing the universal legal capacity model, as enunciated by the CRPD Committee, on empirical evidence,

[153] Ibid. 901.

[154] A Arstein-Kerslake, Restoring Voice to People: Realizing the Right to Equal Recognition Before the Law of People with Cognitive Disabilities (PhD Thesis, National University of Ireland, 2014) 4.

[155] Ibid. 12.

[156] Rachlinski, above n 150, 912.

[157] See JJ Donohue and J Wolfers, 'Uses and Abuses of Empirical Evidence in the Death Penalty Debate' (2005) 58 *Stanford Law Review* 791, 792–4.

[158] Ibid. 792–4.

even as it remains an important concern for identifying and developing good practice and avoiding harm.

C CONCLUSION

The issues listed in this chapter reveal a number of areas that require further attention in debates about the CRPD, mental health and the law. Unresolved issues remain on a number of points, namely determining the justifiable limits on individual agency which can be imposed by the state and made applicable to everyone, regardless of disability or decision-making ability; accommodating the substantially different manner in which various people exercise legal capacity, and arbitrating what it means to do so on an equal basis with others; and operationalising support and safeguards in ways that do not create discriminatory toeholds for historic patterns of abuse, neglect and exploitation. Addressing these concerns would require, among other things, tighter definitions of exceptional circumstances to justify overriding legal agency in emergency crises, which *may* include involuntary treatment. Such reform efforts would need to bring together various groups, including policymakers, disabled people's organisations, independent human rights bodies and professional bodies, in order to conceive and implement alternatives. Other concerns not raised in this chapter are also worthy of attention. Distinct challenges are likely to arise, for example, if previously informal relationships are formalised under supported decision-making schemes.[159] Determining the legal responsibility of supporters and representatives, including consequences where duties are breached, will also require attention. Clearly, research is required on a number of fronts.

Yet, despite these gaps, the issues raised in this chapter provide no plausible reasons as to why domestic law, policy and practice could not be generally reshaped in accordance with the support framework of the CRPD. The concerns and counterarguments listed here resolve some, although clearly not all, ambiguities raised by the CRPD support framework. The issues were listed to provide a more complete analysis of ideas being applied increasingly in law, policy and informal/formal support practices for persons with disabilities and others. While certain tenets of a support framework could be set, some of its boundaries will remain fluid – and necessarily so. This flexibility is required to accommodate the complex tensions inherent in human rights, which concern the intersections between individual needs and broader social and legal

[159] See A Arstein-Kerslake, 'An Empowering Dependency: Exploring Support for the Exercise of Legal Capacity' (2016) 18(1) *Scandinavian Journal of Disability Research* 77.

change; between informal and formal supports; between the state and civil society; and in competing accounts of equality and other core rights.[160] The findings listed in this chapter can assist governments and civil society organisations to navigate dilemmas in the field. For courts, the findings illustrate how the CRPD offers a rights framework which targets the issues (and rights) at stake in difficult cases concerning support, crisis and decision-making in the mental health context.

160 Carney and Beaupert, above n 7, 180–1.

Conclusion

> Few things have done more harm than the belief on the part of individuals or groups (or tribes or states or nations or churches) that he or she or they are in *sole* possession of the truth: especially about how to live, what to be and do – and that those who differ from them are not merely mistaken, but wicked or mad: and need restraining or suppressing. It is a terrible and dangerous arrogance to believe that you alone are right: have a magical eye which sees *the* truth: and that others cannot be right if they disagree.
>
> Isaiah Berlin[1]

> One must drop all presuppositions and dogmas and roles – for these only lead to stalemate or disaster; one must cease to regard all patients as replicas, and honour each with individual attention, attention to how *he* is doing, to *his* individual reactions and propensities; and, in this way, with the patient as one's equal, one's co-explorer, not one's puppet, one may find therapeutic ways which are better than other ways, tactics which can be modified as occasion requires.
>
> Oliver Sacks[2]

A INTRODUCTION

This concluding chapter will bring together the themes of earlier chapters to present a final set of recommendations for advancing the CRPD[3] support framework in domestic law, policy and practice in the mental health context.

Throughout this book, I have argued that both conceptual and practical issues must be addressed when considering mental health law. A narrow focus

1 I Berlin, 'Notes on Prejudice', *The New York Review of Books*, 18 October 2001 (emphasis in original).

2 O Sacks, *Awakenings* (Pan Books, 1991) 259 (emphasis in original).

3 Convention on the Rights of Persons with Disabilities, opened for signature 30 March 2007, Doc.A/61/611 (entered into force 3 May 2008).

on the conceptual inconsistencies between the support framework of the CRPD and current mental health law and policy runs the risk of overlooking the needs of people within existing legal frameworks, as well as downplaying the utilitarian reform objectives of policymakers or the day-to-day efforts of clinicians to provide support at the coalface of mental health services. Equally, an analysis that simply addresses pragmatic reform without critically engaging with underlying theoretical and structural inconsistencies could have negative consequences. This dual consideration is long-standing in the area of disability justice, which Jerome Bickenbach describes in the following terms: 'Realists argue that disability law and policy must be assessed, not by its theoretical foundations but by what it actually delivers. Others argue that however attractive specific reforms may be, they will be temporary and fleeting unless grounded in a solid commitment to human rights'.[4] The CRPD provides a more recent anchor for grounding such reform. Nevertheless, I have sought throughout the book to bridge theory and practice by clarifying steps along the continuum between ideal and pragmatic concerns.

The danger in current efforts to introduce singular elements of the CRPD within mental health law – for example, introducing advance planning and nominated persons schemes, or applying formally non-discriminatory mental capacity assessments – is that such efforts will be advanced by governments using the language of the CRPD, but without meeting core obligations. Such steps will undermine States Parties' claims to hold, in Bickenbach's terms, a 'solid commitment to human rights'.[5]

It is also true, however, that it is unwise to apply the CRPD in any immediate manner in law without establishing the processes for deliberative contributions, particularly by people with psychosocial disabilities, their supporters, professionals and others, in ways that seek to avoid the pitfalls of past reform endeavours. For example, some rights-based reform has resulted in change to the language and terms of mental health policy, without necessarily improving the substantive rights of people with disabilities themselves.[6] If the governments considered in this book were to abolish mental health law in the short term, significant risks would follow. There may be insufficient cultural change in mental health services and other relevant government agencies, such as the police, as they shift towards a CRPD-based support system, where the absence of regulation afforded by mental health legislation could have

4 JE Bickenbach, 'Disability Human Rights, Law, and Policy' in GL Albricht, KD Steelman and M Bury (eds), *Handbook of Disability Studies* (Sage, 2001) 565, 567.

5 Ibid.

6 See Chapter 3, Section C(2).

grave consequences, including large-scale, unregulated coercive practices. The risk of these shortcomings occurring in the jurisdictions considered in this book is substantial.

In this respect, it is clear that mental health law is at a crossroads. In one direction is a continuation along the same path, on which certain *'add-on'* measures appear – for example, the introduction of mental capacity assessments, advance directives, nominated persons schemes and so on.[7] In the other direction, a less certain road requires that law and policy respond to the inevitable human experience of profound mental distress, disorder and disablement *within* a human rights framework.[8]

Advocates for this second, broad approach are calling for the abolition of substituted decision-making under mental health legislation and the creation of a 'supported decision-making regime' in its place. This transformation in the way law addresses mental health crises and long-term support for persons with psychosocial disabilities will pose major difficulties in both legal and political terms. However, new pathways are emerging that invite reformers to address the many *external* determinants of disablement, including removing 'special' laws that create different standards of rights for people with psychosocial disability.

The question remains as to whether this political will could be built upon to repeal or fundamentally alter mental health legislation. Are the societies considered in this book willing to discriminate against people with psychiatric diagnoses through current mental health laws? In my view, they are – although there is scant debate in the public sphere, so it is unclear whether the broader public is openly willing in this respect. Fostering public debate on these issues will be an essential step towards building CRPD-compliant mental health support systems. Nonetheless, the findings in Chapter 3 show that key justifications for maintaining current mental health legislation are not sufficient to warrant the significant restriction of liberties and other human rights that they entail.

From this conclusion, it is possible to answer the question posed at the beginning of this book: How can the support framework of the CRPD address

7 McSherry and Wilson describe a particular view of human rights amongst mental health professionals as an 'add-on' approach, wherein human rights are seen as 'only a secondary part of a much larger "balancing act" between the competing interests driving mental health law'. In their interview sample, one participant saw human rights as 'a separate "add-on" rather than an integral part of balancing the needs of the person and the community'. B McSherry and K Wilson, 'Detention and Treatment Down Under: Human Rights and Mental Health Laws in Australia and New Zealand' (2011) 19(4) *Medical Law Review* 548, 564.

8 Ibid. 580.

the major conceptual and practical issues of mental health law? The CRPD's formulation of the support owed to persons with psychosocial disabilities appears to address major issues in mental health law, but it is the application of this support framework *outside* mental health legislation where the concept holds promise for comprehensively addressing the major issues addressed in this book.

In other words, the support framework cannot be reduced to an isolated mechanism 'bolted on' to existing mental health law. Such an approach might diminish the nuances of concepts such as support to exercise legal capacity or the right to the highest attainable standard of health and social protection, and thus fail to capture the complexity of the CRPD support framework. It is possible that well-defined mechanisms, such as advance directives and nominated persons schemes, can provide political mileage which might spur broad interest and add momentum to the search for human rights–based support. However, such pragmatic steps must be weighed and assessed against core CRPD obligations and the damage caused by current systems. The CRPD Committee, the UN Office of the High Commissioner for Human Rights and the UN Special Rapporteurs on Disability, Health and Torture have repeatedly called for the abolition of substituted decision-making approaches in mental health law.[9] The specific concern of these UN agencies establishes a strong standard against which to measure law and policy reform proposals.

Throughout this book, my aim has been to contribute to such reform efforts. I have sought to outline key legal issues, expose disagreements and resolve differences – and to advance reform recommendations, which are set out in the next section.

B RECOMMENDATIONS

The governments under consideration in this book should:

1. Adopt robust CRPD implementation and monitoring strategies;
2. Closely consult with and actively involve persons with disabilities, including children, through their representative organisations when developing and implementing the CRPD support framework in law, policy and programming in the mental health context;
3. Incorporate a human rights and disability perspective into mental health law, policy and practice;

[9] See Chapter 2, Section D.

4. Introduce legislation to ensure that support to exercise legal capacity is available for all;
5. Take steps to immediately repeal substituted decision-making powers under mental health law;
6. Pursue 'support reinvestment' by shifting resources from coercion to a wide range of supports in health and social policy and programming; and
7. Research ways to strengthen support and self-determination for persons with psychosocial disability in law, policy and practice.

Each of these recommendations will be discussed in turn.

1 *Adopt CRPD National Implementation and Monitoring Strategies*

The text of the CRPD advances a three-pronged approach to changing national law and policy. Article 33 directs governments to: (1) designate a specific agency of government to direct policy reform (with the active input of people with disabilities); (2) appoint a major independent monitoring body (typically a human rights monitoring body); and (3) ensure the involvement of representative disabled people's organisations.[10] The national approach seems particularly necessary when considering the reform avenues that are required by the CRPD across multiple areas of law, policy and practice. Gerard Quinn draws on a useful visual metaphor to describe this broader view when he suggests that 'we need to first zoom out rather than in to perceive the deep structure of the text' of the CRPD.[11] In a similar vein, John Brayley argues that '[i]t is not possible for one part of the system to move unilaterally in the direction of Supported Decision Making'.[12] A multilateral approach would be especially useful in the mental health context, in which issues such as employment, housing, social protection and inclusion are generally viewed as crucial for the enjoyment of a range of human rights. Mechanisms adopting this approach necessarily draw the focus beyond mental health law, which is in keeping with prominent implementation strategies for CRPD-based national law and policy.[13]

10 CRPD art 33.

11 G Quinn, 'Personhood and Legal Capacity: Perspectives on the Paradigm Shift of Article 12 CRPD' (Paper presented at the Conference on Disability and Legal Capacity under the CRPD, Harvard Law School, 20 February 2010) 4 <www.nuigalway.ie>.

12 J Brayley, 'Supported Decision Making in Australia: Presentation Notes' (Presentation to the Victorian Offices of the Public Advocate and the Law Reform Commission, 2009) 4 <www.opa.sa.gov.au>.

13 See, e.g., Centre for Disability Law and Policy, *Submission to the Oireachtas Committee on Justice, Defence and Equality on Scheme of the Mental Capacity Bill 2008* (National University

Matters of equality, disability and legal capacity touch upon myriad laws that may require reform (including criminal law, consent to treatment, family law, property law and so on). The three-pronged implementation approach of Article 33 would help take into account the full spectrum of interconnected human rights, which includes strengthening adult protection laws in line with Articles 16 and 28, in order to disentangle protection from substituted decision-making[14]; moving disability services from group-based to individualised arrangements and, at the same time, fostering social inclusion in line with Article 19[15]; and providing reasonable accommodation and accessibility in healthcare services for people with disabilities in line with Articles 5, 9 and 25.[16] The broad scope of these reform suggestions rests upon recognition that providing mental health support services and strengthening self-determination cannot be de-contextualised from the broader aims of the CRPD as a whole. Prioritising different elements of the support approach requires democratic debate, for which the three-pronged implementation strategy of the CRPD offers a sound deliberative strategy.

2 *'Co-Production' and Leadership by Disabled People's Organisations*

The CRPD requires the participation of persons with disabilities in the development of laws, policies and practices that affect them. This requirement appears as a general principle (Article 3), as a general obligation in implementation (Article 4) and monitoring (Article 33), as a specific right (Articles 29 and 30) and via the inclusion of experts with disabilities on the relevant CRPD Committee (Article 34). The CRPD explicitly directs that people with disabilities 'should have the opportunity to be actively involved in decision-making processes about policies and programmes, including those directly concerning

of Ireland, 2011) <www.nuigalway.ie>; M Bach and L Kerzner, A *New Paradigm for Protecting Autonomy and the Right to Legal Capacity* (Report to the Law Commission of Ontario, 2010) 21 <www.lco-cdo.org>.

14 J Brayley, 'Supported Decision Making: A Case for Change' (Office of the Public Advocate, South Australia, 2013) 19 <www.opa.sa.gov.au>; D Chartres, 'Churchill Fellowship Report: To Investigate Supported Decision Making Practices, Capacity Building Strategies and Other Alternatives to Guardianship' (Winston Churchill Memorial Trust of Australia, May 2012) 36 <www.churchilltrust.com.au>.

15 See G Quinn and MA Stein, 'Challenges in Realising the Right to Live in the Community' in ECCL European Coalition for Community Living Focus on Article 19 of the United Nations Convention on the Rights of Persons with Disabilities (report) (ECCL, 2009).

16 See, e.g., B McSherry, 'The Right of Access to Mental Health Care: Voluntary Treatment and the Role of the Law' in B McSherry and P Weller, *Rethinking Rights-Based Mental Health Laws* (Hart, 2010) 379.

them'.[17] Such input could also occur in reporting and evaluation, including the development of human rights indicators.[18]

Part II of the book highlights the evolving development of the CRPD support framework. This development is likely to be as participatory as the CRPD itself. Janet Lord, David Suozzi and Allyn Taylor have argued that '[t]he Convention – in its embrace of a highly participatory implementation framework in which civil society, national human rights institutions, and intergovernmental organisations can play roles – implicates a wide range of actors and thus embodies due process values much more so than many other international public health law processes'.[19] Maya Sabatello provides a detailed account of how due process values played out during CRPD negotiations, and proposes ways that this 'new diplomacy' might be translated into participatory measures for developing domestic law and policy.[20]

'Active involvement' in the practical, political sense remains ambiguous. Developing law, policy and practice through collaborative processes will challenge governments, disabled persons' organisations (including mental health service-user organisations), professional bodies and the like. Yet such participation appears crucial to the creation of effective and lasting support arrangements, and they are not without precedent. Most, if not all, exemplary policies and practices noted throughout this book were developed with the active participation of persons with disabilities and their peers, families and other supporters.

Collaborative processes should then become a key focus for governments, services and advocates concerned with implementing human rights–based law and policy in the mental health context.[21] Michael Hess and David Adams emphasise process as much as content in the development of public policy, calling for an 'iterative and learning policy process in which policymaking networks become the functional organisational form'.[22] For Hess and Adams,

17 CRPD Preamble para (o), art 33(3).

18 Ibid.

19 J Lord, D Suozzi and A Taylor, 'Lessons from the Experience of UN Convention on the Rights of Persons with Disabilities: Addressing the Democratic Deficit in Global Health Governance' (2010) 38 *Journal of Law, Medicine and Ethics* 564, 577.

20 M Sabatello,'The New Diplomacy' in M Sabatello and M Schulze (eds), *Human Rights and Disability Advocacy* (University of Pennsylvania Press, 2013) 239.

21 M Bach, 'Key Rights – Personhood – The Right to Make Your Own Decisions and Have Them Respected by Others (Article 12 and Legal Capacity)' (Presentation, Centre for Disability Law and Policy, National University of Ireland, Galway, 19 June 2012).

22 M Hess and D Adams, 'National Competition Policy and (the) Public Interest' (Briefing Paper, No 3, National Centre for Development Studies, 1999) 3 <www.digitalcollections.anu.edu.au>.

it is through the active input of people whose lives are most affected that public interest can be established and policymaking can be responsive to those it serves.[23] In the mental health context, implementing human rights–based practices will require new partnerships and institutional mechanisms that are particularly responsive to the demands of the most disadvantaged. This is especially necessary when involving those who have first-hand experience of civil commitment. Another major gap in deliberative policy development is the involvement of persons with *intellectual* disability, who are overrepresented in mental health services[24] yet have faced almost total exclusion from the development of mental health policy and practice.

In other words, achieving CRPD-compliant deliberative processes will require that those who may not yet – or may never – have formal language can still engage. Theodor Adorno highlights the power of marginalised voices in public deliberation when he writes:

> If a stroke of undeserved luck has kept the mental composition of some individuals not quite adjusted to the prevailing norms – a stroke of luck they have often enough to pay for in their relations with their environment – it is up to these individuals to make the moral and, as it were, representative effort to say what most of those for whom they say it cannot see or, to do justice to reality, will not allow themselves to see. Direct communicability to everyone is not a criterion of truth. We must resist the all but universal compulsion to confuse the communication of knowledge with knowledge itself.[25]

As well as ensuring that existing consultation processes are accessible to those most marginalised, it may be that individuals with disabilities and disabled people's organisations will require resources to develop their potential to contribute to human rights–based law and policy in the mental health context, including through research, evaluation and monitoring.[26]

3 *Integrate a Human Rights Perspective into the Mental Health Context*

Jonathan Mann argues that the values and language of human rights are better suited to addressing public health issues than a strict medical

23 Ibid.

24 See, e.g., J Trollor, 'Making mental health services accessible to people with an intellectual disability' (2014) 48(5) *Australian and New Zealand Journal of Psychiatry* 395.

25 T Adorno, *Negative Dialectics* (EB Ashton trans, The Seabury Press, 1973) 41.

26 See, generally, O Lewis and P Munro, 'Civil Society Involvement in Mental Health Law and Policy Reform' in M Dudley, D Silove and F Gale (eds), *Mental Health and Human Rights* (Oxford University Press, 2012).

model.[27] The same can be argued of human rights– and disability-based perspectives for addressing issues in mental health law, policy and practice. This general recommendation was advanced in a 2016 statement on mental health by the Human Rights Committee,[28] which recognised 'the need to protect, promote and respect all human rights in the global response to mental health–related issues, and stressing that mental health and community services should integrate a human rights perspective so as to avoid any harm to persons using them'.[29] As Chapters 5 and 6 noted, the language and values of disability advanced in international human rights law, while not without limitations, provide distinct advantages over the often reductive, individualistic, deficits-based models that tend to underpin current mental health law and policy.

This conceptual shift will be challenging for a number of reasons. Phil Fennell has argued that bringing 'the rights of mentally disordered individuals under the umbrella of disability rights will not be an easy task, either in technical legal terms, or in political terms'.[30] Additionally, developing a vocabulary for public spending using human rights language is likely to be equally challenging.

It is generally agreed that reforming mental health systems requires the collaboration of clinical professionals. Lance Gable has argued that 'CRPD values' can be used in the governance of health systems.[31] In doing so, effort is needed to bridge the language gap between lawmakers, human rights advocates and mental health professionals. According to Ian Kennedy, some clinicians are resistant to enter the public discourse, where 'talk of rights is often represented to the doctor as if it inevitably involves confrontation, legalism, and strict or rigid restrictions on what the doctor may do'.[32] Bernadette McSherry and Leanna Darvall suggest that the challenge becomes one of 'enabl[ing] individual human rights to be viewed as complementing existing medical values and ethics rather than restricting

27 JM Mann, 'Health and Human Rights: If Not Now, When?' (1997) 2(3) *Health Human Rights* 113.

28 UN Human Rights Committee, 'Promotion and Protection of All Human Rights, Civil, Political, Economic, Social and Cultural Rights, Including the Right to Development', adopted 29 June 2016, A/HRC/32/L.26, 2.

29 Ibid. 2.

30 P Fennell, 'Institutionalising the Community: The Codification of Clinical Authority and the Limits of Rights-Based Approaches' in McSherry and Weller, above n 16, 13, 49.

31 L Gable, 'The Proliferation of Human Rights in Global Health Governance' (2007) 35(4)*The Journal of Law, Medicine and Ethics* 534–44.

32 I Kennedy, *Treat Me Right* (Clarendon Press, 1991) 386.

them'.[33] Yet it also appears that, in some instances, existing medical values and ethics *will* be challenged by individual human rights enunciated in the CRPD. This will require policymakers and others to provide opportunities for drawing these tensions out into the open, thus creating the opportunity for them to be acknowledged, deliberated upon and perhaps resolved. Overall, introducing the vocabulary of human rights to the mental health context will require political imagination. Efforts could centre on various levels of government and service delivery, from local-level services to the work of specific government agencies, as well as national mental health strategies.

4 *Additional Statutory and Non-Statutory Support to Exercise Legal Capacity*

Legislation that provides support to exercise legal agency will be an essential element in applying the CRPD support framework to the mental health context. One broad approach is to introduce the support principles of the CRPD into existing legislation. John Brayley has pointed to the principles set out in Australia's National Disability Insurance Scheme Act 2013 as one such instance.[34] Section 3(1)(e) of the act, for example, states that one of its objectives is to 'enable people with disability to exercise choice and control in the pursuit of their goals and the planning and delivery of their supports'.[35] However, as Brayley concedes, the difficulty with relying on principles is that 'unless there is clear case law there can be significant variation in the conversion of principles to practice'.[36] Further, '[a]ssistance and support cannot be vague notions, they need to be operationalised or they may not really happen'.[37] Nonetheless, the adjustment of principles in existing laws and the introduction of CRPD-based support principles in proposed laws seems an important (and quite feasible) short-term step towards implementation.

More robust legislative reform would see statutory recognition of different categories of support in the disability context, including formal recognition of support relationships and representational supports.[38] As noted in Chapter 5, a

33 B McSherry and L Darvall, 'Public Health and Human Rights' (2008) 15(5) *Journal of Law and Medicine* 665, 666.
34 National Disability Insurance Scheme Act (No 20) 2013 (Cth) pt 2.
35 Ibid. s 3(1)(e).
36 J Brayley, 'Supported Decision Making: A Case for Change' (Presentation, Supported Decision Making Forum, Queensland Advocacy Incorporated and the Queensland University of Technology Health Law Research Centre, Brisbane, June 2013) 7.
37 Ibid.
38 Ibid.

key task for such legislation is to define legal capacity and recognise the range of ways in which people can exercise that legal capacity. Another function would be to facilitate support and provide arbitration to resolve any disputes about that support, including disputes about the 'best interpretation of a person's will, preferences and rights'. As discussed in Chapters 5 and 6, legislation could include formal mechanisms for the selection and registration of support persons, and the legal recognition of both 'independent' and 'interdependent' decision-making arrangements of varying degrees of intensity. Registration of support persons would also assist third parties (such as banks and other institutions) to identify authorised supporters.[39] Registration could also activate the provision of resources for informal supporters to assist them in their role. Resources could include coaching, peer support, assistance to create 'circles of support', local area coordination and family leadership materials. (It would be important that such materials are also available to those who may *not* wish to enter specific statutory support agreements, so as to avoid incentives to over-regulate informal relationships.) Legislation could also mandate the extent to which third parties should have a duty to accept people's supporters, although these duties could be integrated into anti-discrimination laws regarding the accessibility and reasonable accommodation owed to persons with disabilities. Such mandated duties on third parties could ensure that, even without a formalised 'supported decision-making agreement', there remains a duty to reasonably accommodate people with disabilities, including the involvement of family and other supporters. Other laws relating to disability and equal recognition before the law will need to be amended to interface with assisted decision-making legislation.[40]

A number of corollary laws would seem to be required to respond to some of the issues to which mental health legislation currently responds. The need for non-discriminatory legislation to respond to emergency situations, including mental health crises, seems unavoidable. Anne Plumb's suggestion for developing places of 'sanctuary', to which emergency interventions could facilitate access, seems a fruitful line of enquiry which could well galvanise a range of mental health commentators.[41] Legislation is likely required, at least in some cases, to regulate interim measures when a person's wishes are unclear, but some emergency response is needed.[42] From a policy and practice perspective, the involvement of skilled facilitators and communication specialists could

39 See, e.g., Representation Agreement Act R.S.B.C. 1996 c 405 s 9.
40 Centre for Disability Law and Policy, above n 13, s 1 (c)(d).
41 See Chapter 7, Section B(6).
42 See Chapter 7, Section B(3).

be especially useful in this respect; for example, when a person is confused or non-responsive during a severe mental health crisis.[43] Where communication fails despite best efforts, and where efforts to communicate continue, any decision regulated by law made in the absence of the person (according to the 'best interpretation of his or her will, preference and rights') ought to have the least possible irreversible effects, whereby the person could potentially revise the decision in the future.

States Parties are likely to insist on the need to retain some element of the public protection function currently provided by mental health legislation. Where this remains the case, law reform could *conceivably* impose liberty restrictions on 'dangerous persons' in a disability-neutral manner.[44] This avenue of law reform will be challenging, given the highly controversial nature of such suggestions and the myriad human rights issues raised by preventative detention laws and laws related to 'dangerous persons'[45] (not to mention the limited empirical basis for assessing risk). Peter Bartlett articulates a number of these concerns:

> If it is dangerousness that is of concern, for example, a disability-neutral law could be introduced to detain people who are perceived as dangerous, irrespective of disability. While this might satisfy the problems of interpretation of Article 14, it is difficult to see that it is a good idea. It is difficult to see that it would be wise in human rights terms to encourage autocratic regimes to introduce laws allowing detention of people perceived as dangerous (whether mentally disabled or not), as such a law invites political abuse.[46]

As Bartlett notes, the task of creating provisions that are non-discriminatory in form and effect does not seem insurmountable, although further research and broader public debate – including full consideration of the potential flow-on effects – are clearly required. The proposal to use new thresholds, such as 'serious adverse effects', to impose potentially coercive interventions *may* also present an important (though fraught) line of enquiry in creating non-discriminatory grounds for emergency intervention in a range of circumstances.[47]

[43] International Disability Alliance, 'IDA CRPD Forum, Principles for Implementation of CRPD Article 12' (2008) s 13 <social.un.org/ageing-working-group/documents/egm/Article12.pdf>.

[44] See Chapter 4, Section C(9).

[45] B McSherry, *Managing Fear: The Law and Ethics of Preventive Detention and Risk Assessment* (Routledge, 2013).

[46] P Bartlett, 'The United Nations Convention on the Rights of Persons with Disabilities and Mental Health Law' (2012) 75 *Modern Law Review* 752, 773.

[47] See Chapter 5, Section C(1) and Chapter 7 Section B(5). See also M Bach and L Kerzner, *A New Paradigm for Protecting Autonomy and the Right to Legal Capacity* (Prepared for the Law

5 *'Take Steps to Immediately Repeal Substituted Decision-Making'*

These words, taken from the CRPD Committee's General Comment No 1, are premised on the view that introduction of the support framework will necessarily entail reforming and, in some cases, repealing certain laws. It is generally agreed that, in their current form, some laws violate the CRPD, and it is particularly difficult to argue that current mental health law satisfies its anti-discrimination requirements.[48] The challenge of overcoming this divergence goes to the heart of the tension between pragmatic and ideal pathways explored in this book.

As a starting point, calls to repeal involuntary outpatient treatment provisions have attracted an unusual consensus in some places, including from the CRPD Committee, disabled people's organisations and senior figures in the Royal College of Psychiatrists (United Kingdom).[49] From a political perspective, such a consensus suggests that repealing community treatment orders and similar coercive measures, in some places, offers governments a reasonable short-term goal for replacing substituted decision-making in the mental health context with CRPD-based support. Repealing compulsory treatment in the community offers a far less demanding avenue of reform than reimagining mental health legislation in its entirety.

Community treatment orders were introduced in many jurisdictions as a 'common-sense' and benevolent measure, despite a general lack of empirical grounding. It bears repeating, therefore, that mental health legislation is not a pragmatic administrative tool based on neutral clinical management. Whilst it might be tempting to view coercive interventions as purely practical in nature, they are essentially grounded in politico-ideological decisions. These decisions include the relative value attributed to particular viewpoints, the distribution of resources and (often unstated) claims about rationality, autonomy, distress and disablement. This is not to suggest that proponents of mental health legislation are disingenuously presenting civil commitment as a value-free, clinical intervention; instead, it is to highlight that a range of political and ideological decisions guide civil commitment which often remain unacknowledged, and therefore uninterrogated. It may come as a surprise to many mental health professionals that people with psychosocial disability,

Commission of Ontario, 2010) 144 <www.lco-cdo.org>; P Gooding and E Flynn, 'Querying the Call to Introduce Mental Capacity Testing to Mental Health Law: Does the Doctrine of Necessity Provide an Alternative?' (2015) 4(2) *Laws* 245.

48 See Chapter 2.

49 R Heun, S Dave and P Rowlands, 'Little Evidence for Community Treatment Orders: A Battle Fought with Heavy Weapons' (2016) 40 *BJPsych Bulletin* 115.

their families and other supporters even *perceive* a power imbalance in their engagement with services. Unmasking and acknowledging these imbalances is an important step towards 'rebalancing the scales'.

Since the CRPD came into force, a division has emerged amongst reformers committed to strengthening the self-determination of persons with psychosocial disability and the support that they are owed. On the one hand, there are those calling for the gradualist discovery of alternatives; on the other, there are those calling for the immediate repeal of mental health law. The question of how to resolve this difference is an extremely difficult one. The CRPD Committee unequivocally argues that '"[p]rogressive realization" (art 4, para 2) does not apply to the provisions of article 12'.[50] This is justified on the grounds that '[t]he right to equality before the law has long been recognized as a civil and political right, with roots in the International Covenant on Civil and Political Rights'.[51] As such, upon ratifying the CRPD, States Parties 'must *immediately begin taking steps* towards the realization of the rights provided for in article 12', steps which must be 'deliberate' and 'well-planned'.[52] In contrast, the European Foundation Centre describes establishing the support model of the CRPD as 'a complex task' requiring 'careful consideration of different proposals', which are 'clearly determined in consultation with key actors, and (which) should be *gradually* implemented'.[53] Similarly, Inclusion Europe has recommended that States Parties 'set up a plan to implement gradually the newly adopted supported decision-making system'.[54] Responding to pragmatic political concerns and conceivable objections, Inclusion Europe notes:

> This system will take time to develop and would run the risk of becoming dysfunctional if all existing [substituted decision-making] measures ... were

50 Committee on the Rights of Persons with Disabilities, *General Comment No 1: Article 12: Equal Recognition Before the Law*, 11th sess, UN Doc CRPD/C/GC/1 (19 May 2014) 7 [30]. Article 4(2) of the CRPD states: 'With regard to economic, social and cultural rights, each State Party undertakes to take measures to the maximum of its available resources and, where needed, within the framework of international cooperation, with a view to achieving progressively the full realization of these rights, without prejudice to those obligations contained in the present Convention that are immediately applicable according to international law'.

51 Ibid. 7–8 [30].

52 Ibid. 7 [30] (emphasis added).

53 European Foundation Centre, Study on Challenges and Good Practices in the Implementation of the UN Convention on the Rights of Persons with Disabilities (VC/2008/1214, 2010) 93 (emphasis added).

54 They also direct States Parties to '[r]eview all national laws in light of Article 12 and to ensure that the right to self-determination and to equal recognition before the law without discrimination on the basis of disability is enshrined in the law'. Inclusion Europe, *Key Elements of a System for Supported Decision-Making: Position Paper of Inclusion Europe: Adopted at the General Assembly 2008* (2008) 6 <www.inclusion-europe.org>.

> declared illegal at the same time, without the conditions in place that made supported decision-making effective for a particular individual. The system of [substituted decision-making] and the system of supportive decision-making should therefore exist in parallel during the period of time until the transition is completed.[55]

Resolving the differences between those promoting either a 'progressive' or an 'immediate' realisation of the support model will be more likely to occur if law reform is genuinely 'co-designed' (as per Recommendation 2). Australia's 2012 'shadow report' to the CRPD Committee, for example, recommended that 'in consultation with people with disability through their representative, advocacy, and legal organisations, Australia conducts a comprehensive audit of laws, policies and administrative arrangements underpinning compulsory treatment'.[56] The audit would occur 'with a view to … introducing reforms to eliminate laws and practices that relate to compulsory treatment that inherently breaches human rights'.[57] In this way, collaborative processes could be used to develop a range of short- and medium-term recommendations applying human rights to a framework of legislation, policy and practice.

However, it is misleading to suggest that a major narrowing of grounds for involuntary intervention will necessarily lead to 'dysfunction'. As noted, the invalidation of some German laws regulating involuntary medication in 2011[58] has not resulted in reports of chaos and egregious rights violations against people in mental health crises. Instead, there are some initial reports, although data are limited, of a significant reduction in rates of involuntary treatment and the development of creative responses to promote voluntary treatment.[59]

However, merely restraining the scope for coercive intervention will not result in people in mental health crises or those with long-term psychosocial disabilities having their human rights respected. Individuals will still be susceptible to neglect, abuse and exploitation, particularly where they cannot

55 Ibid.

56 Disability Representative, Advocacy, Legal and Human Rights Organisations Australia, *Disability Rights Now: Civil Society Report to the United Nations Committee on the Rights of Persons with Disability* (August 2012) 15 <www.disabilityrightsnow.org.au>.

57 Ibid.

58 Federal Constitutional Court (Germany), Press office – Press release No 28/2011 of 15 April 2011, Order of 23 March 2011, 2 BvR 882/09 <www.bverfg.de>. The laws allow for involuntary treatment as a last measure where a person is deemed to lack mental capacity, 'particularly after intensive attempts to convince the patient', and is implemented following application to a separate court, and 'taking into account the review of an independent expert'. E Flammer and T Steinert, 'Involuntary Medication, Seclusion, and Restraint in German Psychiatric Hospitals after the Adoption of Legislation in 2013' (2015) 6 *Frontiers in Psychiatry* 153.

59 Ibid.

access adequate support. Government inaction or an emphasis on 'negative rights' does not leave space for human freedom in this area; instead, government inaction may amount to an indifference to the loss of freedom, hence the need to shift resources from coercion to voluntary support (as per Recommendation 6). Thus, law and policy are required that provide all citizens with 'positive rights', such as the right to enjoyment of the highest attainable physical and mental health and the right to an adequate standard of living and social protection. Such a legislative framework, instead of regulating involuntary interventions, would be concerned with providing a range of voluntary supports, including support for people in their homes and communities, advocacy services and the creation of places of 'sanctuary' for people facing acute illness and extreme mental health crises.

The fundamental alteration or repeal of existing mental health law appears to require the development, elsewhere in law, of 'disability-neutral' grounds for: (1) emergency intervention, including intervention in mental health crises, particularly when a person's will and preferences are unknown or unclear; and (2) sustained 'facilitated decision-making', where ongoing support is required in certain 'hard cases'. There may also be a need to define restrictive measures developed related to dangerous persons (who may or may not have mental impairments), given that states appear committed to pursuing such measures for the long term.[60] Separating these state impulses – in contrast to their entwinement in current mental health legislation – would help resolve some of the issues with mental health law identified in Chapter 3. Distinguishing the relevant areas of law for each impulse (such as criminal law, laws of public order, adult protection law or the doctrine of necessity), which are often unhelpfully conflated in discussions about mental health legislation, would help isolate and address specific issues, including identifying the specific human rights at stake.

6 *'Support Reinvestment': Shifting Resources from Coercion to Support*

The main issues confronting people with disabilities and their supporters are not theoretical in nature; instead, they are practical, relating to the support people do or do not receive. Policy reform strategies need to be developed in the real-life contest over resources. Current financial constraints in many countries will clearly present barriers to certain types of legal change. Yet a number of the policy and programming measures discussed in this book

[60] See Chapter 4, Section C(7) and (9); Chapter 7, Section B(5).

represent low-cost or 'no-cost' initiatives, many of which could be developed through the redistribution of existing resources.

'Support reinvestment' could involve the movement of resources currently used for coercion to voluntary support. For example, costs associated with involuntary outpatient treatment currently include clinical administration and delivery, monitoring and regulation by mental health tribunals, and the resources needed for ordering people to hospital (the latter of which could include multiple emergency services, such as police, ambulance and emergency departments). It is difficult to argue, on either moral or pragmatic grounds, that these resources would not be better directed to the support measures discussed in Chapter 6, including independent advocacy and local area coordination, as well as voluntary clinical support.

Catalina Devandas, the UN Special Rapporteur on Disability, has described how the CRPD has invited a shift from welfarist concerns to 'systems that promote active citizenship, social inclusion and community participation, while avoiding paternalism, dependence and segregation'.[61] Thus, a supported decision-making regime appears to require a 'new wave' of disability service provision which prioritises the 'personalisation of support'.[62] Chapters 4, 5 and 6 highlighted the importance of personalised support as a means of strengthening self-determination, while also avoiding abandonment. The personalisation of support advances the Article 19 right to independent living and being included in the community in particular, and invites a reconceptualisation of the way in which traditional disability and mental health services operate.[63] Indeed, in many of the jurisdictions examined in this book, disability and mental health services are moving away from the typical 'command-style' service provision which emerged in the post-war welfare state, and towards more personalised assistance. Andrew Power, Janet Lord and Allison deFranco conducted an international comparative study of the ways in which self-determination and personalisation are advanced in disability law and policy in the United States, Canada, England, Northern Ireland, Sweden, France and

61 UN General Assembly, *Report of the Special Rapporteur on the Rights of Persons with Disabilities*, 70th sess, UN Doc A/70/297 (7 August 2015) 8 [24].

62 G Quinn, 'Liberation, Cloaking Devices and the Law: Or a Personal Reflection on the Law and Theology of Article 12 of the UN CRPD' (Presentation, BCNL Conference, Sofia, Bulgaria, 16 October 2013) <www.nuigalway.ie>. See also A Power, J Lord and A deFranco, *Active Citizenship and Disability: Implementing the Personalisation of Support* (Cambridge University Press, 2013).

63 Oliver Lewis makes this point, and argues that the CRPD invites States Parties to reconceptualise the role of services in the lives of persons with disabilities, calling for a 'holistic' approach to the development of law and policy. O Lewis, 'The Expressive, Educational and Proactive Roles of Human Rights' in McSherry and Weller, above n 16, 96, 124.

the Irish Republic.[64] Drawing on case studies, they highlight how disability law and policy reform can be reconfigured in various ways to maximise choice, independence and support for people with disabilities.[65] The move towards inividualised funding schemes, in which a person with a disability determines what services are purchased with the dollars the government provides, exemplifies this shift. Examples include the Canadian cities of Toronto, Thunder Bay and Windsor, where community service agencies shifted from a 'block-funded approach' to disability services to individualised funding.[66] In Western Australia, a similar small-scale trial for mental health service users has commenced, with positive initial evaluations.[67] In addition, the current rollout of Australia's National Disability Insurance Scheme holds promise for the development of more personalised support in the mental health context.[68]

For the most part, those who promote individualised funding arrangements remain aware that self-determination is defeated if resources are not available to create conditions for choice-making, independence and a good life. The conditions could include a person having good clinical support if needed, or a network of friends and acquaintances to help generate opportunities related to, for example, accommodation, relationships and employment – all of which can contribute to the enjoyment of one's rights as a person before the law.

Incorporating support reinvestment into budgetary analysis would be challenging. Policymakers wishing to restructure their budgets and explore available options could consider ways of encouraging families and NGOs to implement the broad CRPD support approach, and to measure and tie funding to certain requirements. On the issue of mental health spending, Mary Donnelly has suggested that units of budgetary measurement could expand from a dominant focus on 'hospital beds' to include 'interdisciplinary teams based in the community'.[69] Finally, there do not appear to be any budgetary

64 Power, Lord and deFranco, above n 62.

65 Ibid. 85–340.

66 Linking Individualized Supports and Direct Funding: Making Money Work for People – A Pathway to Self-Determination and Community Involvement for People with Disabilities (Report of the Ontario Round Table on Individualized Funding, May 2000) 12 <www.individualizedfunding.ca>.

67 The Mental Health Commission of Western Australia has published two reports that detail the rationale for individualised support and funding, also known as self-directed supports and services, including references to the positive benefits and outcomes of this approach. See, generally, *Mental Health 2020: Making it Personal and Everybody's Business* (Mental Health Commission [WA], 2009) <www.mentalhealth.wa.gov.au>; *Putting the Public First: Partnering with the Community and Business to Deliver Outcomes* (Economic Audit Committee, Final Report, October 2009) <www.dpc.wa.gov.au>.

68 National Disability Insurance Scheme Act (No 20) 2013 (Cth).

69 M Donnelly, 'Mental Health Law Reform: New Perspectives and Challenges' (Presentation, International Mental Health Conference, National University, 23 June 2012).

formulations that have specifically invited the input of persons with psychosocial disabilities, which would seem a constructive avenue of participatory deliberation.

Policy measures should also be directed to identifying and eliminating barriers to realising the CRPD support framework. For the mental health sector, as Chapters 3 and 6 identified, risk aversion is a major barrier to realising supported decision-making in practice. Policy aimed at addressing risk aversion in mental health services, such as that advanced by the United Kingdom Department of Health in 2007,[70] will be useful for explaining ideas such as 'dignity of risk' to staff. Policymakers, service providers and disabled people's organisations may wish to work strategically with the media, given its role in shaping public understanding of risk and mental illness.[71] Another likely barrier to achieving a CRPD support framework is the prejudicial attitudes of service providers.[72] In a small study of mental health service users, Janet Lammers and Brenda Happell note that most participants 'reported experiences of providers who seemed unprepared to accept that the consumers had anything to contribute'.[73] Lammers and Happell conclude that 'there is a need to influence the attitudes of health professions to become more appreciative of a consumer perspective'.[74] Isabel Collins has argued that significant cultural change and targeted capacity building are required before people with psychosocial disability can truly benefit from choice:

> [T]hose of us who work in mental health know only too well that we have, more often than not, conditioned people with a psychosocial disability to not expect much out of life or services. In order for them to truly choose, much work is going to need to be done to 'un-condition' people from their low expectations of life. We will also need to condition staff to stop deciding for the consumer community. Who is going to assist people to develop a better

70 Department of Health (United Kingdom), *Best Practice in Managing Risk: Principles and Evidence for Best Practice in the Assessment and Management of Risk to Self and Others in Mental Health Services* (Prepared for the National Mental Health Risk Management Programme, June 2007).

71 Indeed, in a supported decision-making initiative produced by the department itself, it suggested 'that good practice in media management is vital to the reputation of the organisation and its corporate approach to managing risk'. See Department of Health (United Kingdom), *Independence, Choice and Risk: A Guide to Best Practice in Supported Decision-Making* (May 2007) 5, s 22.

72 J Lammers and B Happel, 'Consumer Participation in Mental Health Service: Looking from a Consumer Perspective' (2003) 10 *Journal of Psychiatric and Mental Health Nursing* 385.

73 Ibid. See also V Cowling et al., 'Mental Health Consumer and Carer Participation in Professional Education: *'Getting There Together'* for Children of Parents with Mental Illness and Their Families' (2006) 59(4) *Australian Social Work* 406.

74 Lammers and Happel, above n 72, 385.

sense of self and entitlement so that they eventually genuinely choose what they want?[75]

Finding the most effective ways to strengthen support and self-determination for people experiencing mental health crises, as well as those with ongoing disability, will be an essential step towards human rights–based law, policy and practice.

7 *Develop Research to Strengthen Support and Self-Determination for Persons with Psychosocial Disability*

This final recommendation concerns research into the most effective law, policy and practice to strengthen the self-determination of and support for persons with psychosocial disability. George Szmukler and Diana Rose define self-determination in the mental health context as 'freedom from forms of control or coercion deriving from external limitations imposed through common treatment practices and social institutions'.[76] 'Support', here, refers to the resources provided by services and other social institutions which help create the fundamental conditions of a good life. Clearly, the scope for research promoting these aims is quite broad, and I will list a select number of key issues that have reappeared throughout this book.

Some pressing research priorities have been noted in previous recommendations, particularly the need to identify the justifiable limits on individual agency which are applicable to everyone, regardless of disability or decision-making ability. Research could be undertaken to ensure that implementation mechanisms are responsive to any adverse consequences that may arise. Forms of indirect discrimination will almost inevitably appear, particularly given existing levels of stigma and prejudice, in relation to which tools for preventative monitoring will be useful.

It is logical that any research aimed at boosting the self-determination of persons with disabilities should be led by or undertaken with the active involvement of those people themselves. Involvement could include persons with disabilities as partners or leaders in conducting research, including in its design, delivery and dissemination.[77] Involving service users and others with disabilities in research displaces the traditional role of patients as research

[75] I Collins, 'What Do Consumers Want, Need and Deserve from the NDIS?' (2014) *Australian Journal on Psychosocial Rehabilitation*13, 14.

[76] G Szmukler and D Rose, 'Strengthening Self-Determination of Persons with Mental Illness' in J Clausen and N Levy (eds), *Handbook of Neuroethics* (Springer, 2015) 879.

[77] This definition was adapted from one offered by Szmukler and Rose. Ibid. 887.

'subjects', and instead positions them as collaborators. Such participatory, 'co-produced' and 'user- and survivor-led' research[78] is being increasingly incorporated into government research agendas.[79] The call for participatory methods can be based on moral and human rights claims, but can also be made on pragmatic grounds, given that 'community-engaged' research often benefits from 'improved credibility, design and quality, trial recruitment, and dissemination'.[80]

There remains the potential for service user perspectives to be devalued in research. Trisha Greenhalgh and colleagues have argued that 'evidence-based medicine', even outside the mental health context in general medicine, may 'inadvertently devalue the patient and carer agenda', including through 'limited patient input to research design, low status given to experience in the hierarchy of evidence, a tendency to conflate patient-centred consulting with use of decision tools, insufficient attention to power imbalances that suppress the patient's voice, over-emphasis on the clinical consultation, and focus on people who seek and obtain care (rather than the hidden denominator of those that do not seek or cannot access care)'.[81] The authors suggest a number of ways to reduce such 'biases',[82] which adds to a growing body of literature aimed at improving user involvement in research.[83] Such methods can be integrated into research agenda–setting mechanisms, such as national research guidelines, disability strategies, research funding rules and so on. As Szmukler and Rose point out, participatory research offers 'the opportunity to influence the research agenda, including the questions that should be asked and thus what knowledge is deemed important in mental health care'.[84]

Outcome studies, which are a key aspect of health economics and public health efforts, will be particularly useful for informing governance. Developing and evaluating programs in the mental health context could include intentional peer support; advance planning; personal advocacy programs; the use of interdisciplinary teams supporting people in their homes and communities;

78 See, e.g., S Sweeney, et al., *This Is Survivor Research* (PCCS, 2008); A Faulkner and P Thomas, 'User-Led Research and Evidence-Based Medicine' (2002) 180(1) *The British Journal of Psychiatry* 1; J Wallcraft, B Schrank and M Amering, *Handbook of Service User Involvement in Mental Health Research* (John Wiley & Sons, 2009).

79 See, e.g., H Kara, 'Mental Health Service User Involvement in Research: Where Have We Come From, Where Are We Going?' (2013) 12(3) *Journal of Public Mental Health* 122.

80 Szmukler and Rose, above n 76, 888.

81 T Greenhalgh et al., 'Six "Biases" Against Patients and Carers in Evidence-Based Medicine' (2015) 13(200) *BMC Medicine* 1.

82 Ibid. 8–9.

83 See above n 78.

84 Ibid. 878.

informal safeguarding, social inclusion and community development; the provision of resources for clinical staff to ensure that service users can take risks on an equal basis with others; and a range of other practical endeavours which have been noted throughout this book.[85]

Another strong theme to emerge from the investigation conducted for this book is the importance of relationships – a topic that would benefit from further research. Helen Gilburt and colleagues conducted a small, user-led study to explore mental health service users' experiences of hospitalisation, and reported that 'relationships formed the core of service users' experiences'.[86] The authors identified that the key elements of valued relationships are effective communication, a sense of safety, trust, cultural competency and the absence of coercion.[87] There is surprisingly little research and policy concerned with fostering such relationships – whether between clinicians, services and service users, or between individuals and families, friends and so on. Future research could usefully explore ways to foster relationships that promote agency amid the complex dilemmas raised by mental health crises and that avoid encouraging compliant and passive behaviour or persecuting anger or dissent.

In relation to Article 4(1)(i) of the CRPD, further research is required concerning the obligation of States Parties to 'promote the training of professionals and staff working with persons with disabilities in the rights recognized in this Convention so as to better provide the assistance and services guaranteed by those rights'. Specifically, research to discover the most effective ways of 'provid[ing] the assistance and services guaranteed' by the CRPD will be crucial. Interdisciplinary work in this area will help clarify the human rights obligations of relevant parties, professionals, disabled people's organisations, families and their representative organisations, legal professionals and others. Bernadette McSherry and Ian Freckelton note that the CRPD asks 'how best in a practical sense can clinicians transcend the temptations of paternalism and work toward maximizing the capacity of those with disabilities'.[88] In particular, clarifying core CRPD concepts will help professionals to identify criteria for success; for example, differentiating mental capacity from legal capacity, or distinguishing 'best interests' from the CRPD emphasis on 'rights,

[85] See Chapter 6.

[86] H Gilburt, D Rose and M Slade, 'The Importance of Relationships in Mental Health Care: A Qualitative Study of Service Users' Experiences of Psychiatric Hospital Admission in the UK' (2008) 8(1) *BMC Health Services Research* 92.

[87] Szmukler and Rose, above n 76, 880.

[88] B McSherry and I Freckelton (eds), *Coercive Care: Rights, Law and Policy* (Routledge, 2014) 286.

will and preference'. At present, the 'best interests' formulation appears to remain entrenched in mental health service provision,[89] which is likely to pose a significant challenge to implementing the CRPD.

This list of research goals is clearly not exhaustive, and a range of other issues could easily take priority. For example, this book has paid little attention to the increasing marketisation of health and welfare services,[90] which has significant implications for the provision of mental health services. Gender is another matter that is largely absent from my analysis, whether in relation to women's experiences of coercion or in informal support and caring. Support for older persons along with the legal and political issues raised by an ageing population present another unexamined but important intersection with the issues considered in this book.

C CONCLUSION

The purpose of this book has been to address a gap in the literature on international human rights law and to consider the implications of the CRPD support framework for mental health-related law, policy and practice. I have sought to demonstrate why the CRPD framework should not be viewed as a 'top-down' directive in which change is suddenly imposed from above. Instead, it is more accurate to view ideas like 'supported decision-making', 'accessibility' and 'independent living' as emerging from the consolidated input of diverse grass-roots coalitions, including persons with psychosocial disabilities and with physical, sensory and intellectual disabilities, as well as families, professionals and others. These diverse coalitions have contributed to the realisation of human rights in the lives of people with psychosocial disabilities in a manner that often has been incremental and quite practical in nature, with an occasional, highly strategic, elevation of ideas to the macro level of policy and law at the national and international levels.

Applying these ideas to the majestic generalities of international human rights law has helped to create a global framework with the potential to address persistent issues regarding mental health and the law. The roles of persons with psychosocial disabilities and their representative organisations in this process, should not be understated, particularly with regard to the innovation of Article 12. The resulting convention offers alternative ways to provide

[89] P Gooding, 'In a Format that They Can Actually Utilise Meaningfully' – Psychiatrists' Perceptions of Supported Decision-Making: A Victorian Empirical Study' (2014) 22(5) *Psychiatry, Psychology and Law* 701.

[90] AM Eikenberry and JD Kluver, 'The Marketization of the Nonprofit Sector: Civil Society at Risk?' (2004) 64 *Public Administration Review* 132.

substantive rights to people with psychosocial disabilities, while also offering a 'shield' against discriminatory intrusions into the lives of an already marginalised group. These mechanisms for providing support to enjoy equality before the law, for realising the right to physical and mental health on an equal basis with others, for living independently and participating in the community, and so on, can help transcend the stalemate caused by a narrow focus on negative rights in debates about mental health law. These concepts offer alternative pathways away from risk aversion and the increasing use of compulsory drug intervention.

It is true that ambiguities remain, and it would be an overstatement to suggest the CRPD can address every practical and conceptual issue raised by the dilemmas of mental health and the law. However, while it is important to consider the potential problems with a CRPD support approach, it can be misleading to make these problems the starting point of discussions. To do so is to potentially lose sight of the serious problems in current legislative arrangements, particularly the danger associated with substituted decision-making even with formal safeguards, where people cannot make choices about their own lives. Instead, this book has sought to focus on propositions for change, and on law and policy being tried and tested. In this way, it is possible to encourage governments and others to work with the inevitable tensions that arise when applying human rights to the mental health context.

Today, innovation is occurring in law and policy, and in the work of non-government actors, including among clinical and community-based service providers, in informal and formal peer support groups, and within families. These efforts will be influenced by – and will influence in turn – major debates that seek to reconcile human rights obligations with formal and informal responses to mental distress, disablement and 'madness'. Once again, facilitating the active involvement of people with psychosocial disabilities and their supporters in these matters will be crucial. After all, the success of any human rights–based change to law, policy or practice can only be truly measured 'on the ground', in the lives of those it is meant to assist.

Index